SOCIAL STRATIFICATION
AND MOBILITY
IN THE USSR

EDITED AND TRANSLATED WITH AN INTRODUCTION

by Murray Yanowitch HOFSTRA UNIVERSITY

and Wesley A. Fisher COLUMBIA UNIVERSITY

WITH A COMMENTARY BY
S. M. LIPSET HARVARD UNIVERSITY

 International Arts and Sciences Press, Inc.
White Plains, N.Y.

To Our Soviet Colleagues
in the Study of Social Inequality

Acknowledgments

The editors are most grateful to Fred Ablin, Editorial Director of International Arts and Sciences Press, for his invaluable assistance in seeing this volume through its many stages from inception to final publication. Our thanks also to Michel Vale for his translation of the article by M. Kh. Titma (the final version is, of course, our responsibility), and to Lynn V. Fisher and Mirra-Renée Visson for assistance in solving some of the thornier linguistic problems.

Contents

Contents

Contents

Introduction: The Development of Soviet Studies on Stratification and Mobility

MURRAY YANOWITCH AND WESLEY A. FISHER

The selections from Soviet sociological literature presented in this volume are significant from at least three standpoints. First, they reveal the extent to which the issue of social and economic inequality has become a subject for legitimate public discussion in the Soviet Union. In a society whose political leaders and mass media frequently reaffirm the goals of achieving "full social equality" and the building of a "socially homogeneous society," sociologists' studies of Soviet social structure have become part of a public discourse whose audiences and participants are vastly broader than the ranks of Soviet sociologists. Indeed, the latter — including some whose work is represented in this volume — are not infrequently called upon to discuss their work in mass-circulation newspapers and magazines. (1) Hence the selections, although drawn largely from the "professional literature," provide at least a rough picture of the way in which problems of social and economic inequality are defined and presented to the Soviet reading public at large.

Second, these selections offer the reader a means of appraising the quality of work in what, under Soviet conditions, is the formative period of a new intellectual discipline. The Soviet Sociological Association was founded as recently as 1958. (2) (With two exceptions, the materials included in this volume were originally published in the Soviet Union in 1970-1971.) Soviet academic sociology — stratification and mobility research in particular — has thus had little more than a decade in which to develop. Nonetheless, enough serious work has been produced in this relatively brief period to justify its presentation to Western sociologists interested in discovering for themselves the range of interests, conceptual apparatus, and degree of technical sophistication exhibited by their Soviet colleagues.

Third, the selections provide abundant empirical evidence bearing on the forms and degrees of inequality currently found in Soviet society. The samples on which the empirical studies are based encompass a wide spectrum of occupational groupings and are drawn from a variety of locales. Much of the data gathered in these studies on differences in income, prestige, decision-making power, life-styles, and access to education appear in the selections presented below. Thus, readers interested primarily in comparative social structure, social inequality, and mobility should find a rich harvest of materials here.

The remainder of this introduction will briefly consider: (a) some factors contributing to the emergence of Soviet studies of social stratification, (b) changing Soviet conceptions of social structure, and (c) the explanations offered by Soviet sociologists for the perpetuation of social inequality in the USSR.

Why the Emergence of Soviet Studies of Social Stratification

A good many of the Soviet scholars working in the newly legitimated area of sociology in the USSR have turned their attention to problems of social stratification. Indeed, stratification is a relatively more popular topic among Soviet sociologists than among American sociologists. "Social Structure of Soviet Society" ranked fifth in popularity in a list of forty current research topics of the members of the Soviet Sociological Association in 1970. In contrast, "Stratification and Mobility" ranked only fifteenth out of thirty-three areas of competence listed by members of the American Sociological Association in the same year. Proportionately more Soviet than American sociologists are currently engaged in research on problems of stratification (approximately 4.4% of the members of the SSA as opposed to 3.0% of the members of the ASA in 1970). (3)

In part this emergence of stratification and mobility research in the Soviet Union has been a response to the needs of state authority. Certain new social problems ("disproportions" in Soviet parlance) bearing on stratification and mobility appeared in Soviet society in the 1960s. The possibility that the work of sociologists in this area could be used to meet these problems undoubtedly made the authorities receptive to certain kinds of stratification research, and provided an opportunity for sociologists to legitimate their discipline further through proof of its potential service in the management of public affairs.

Perhaps the most obvious example of a new "disproportion" was the appearance of a significant gap between the occupational aspirations of young people and the actual structure of job opportunities. The steady extension of secondary education and the frequently reiterated refrain by socializing agencies that "all paths are open" to Soviet youth began to hamper the recruitment of young workers to the many unskilled and unpopular jobs which remained to be filled. (4) In these circumstances sociologists' interest in occupational prestige studies, for example, was undoubtedly reinforced by their "practical" implications for planning agencies interested in the efficient management of labor resources. The pioneer of Soviet occupational prestige studies, Vladimir N. Shubkin, explicitly stressed their potential service to state authorities: (5)

> The management of occupational prestige, increasing the attractiveness of some occupations and reducing the attractiveness of others — this is essentially one of the possible approaches to the management of labor resources, based not on administrative measures but on reckoning of the motives, interests, and aspirations of different groups of the population. Without studying these problems it is impossible to manage successfully the mechanical movement of the population — migration, turnover — and to ensure the creation of stable cadres in various branches and regions of the country.

So, too, Soviet studies of social mobility, especially those that focused on the social composition of students in higher educational institutions, had a bearing on another new problem confronting state authorities. Until the mid-1950s a substantial

proportion of secondary-school graduates had the opportunity
to go on to a higher education, regardless of their social background. A decade later the situation had changed markedly. The
rapid extension of secondary education had substantially out-
paced the growth of admissions to higher educational institutions. Under the system of competitive entrance examinations,
secondary-school graduates from worker and peasant homes
found it increasingly difficult to compete with children from intelligentsia families. Soviet authorities could not be indifferent
to the prospect of a declining proportion of worker and peasant
children among students at higher educational institutions. Thus,
as in the case of studies of occupational prestige, studies of social mobility and inequality in access to advanced education
could shed some light on problems of concern to state authorities. The solutions to these problems were not obvious but —
once again in Shubkin's words — the problems "have to be seen"
in order to be solved, and the work of sociologists could be of
assistance in this regard. (6)

It would be a crude mistake, however, as well as an injustice
to the authors represented below, to explain the emergence of
Soviet stratification research (and therefore the contents of this
volume) as reflecting mainly the response of Soviet sociologists
to the needs of state authority. As the reader will discover,
there is too much in this volume that does not fit into this narrow utilitarian framework. The opportunity afforded Soviet sociologists to study their country's social structure has undoubtedly been enhanced by the possibility that political authorities
could "use" their work to meet new and old problems, but it
has also had its own intellectual momentum. In several important senses the emergence of the kind of stratification and mobility studies included here is quite independent of any "directives" from political authority.

Perhaps most obvious in this respect is the fact that Soviet sociologists have been reared in the Marxist intellectual tradition, in
which concepts of "social class" and "class structure" play a central role, a tradition which is permeated by a concern with social
inequality. It is hardly surprising, therefore, that some of them
have turned their attention to problems of social stratification

in the USSR. If the Marxist tradition can inspire scientific interest in the study of social stratification by sociologists in the
United States, it can surely do so in the Soviet Union. Thus,
once sociology was "officially" recognized and encouraged, at
least some Soviet sociologists could be expected to focus their
attention on problems of social and economic inequality.

Indeed, it is arguable that by so doing, Soviet sociologists
have helped legitimate their field. By dealing with problems of
class structure, these scholars tie their discipline to the central concerns of Marxist-Leninist ideology and thus enhance
sociology's prestige in the USSR. Stratification is an area of
sociology where the links with prevailing ideology are quite direct, and it is these very links which — under appropriate circumstances — enhance the feasibility of theoretical elaboration
and empirical research in this area. (7)

The studies of social structure by East European sociologists,
particularly in Poland and Czechoslovakia, must also have acted
as a stimulus to Soviet sociologists beginning to work in this
area in the 1960s. Both theoretical and empirical studies of social stratification flourished in Poland during the first half of
that decade, while the first all-union conference of Soviet sociologists on problems of social structure did not meet until
1966 and most of their major studies in this area did not appear
until the end of the decade. Some Soviet sociologists have acknowledged, at least implicitly, the important role which their
contacts with East European colleagues and acquaintance with
their writings on social structure played at a time when their
own studies had barely begun. (8)

Finally, we suggest that certain aspects of the social position
of sociologists in Soviet society are consequential for their interest in questions of stratification. Since their contact with
political authorities is necessarily extensive, Soviet scholars
in the field are perhaps acutely aware of their own subordination. Consciousness of their own dependence on state authority
probably makes them particularly sensitive to problems of hierarchy and inequality in the society as a whole.

Changing Soviet Conceptions of Social Structure

What are the conceptions of Soviet social structure that have
emerged in Soviet social thought in recent years and that under-
lie most of the selections which follow? Although the serious
study of social classes and strata is a recent phenomenon in the
Soviet Union, a simple "vision" of the country's social structure emerged in the 1930s and was repeatedly and officially reiterated. A useful way of approaching more recent modes of
perceiving Soviet social structure is to see them as simultaneously elaborating and transcending the simple "vision" of social differentiation which appeared in the 1930s.

From the late 1930s to the early 1960s the typical references
in Soviet publications to domestic social structure were largely
confined to asserting and illustrating the existence of a threefold structural division in Soviet society: the working class, the
collective farm peasantry, and the intelligentsia. The first two
were "nonantagonistic classes" and the third was a "social
stratum." The two classes were associated with different forms
of socialist property — the working class with state property
"belonging to the whole people," the peasantry with the "group"
or "cooperative" property of particular collective farms. The
intelligentsia was distinguished by its employment in "mental
labor." The three groups lived and worked under conditions of
"friendly collaboration" with no possibility for one of the groups
to appropriate the labor of the others. To the extent that any
empirical data were introduced into the discussion, their function was mainly to illustrate the harmonious and simple picture
of social structure outlined here. (9)

If Soviet social structure was to become a subject for serious
study, this narrow framework had to be extended. In 1965-1966
a broader framework for the analysis of social structure
emerged in the writings of men like G. E. Glezerman, V. S. Semenov, and Ts. A. Stepanian. These were the men whose articles on
social structure appeared in Kommunist, whose remarks opened
or concluded sociologists' conferences, and who edited collections
of papers on social structure. In this sense the new "official"
conception of social structure may be traced in their writings. (10)

In this new conception the framework for discussion of social structure was established by specifying a variety of "social differences" that presumably continue to prevail following the establishment of socialism and are therefore appropriate subjects for investigation. These include differences (a) between classes (i.e., the working class and the collective farm peasantry); (b) between those employed in manual and non-manual work (with the latter divided into the "intelligentsia" and non-specialist "employees"); (c) between groups within the working class, peasantry, and non-manual category (frequently referred to as "intraclass differences"); (d) between urban and rural members of the same class or stratum.

In some ways this appeared to be merely an extension of the earlier simple "vision" of social structure introduced in the 1930s. The two (and only two) basic classes remain. The single intelligentsia stratum has been split into two non-manual categories — an intelligentsia proper (specialists with advanced education) and ordinary white-collar employees. "Intraclass" and urban-rural divisions have been added as distinct bases for social differentiation. The impression of continuity with earlier formulations is reinforced when we read that the various social groups are "nonantagonistic" and that relationships of "exploitation" are absent. (11) However, maintaining continuity with earlier formulations is often a necessary means of establishing the legitimacy of new approaches. What is important about the "official" conception of social structure that emerged in the mid-1960s is that it permitted consideration of a much broader range of social differentiation and social inequality than was possible earlier.

It is true that some recent Soviet literature on social structure seems to have been little affected by the possibilities offered by the new approach. This is particularly true of those writers who continue to stress the current importance of class divisions compared to other types of social cleavages. For A. K. Kurylev, for example, "social structure under current conditions of socialism means primarily the class structure." (12) Similarly, for Ts. A. Stepanian class differences are still the "decisive" ones, and excessive focus on other structural divisions

is obviously premature ("running ahead"). (13) When we recall
that the only classes whose existence is recognized are workers and collective farm peasants, and the main criterion of
class division is the nature of property ownership, it is clear
that the position taken by these writers tends to minimize the
range of social differentiation.

Most of the Soviet writers who have continued to stress the
priority of class differences appear to be older "social philosophers" rather than the new generation of sociologists proper.
Those who have gone furthest in the study of social differentiation are a group of sociologists who have, in effect, "paid their
respects" to the continuing importance of the class division and
have then proceeded to focus on "intraclass" and "intragroup"
differences in Soviet society. The opportunities which this approach provides for serious empirical research and the posing
of new questions on Soviet social structure is perhaps best ex-
emplified in the selections below from the work of Shkaratan,
Arutiunian, and Volkov.

Shkaratan's work focuses on "intraclass social differentiation" within the urban working class. Although interclass differences are still the "main" ones, this is a temporary situation.
As differences in forms of property ownership diminish in significance, the principal social cleavages in Soviet society are
becoming those determined by differences in the character and
complexity of work within a common form of property ownership, with particular emphasis on the differences between manual and mental labor. This type of social division is best studied as an aspect of intraclass social differentiation. Shkaratan
then takes the significant step of including the technical intelligentsia employed in state industry (ranging from foremen to
plant directors) as part of the working class and comparing its
economic and social status not with a single undifferentiated
mass of manual workers but with a series of distinct, stratified
workers' groups. The comparisons within this enlarged version
of the working class encompass some eight to nine occupational
groupings ranging from unskilled manual workers at one extreme
to "organizers of production collectives" (plant directors and department heads) at the other. What emerges is an implicit rank

order of a rather wide range of occupational categories whose
incumbents are differentiated with respect to income, education,
extent of Party membership, as well as social origins and
"modes of life" (cultural interests, leisure activities, patterns
of association). This is not simply a scheme of social differentiation, but a picture of vertical gradations within the working class.

Shkaratan's approach implies no sharp divisions between adjoining occupational groups and has the important virtue —
from the Soviet standpoint — of leaving undisturbed the traditional vision of Soviet society as consisting of "nonantagonistic"
social groups. But it underscores the range of inequality between the extremes of this structure, and the variety of forms
which inequality assumes, in a way that was impossible within
the confines of the traditional "two classes and one stratum"
framework.

Shkaratan's focus on intraclass vertical gradations among
urban workers has been extended to the countryside in
Arutiunian's studies of rural social structure. For Arutiunian,
"socio-occupational" groups rather than classes have already
become the "primary elements" of social structure. (14) The
boundaries of classes in the countryside are extended so as to
embrace skilled agricultural specialists and managerial personnel at one extreme and ordinary field hands at the other, all
within the same class. Throughout his empirical studies of rural social structure Arutiunian emphasizes the importance of
occupational position rather than the form of property in determining social and cultural differentiation. Perhaps most important is his readiness to move beyond Shkaratan in treating
inequality of participation in decision-making at economic enterprises as a legitimate area in the study of social inequality.

The work of Iu. E. Volkov on Soviet social structure is significant chiefly for its attempt to touch directly on broad questions
of power. Like Shkaratan and Arutiunian, Volkov moves beyond
the earlier "two classes and one stratum" framework by adopting a "differentiated" approach to what was earlier treated as
a single social group. He centers his attention on a "special
stratum" which is part of the broader non-manual or mental

labor category. This stratum encompasses individuals "performing the administrative-managerial function." They are obviously distinct from that portion of the intelligentsia which is
engaged in artistic endeavors, but also from all those who are
mere "executors" rather than initiators of decisions. These
"higher-level" (rukovodiashchie) individuals occupy positions
as "heads and deputy-heads of enterprises, institutions, and their
structural subdivisions." The organizations which they "manage" are not only economic enterprises but also educational,
scientific, and medical institutions, as well as organs of government administration. (15) Their most distinguishing characteristic is their "right to make decisions which are binding on
others and to put these decisions into practice with the use of
measures of coercion if necessary" (p. 54 below). It is this
"very significant distinguishing trait" which sets them apart
from all other structural elements in the population, including
other strata within the non-manual or mental labor category.

In the selection from Volkov's work included in this volume,
he suggests that the social differences between those possessing and lacking this managerial power "in certain respects are
no less important" than those between classes or between the
manual and non-manual categories as a whole (pp. 53 and 54 below).
This formulation does not appear in his more recent writings.
But what seems to us most significant about Volkov's work is
that he has posed certain new questions concerning higher-
level managerial personnel and has treated them as legitimate
subjects for sociological inquiry: "What is the social nature of
this stratum; what is its status in current social structure;
what are its interrelations with other strata and groups in society." (16) The transcendence of the earlier "vision" of Soviet
social structure has thus made possible the beginnings of an
approach to the study of power.

Along with the "objective" attributes of occupational position,
the latter's impact on value orientations has also come within
the purview of social research (see particularly the selection
by Titma as well as Vodzinskaia's study of occupational prestige). When these latter works are considered jointly with the
empirical studies of Shkaratan and Arutiunian, and with the

issues raised by Volkov, it is clear that the conceptual apparatus of Western stratification studies has begun to permeate Soviet Marxists' perception of their own social structure. The
conception of social structure as embracing a hierarchy of occupational strata differentiated by income, prestige, cultural
levels, value orientations, and power has now become — implicitly or explicitly — part of the normal discourse of Soviet
social thought.

The process of assimilating the very concept of stratification
into Soviet Marxism has also proceeded apace. Soviet references to Western stratification and mobility studies continue
to be largely, but no longer exclusively, critical. (17) Social
structure under capitalism is still seen as sharply dichoto-
mized along either side of the property ownership line, and the
stratification approach, with its focus on a multiplicity of occupational gradations, is viewed as blurring the principal source
of social divisions (class membership in the Marxian sense).
On the other hand, when property relationships are essentially
homogeneous, as they presumably are in the Soviet Union, occupational gradations become a more reliable indicator of social and economic position than they are under capitalism. The
Marxist approach to social structure is now regarded as en-
compassing "all that is positive" in Western stratification studies. (18)

The explicit recognition of a variety of vertical gradations in
social structure has also stimulated study of the "openness" of
Soviet society, i.e., the extent to which the higher-ranking occupational positions are accessible to the offspring of different
strata. The studies bearing on rates and patterns of social mobility which have appeared center on parental occupational status of students in higher educational institutions and of individuals in various occupational positions (see the selections by
Rutkevich, Liss, Shkaratan, and Arutiunian in Part III). The extent to which Soviet institutions transmit or reduce inequality
across generations is thus becoming subject to empirical verification.

Finally, along with the emergence of occupational stratification and mobility studies, another "new direction" has appeared

in Soviet investigations of social structure. Sociologists like
Gordon and Klopov (in Part I) argue for the independent causal
role in the creation of inequality of variables other than occupation and class position — variables such as sex, age, and
place of residence. They suggest that "cultural strata" based
on these variables exist that are independent of either class or
occupational groupings.

The Confrontation with Inequality

Soviet sociologists recognize that social inequality is not only
a heritage of the previous social order; it is also "reproduced"
by socialism (pp. 13 and 25 below). But why should substantial inequalities in economic and social status continue to prevail long
after the nearly complete abolition of private ownership of the
means of production? Given the central role which the private and
unequal ownership of property plays in the Marxian interpretation
of social inequality under capitalism, as well as the continuing
and obvious evidence of inequality in current Soviet society, it
is hardly surprising that this question should have been posed
fairly early in the discussions of social structure which emerged
in the 1960s. Those sociologists who have confronted this question (the selections by Shkaratan and Mokronosov in Part I are
examples) have sought to explain the necessity for current inequality by drawing on the concept of "the social division of labor" and the impossibility of transcending it during the first
phase of the postcapitalist society.

In this view the crux of the problem is that work activities
which differ in complexity, scope for creativity, and contribution
to economic development must frequently remain the more-or-
less permanent life-fates of distinct population groups. It is
not simply the continued existence of both manual and nonmanual job operations, of skilled and unskilled work activities,
of "organizational" and "executor-like" functions, but the necessity of distributing these economically dissimilar functions
among different social groups that makes the perpetuation of
social inequality unavoidable during the "lower phase of communism." The inadequate level of technological development

means that the normal functioning of the economy requires the
more-or-less stable attachment of some strata to heavy, physical labor and of others to more skilled, creative labor (p. 23
below). Perhaps the most explicit statement linking technological inadequacy and the social division of labor appears in the
work of V. Ia. El'meev and his colleagues: (19)

> In the lower phase of communism society has not yet at-
> tained the increase in productive forces which would per-
> mit the full liquidation of economic differences in the con-
> ditions and character of labor of all working people in ma-
> terial production, and by reducing their working time to a
> minimum, ensure the performance of intellectual functions
> in the economic and social spheres by all individuals. As
> long as these conditions have not been prepared there re-
> mains the historical necessity for the existence of a par-
> ticular social group of people who are freed from direct
> physical labor in the sphere of production of material
> goods and are attached to activities in the management of
> production, state administration, the development of sci-
> ence, art, etc., to intellectual activity. In the sphere of
> material production the higher scientific functions of labor
> cannot yet be directly realized by all producers, which
> again requires the existence of a special category of
> engineering-technical and scientific personnel. As a re-
> sult of all this, mental and manual activities...are divided
> between different individuals....

Thus the social division of labor, which in presocialist societies was most clearly expressed in the private and unequal
distribution of property and the existence of antagonistic
classes (20), now engenders the principal classes and strata
of a society in which property is socialized.

But why should the necessity for a social division of labor
generate unequal rewards for those who hold different occupational positions? Dahrendorf has correctly noted that the division of labor cannot explain the existence of social inequality
without "an additional act of evaluation" which transforms social differentiation into social stratification. (21) This point
seems to have been clearly recognized by Shkaratan, whose

explanation for inequalities in economic and social status in
Soviet society rests explicitly on just such "an additional act
of evaluation."

For Shkaratan the social division of labor in its present form
means that different occupational groups have unequal opportunities to contribute to society's economic and cultural development. Their unequal contributions are inherent in the occupational roles that must be performed and do not necessarily reflect the differing merits or potentials of the individuals concerned. But the critical point is that until technological advance
permits economic abundance and high cultural levels to be
achieved, it is unavoidable that society "evaluates and will continue to evaluate its members primarily according to their contribution to the development of social production" (p. 13 below).
This differential social evaluation of occupations — and therefore of their incumbents — assumes the form of unequal economic rewards and social esteem.

At least for Shkaratan, inequality of rewards is not regarded
primarily as part of an incentive mechanism required to fill
occupational roles of differing social importance. Given the
continuing scarcity of economic resources, the members of society are rewarded according to their contribution to overcoming this scarcity. As such, unequal rewards involve the application of a kind of "just price" principle in a society in which the
urgency of rapid economic and cultural development is presumably a commonly shared value. But the resulting inequality
is treated as reflecting the "immaturity of socialism" (22)
rather than as a requirement of all forms of social organization — and certainly not of the communist society of the future.

It is all too easy to dismiss these discussions of social inequality as merely providing scholastic justifications for systems of privilege imposed by state authority. Whatever may be
the validity of this interpretation, it surely does not exhaust
the significance of Soviet sociologists' confrontation with social inequality. It is particularly worth noting that the interpretation of social inequality as inherent in the social division of
labor has not served to close off discussion of the problems
which its continued existence engenders. Thus some sociologists

have stressed that recognition of the inevitability of inequality
for the present does not resolve "the problem of the degree of
inequality." (23) Warnings against a tendency toward the "self-
reproduction" of the intelligentsia and the emergence of a "privileged stratum" have been voiced by sociologists in arguing for
changes in the admissions practices of educational institutions. (24) Others have stressed the desirability of democratization of economic management and the problematic consequences
of future technological change for the possibility of such democratization. (25) The raising of all of these issues has been compatible with the acceptance of the inevitability of social inequality rooted in the social division of labor.

What is perhaps most significant is that inequality — at least
in some of its forms — is becoming a subject for social research, rather than a theme discussed mainly in the context of
a struggle against "petty bourgeois equalitarianism" or "right-
wing revisionism." Western sociologists should be the first to
recognize that the admission of the inevitability of social inequality — if only for the present — may promote its serious
study.

Notes

1) See, for example, V. N. Shubkin in Literaturnaia gazeta,
December 9, 1970; Shubkin, "Occupations: Problems of Choice,"
Nauka i zhizn', 1971, No. 5, pp. 68-73; M. N. Rutkevich in
Izvestia, December 10, 1967.

2) Discussion of the formative period of Soviet sociology may
be found in George Fischer, Science and Politics in the Soviet
Union (Ithaca, N. Y.: Center for International Studies, 1964).

3) See Wesley A. Fisher, "The Social Composition of the Soviet Sociological Association," paper presented at the 67th Annual Meeting of the American Sociological Association, August
28-31, 1972; Nico Stehr and Lyle E. Larson, "The Rise and Decline of Areas of Specialization," The American Sociologist,
7 (August 1972), p. 5.

4) See Murray Yanowitch and Norton Dodge, "The Social
Evaluation of Occupations in the Soviet Union," Slavic Review,

December 1969, pp. 637-641.

5) V. N. Shubkin, "On the Stability of Ratings of Attractiveness of Occupations," in R. V. Ryvkina, ed., Sotsiologicheskie
issledovaniia, Novosibirsk, 1966, p. 265.

6) V. N. Shubkin, Sotsiologicheskie opyty, "Mysl'" Publishing House, Moscow, 1970, p. 235.

7) Fischer, op. cit., Chapter VII, passim.

8) S. A. Kugel', Novoe v izuchenii sotsial'noi struktury
obshchestva, Leningrad, 1968, p. 5; O. I. Shkaratan, Problemy
sotsial'noi struktury rabochego klassa, "Mysl'" Publishing
House, Moscow, 1970, p. 13.

9) For a typical presentation of the threefold, nonantagonistic social division, see F. V. Konstantinov, ed., Istoricheskii
materializm, Moscow, 1954, pp. 177-182.

10) Some examples of the "official" conception appear in
V. S. Semenov, "Social Structure of Soviet Society," Kommunist,
1965, No. 11, pp. 39-48; same author, "The Obliteration of Social and Class Differences and the Transition to a Classless
Society," Voprosy filosofii, 1965, No. 9, pp. 141-151; the comments of Semenov, Glezerman, and Stepanian at the 1966 conference on social structure, as reported in Voprosy filosofii,
1966, No. 5, pp. 143-154; Akademiia nauk SSSR, Institut filosofii, Problemy izmeneniia sotsial'noi struktury sovetskogo
obshchestva, "Nauka" Publishing House, Moscow, 1968, Introduction and Chapters 1 and 2 (cited henceforth as Problemy
izmeneniia).

11) See, for example, Akademiia nauk SSSR, Institut filosofii,
Stroitel'stvo kommunizma i razvitie obshchestvennykh otnoshenii,
"Nauka" Publishing House, Moscow, 1966, Chapters 1, 2, 4.

12) Problemy izmeneniia, p. 64.

13) Ibid., p. 11.

14) Iu. V. Arutiunian, Sotsial'naia struktura sel'skogo
naseleniia SSSR, "Mysl'" Publishing House, Moscow, 1971,
p. 99.

15) Iu. E. Volkov, "The Organization of Management of Society and the Character of Social Relations," Voprosy filosofii,
1965, No. 8, pp. 21-22.

16) Ibid., p. 18.

17) See, for example, Rutkevich's favorable comments on the work of D. Glass and his colleagues on mobility in Great Britain (M. N. Rutkevich, in Nauchnye doklady vysshei shkoly, filosofskie nauki, 1970, No. 5, p. 18).

18) Ibid., p. 19.

19) V. Ia. El'meev, V. R. Polozov, and B. R. Riashchenko, Kommunizm i preodolenie razdeleniia mezhdu umstvennym i fizicheskom trudom, Leningrad University Publishing House, Leningrad, 1965, pp. 12-13.

20) Here Soviet writers cite Engels's remark: 'It is therefore the law of the division of labor which lies at the root of the division into classes" (F. Engels, Anti-Dühring, International Publishers, New York, p. 307).

21) R. Dahrendorf, "On the Origin of Inequality Among Men," in A. Béteille, ed., Social Inequality (Baltimore: Penguin Books, 1969).

22) O. I. Shkaratan, "The Social Structure of the Soviet Working Class," Voprosy filosofii, 1967, No. 1, p. 33.

23) V. I. Mishin, I. E. Rubtsov, and A. A. Terent'ev, "Problems of the Social Composition of Today's Student Body," in Gor'kovskii Gosudarstvennyi Universitet, Sotsiologiia i vysshaia shkola, Gorky, 1970, p. 15.

24) Ibid., p. 11; M. Kh. Titma, "The Role of Social Origins in the Formation of Values of Occupations," in Uchenye zapiski Tartuskogo Gosudarstvennogo Universiteta, Trudy po filosofii, Vol. XV, Tartu, 1970, p. 198.

25) O. I. Shkaratan, in Voprosy filosofii, 1968, No. 11, p. 24.

A Note on Selections

Soviet sociologists, like their colleagues in other countries, are not immune to the use of jargon and clichés. Readers may find some passages in the selections that follow tedious and/or reminiscent of the ideological statements of an earlier era. In the belief that Soviet sociologists should be heard in their own voice and that their style of communication is of interest in its own right, however, we have chosen to retain such "ideological" passages even though their elimination would have made the volume more readable.

Each article contains either new theoretical formulations or significant empirical findings. The theoretical selections in Part I were chosen mainly to illustrate various departures from the traditional "two classes and one stratum" approach to social structure. In one form or another, the selections by Shkaratan, Mokronosov, and Volkov all represent attempts to apply the concept of "the social division of labor" to the explanation of social inequality, and are justifications for disaggregating the broad social categories of which social structure was composed in the traditional approach. Gordon and Klopov take this disaggregation one step further and argue for the independent importance of groupings other than those based on occupation and class. Levada's article, although not concerned primarily with Soviet social structure, seeks to broaden the conceptual framework within which Soviet Marxists analyze all social systems.

The empirical studies in Part II encompass both urban (Shkaratan) and rural (Arutiunian) settings, as well as a special

I. SOCIAL STRATIFICATION: NEW DIRECTIONS IN SOVIET THEORY

1 Social Structure

IU. A. LEVADA

Social structure is one of the basic categories of the sociological analysis of society. It designates the network of ordered
and interdependent relations among the components of a social
system. The term "social structure" includes the mode of division of labor peculiar to a given society, the interrelations of
classes and other social groups, the nature of the functioning
of social institutions, and the forms of social organization and
of social action.

The economic, political, cultural and other structures of a
society can be viewed as separate aspects of its social structure. The Marxist approach to the development of society reveals the determining role of the system of economic relations
(the economic structure) in relation to other societal structures,
noting at the same time the significance of the reverse influence
of the latter on the economic structure. The relations determining the functioning of separate spheres or institutions of societal life make up the social structure of production, politics,
science, leisure, and so forth. Finally, social structure — more
precisely, social composition — is commonly understood to
mean the distribution and quantitative interrelation of classes,
of social groups, as well as of strata, professional, cultural,
and other groups. This important, comparatively strictly fixed,
statistical indicator of social structure can be correctly understood only in conjunction with the interrelations of appropriate

From Filosofskaia Entsiklopediia, Vol. 5, "Sovetskaia
Entsiklopediia" Publishing House, Moscow, 1970, pp. 142-144.

institutions, spheres of society, and types of division of labor,
i.e., only through the social structure of a society as a whole.

The social structure of a society can be considered on three
planes: (a) the <u>functional</u> plane, i.e., as an ordered system of
forms of social activity assuring the functioning and development of a particular whole; in this case the units of analysis are
separate spheres of the social division of labor and social institutions; (b) the <u>organizational</u> plane, i.e., as a system of relations forming various types of social groups characteristic of
a given social system; the units of analysis here are collectives,
organizations, and their structural elements; and (c) as a certain
system of <u>orientation of social action</u> (collective and individual);
the units of analysis in such an approach to social structure are
the elements of social action (goals and means, motives and
stimuli, norms and standards, programs and their elements,
etc.). These approaches to the social structure of a society can
be considered different cross-sections that complement each
other; each permits theoretical and empirical analysis, although
the degree and forms of their correspondence to each other are
not alike.

Some peculiarities of the reflection of social structure in social and, later, sociological thought are also associated with the
distinguishing of these planes. The primary, as though "immediately given" concern of sociological thought was the actions
of separate individuals and collectives (rulers, armies, etc.).
Interest in distinguishing particular types of social organization
(for example, Thierry's political classes, and others) appeared
considerably later. Having demonstrated the connection of social classes with particular phases of the development of production, Marx revealed the functional structure (the division of
labor and private property) that serves as the basis of the existence of the corresponding social group. It was precisely this
step that made it possible to approach scientifically both the organizational structure of society and social action. An example
is the socio-economic definition of classes introduced by Marx
in connection with the differentiation of social production. Such
a statement of the problem does not signify economic determin-
ism, inasmuch as the whole process of production by people of

their own lives is taken into account (see Marx and Engels, Sochineniia, 2d ed., Vol. 3, p. 27).

Approaching society as an organized system of social relations presupposes analysis of such processes as the division, specialization, and cooperation of the forms of labor and of management in terms of the functioning and development of a specific whole. Elements of this process are the differentiation and institutionalization of separate spheres of social life, leading to corresponding changes in the social composition of the population.

"Nonsystemic" processes — conflict, the reciprocal influence of heterogeneous structures (connected, for example, with clashes of local cultures) — also influence the formation of and changes in social structure. Social structures that differ in level and type of development are capable, to differing degrees, of integrating external social formations and thus making them functional. Historical examples of such a process are the integration of agricultural and pastoral tribes in a single social organism, the transformation of ethnic and religious dissociation into elements of a division of functions (labor, power, prestige, communication, and others) under the conditions of bourgeois society. Having been transformed into an element of social structure, such "naturally" given characteristics as sex, age, ability to work, and others are also made functional. A characteristic feature of the structure of bourgeois societies is the transformation — manifest or latent — of certain forms of anomie, revolt, and asocial behavior (crime, drug addiction, certain types of religious and other movements) into means of diminishing psychological conflicts and reducing tension in the system. Conflict mechanisms can serve as a regulator of the interrelations of the various elements of a social structure, of the distribution of a population by spheres of social production.

The basic factors in the development of social structure are: (a) "horizontal" differentiation of functions between separate complementary spheres of social activity (an example is the division of spheres of social production); (b) "vertical," hierarchical differentiation of functions between different levels of social management (an expression of this is the corresponding differentiation of social institutions, mechanisms of social control, and programs of activity of a social system); (c) functionalization of social structures "foreign" to the given system of social structures.

The mechanisms of integration of a social structure are: (a) the formation and development of objective preconditions for the cooperation of different spheres and elements of social life; (b) the action of spontaneously arising social-psychological attitudes and orientations (to which should also be added the compensatory mechanisms of psychological tension reduction); (c) the influence of organized ideological systems called upon to preserve such attitudes and orientations; (d) the action of mechanisms (including specialized institutions) of social control directed toward the realization of the normative system accepted in the given culture. The system of social norms functioning in a given society ensures the preservation and reproduction of its social structure.

Behind the multiplicity of historically concrete forms of social structure may be observed several general types characterized by such fundamental parameters as the degree of functional differentiation (horizontal and vertical in the sense indicated above), the type of connection between functionally dependent elements, and the ways of reproducing role positions. The breakdown of a program of social activity and of the institutionalization of functions may be considered derivative characteristics.

In "primitive" social structures (primordial as well as other "traditional" systems of relations) functional differentiation of both types is practically nonexistent; and the attachment of individuals to social roles is comprehensive (i.e., any dominant type of connection is lacking), lifelong, and inherited. Corresponding to such a structure is a "one-level" program of social action consisting of a certain sequence of categorical demands, digression from which threatens the whole social structure with destruction.

Under the conditions of ancient, Asiatic, and feudal social relations, elements of social structure such as the following developed: (a) differentiation and isolation of spheres of social activity and, to some extent (in the sphere of government and control), of its levels; (b) systems of institutional consolidation and hereditary transmission of social status (privileges, titles, etc.). A requirement for these types of social relations was the institutionalization of a normative structure in the form of cult systems — later, legal and ideological systems — partly fixing standards of "normal" behavior, and basically called upon to eliminate anomalies.

In bourgeois society of the laissez-faire period, social structure was characterized by: (a) growing differentiation of spheres of social activity, in which the mechanisms of interrelation of these spheres (exchange, upbringing) isolate themselves; (b) development of a multilevel hierarchy of rule ("vertical" differentiation); (c) the dominant significance of conflict (competition) mechanisms for the regulation of social relations that presuppose mobility and autonomy of separately acting units oriented toward the achievement of individual success; (d) private, inherited, and alienated property as a defining indicator of this success, and also of social role, status, and prestige. It is precisely this peculiarity of bourgeois society that made possible the selection by Marxism of property, socio-economic relations, and social classes as the basic categories in the materialist analysis of a social system.

The indicated types of social structure must not be directly identified with historically real structures — they can be superimposed and influence each other in one and the same given social system. In the contemporary state-monopolistic stage of bourgeois development in various countries, "traditional," "Asiatic," and other such elements of social structure retain their significance to some extent. At the same time, the concentration of political power and the isolation of the entire sphere of social rule, together with the development of monopolistic mass communications, place increasingly significant limits on the whole mechanism of action of the social system formed in the laissez-faire period and create conditions for the appearance of totalitarian and fascist social forms. Under conditions of tremendous growth of the service sector and of the governing apparatus, indicators of property and personal success lose their universal meaning, giving way to a certain extent to indicators such as status in a bureaucratic system and conformity to the accepted standards of that system's functioning. Correspondingly, positions of status and prestige are isolated as elements of social role.

The social structure of a society determines the nature of the corresponding interests of separate social groups and organizations, the direction and significance of social conflicts in the functioning mechanism of the corresponding social system, and the types of social mobility. If for capitalist society the determining factor is the conflict of socio-economic interests that directly make for class struggle, in precapitalist societies this conflict of social forces can express itself in a struggle of political and ideological (religious) interests and traditions.

The increased complexity of the social structure of contemporary capitalist society finds expression partly in the fact that the objects of class struggle of the working masses include demands connected with ensuring access to education, culture, services, and prestige.

In socialist society, centralized state regulation of the spheres of societal production, services, and culture, plays the determining role in social structure; the differentiation and institutionalization of the spheres of management, planning, and education correspondingly take on new meaning. The rule of social ownership of the means of production changes the meaning of property itself as a structure-forming factor and as a measure of social status; the latter is measured, according to the principles of socialism, by the participation of separate individuals and collectives in the satisfaction of socially recognized needs, i.e., by their functional activity. Destroying such institutions as the inheritance of social status, property and power, socialist society creates a system of state-organized commensurability and evaluation of the role of separate individuals, collectives, and groups; the means of such evaluation take the form of value expressions of the results of labor, as well as the juxtaposition of the latter with indicators of the plan and other directives; varied systems of incentives of a temporary or lifelong nature (titles, etc.) are widely developed. The exchange of

human and material resources among separate spheres of societal life and production depends, under these conditions, on
a complicated conglomerate of economic and socio-ideological
factors that become more fully developed in the process of per-
fecting socialist social relations.

2 Sources of Social Differentiation of the Working Class in Soviet Society

O. I. SHKARATAN

The social inequality that persists during the stage of social-ism is a "legacy" from antagonistic social orders. Because of the social nature of property, the equality of all members in re-lation to the means of production, the equality in leadership functions, and the community of basic economic interests, there are no antipodal or antagonistic social groups in a socialist so-ciety. However, differences still remain (a) in relation to so-cialist property, associated with its existence in two principal forms (this is the chief basis for the residual social differences between the working class and the collective-farm peasantry), and (b) in the degree of utilization of property (this is the basis for differences under socialism between workers of differing skills and complexity of labor, between personnel in mental and manual labor, between urban and rural residents).

Since differences of the first type — in relation to the means of production — are not inherent in the first phase of commu-nism, they are overcome more rapidly than differences of the second type, which are conditioned by an unequal degree of ac-tual utilization of property and which persist considerably longer.

Our title. From O. I. Shkaratan, Problemy sotsial'noi struktury rabochego klassa SSSR, "Mysl'" Publishing House, Moscow, 1970, pp. 50-52, 153-162. Our notes numbered 1-4 be-low correspond to footnotes numbered 246-249 in Chapter 1 of the Shkaratan volume. The chapter is entitled "Methodological and Systematic Principles of Analysis of Social Structure of the Soviet Working Class."

The totality of all such socio-economic differences characterizes that system of social relationships which is reproduced
on the basis of socialist production relations, but which is developing in the direction of the gradual elimination of these differences. Such are the changes being undergone by the differences reproduced in the social structure of a socialist society
in the process of transition to communism. In the foreseeable
future, a society that has eliminated classes, although it has
not yet achieved full social equality — for which considerably
more time is required — will be an established fact. The social and economic inequality of individuals is both historically
and, in its sphere of application, broader than the inequality of
classes. Hence it is particularly important to study carefully
all aspects of the process of overcoming social heterogeneity
that is taking place in socialist society, including the structural
changes in class groupings.

The correlation and subordination of social elements and relationships change in the course of development of social relations during the transition to communism. Thus, as the development of social relations in the USSR has shown, the significance of differences between workers in mental and manual labor increases. This is connected with the sequence in which social differences disappear. Differences between workers in
mental and manual labor are not heightened, of course; rather,
they move to the foreground by comparison with the more rapidly disappearing interclass differences.

When socialism liquidates private property, it eliminates the
consequences of private property — antagonistic classes — but
it does not eliminate the original cause of social inequality:
the division of labor into socially heterogeneous types. This
task, whose solution requires a much longer period of time, is
a matter for the transition to full communism. It requires, during the stage of socialism, the planned regulation of social relations and the elaboration of methods for consciously resolving
the continuing social contradictions between groups of people
employed in socially heterogeneous labor. The transformation
of social relations connected with changes in the productive
forces proceeds through qualitative changes in the division of

labor that embrace society as a whole.

The social structure of a socialist society is extremely complex. Along with components reflecting the existence of social and economic inequality (classes, etc.), it encompasses other societal relationships and structural formations that will persist under communism: labor collectives, residential collectives, families, and nations and nationalities (the merger of the latter into a single non-national community will occur only after a whole series of stages of development of a fully formed communist society).

In addition, we must keep in mind the difference between a socialist social structure in its "pure form," so to speak, and the actual social structure of a concrete socialist organism, as well as the totality of socialist organisms — the world socialist system in its historical reality. There are certain differences here that can be understood and perceived only by investigating the historical path of formation of concrete social structures (the presence of residual social groups, presocialist types of relations in individual spheres of vital activity, etc.).

That social structure whose elements are groups of individuals unequal in social and economic relations is a historically transient one. It encompasses that part of a structural organization which — as the highest expression of social inequality — arose later in historical terms and will disappear earlier than other structural organizations based on social and economic inequality. We refer to the class structure of society.

.   .   .

Those aspects of production relations which are common to both phases of the communist social order, above all, the directly social relations of the whole collectivity of members of society to the means of production, become the decisive aspects in the mechanism of social structure under socialism. This is the economic foundation of the nonantagonistic character of the relations between social groups, of the deep community of their interests, and of the objective tendencies of the development of the social structure inherent in socialism into a social structure of the communist type.

At the same time, the totality of socialist production relations still contains elements that reproduce social and economic inequality. Because social and economic heterogeneity of labor continues to exist, the members of society, socially attached to its economically different forms, have unequal opportunities to utilize the means of production, i.e., they participate unequally in the organization and improvement of production and contribute unequally to economic and cultural development. They do not develop their abilities and talents to the same degree, nor are they equally the subjects of society's activity. In other words, the social and economic heterogeneity of labor leads to a situation in which the members of society, although equally co-owners of general public property, in actual fact do not equally perform the functions associated with that form of ownership. The social division of labor inherent in socialism thereby emerges as the foundation of actual inequality of groups of workers who, owing to the operation of the law of distribution according to work, end up with unequal shares in the national income of society.

This fundamental division will continue to exist right up to the building of full communism, when the level of development of production will permit us to realize in actual practice the principle of "to each according to his needs." Until that time, socialist society evaluates, and will continue to evaluate, its members primarily according to their contribution to the development of social production, i.e., according to the quantity and quality of their labor. Thus the historically conditioned inequality of this contribution operates as a decisive feature of the structural characteristics of classes under socialism, as an important expression of differences between social groups. (1) Insofar as methods of social evaluation of the contribution of each individual to the development of production are concerned, the most appropriate is based on the degree of complexity of labor (its degree of skill in the broad sense of the word). This method of evaluation arises objectively from the production relations of socialism, with their inherent commodity-money relations and, consequently, also the law of value. A necessary category in this connection is abstract labor, which measures differences based on the differing complexity of labor.

There is thus a close association among: (a) the primary factor making for the social differentiation of the working class — the social and economic division of labor; (b) the dominant factor in this differentiation — the degree of utilization of property (realized, in particular, in the contribution to its development); and (c) empirical measures of actual inequality in the utilization of property, one of which — differences in the complexity of labor — is an expression of the social and economic heterogeneity of labor. This association reflects the unity and integrity of the system of production relations in their interdependence with the social structure of society.

Although under socialism the division of the working class into basic social groups is based on the persisting social and economic heterogeneity of labor and the inequality in the utilization of, and contribution to, the development of socialist property associated with that heterogeneity, as well as on the group's role in the social organization of labor, socialist society grants every person in one or another group extensive opportunities for developing himself as an individual. This is the objective of all social institutions under socialism, within which the role of a specific individual is determined not only by his position in the system of socially differentiated, heterogeneous labor but also by his individual abilities and their utilization for the benefit of society.

The intraclass division of workers into groups according to employment in socially heterogeneous labor sets the conditions for the social makeup of the members of these groups: their social status, the nature of their interpersonal contacts, the structure of their leisure, their social and political functions, their informal production and managerial functions — in short, everything that transforms a category of individuals into a social group with its own specific characteristics.

That is why we cannot state that when a new occupational category of individuals arises in the process of development of production, there immediately arises a new social group, that the latter is created instantaneously from the former. The

transformation of the whole system of social ties and the acquisition of specific social characteristics, including social-
psychological characteristics such as group consciousness,
group solidarity, stability, and self-recruitment, require a considerable interval between the appearance of a new category of
individuals in the occupational-skill structure and their emergence as a social group. Therefore, the formation of an
occupational-skill group based on the social division of labor
serves as the initial, not the final, phase in the reproduction of
the social structure of the working class.

The socio-economic aspect of the division of labor manifests
itself in the division between executive-type [organizatorskii]
and executor-type [ispolnitel'skii] labor and, in the case of the
latter, between mental and primarily manual labor and between
skilled and unskilled labor.

An approach to the determination of specific criteria for the
social differentiation of the working class under socialism follows from the system of propositions presented above. One
such criterion, above all, is the division into groups employed
in mental and primarily manual labor. Naturally, at the present stage in the process of overcoming this division there is
no longer a sharp differentiation between two groups with a
clear boundary between them; the division exists as a gradual
transition through a series of intermediate types, from workers in creative, intellectual labor, to workers in manual labor
with intellectual content, and then to workers performing heavy,
monotonous, manual labor.

Another criterion is the division into executives and executors in the production process, again characterized by a gradual transition from professional executives, through mixed
types of participants in social self-management, to executors
who do not yet exercise their rights to participate in managerial functions.

A third criterion, when applied to workers in primarily manual labor, is the attachment to groups of occupations with different skill levels, and, when applied to workers in mental labor, a functional-skill division into workers performing functions of social management (executives of labor collectives),

functions of guidance and control of production processes (technologists and similar specialists), and functions of executor-type scientific-technical labor (researchers, designers, etc.).

All these basic empirical criteria for identifying social strata are measured by certain indices: type of labor activity, job position, occupation, and participation in social self-management.

The existing schemes of differentiation of the working class, including those examined above, depict the types of intraclass structure that have prevailed up to now. These types are basically associated with two major stages undergone by the social dynamics of the working class.

During the first stage, when property relations exercised the main differentiating impact on the structure of hired labor, the principal elements in this structure were the workers' aristocracy, regular workers ("pure" proletarians), and the stratum of newly emerging workers. Under capitalist conditions this kind of differentiation outlives itself in developed countries that have attained a high level of maturity, have completed industrialization, and have a stable social-class structure with social-class groups that are predominantly self-reproducing. In countries where the process of urbanization and industrialization has not yet been completed, the above criteria of differentiation are the dominant ones. In socialist countries, independently of the extent of industrialization and urbanization, these criteria cease to exercise an important influence; they cease to be dominant in the social structure following the socialist transformation of agriculture.

During the second stage, when the division of labor becomes the foundation of the existence of intraclass strata, social differentiation is connected with different levels of skill. But here, also, this connection is mediated through the system of property relations. Under capitalism this is expressed in differences in the amounts of surplus value created, and under socialism, in the unequal utilization of the means of production belonging to society. Under socialist conditions the significance of differences associated with one's role in the social organization of labor is heightened; and this, in turn, is determined by the social and economic heterogeneity of labor.

The scientific-technical revolution currently in progress leads to a new, third stage in intraclass social differentiation, a stage organically connected with, and a direct sequel to, the second stage. The point is that the functional, technical division of labor changes qualitatively in connection with the transition from the first and second phases of large-scale machine production (small-scale serial production on the basis of general-purpose equipment and conveyor-belt production) to its third phase — partially automated production with extensive use of artificial materials of special quality, and the like. From this there naturally follow important changes in the structure of the aggregate worker, primarily those changes which we considered in the section devoted to the historically changing boundaries of the working class.*

Changes in the structure of the aggregate worker in turn influence the social structure of production collectives.

The result is that currently proposed schemes of differentiation are to a considerable extent outdated insofar as groups of workers in predominantly mental work, purely mental executor-type work, managerial work, and service work, which in earlier periods were less differentiated groups, have now not only increased their share in the aggregate worker but have become significantly more complex in their internal composition. At the same time, groups employed in low-skilled, primarily manual labor exhibit a tendency toward increasing similarity in their social makeup. In other words, the lower groups on the scale of socio-occupational differentiation are tending to merge, and the higher groups are tending to split up and form subgroups with specific social characteristics. (2)

Apparently, we must proceed from the following general proposition: the process of development of the division of labor under conditions in which its socio-economic heterogeneity continues to prevail is accompanied by certain social divisions

---

*Shkaratan is referring here to his argument that under conditions of modern technology, large portions of the intelligentsia should be regarded as "a scientifically educated stratum of the working class" (Shkaratan, op. cit., p. 118).

among the groups employed in mental work. In this situation differentiation must be based on the degree of skill of labor. Various approaches to the operational use of this general principle are possible.

One of the approaches is connected with the actually observed division of personnel in mental work on the basis of their skill-functional differences: (1) individuals employed in the management and organization of management of a system of machines, i.e., those employed in functions involving the organizational-technical and technological servicing of production; these are the so-called "technologists" and groups having similar functions; (2) people employed in the creation of basically new schemes of production and their scientific-technical maintenance, i.e., scientists and designers; (3) those employed in the management of production collectives of complex composition (including small groups — the units of production collectives); it is from this group that professional executives are drawn; (4) individuals who implement management decisions, i.e., personnel in the managerial apparatus whose function is not to make decisions but to carry them out.

The material examined in the following chapters shows substantial differences in the social characteristics of these groups. Above all we may observe considerable variation in the level of education and the nature of social "careers," including social origins.

However, one should not conclude that this approach is the only possible one. We may postulate a relatively independent differentiation according to a skill-job position scale based on the required level of education. This approach produces three principal groups: (1) personnel employed in positions requiring specialized training in addition to general secondary education (in actual practice this group coincides with the managerial-apparatus group); (2) personnel employed in positions requiring secondary specialized education; (3) personnel employed in positions requiring higher education.

While the first classification (the skill-functional) does not yield a clearly distinguished scale of roles and positions along the lines of "lower to higher," the second (the skill-job position) does not take specific social functions into account. Both are characterized by inadequate differentiation, and require greater specification and subdivision into a larger number of subgroups in order to forecast the social characteristics of a person who may appear in one or another social role.

Apparently, we can verify which of these schemes of differentiation is most adequate by determining the range of fluctuations of the principal socio-economic characteristics of groups with respect to mobility, income, wages, cultural level, family ties, etc., since the most adequate classification is the one that yields the lowest coefficient of variation. A more thorough method of verification, of course, involves use of pattern recognition [raspoznavaniia obrazov] (the taxonomic method); and the most appropriate method of classification of characteristics according to their significance for social differentiation involves the use of entropy analysis.

Finally, we can assume that a practicable grouping would be based on the interaction of indices comprising the foundation of both the skill-functional and the skill-job position classifications.

In all cases, however, we must keep in mind that up to now we have been concerned with differentiation essentially within the social structure of the enterprise.

The actual differentiation of the working class as a whole is much more complex, since the social position of a category of individuals is not fully determined by the position of each category in the formal structure of the enterprise: it is also defined by indices of the individuals' position in the community, the social status of those associated with them, including, above all, members of their families, etc. It is only in this whole system of relations that the real social status of one or another category of individuals emerges, while the basic elements and determining relationships are revealed in the social structure.

The social structure of the working class at the present stage of its development is given, therefore, by two composite indicators: (1) the structure of jobs according to the complexity and social importance of labor (3); and (2) the social structure of the population as a whole, involving the reproduction of social groups (including socio-occupational groups) in certain proportions.

These social-historical determinants of social structure also condition the factors determining the fate of individuals. Such factors include education, general cultural development, occupational skills (including managerial skills), and special abilities whose development is affected, in turn, by the impact of the socio-economic conditions of socially divided, socially heterogeneous labor. Given equal access to education and other cultural values, the members of different social groups make unequal use of them.

The features characterizing social intraclass groups can be reduced to three basic sets of indices:

1. Resultant (determining) features reflect the main socioeconomic characteristics and functions of groups. They are determined, as already noted, by the socio-economic heterogeneity of labor and are expressed in such indices as occupation (or, more precisely, the category of occupations from the standpoint of the degree of skill of labor), skill (in terms of rank, let us say), job title, participation in the management of society and production, and wages. In this connection, not one of these indices taken separately can serve as the basis for placing an individual in any particular social group.

2. Factor (or genetic) features reflect the causes that have led specific categories of workers into a given intraclass group. These include social origin, cultural surroundings, education, and individual special abilities. (4)

3. Attribute (supplementary) features refer to peculiarities of everyday life, culture, attitude toward work, and other forms of social conduct in which the specific characteristics of intraclass groups are reflected.

The structure of the working class is highly complex. In this study we have confined ourselves primarily to the characteristics of only the determinant structure of organizations. A multifactor model of the structure of the Soviet working class must reflect the sex, age, national, and other such structures, and — what is extremely important — in such a model the whole

working class should be regarded as a system, with the enterprise collective as the basic social cell. But all these aspects
of structural organization are subordinate to the skill-
occupational structure, through whose mechanism the social
structure of society — growing into a communist society — operates on the process of development of classes. The scientific-
technical revolution, determining changes in the productive
forces of modern society, emerges as the primary factor in
changes in the social division of labor and is thus the condition
and prerequisite for the social development of the working
class.

Notes

1) This reveals with particular clarity the superiority of socialism, which evaluates people not according to the amount of
wealth they have appropriated (which is the ultimate basis of
intraclass differences within the ruling classes of antagonistic
social orders), but according to the quantity and quality of labor of all individuals, who are equally owners of social wealth.

2) For a somewhat different interpretation of this question,
see S. A. Kugel', "Changes in the Social Structure of Soviet Society Under the Impact of the Scientific-Technical Revolution,"
Voprosy filosofii, 1969, No. 3.

3) It follows that the guidance and regulation of social structure under socialism includes the exercise of directing influence on trends of scientific-technical progress, since the structure of jobs according to the complexity of labor is predetermined by the level of mechanization and automation of production processes.

4) When we speak of the role of special abilities in the individual's social position under socialism, we should recall that
Marx regarded them as the consequence of the division of labor, which limits the harmonious development of the personality. "The initial difference between a porter and a philosopher is less than that between a mongrel and a wolfhound. The
gulf between them is forced by the division of labor" (Marx
and Engels, Soch., Vol. 4, p. 149).

3 On the Criteria of Intraclass Differences in Socialist Society

G. V. MOKRONOSOV

Why, under conditions of societal ownership of the means of production, do we regard as social differences the significant differences between industrial and agricultural labor, manual and mechanized labor, mental and physical labor, simple and complex labor, and, correspondingly, between the people connected with these types of activity?

In other words, why are the significant differences in the content as well as in the conditions of performance of mental and physical, industrial and agricultural, and manual and mechanized labor considered a manifestation of the social heterogeneity of labor, while the differences between people engaged in these types of labor are regarded as social differences?

The answer to this question, in our opinion, can be obtained from analysis of the basic economic law of the socialist mode of production, expressing the essence of socialist production relations. The affirmation of societal ownership of the means of production ensures, in accordance with the achieved level of development of the productive forces, the improvement of the material conditions of existence of the working masses, and subordinates production to achievement of the full well-being and all-round development of the mental and physical abilities of all members of society.

From M. N. Rutkevich, ed., Protsessy izmeneniia sotsial'- noi struktury v sovetskom obshchestve, Sverdlovsk, 1967, pp. 9-13. We have omitted the first half of this article to avoid repetition of material presented earlier.

The level of development of the productive forces under socialism is still not sufficient, however, for the creation of such
conditions of labor as would ensure equal possibilities for the
all-round development of the abilities of all citizens. For all
its relativity, the criterion which lies at the foundation of the
division of spheres of production and of types of labor according to their social significance, in our opinion, is the degree,
the level of conditions, created by one or another type of labor
for the all-round development of a person's mental and physical abilities.

This criterion directs attention to the objective content of labor and of the productive process that primarily determines the
character of the needs, interests, and consciousness of those
groups who are engaged in that type of labor. The boundaries
between types of labor — between mental and physical, manual
and mechanized, industrial and agricultural labor — are shifting
and relative; but nonetheless they objectively exist and, at their
extreme points, show up very sharply. For example, the conditions of labor of even workers on modern blast-furnaces differ
sharply from the conditions of labor of an engineer, and even
more from those of a teacher, doctor, etc. This is particularly
true of groups and strata of workers and peasants involved in
heavy manual labor. We suggest that the degree of mechanization, the creation of favorable conditions of labor and of possibilities for changes in activity, in the degree of its monotony
and fatigue for the worker — i.e., all those indicators that in
the aggregate determine the extent of possibilities for the all-
round development of personality — are the basis of differences
within the classes and social groups of socialist society.

Can one, then, deduce them directly from the content of mental or physical, industrial or agricultural labor? Our literature
examines in detail the reasons for the existence under socialism of significant differences between such types of labor as
mental and physical, agricultural and industrial, manual and
automated labor, etc. It is well known, for example, that agricultural labor still differs significantly from industrial labor
in level of mechanization, in use of technology and energy, in
utilization of the achievements of science, etc. In the sphere of

material production there are still many occupations involving manual labor, which for the most part is fatiguing, demands much expenditure of muscular energy, and is monotonous. About 47% of the workers in our industry are engaged in manual labor; in agriculture the percentage is even higher.

The specific nature of socialism, its difference from developed communism, consists in the fact that at this stage of the development of production the normal functioning of the latter is possible only on the basis of the constant attachment of particular groups of society to qualitatively dissimilar types of labor. This does not occur by law; it is caused by the objective conditions of societal production.

The socialist system of the social division of labor is in essence the expression of the social heterogeneity characteristic of society in that stage of development at which it emerges, after long birth pains, from capitalist society. The particular nature of this historically transient system of the social division of labor consists in that, affirming the equality of all in relation to the means of production (at least in the public sector), it does not ensure equality in the conditions of labor. This appears in the constant attachment of particular groups of people to qualitatively dissimilar types of labor, and this in turn creates social inequality among people. This is expressed concretely in the fact, for example, that for particular groups of people, physical labor, including heavy manual labor, remains the sphere in which they apply their labor throughout their lives.

Marx, characterizing precisely this feature of socialism, wrote that along with equal rights to the means of production, there are unequal rights for unequal labor. People engaged primarily in physical labor — especially in heavy manual labor — have fewer possibilities for the development of their potential abilities, for the assimilation of all the spiritual wealth that has been amassed by humanity. We are speaking here not of the payment of labor — heavy physical labor is often paid more than skilled labor — but of the conditions under which this labor is performed, their influence on the development of man's abilities. And abilities cannot be reduced to level of skill in the sense of knowing how to perform particular work operations,

but express themselves in the ability of a personality to assimilate, to transform into its internal content, all the wealth of social relations expressed in social activity, in the assimilation
of culture, etc.

We therefore see the determining criterion of intraclass differences among workers in the level of the technical, scientific
foundations of labor; and this is expressed in such indicators
as level of energy supply and of mechanization and automation
of production in the conditions of the realization of labor. The
level of skill, the cultural-technical level of a worker, is rather
a factor conditioning the possibility of employment in one or another type of labor, of moving from one stratum to another, or
of raising an entire stratum to a higher level.

The level of development of the productive forces under
socialism is still such that it is not possible to eliminate the
division of labor into "dirty" and "clean" work. It is inevitable
that some strata of society must be engaged primarily in heavy
physical labor and others in lighter labor, some in less skilled
labor and others in more skilled labor. Insofar as society needs
every type of labor in given proportions, the number of people
engaged in a particular type of labor has its limits. Which
groups of society will occupy one or another area of labor in
the conditions of socialism is determined primarily by the
cultural-technical level, by the skill of working people.

The population census of 1959 showed that the strata of workers involved in heavy manual labor as a rule have comparatively
low general educational preparation. For example, for every
thousand metallurgical and metal workers engaged in the occupation of smith, 812 did not have even an incomplete secondary
education, and for workers in such occupations as lathe
operator and milling-machine operator this indicator was 333
and 327, respectively. (1)

Unequal conditions for unequal labor are reproduced by the
relations of production themselves, since those societal groups
that are engaged in labor that offers less possibility for the all-
round development of the personality, being constantly attached
to these types of labor, have fewer possibilities for transcending these boundaries.

The fact that, for people at a low cultural-technical level, the main area of application of labor remains manual labor in the sphere of material production, which does not increase the chances of that category of working people in competition with other members of society in the all-round development of their abilities, is basically a manifestation of the same inequality in social position.

One of the facts that testifies to this is that among workers engaged in various types of study, the bulk are workers connected with occupations of mechanized or complex labor.

Surveys carried out in the Uralkabel' factory show that of the total number of workers in a given occupation, 69.9% of machine operators, 10.7% of auxiliary workers, and only 3.9% of loaders are engaged in various types of studies.

Thus, differences in the nature of labor are basic for intra-class differences under socialism. The social inequality characteristic of socialism finds its expression in this difference, since possibilities for the development and satisfaction of needs remain, for the moment, unequal for different strata. In accordance with the transformation of socialist production relations into communist ones, the overcoming of social differences among workers, peasants, and intelligentsia, and between strata within these classes and social groups, is proceeding.

Note

1) Itogi Vsesoiuznoi perepisi naseleniia, Moscow, 1959 (summary volume), p. 177.

4 Some Problems of the Social Structure of the Soviet Working Class

L. A. GORDON AND E. V. KLOPOV

It is generally recognized that problems of the contemporary working class and the contemporary city have a plethora of "points of intersection" and even whole "border areas," study of which is necessary for a more or less fruitful analysis of both of these types of problems. It appears, however, that not all aspects of the intersection, coincidence, and interpenetration of these problems have received enough elucidation in the literature.

One such aspect is the territorial (spatial) interrelation of these social categories.

Historically, under capitalism the working class was formed primarily in urban areas — even more narrowly, in such primarily urban branches of the economy as industry and construction. The organic tie with the city of the antagonistic classes, the proletariat and bourgeoisie, partly determined the city's leading role in society. "The town cannot be equal to the countryside," wrote V. I. Lenin. "The countryside cannot be equal to the town in the historical conditions of this era. The town inescapably pulls the countryside after it. The countryside inescapably follows the town." (1)

No major changes in this regard have occurred under socialism: as before, the working class is connected primarily with the city; as before, the city plays a leading role in all the major

From Akademiia Nauk SSSR, Institut mezhdunarodnogo rabochego dvizheniia, Urbanizatsiia i rabochii klass v usloviiakh nauchno-tekhnicheskoi revoliutsii, Moscow, 1970, pp. 191-211.

spheres of society's life. In the contemporary stage of development of Soviet society, however, processes are at work that are
causing both a change in the concept of "the working class" itself and some new features in the relations between the working
class and the city. Not the least important of these changes is
the widening of the boundaries of the working class. In essence
the working class now encompasses not one or another part, but
practically all of the city, as well as important groups of the
population outside it.

The traditional conception of the working class that underlies
all official statistical data assumes that workers include people
engaged primarily in manual labor and working for hire in state
enterprises and institutions. In this case the composition of the
working class does not include: (1) persons engaged in manual
labor but not working in state enterprises (i.e., mainly collective farmers); (2) persons engaged in mental labor as such, no
matter where they work (the intelligentsia); (3) persons engaged
in nonmanual labor fulfilling auxiliary and service functions
(conditionally, employees).

In the USSR the quantitative relation of the enumerated groups
to each other (according to rounded figures for 1959-1960 and
1966-1967) is as follows (in percentages of all those employed):

	1959/1960	1966/1967
Workers engaged primarily in manual labor for hire (the working class in the traditional sense)	50	55
Those engaged primarily in manual labor not for hire (mainly the collective farm peasantry)	30	20
Those engaged in nonmanual service work (primarily nonspecialists-employees)	$10^{(2)}$	$11^{(2)}$
Those engaged in mental labor as such (the intelligentsia)	$10^{(2)}$	$14^{(2)}$

However, the socio-economic nature of several groups of working people has changed so much that the division introduced above no longer reflects the boundaries of the working class.

Particularly noticeable today is the fact that the stratum of those engaged in nonmanual service work in state enterprises and institutions has many characteristics in common with the working class. (3) At the time of the 1959 census, this group was taken to include salespeople, mechanics, rate-setters, laboratory technicians, cinema operators, foremen, nurses, telegraph operators, postal clerks, typists, clerks, heads of storage houses, hairdressers, and other such categories of working people. The overwhelming majority of these working people differ from workers neither in their relation to the means of production nor in their role in the organization of labor (in particular, as a whole they also are not involved with the management of people).

The proximity of nonspecialists-employees to the traditional workers is confirmed also by the repeated changes of place of work in the course of a man's life in which those engaged in auxiliary nonmanual labor become workers and vice versa. A no less striking illustration of their social proximity is the "daily-life unity" of workers and the group of employees under consideration: in the great bulk of families of those engaged in auxiliary nonmanual labor there are also workers — husbands, wives, children. According to the data of one of our studies conducted in 1967-1968 in a typical industrial center, about 80% of employees without specialized education live in families which include workers. (We should point out that only a few decades ago the situation was entirely different in this regard.)

These facts permit the conclusion that in contemporary Soviet society those engaged in nonmanual service work have already become, or are becoming, a part of the working class.

At the same time, the majority of them, in particular those who are employed outside the sphere of material production, form a particular group within the structure of the working class that differs from industrial workers with respect to the character of labor, degree of concentration, and closeness to a collective in the process of production. Incidentally, in the

era of the present scientific-technical revolution, even these
differences have a tendency to be smoothed out; enormous enterprises are appearing in the service sector, and they are
employing hundreds and thousands of people in work that is essentially industrial in character. The further progress of science and technology, as well as the policy of broadening and
"industrializing" the service sector, suggests that in the not
very distant future this group, too, will become a segment of
the working class.

In a developed socialist society a tendency toward increasing similarity between the working class and a significant portion of the intelligentsia (personnel in mental labor proper,
specialists) is also sharply intensified.

Antagonistic or semi-antagonistic differences between the
working class and the intelligentsia disappeared in the USSR
comparatively long ago, and since that time the great bulk of
the intelligentsia differs from workers neither in their objective relation to the means of production nor in their origins,
ideology, or political attitudes. The present stage of socio-
economic development brings new features into this process.
The overall numbers of the intelligentsia and its role in the
life of our country have increased sharply. Thus, for example,
if at the end of the 1930s and the beginning of the 1940s there
were 2-2.5 million specialists employed in the economy, and
in the middle of the 1950s, 5-5.5 million, by 1966 their number
had reached 13 million.

In connection with the question of rapprochement with the
working class, it is particularly important to point out that
about 4.5 million specialists (approximately 35% of their total
number) are employed in the sector of material production: in
industrial enterprises, in construction organizations, in transport enterprises, in state farms and other state agricultural
enterprises, in material-technical supply. In addition, scientific institutions, the majority of which are today inseparably
linked with material production, employ approximately another
8% of specialists. (In 1940-1941, only 20% of specialists were
engaged in material production.)

The overwhelming majority of specialists engaged in material production work within the framework of large collectives, and are subordinated to their discipline, organization, and interests. The economic reform further strengthens the effect of this factor by increasing the role of the collectives. Moreover, the technological revolution is bringing with it an increase in a group of specialists whose work is in no way connected with the management of people and in degree of breakdown differs little from the labor of workers. Even now, not only the relation to property but also participation in material production, collectivity, concentration, and organization of work are making important strata of the intelligentsia increasingly similar to the working class. Simultaneously, many groups of workers are rising to the level of the intelligentsia.

It stands to reason that the nature of mental labor itself, as well as cultural level and many features of life-style, distinguish the intelligentsia from the workers. Incidentally, even these differences are no longer absolute. For example, in the industrial center that we studied, 30-40% of specialists live in families that also include workers engaged primarily in manual labor. This figure is rather large, although noticeably smaller than that indicating the proximity in family and daily life of workers and nonspecialist employees.

Also extremely interesting in this connection are data concerning the daily behavior of workers, employees, and engineering-technical personnel obtained as a result of the study of time-budgets of those employed in industrial enterprises of several cities of the European USSR. Typological analysis of these data showed that the industrial intelligentsia does not form a group with a specific way of spending time. The structure of time expenditure of the bulk of engineers and technicians studied does not differ, for all practical purposes, from the corresponding indices of a large group of more developed workers engaged in manual labor.

On the whole, changes in the position of several groups of those engaged in mental labor in production, and, to some extent, in their daily life have gone so far already that it is possible, if you will, to speak of their transformation into a part of the working class. In its ranks they form a completely new layer that is changing the composition and entire structure of the working class in a fundamental way. Thus, in socialist society as in the developed capitalist countries, there is taking place, although on a different socio-economic base, a universal process of consolidation of hired laborers into a single class. It is evident that working people of almost all the "urban" sectors of the economy are now becoming members of the working class. This means that already not a greater or lesser part of a socialist town's labor force belongs to the working class, but an overwhelming majority of it.

The results of the shifts occurring in Soviet society in its social structure and, correspondingly, in the composition and structure of its working class are not limited to the above, however. Among these shifts, the switch-over of a large part of the collective farm peasantry to work in state agricultural enterprises, mostly in state farms, attracts one's attention: the number of workers and employees in agriculture had not yet reached 3.5 million at the beginning of the 1950s, but by the end of the 1950s it had surpassed 7 million, and in 1967 it was 9.5 million (which accounts for about 12% of all workers and employees in the nation). Workers and employees now make up about 1/3 of all those engaged in public agricultural production.

Of course, workers of the state farms still retain many traits characteristic of the collective farm peasantry: the private subsidiary economy remains an important source of their income; the way of life and culture in the state farms do not differ too much from those in the collective farms and, on the contrary, they differ very noticeably from the conditions of life of urban workers. Nonetheless, the formation of a new and numerous segment of the working class on the basis of a change in the social nature of those engaged in agriculture cannot be doubted. One can assert, therefore, that in the contemporary stage of development of Soviet society, the working class's sphere of vital activity is already not only the town but also the countryside, and it is now impossible to make the mechanical association "town-working class," "countryside-peasantry," which was justifiable as a first approximation several decades ago.

*   *   *

Up to now we have been examining processes occurring in the working class and in Soviet society as a whole under the influence of production and socio-occupational factors (such as relation to property, position in production, character of work, and so forth). At the same time, the smoothing over and relocation of class boundaries, the transformation of them, in part, into intraclass divisions, by no means exhausts all the complexity of changes in the working class's structure in the stage of mature socialism. Another remarkable feature of this period is the gradual growth of the relative significance of non-class divisions and, in general, of divisions unrelated to production. We refer specifically to social mode of life and cultural and socio-demographic divisions (i.e., divisions arising not only due to a man's position in production but also in connection with his family status, level of education, everyday environment, etc.). Thus, in the workers' milieu strata are being distinguished ever more distinctly which differ not "by the place they occupy in a historically determined system of social production," not "by their relation...to the means of production" (4), etc., but by their level of culture in the broad sociological sense of this term as a designation of the totality of life conditions, norms, traditions, and knowledge directly determining man's behavior. (It is precisely in this sense that culture is understood, for example, in the last works of Lenin, where culture, daily life, and habits are viewed as a unified whole.) (5)

Cultural divisions were, of course, always one of the elements of the structure of the working class. However, in a society with a developed class structure, cultural divisions as a whole occupy a subordinate position since they depend directly and immediately on class membership, i.e., actually on a man's position in the system of production, which predetermines in this case the main features of all other conditions of life — family, daily-life, educational, etc. For example, when we talk about workers and bourgeoisie, we actually distinguish large groups of people differing not only in their relation to property but, in Lenin's expression, in their whole "order of life," "order of family relations," "level of needs, both material and spiritual." (6) This is also true in relation to the most important groups in the workers' milieu: the experienced nucleus of the proletariat, the workers' aristocracy, quasi-proletarian groups, etc. In essence, class and even intraclass divisions have, so to speak, a culture-forming character.

In developed socialist society the situation changes noticeably. The tendency toward the erosion of class boundaries, the general dynamism and mobility of social life are such that social production factors begin gradually to lose their exclusive culture-forming properties. Membership in one or another production layer no longer determines all conditions of life (or, as Lenin said, the entire "life situation" [7]) with such strength as was the case only a few decades ago.

Under present conditions there are no grounds for talking about the conditions and way of life of the industrial proletariat distinct from the "order of life" of workers in the urban sphere of services (we should remember that, as a rule, they are members of the same families). The daily life of agricultural workers, noticeably different from the daily life of urban industrial workers, is very close to the way of life of those nonagricultural workers and employees who live in the village.

In other words, "conditions of life situation" are not as closely connected with social production factors as they once were; in the contemporary stage they take on a relative autonomy of a sort. (8) Cultural divisions, cultural strata in society as a whole and in the workers' milieu in particular, are formed under the influence of the totality of conditions both in the realm of work as well as outside it. Moreover, the latter already function as independent variables, so to speak. It is not surprising that differences in "life situation" and the cultural strata connected with them in the workers' milieu do not coincide with the basic intraclass layers formed on socio-occupational grounds. Therefore, analysis of the structure of the working class in these conditions demands a characterization not only of the socio-occupational but also of the cultural divisions in its milieu.

Unfortunately, the present level of study of the problem still does not allow one to describe the entire mechanism of the formation and functioning of cultural strata in society. However, the results of a series of sociological surveys already make it possible for us to note several objective factors influencing the conditions of the "life situation" of various groups and, consequently, determining the formation of their culture (understood in the sense described above).

Among the factors determining the emergence and functioning of various cultural strata in the working class, and of divisions independent of socio-occupational ones or not coinciding with them, the nature of the milieu in which a man's life activity flows has great significance. This manifests itself most clearly in the juxtaposition of economic and cultural conditions of everyday life in town and countryside. (We should keep in mind that today the countryside has also become a realm of life activity — not the chief one, of course — of the working class.) In essence this is a question of the level and degrees of development of urban culture and urban conditions of daily life — i.e., of the level of urbanization of conditions of life in settlements of various types.

Let us remember, first of all, that the private subsidiary economy plays a not unimportant role as an additional source of income for the overwhelming majority of rural inhabitants, including workers and employees engaged in the nonagricultural sectors — i.e., for people whose position in social production is identical in principle with the socio-occupational structure of city-dwellers. It is natural that work at housekeeping and in the garden is a characteristic feature of the everyday behavior of these strata of working people.

Another very essential factor that gives rise to dissimilar conditions of "life situation" in town and countryside is the lower level of development of material and cultural services in rural locations: for the 45% of the population concentrated here, there are only about 38% of those engaged in education, 23% in health, 19% in trade, public catering, etc.

The cultural revolution that has come to pass in our nation has had the result that many important preconditions for the development of mass culture have reached almost the same level in the countryside as in the town. For example, in 1967, public libraries in rural locations possessed 506 million copies

of books and journals, while libraries in towns and settlements
of the urban type had 599 million. Rural locations even have
significantly more film projectors than do the cities: for more
than 5,000 towns and settlements of the urban type, there are
23,000 film projectors; for 40,000 rural soviets — 129,800.
Nonetheless, at the moment the countryside still has a somewhat lower level of cultural services on the whole. A graphic
indicator of the countryside's backwardness is differences in
the educational level of the urban and rural populations in general and, in particular, of workers living in town and countryside. The following figures of the All-Union Census of Population of 1959 on the number of persons with incomplete secondary education and higher (per 1000 employed) bear witness to
these differences:

	Urban population	Rural population
All societal groups	564	316
Of these, workers	424	311

The depths of cultural-daily life differences between town and
countryside and the difficulty in overcoming them become particularly appreciable when we turn from statistical to dynamic
indicators.

Conditions of life in rural areas in the period of full-scale
building of communism are improving at a rapid pace. In rural
areas, increasingly numerous and varied elements of urban culture and urban daily life are "acclimating themselves" — from
television sets and water and gas supply in millions of homes and
apartments to personal service shops and mobile exhibitions of
paintings. An intensive rapprochement of the countryside with
the town is occurring. However, a rise in the standard of living — in particular, a development of the service sector — is
also taking place with great speed in urban areas. As a result — and herein lies the complexity of the problem — with an
absolute growth of all indicators, the relative gap remains in
certain respects, and at times it is even increasing. Characteristic, for example, are the following data on the dynamics of

several branches of cultural and material services in town and countryside:

	1950		1966	
	In towns and settlements of the urban type	In rural locations	In towns and settlements of the urban type	In rural locations
Number employed per 1000 inhabitants				
in education	23	16	35	24
in health	20	6	27	9
Commodity circulation of trade and public catering (rubles per capita)	390	79	690	243

Behind the dissimilar material-economic, educational, and other conditions, lie deep differences between many other elements of culture — customs, morals, traditions, norms of behavior. It is not surprising that from the point of view of daily way of life, differences between the "life situations" of the urban and rural populations today are hardly less significant than the differences between the basic socio-occupational groups.

In characterizing the social, daily-life and socio-cultural differences between town and countryside, one must keep in mind at the same time that the city itself as a social environment is not a single whole.

The differences between major cities and large towns on the one hand, and many small towns and workers' settlements on the other, are especially great. (We note parenthetically that almost half of the entire urban population lives in urban settlements with populations of less than 100,000.) The majority of

small towns and workers' settlements seem to be in an intermediate position between big cities and the countryside in terms
of conditions of life, level of development of service sector, and
general character of culture.

Some small towns — old ones in particular — notwithstanding
the rather intensive industrial development which at times occurs in them, still retain many features of the tenor of rural
daily life. Not without interest in this connection are several
traits that came to light in the course of studying the conditions
of life of workers of the same socio-occupational categories in
a large and a small town. As in the countryside, the private
subsidiary economy plays an essential role in the life of workers of a small town. Here kitchen gardens are possessed by almost 3/4 of the workers studied, while in a major city the figure is less than 1/4. In contrast, the service sector — in particular, communal services — is much more strongly developed
in major cities. It is characteristic, for example, that from 2/3
to 3/4 of the workers studied in a big city live in government
housing with all basic communal conveniences, while in the
small town the government supply of housing provided with conveniences satisfies the needs of only 1/2 of the workers.

Differences in level of education are also quite large. In our
study, for example, it turned out that one-and-a-half times
more workers had finished more than seven grades of school
in the major center than in the small town.

In essence, we have here entirely different stages of development of urban culture and urban conditions of daily life; they
testify to the presence, in the contemporary stage, of at least
two types of urban realms — highly developed contemporary
cities and urban settlements, for which quasi-urban conditions
of "life situation" are characteristic. In scale, the difference
in conditions of life in big cities and small towns (developed
urban areas and "quasi-urban" areas) is comparable to the
difference in conditions between countryside and town as a
whole.

It follows that the degrees of urbanization of "life situation" —
including conditions of life in the countryside as the first of
these — create objective foundations for distinguishing within

the working class no less than three (and not two, as is usually done) categories distinct from socio-occupational groups, namely: urban, semi-urban and rural (but not necessarily agricultural!) workers.

Although differences in life conditions at various stages of urbanization give rise to groups for which the urban, semi-urban and rural way of life is characteristic, their demarcations by no means necessarily coincide with territorial divisions into big and major city, small town and suburb, and village. The high social, territorial and cultural mobility of the Soviet population is accompanied by a sort of "transmission" (9) of traditions, norms, habits of daily life, and attitudes from the countryside to the towns, from small towns to big ones, and partly also in reverse. As a result of the differences in objective living conditions, such an "overflow" does not lead to a merging and disappearance of the division into cultural-daily life strata itself. However, as a result of this process the boundaries of the strata are displaced in such a way that people belonging to a semi-urban or to a rural cultural-daily life environment can turn out to be inhabitants of major cities, and vice versa.

On the other hand, in small towns and even villages there are groups of people who live in conditions that do not differ too much from the life situation in major centers. The so-called "demonstration effect" of contemporary mass culture, which causes many elements of the urban style of life to penetrate into villages and "semi-urban" areas where conditions often have not yet been developed for their general distribution, also facilitates the displacement of territorial boundaries of cultural strata.

In light of these facts, the results of the above-mentioned special research study devoted to a typology of the everyday behavior of a group of urban industrial workers are not without interest. As the analysis showed, in this group two strata are clearly distinguishable — one with an urban and the other with a "quasi-urban" type of behavior. Some distinguishing features of urban daily life that emerged were an orientation toward broad participation in mass urban culture, self-education, and contact with one's family. Quasi-urban daily life is distinguished by the great role of work in the household and in the garden, by the broad development of ties with neighbors and, in general, of socializing outside the family, all at a somewhat lower level of cultural activity. The genetic link of this type of behavior with the countryside and small town is obvious, and indeed, people with a quasi-urban style of daily life make up 2/3 to 3/4 of all those who were studied in the small town. In major cities, too, this stratum encompasses more than 1/3 of those studied, however, although here the predominance of daily life of the urban type proper is natural. It appears that these data support the very existence of a connection between stages of urbanization and the character of daily-life culture, as well as the impossibility of a total coincidence of socio-cultural and territorial divisions.

*   *   *

In studying the character and conditions of life activity of the working class, one must also take into account those circumstances which, in one way or another, depend on the influence of "eternal" natural factors — such as the age, sex or family status of workers and the members of their families. Earlier, under capitalism and even in the early stages of socialist construction — in short, in societies with a developed class structure — their meaning was as if overshadowed by the much stronger effect of class and socio-occupational factors. Today, in the framework of mature socialist society, in connection with the process of erosion of class boundaries noted above and under the influence of scientific-technological progress, family and sex-age differences not only take on a relatively independent significance but become important aspects for the scientific management of society.

Thus, for example, the mass inclusion of women in societal production poses very pressing problems.

Today women comprise 1/2 of all workers and employees in the Soviet Union as against 1/4 in the 1920s. But the equality achieved by women with respect to their participation in societal labor is by no means complemented by equality in daily life. Even under conditions of developed urban daily life, female working people are occupied by housework approximately twice as much as males and, correspondingly, have 1/2 the free time. It is not surprising that from the point of view of way of life, one of the deepest differences in the working class is precisely that between men and women. The double burden lying on the shoulders of women leads, in addition to many other socially significant losses, to the fact that in the majority of cases women have fewer possibilities for raising their qualifications, for mastering the more complicated and responsible types of jobs. It is characteristic that the average wages of women are lower than those of men (for example, in one of the industrial centers we studied, this difference is approximately 1/3 less: 84 rubles per month for women as against 131 rubles for men).

In contemporary conditions, age divisions among workers also have a specifically social meaning.

As a result of the rapid cultural progress in our country over the course of several decades, an uneven rise is occurring in the educational level of each succeeding generation in comparison with the preceding one. In sum, a situation has come to pass in society in which the school preparation of different generations differs distinctly. The following figures of the 1959 All-Union Census of Population bear graphic witness to this (see table on following page). In other words, age divisions have to some extent taken on a cultural-educational character.

Age divisions have not only a cultural meaning, incidentally; they also have a material-economic meaning. We should be more precise and speak not of age divisions but of family-age stages of the life cycle (in an individual's active work career there are, with some simplification, three stages: youth until the founding of a family; family life with children not yet of age; middle age after children have entered upon an independent working life). These stages are more or less directly and immediately related to a person's standard of living, and specifically to such an indicator as income per capita.

The fact is that although payment according to the quantity and quality of labor is a most important principle of the distribution of material benefits under socialism, actual consumption depends not only on wages but also on the so-called "co-

| Age | Number of persons with education of not less than 7 grades per 1000 population | | |
	Workers	Employees	Collective farmers
20-24 years	617	917	502
25-29	342	905	216
30-34	399	902	277
35-39	353	895	239
40-44	208	891	91
45-49	102	682	31
50-54	73	622	19
55-59	49	554	13
60-64	34	459	10
65-69	24	355	8
70 and older	15	228	6

efficient of family burden" (measured by the number of dependents in the family per working person). As the materials of one of our studies demonstrate, after having shown a direct link between the character of labor and wages, the size of per capita income of socio-occupational groups with dissimilar character of labor varies much less than do the wages of these groups:

	Average monthly wages (rubles)	Average monthly income per capita (rubles)
Unskilled and low-skilled workers	74	62
Skilled workers	111	69
Highly skilled workers	144	72
Employees in management positions	169	81
Teachers, scientific, medical, and other specialists not in the sector of material production	110	81
Engineering-technical personnel and other specialists in the sector of material production	117	78
Employees without specialized education	84	66

The reasons for the lack of direct dependence of income per capita on the character of labor and, correspondingly, on the level of wages become obvious if one juxtaposes the amounts of income per capita with the "coefficient of family burden" mentioned above:

Average monthly income per capita (rubles):	30 and less	31-40	41-50	51-60	61-70	71-80	81-90	91-120	121 and higher
Coefficient of family burden:	1.33	1.11	0.88	0.54	0.41	0.34	0.27	0.17	0.04

Tentative calculations allow us to suggest that, overall, income per capita depends no more on the level of wages than on the number of dependents in the family (in the majority of cases these are children of minor age) per working person, i.e., to a considerable extent on what stage of the life cycle that working person is in. And correspondingly, one of the most important bases for the grouping of workers and of working people in general according to their conditions and level of life is their family-age divisions: into "youth" (in respect to family status), married people with children, and middle-aged people without children of minor age.

*   *   *

Thus, we find that a characteristic process for developed socialist society is the erosion of class and intraclass boundaries and, correspondingly, the "appearance," the rise of the relative significance, and the strengthening of the effect of the non-class aspects of its structure (not only educational, cultural and daily

life, etc., but also family-demographic aspects), of their transformation into a relatively independent "level" of structure. In
the era of mature socialism, this "level" coincides less and
less with the divisions resulting from socio-occupational differences and, even more important, does not directly depend
(or depends comparatively weakly) on them.

Let us remark once more that class social structure in any
society includes several levels, and always consists of several
grids built from various bases (above all those of class and
production, but also those of daily life, culture, family, etc.).
Under circumstances of developed class relations, however, including the early stages of socialism, the boundaries of the
socio-occupational grid have a distinct culture-forming character, and therefore divisions on the other levels coincide with
these first ones. All other "social grids" here are practically
set synonymously onto the socio-occupational grid. Under these
conditions, a social group distinguished by a particular position
in the sphere of production generally has a more or less identical level of culture, lives in comparatively similar cultural
and daily-life conditions, and is distinguished by approximately
the same tenor of family life. In this sense one can consider
such a socio-occupational group — of industrial workers, let
us say — a prime element of intraclass social structure. In
contrast, in the period of formation of social homogeneity in a
society which already is not a class society in its pure form,
divisions according to various bases cease to coincide with
each other. The boundaries that earlier corresponded comparatively strictly to each other on all levels seem to shift, forming a system of several "social grids" set one upon another,
but now criss-crossing.

The structure of the Soviet working class is ceasing primarily to be uniformly production-based, socio-occupational
in nature. It presents itself today in the form of a complicated
interweaving of socio-occupational layers with socio-cultural,
socio-daily life, socio-demographic strata; it takes on, so to
speak, a voluminous, manifold character. As a prime element
necessary for the understanding of such a structure, one must
consider not simply a socio-occupational group but a cultural-

production group distinguished not only on the basis of its position in production but also on the basis of many other circumstances. For example, if earlier one could examine, as one of such prime elements, the single stratum of industrial workers, it is now necessary to speak of several prime groups within this stratum: well-educated young industrial workers in a major city; well-educated young industrial workers in a small town; less-educated married workers of a major city, etc.

The dialectics of the formation of social homogeneity of Soviet society (and of the working class as its basic part) consists above all else in the fact that the gradual erasing of social boundaries is being accompanied by a certain complication of the entire social structure. Differences between separate social strata within the working class (as well as within society as a whole) are decreasing, but the very quantity of these groups, the number of elements of the social structure, is increasing.

Of course — and it is necessary to emphasize this with all seriousness — the thoughts expressed here reflect not so much a situation which has already come to pass as tendencies, the general direction of changes in the social structure of the working class. Today socio-occupational divisions among workers still remain decisive, and the independence of other, non-production levels is rather relative. In this sense our assertions have a partly prognostic character; they touch on phenomena and processes whose full development will not occur today but tomorrow. However, the tasks of successful management of social processes demand intensive study of shifts that are occurring or are beginning to manifest themselves.

Notes

1) Lenin, Poln. sobr. soch., Vol. 40, p. 5.

2) Approximate evaluation, based on the number of specialists with diplomas in the USSR economy.

3) In view of insufficient space, we do not examine the question of the position of persons engaged in mental and nonmanual labor who are members of collective farms; besides, their number is relatively small — approximately 3% of the employed

population (according to the data of the 1959 census).

4) Lenin, op. cit., Vol. 39, p. 15.

5) Lenin, op. cit., Vol. 45, p. 390.

6) Lenin, op. cit., Vol. 3, p. 547.

7) Lenin, op. cit., Vol. 1, p. 430.

8) In order to avoid misunderstanding, we emphasize that the question is one of "independence" precisely from disappearing class divisions but by no means from relations of production: the latter, it stands to reason, determine (although in a complex manner, indirectly) all sides of social life.

9) The term is proposed in the article of A. C. Akhiezer, L. B. Kogan, and O. N. Ianitskii, "Urbanization, Society, and the Scientific-Technical Revolution," Voprosy filosofii, 1969, No. 2.

5 Social Structure and the Functions of Management

IU. E. VOLKOV

One of the most important aspects of the development of the social structure of socialism and the formation of the social homogeneity intrinsic to developed communist society is the assurance of increasingly broad and, eventually, universal participation of the working masses in the management of social life. This process is rather extensively considered in our literature, but only from the standpoint of the development of the masses' creative activity and the development of socialist state organization. It seems to us, however, that the real essence of this process, leading ultimately to an order "in which no one will govern because all will govern" (V. I. Lenin), is that it signifies a change in a particular aspect of the social structure of society and represents one of the most important directions in the formation of communist social homogeneity. And it is precisely in this sense that this problem is not considered in our literature. On the other hand, even when consideration is given to the social structure of socialist society, with its characteristic significant differences among separate groups and strata of the working people, attention is not usually paid to the significance of differences in the role of separate categories of working people in carrying out the functions of managing society, to the

Our title. From M. N. Rutkevich, ed., Izmenenie sotsial'noi struktury sotsialisticheskogo obshchestva, Sverdlovsk, 1965, pp. 32-43. The original title of this selection is "The Increasing Role of the Masses in Management as a Factor in the Development of Socialist Society Toward Social Homogeneity."

presence of a particular category of mental workers who are primarily occupied in carrying out these functions.

Study of the special nature of the position in the social struc-ture of socialist society of that category of people who are spe-cifically engaged in the performance of management functions, as well as of changes that are occurring in this area in the pro-cess of the formation of communist social relations, is impor-tant from the standpoint not only of a deeper understanding of the latter process but also of the struggle against the ideology of anticommunism. It is well known that bourgeois ideologists, in striving to distort the essence of socialism and, in the same breath, to "prove" its "kinship" to capitalism and its "inability" to overcome the "irremovable" traits of the latter, deliberately circulate fabrications regarding the presence in our country of a "new ruling class," a new "elite," etc. In this context it is necessary to stress that for our ideological opponents this is not a question of the intelligentsia in general. The "new ruling class" is depicted precisely as that stratum which is specially engaged in performing management functions in administrative-political, economic, and other organs, and which is allegedly in a governing, privileged position in relation to the other strata of our society. Let us add that to these fabrications of the frank ideologists of anticommunism are joined the voices of revision-ists of various sorts and, in general, of many of those who ver-bally advertise their loyalty to Marxism-Leninism but, at the same time, counter to the sense of Marxist theory and the facts, slanderously characterize our party and state leadership as rep-resentatives of a "new bourgeois class" in antagonistic relations to the broad masses of the working people, etc.

In reality, through a scientific Marxist approach to this prob-lem, it becomes obvious that although under socialism the role of various categories of working people in the performance of management functions is extremely dissimilar, and although there are differences between those who are engaged primarily in performing such functions and those who are — again, pri-marily — only "executors," basically all this differs qualita-tively from the nature of the interrelations between the "man-agers" ("rulers") and the "managed" in an exploitative society.

Moreover, along with the development of socialism into communism, even the existing significant differences are disappearing on the basis of the involvement of ever broader masses in
the management of social life. And all this is connected with
the regularities of changes in society's social structure.

*   *   *

Management is a necessary feature of the vital activity of any
human community. It is necessary to state immediately that the
managerial activities of people are an aspect, on the one hand,
of the functioning of the productive forces, including the human
activity that goes into the technical process, and, on the other
hand, of the regulation of production and all other social relations among people. The first can be called technical management; the second, social management. Social management, manifested externally in the activity of a particular system of institutions, in its essence is one of the elements of the system of
societal relations characteristic of any given formation: the relation between those who manage and those who are managed.
What the character of this relation is — i.e., what group of people governs and what its relations with other members of society are — depends on the essence of the societal formation, on
the governing societal (in the final analysis, production) relations.
In an exploitative society the system of social management,
which finds its fullest embodiment and ultimate form in the state
system, is in its essential nature an expression of class rule.
The particular role performed in the organization of social production, and consequently in the management of all social life
(the role of managers or executors), serves, as we know, as one
of the signs of class formation. It is indissolubly linked with the
most basic of these signs — relation to the means of production.
The class that owns the means of production and occupies a ruling position in the economy manages and gives orders in society,
both directly (as in its enterprises, so on the scale of society as
a whole, through the composition of the organs of public power)
and through the use of hired personnel. The latter, naturally,
carry out the will of those they serve — i.e., of the same ruling

class of owners of the means of production. This applies both
to employees in the private sector and to employees of the state
apparatus, whose activity, as we know, is directed by the same
class of the bourgeoisie organized in state form. Of course, in
the immediate production sphere, the purely technical direction
of production occupies a large place in the activity of engineering-
technical personnel. But interwoven in this is the performance
of functions of social management, consisting in the realization
of the will of the masters of the means of production and the sub-
jugation of the working people to this hostile will. Thus, on a
social plane the relations of management, the relations between
managers and managed in an exploitative society, are one of the
manifestations of that antagonism between classes that constitutes the essence of the social structure of this type of society.

Under socialism the system of societal management is externally similar to those that existed in previous formations: management is carried out in a state form; there is a particular
stratum of persons occupied exclusively with the performance
of the respective functions. On the gnoseological plane, this is
precisely what makes possible the fabrications, mentioned
above, of the ideologists of anticommunism and of various op-
portunists. In reality, no matter how the apparatus of management in socialist society is formed and functions, and no matter
how externally similar it is to that existing under capitalism,
the essence of management, of the relations of management, has
a qualitatively different character than under capitalism, being
defined by the specific nature of the social structure of socialist
society. Here exploitative classes and class antagonisms are
absent, and management simply cannot be the imposition of the
will of one class on another. Because of the reign of societal
property, the only masters in the economy, and therefore in societal life as a whole, are the working masses. It follows that
only they, forming an all-encompassing social unity led by the
working class, can assume the function of societal management.

Under such conditions, what is the nature of that particular
stratum of persons who in our country are specially occupied
with the performance of management functions, and what is the
nature of the relations between them and other social strata and

groups of the working masses? This stratum, as in any society, is not, and cannot be, a particular class; it manages in the interests of the owners of societal production, and under socialism that owner is the society as a whole, consisting of the working people. It is another matter that, in particular manifestations of managerial activity, the interests of the working masses as a whole can be expressed in some situations to a greater extent, in others to a lesser extent, less correctly (in such a case we characterize this as a manifestation of subjectivism, of bureaucratism, etc.). But in general, essentially as a result of the very socio-economic foundations of socialist society, management cannot be the expression of the self-seeking interests of a minority, the imposition of their will on the other members of society. It can only be a more or less exact expression of the will and interests of the whole society. And people specially engaged in the performance of the corresponding functions can be only one of the strata of working people (aside from working people there is no one else in a socialist society). Further, the relations between them and the other strata of society represent not an antagonism, as in an exploitative society, but simply a social difference between various groups of working people. It is true that, corresponding to the nature of the socialist societal division of labor, this difference is a significant one. Herein, by the way, also lies the possibility of a not very precise expression in managerial activity of the general interests of the people, the possibility of bureaucratism, etc.

It is generally recognized that the structure of socialist society in particular presupposes the presence of a particular stratum of people engaged in mental labor, between whom, on the one hand, and people engaged in manual labor, on the other hand, there are still essential differences that are gradually being erased with the building of communism. But these differences (and, consequently, the problem of overcoming them) are usually considered, in our view, one-sidedly, according to a tradition formed in past decades: everything was reduced only to differences in the proportion of elements of manual and mental labor in the productive activity of separate categories of working people and, correspondingly, to the differences in their cultural-technical level. However, in such an approach the category of those engaged in mental labor actually is restricted to only the production-technical intelligentsia (including researchers in the technical sciences), and only those of its functions are considered which directly relate to the production of material goods. It is true that sociological studies more and more frequently consider aspects of the cultural growth of those engaged in manual labor such as their becoming accustomed to artistic creation. This means that the specific character of artistic creation is taken into account as a particular kind of mental labor and, consequently, the specific character of a category of individuals engaged in mental labor — the artistic intelligentsia. Already, in connection with this, attention must be paid to the fact that mental labor encompasses several different types of activity, various functions of social labor. This is extremely essential for understanding the process of the erasure of social distinctions in the transition to communism and the formation of a socially homogeneous society.

No matter how important may be the erasure of existing differences between those engaged in manual labor and the production intelligentsia that is taking place on the basis of unification of elements of mental and manual labor in production activity, it does not exhaust entirely the problem of the erasure of differences with respect to all those engaged in mental labor.

In the lower stage of communism, significant differences between those engaged in mental and manual labor represent one of the manifestations of the social division of labor in that specific form which is characteristic for socialism. Its particular nature consists in the fact that remnants of the division of labor characteristic of previous class formations are still preserved. The various functions of societal labor are still unevenly, unhomogeneously distributed among different strata of society. One function is primarily or entirely fulfilled by one social group, another by another group, and so on. True, as opposed to exploitative formations, this is not connected with the monopolization of the means of production and with class privileges, so the more pernicious manifestations of the previous type of division of labor are here eliminated.

The functions of mental labor are fulfilled — at least primarily — by a specific stratum, the intelligentsia. But even
within this stratum — insofar as the functions of mental labor
themselves are heterogeneous — various categories can be distinguished, including both the above-mentioned production-
technical and artistic intelligentsia and others. In addition, social differences not only exist between the intelligentsia as a
whole and those engaged in manual labor, but also among the intelligentsia — i.e., between various categories of the intelligentsia, just as there are intraclass differences between separate
categories of workers and between separate categories of collective farmers. And intraclass differences under socialism in
certain respects are no less important than interclass differences.

One of the categories of people engaged in mental labor under
socialism consists of those occupied in the performance of management functions. Quantitatively this group makes up a large
portion of the general mass of those engaged in mental labor,
and with the development of our society its numerical strength
in absolute terms not only is not decreasing but is growing. In
1941 the group numbered 5,515,000; in 1958 — 5,579,000; and
in 1960 — 5,753,000. (1)

There are no published statistics for subsequent years, but
analysis of statistical reports for the RSFSR available in the
Central Statistical Administration of the Republic shows that the
tendency toward numerical growth of the category in question
continues.

It is entirely proper, from the point of view of financial and
other purely practical considerations, to consider the correspondence of this numerical strength and its growth to objective
needs, as well as possibilities for reducing the administrative-
managerial apparatus, etc. But, in the first place, upon deep
analysis of societal needs and the tendencies of their development, it becomes clear that whatever the possible reductions of
unnecessary management units, the absolute number of personnel under consideration cannot be reduced by any means. In the
second place, no matter what its numerical strength may be,
this cannot affect the evaluation of the social nature of the group.
It is not some sort of particular class since, in relation to the

means of production, it is in the same position as the other groups of the working masses, including the entire stratum engaged in mental labor, of which it is a part. Therefore, on the social plane the problem is not one of numerical changes, but of what internal changes should take place in the specific features of the group's social position and its relations with other groups on the path to the formation of the social homogeneity of communist society. It is obvious that in order to disclose the specific character of the position of administrative-managerial personnel in the social structure of socialist society, more is required than a general indication that their position as a whole is defined simply by belonging to the stratum of those engaged in mental labor and, as such, essentially differs, in a general way, from strata primarily engaged in manual labor. The specific nature of the given type of mental labor is of the greatest significance, since it primarily involves the performance of such a particular social function as management — just as the position of other categories of the intelligentsia is related to the specific nature of various types of mental labor "specialized" in the performance of distinct social functions. Within the framework of the general difference between those engaged in manual and mental labor that exists under socialism (although it has lost its oppositional character and is gradually being eliminated), certain specific differences are characteristic of the activity and, correspondingly, of the social position of administrative-managerial personnel in comparison not only with workers and peasants, but also with other large categories of people engaged in mental labor.

The performance of administrative-managerial functions presupposes the right to make decisions which are binding on others and to put these decisions into practice with the use of measures of coercion if necessary. It is not difficult to see that this constitutes a very significant distinguishing trait of the role of those engaged in management as compared with those categories of personnel who do not possess such rights. This distinction can hardly be characterized as less significant than, for example, differences in the relative weight of elements of mental and manual labor in work activity. Here we see an example of the significant character of differences between separate categories within a basic social stratum of socialist society.

Let us compare those social strata of our society that include individuals employed in primarily manual labor with some categories of individuals engaged in mental labor, namely: (a) engineering-technical personnel who do not perform administrative-managerial functions (employed in designing, technological, and similar jobs); (b) engineering-technical personnel employed in the management apparatus of production (shop superintendents, directors of factories, personnel in plant management and higher organs of economic management); (c) persons employed in state organs of administrative-political management not related directly to production. It is evident that elimination of existing differences between those engaged in primarily manual labor and each of the above-mentioned social groups presents unique features connected with the peculiarities of the present position of each group. By no means can everything here be reduced to the combination of elements of mental and manual labor in direct production activity.

The labor of an engineer or a technician who does not have administrative-managerial functions, with all its differentiation from the labor of a worker, has in common with the latter the fact that both are directly involved in the creation of material goods. Elimination of the existing differences here as regards both character of labor and cultural-technical level really amounts to a change in the nature of production, that is, the organic unification of elements of mental and physical activity, which takes place on the basis of technological progress under the conditions of socialism and the building of communism. But managerial activity, even when connected with production (economic management), not only contains elements that enter directly into the technological process of the creation of material goods, but also elements that do not enter directly into this process, and in the field of administrative-political management it is entirely nonproductive. Consequently, there is no technological progress or change in the character of production that can, by itself, lead to elimination of existing differences between such a specific type of mental labor as managerial labor and other

types of labor, both manual and mental. Solution of this problem obviously requires organic unification of direct productive
labor and managerial labor in the activity of all the working
masses now included in the above-mentioned social groups (and
in those we have not mentioned). In other words, it is necessary
to accustom everyone to work in the management of societal
matters.

Thus, the existence under socialism of a particular stratum
of individuals employed in the performance of management functions means that although in principle all the members of society are the bearers of this function, as a practical matter not
all working people participate in equal measure in its performance. Some do to a lesser extent, some to a greater extent,
and for some this is even their basic occupation. However, the
relations between the latter and the rest of the members of society by no means bear the character of class antagonism; they
are only differences between various groups of working people
within the framework of a social whole that unites them. With
the transition to the higher phase of communism it becomes
possible to overcome also the significant nature of the given social difference (and of all others) that still exists under socialism. With the general and constant participation of all the working masses in the management of societal matters, work in the
management apparatus, as the Program of the CPSU states,
will cease to be a distinct occupation.

We think, however, that some inconsequential differences between members of society in terms of their role in the performance of the management function will also remain in the higher
phase of communism. This is connected with the fact that production, which is such an important sphere of societal life, will
always require a certain number of personnel (primarily directors) for whom management must be their basic activity. But
one must distinguish two different aspects of the management
of production: technical management and social management
(making fundamental decisions concerning the life-activity of
the collective, maintaining labor discipline). And it is precisely
the latter that can be carried out with the general participation
of the members of every collective. In such conditions the role

of a director will amount to that of an authoritative specialist-organizer whose labor will be organically interwoven into the general process of the creation by the work collective of material or cultural goods and into collective managerial activity. Only technical management will remain "individual." And all this means that differences between individuals in terms of their participation in the performance of management functions will exist, but these can be described only as inconsequential differences.

Even now, as we know, substantial success has been achieved in involving the masses in management, particularly with respect to production. The rights of social organizations of the working people — primarily those of the greatest mass character, the trade unions, the active membership of which now numbers 26 million — have been broadened, and their role is constantly growing. More than 20 million people comprise the active membership of the Soviets of Working People's Deputies. The activity of such representative organs of the working masses as the constantly functioning production meetings, in which about 5 million workers and employees participate, has become a necessary element of the management of production. More than 4 million Communists and non-Party people make up the active membership of the Party-State Control Commission. More than a million people work in the public offices of economic analysis and of norm-setting, and in other similar voluntary associations that play a not unimportant role in the management of production. In an extensive study conducted in the town of Krasnoturinsk, it was found that 55% of workers and employees take part in state management to one degree or another.

At the same time, our studies have shown that at this point only the first steps have been taken in involving the broad masses in the performance of management functions. For the most part, only a more or less satisfactory organizational structure has been created. There is still much to be done in order to have that structure function constantly and actively.

At present the participation of the broad masses in the performance of management functions generally has an episodic character and occupies a very modest place in the overall volume of management activity. Studies have come to the conclusion that for a more successful solution of such an important problem, in social terms, as the general involvement of the working masses in management, not only will it be necessary to improve mass political work, but a series of organizational and economic measures will have to be taken. In particular, until recently the fact that enterprise activity was overly regimented from above and that workers did not have the necessary material interest in the general results of the production-economic activity of their enterprises that would spur them on to struggle more actively to improve this activity — i.e., to participate more actively in management — seriously impeded development of the process of involving the working masses in the management of production, as well as the scope of their activity. This was mentioned in the majority of interviews with 1200 workers and engineering-technical personnel of various enterprises. It was also confirmed by several objective indicators. In those production collectives in which principles of cost accounting and collective material interest were, for one reason or another, put into practice more consistently than usual (the Severskii Metallurgical Factory, the cost-accounting brigades of N. Kosarev, V. Ponomarev, M. Laletin and others in various enterprises; the Verkh-Mullinskii State Farm and others), the participation of the working masses in the management of production was incomparably more active.

One can say with certainty that the economic reform enacted by decision of the September Plenum of the CPSU Central Committee — which provides for the broadening of the self-sufficiency of enterprises and the strengthening of the material interest of their collectives in the general results of work — and the improvement of centralized leadership will also have enormous positive significance with respect to the problem we have been considering. Implementation of the intended measures is creating a promising economic basis for the working masses to be involved, in an interested way, in the management of production. One can understand the great significance this will have for the formation of communist social relations, for the gradual transformation of socialist enterprises into communist ones — into self-governing associations harmoniously combined in a general, systematically organized economy (Program of the CPSU). And within the framework of the formation of these self-governing associations, with the increasingly active participation of the working masses in management, there will be an elimination of the existing important role differences in the performance of the management function, which is an important aspect of the formation of communist social homogeneity.

Note

1) Narodnoe khoziaistvo SSSR v 1960 g. Statisticheskii spravochnik, Moscow, 1961, p. 644.

II. SOCIAL STRATIFICATION:
SOVIET EMPIRICAL STUDIES

6 Social Groups in the Working Class of a Developed Socialist Society

O. I. SHKARATAN

The social structure of the working class, as already noted above, is highly complex. It is examined in this section, but by no means in all of its possible dimensions. In particular, division of the working class into its urban and rural parts remains outside the analysis. This problem deserves special study. We do not have at our disposal any concrete studies that would assist us in illuminating this highly complex problem in all its ramifications. As for the rather limited data that are available, they have already been thoroughly analyzed by S. A. Kugel and V. S. Semenov. (1)

The identification and description of the principal social groups proposed below relies on information collected in the course of three empirical sociological investigations covering (1) machine-building personnel in Leningrad (1965-1966), (2) the firm Krasnaia zaria (1967), and (3) the urban population of the Tatar Republic (1967-1968). (2)*

From O. I. Shkaratan, Problemy sotsial'noi struktury rabochego klassa, "Mysl'" Publishing House, Moscow, 1970, pp. 366-368, 377-379, 390-426. Footnotes numbered 1-13 below correspond to the following footnotes in Chapter 3 of Shkaratan's book: nos. 95, 96, 100, 101, 107-115. Tables numbered 1-7 below correspond to Tables 52-58 in Shkaratan.

*The study in Leningrad was based on data drawn from seven machine-building enterprises described by Shkaratan as "typical" (for the city) with respect to the number employed and the composition of the work force (p. 181). The number of respondents

In undertaking the investigations we proceeded from the assumption that the social structure of the working class is reproduced first of all in the basic cell of society, the enterprise, where the individual enters into social relations in the process of appropriating the means of production.

As information was accumulated (its chief source was a "questionnaire for interviews" which we prepared) we tested our initial hypotheses, and in the course of subsequent theoretical analysis, which was combined with an examination of the empirical material resulting from the questionnaire, these hypotheses were formulated more precisely and then checked against the data collected.

Our principal conclusion was that the intraclass structure accumulates within itself intrasocietal differences, and that the subordination of these differences is predetermined by their

---

in the sample is indicated in the tables below. The data for the Krasnaia zaria combine were drawn from enterprises of this combine located in Leningrad, Pskov, Porkhov, and Nevel. The proportion of workers included in the study ranged from 20% to 45% at the different enterprises (p. 188). The data for the Tatar Republic are based on surveys in three cities — Kazan, Almetevsk, and Menzelinsk — covering 7,230 respondents (pp. 188, 190). The principal features of these cities and the nature of their activities are summarized by Shkaratan as follows (p. 189):

"1) Kazan — a large city with a multibranch economy, containing all the main social and occupational groups of the population, and characterized by a high level of vertical and horizontal social mobility;

"2) Almetevsk (a center of the oil-extracting industry) — an average-sized city with a limited group of developed economic branches; it provides scope for high vertical mobility but limited opportunities for horizontal mobility, particularly outside the sphere of material production;

"3) Menzelinsk — a small town with weakly developed industry, in which may be found only individual elements of the social structure of the country's population, and in which the opportunities for social mobility are extremely limited."

subordination in the society as a whole.

Under socialism the state of the productive forces conditions the retention of the socio-economic heterogeneity of labor. This means that, although the members of society are equal co-owners of socialist property, they do not participate equally in the organization and improvement of production, they contribute unequally to the development of the economy and culture, and they are unequal in the degree to which they are the subjects of social activity.

These are the features which make for the division of the working class into basic social groups under socialism, groups which differ in their contribution to the development of the means of production and the degree of their participation in the social organization of labor, and which are rooted in the still remaining socio-economic heterogeneity of labor in society. These are the essential features of the proposed hypothesis that was tested as the special investigation proceeded.

.   .   .

Let us now examine the method of distinguishing the principal social groups in the working class that are formed under the influence of the factors analyzed.

In preparing the initial grouping of occupations and job titles included in the questionnaire that was addressed to machine-building personnel of Leningrad, we took account of the peculiarities of workers' production activity connected with the technical division of labor into its specific forms. (3) The objective of the subsequent grouping was to identify large groups which differ significantly in socio-economic characteristics. The original occupational groups were combined not only by taking account of peculiarities in work activity, degree of mechanization, and level of complexity of jobs (4), but also by using the magnitudes derived in the investigation to test for homogeneity in the average indicators and the range of variations in such features as educational level, wages, skill grades, participation in rationalization and community activities, length of work experience generally and in the particular occupation.

As a result, the following groups were distinguished:

1) unskilled personnel in manual labor — auxiliary workers;

2) personnel in nonmanual labor of medium skills — clerical and office workers, inspectors, sorters, etc.;

3) personnel in skilled, primarily manual labor, employed on machines and mechanisms — machine operators, punch press operators, press operators, machinists, all designations of motor mechanics, etc.;

4) personnel in skilled, primarily manual, hand labor — all designations of metal craftsmen, assemblers and fitters, electricians, etc.;

5) personnel in highly skilled work combining mental and manual functions in operating complex machinery — adjusters; tuners of automatic lines, machine tools, automatic machines; repair mechanics on automatic lines used in production;

6) personnel in skilled mental work — technologists, economists, planning personnel, bookkeepers, etc.;

7) highly skilled scientific and technical personnel — designers;

8) organizers of production collectives; this group initially included all engineering-technical personnel with managerial functions in production collectives.

However, in analyzing the statistical material a certain inadequacy became apparent in this kind of grouping. In particular, the specific features of personnel performing organizational functions did not emerge with sufficient clarity. Therefore, in the final grouping we separated executives of enterprises, shops, and departments from the whole mass of organizational personnel.

In studying the social structure of the urban population of the Tatar Republic, we took into account the fact that the investigation of Leningrad machine-building personnel confirmed the correctness of our hypotheses concerning the principal groups of working people at state enterprises. The urban population of the Tatar Republic was divided into the following socio-occupational groups, reflecting the still existing social heterogeneity of our society;

1) unskilled and low-skilled personnel in manual and nonmanual

labor without special training:

2) personnel in skilled, primarily manual labor, employed on machines and mechanisms;

3) personnel in skilled, primarily manual, hand labor;

4) personnel in skilled nonmanual labor without special education;

5) personnel in highly skilled work combining mental and manual functions;

6) personnel in skilled mental work;

7) highly skilled scientific and technical personnel;

8) highly skilled personnel in the so-called "creative" occupations;

9) executives of labor collectives in public and state organizations.

This kind of grouping reveals the structural characteristics of the population employed in socially heterogeneous labor, and belonging to groups that play different roles in the social organization of labor and perform work functions of differing degrees of complexity and responsibility.

.   .   .

The tables that follow present some data on the social groups employed in industry.

Executives of production collectives (5) have been placed in a separate group. Given the special nature of their functions, they enjoy relative independence in regulating the activity of collectives. Iu. E. Volkov was correct when he wrote: "They are also working people, just like all other members of the socialist society. They are by no means a special class, for they do not monopolize the means of production and therefore do not manage them in their own selfish interests, but in the interests of the whole society. However, insofar as they comprise a distinct stratum specially employed in performing managerial functions, there are essential differences between them and other strata of working people (including personnel in mental work who do not perform administrative and managerial functions), strata which are primarily 'managed,' and in this sense 'executors.' " (6)

Two groups combine individuals in mental work — designers, technologists, economists, etc. They perform special functions in a society that still bears the burden of a division between mental and primarily manual labor.

Individuals performing uncreative, executor-type functions in nonmanual labor (office personnel, etc.) have been placed in a separate group.

Workers engaged in primarily manual labor have been divided into five basic skill-occupational groups according to the nature of their labor.

We used three indicators of length of employment in the study of Leningrad machine-building personnel. The first of these — overall length of employment — in contrast to data in state statistics, includes work experience in collective farms. It would be incorrect to retain the distinctions in calculating length of employment left over from the time when peasants were engaged in private farm operations. While the private peasant, in the course of his work in his own enterprise, acquired socio-psychological habits, traditions, and modes of thinking that were qualitatively different from the proletarian, the situation is completely different with respect to the traditions of collective farm work. Thus, there are no grounds for excluding work on collective farms in calculating overall length of employment in the socialist economy. The second category of length of service which we have considered is length of employment in industry. This indicator permits us to ascertain the impact of large-scale industrial production on the moulding of the rank-and-file socialist worker. The third indicator — length of employment in the given occupation — reflects the accumulation of occupational skills and craftsmanship, but apparently does not involve features associated with the acquisition of social group and class traits.

The general picture revealed by the data from the study of machine-building personnel is seen in Table 1.

Table 1 shows that the machine-building personnel included in the study are individuals with a clearly established social and occupational status. Their average overall length of employment, as well as their length of employment in industry,

Table 1

Age and Length of Employment of Leningrad Machine-Building Personnel, 1965

Groups of employed personnel	Age (in years)		Overall length of employment (in years)		Length of employ-ment in industry (in years)		Number of persons questioned
	$\overline{X}$	σ	$\overline{X}$	σ	$\overline{X}$	σ	Σ
Unskilled personnel in manual labor	39.2	12.5	18.9	8.8	14.5	8.3	115
Personnel in nonmanual labor of medium skills	32.3	10.7	13.6	8.9	11.4	7.9	353
Personnel in skilled, primarily manual labor, employed on machines and mechanisms	35.7	11.1	15.4	9.0	13.5	8.1	837
Personnel in skilled, primarily manual, hand labor	39.1	10.6	15.7	8.9	14.0	8.1	1,002
Personnel in highly skilled work combining mental and manual functions	35.3	11.0	18.5	8.9	15.5	7.7	67
Personnel in skilled mental work	36.8	9.2	15.6	9.1	14.0	8.1	287
Highly skilled scientific and technical personnel	35.7	10.3	14.5	8.6	13.5	7.8	135
Organizers of production collectives	41.8	9.9	20.1	8.0	17.0	7.0	92

is considerable, and in absolute terms exceeds 10 years of
work experience for all the groups. The data on the age of the
people studied also point to the predominance of those who have
already determined their place in society. The average indicator of overall length of employment differs markedly among the
members of the different socio-occupational groups. A characteristic feature is the clearly more advanced age of individuals
employed in unskilled manual labor. Their overall length of
employment, 18.9 years, is higher than that of any other group
except executives, although their length of employment in industry, 14.5 years, is considerably lower. The duration of their
employment in the given occupation, 7 years, is lower than that
of any other socio-occupational group. In other words, this category of workers is a variable group without a stable occupational status. Among skilled workers of the machine-operator
type, i.e., workers employed on machines and mechanisms, the
overall length of employment is 15.4 years. Their work experience in industry is somewhat less, 13.5 years. Their employment in the given occupation, 8.2 years, is still less. Thus,
even among machine operators a considerable proportion of individuals have changed their jobs before beginning work in the
given occupation, although this proportion is very much less
than in the case of unskilled workers in manual labor.

A favorable picture prevails in the case of skilled workers
in manual, hand labor, such as metal craftsmen. Their overall
duration of employment, 15.7 years, is one of the highest among
all workers' groups. Their work experience in industry is 14
years, and in the given occupation — 11.1 years.

The occupational mobility of workers is not exclusively a
negative feature. As our investigation showed, individuals who
have had a second and third occupation similar to their present
one are more productive workers. They are more versatile in-
tellectually, and their production skills are more varied.

The data on executives of production collectives show that
this category of personnel has a high level of both life experience and production experience. Their average length of employment is 20.1 years, while their experience in industry is
17 years, and in the given occupation — 12.5 years. We find

that 56.6% of executives have been employed for more than 20 years. This has its positive as well as negative features. Unfortunately, the promotion of young people to executive positions does not occur with sufficient frequency. The proportion of individuals with 5 to 10 years of work experience among executives — including the lower levels of executive personnel — is only 9.3%, while those with 10 to 15 years of employment comprise 11.3%.

The conclusions derived from the investigation of Leningrad machine-building personnel in 1965 were confirmed by our subsequent research. Thus, at enterprises of the Krasnaia zaria combine (the 1967 survey) in all four cities, the average age of unskilled workers exceeded not only the average for all personnel in the collectives, but also for all age groups*, including even the executives' group. At the Leningrad enterprises of the combine, the average age of unskilled workers was 40.4, as compared to 43.4 for executives of the enterprises, while in Pskov the corresponding figures were 43.9 and 37.9, in Porkhov — 39.0 and 35.6, and in Nevel — 41.5 and 40.3. A more favorable situation prevailed in the cities of the Tatar Republic. In Kazan the average age of unskilled workers was 34.3 years, in Almetevsk — 36.6, and in Menzelinsk — 37.1. The average age of executives in both industrial and nonindustrial enterprises was 39.1, 35.9, and 37, respectively. At the same time, the average age of personnel in skilled, primarily manual labor in these cities ranges from 30 to 32. The cadres of skilled scientific and technical personnel are also young, with the average age in Kazan at about 34 years and in Almetevsk at less than 33. As in Leningrad, these are people with a firmly established socio-occupational position. Thus, the average overall length of employment in all groups and in all cities ranges from 11.5 to 14 years, except, naturally, among the group of executives of labor collectives, whose average length of employment ranges from 18 to 20 years. It should be noted that the length of employment (as well as age) of unskilled workers — 14 to

---

*The term "age groups" appears in the Russian, but Shkaratan is probably referring to occupational groups.

Table 2

Dependence of Average Monthly Earnings
(in Rubles) on Overall Length of Employment,
Leningrad Machine-Building Personnel

Wages	Length of employment (in years)							
	less than 1	1-3	3-5	5-10	10-15	15-20	20-25	more than 25
Average monthly earnings (in rubles)	81	84	100	106	115	120	123	126
Absolute increase (in rubles)	—	3	16	6	9	5	3	3
Average annual increase (in rubles)	—	1.5	8.0	1.2	1.8	1.0	0.6	—

16.6 years — exceeds that of skilled personnel. A similar situation prevails in Pskov, Porkhov and Nevel, except that the
overall length of employment among unskilled workers in these
Russian cities is 5 to 7 years greater than in the Tatar Republic, ranging from 19 to 21 years.

Let us now turn to the influence of length of employment on
the social characteristics of workers. The role of this factor
is most apparent in production-and-occupational indicators, as
is evident from data showing the dependence of workers' wages
on the length of employment (Leningrad, 1965).

It is evident from Table 2 that wages do not increase uniformly with increases in length of employment. The highest
rates of growth are observed in the 3- to 5-year interval. It is
within this period that the molding of the rank-and-file industrial worker occurs. The effect of saturation [nasyshcheniia]

sets in after this. Length of employment does not have an unlimited impact on the production characteristics of the worker.
Average annual rates of growth in wages gradually decline.

Length of employment in the given occupation, under our conditions, promotes the development of workers' love for their
specialties, i.e., it affects their value orientations. Thus, those
who answered "I like it" to a question concerning the degree of
satisfaction with their occupation have an average length of employment in the given occupation of 11.2 years, while the figure
for those who answered "In general I like it" is 8.6 years. Those
who answered "I dislike it more than I like it" were employed
in their current occupation for 7.8 years. Those who were completely dissatisfied with their occupations had also worked in
them for 7.8 years, while the figure for those who had not yet
defined their attitudes toward their occupations or did not want
to express them was 6.5 years.

Thus, workers with more than 7 years of experience are generally able to develop a definite attitude toward their occupations. This attitude becomes increasingly stable. It follows,
obviously, that the problem is primarily one of attaching young
people to particular occupations and taking well-considered
measures to instill in them an enthusiasm for their specialties.

Analogous findings were derived in studying the motives for
releases from employment among Leningrad workers (1963).
After three or more years of work, most workers no longer
strive to change their occupations. After this period the overwhelming majority retain their occupations even when they
leave their places of employment. Naturally, this kind of stability does not develop among auxiliary workers, no matter how
long their period of employment. The concept of "regular auxiliary worker" is unknown in our industry. Workers who have
been employed for longer periods fulfill their shift assignments
better and participate more actively in rationalization activity.
Among those who overfulfilled their shift assignments, the average length of employment was 16.2 years, and their length of
work experience in industry was 13.7 years. Analogous indicators among those fulfilling shift assignments were 15.1 and 12.7
years. Among those not fulfilling shift assignments, the following

indicators prevailed: overall length of employment — 14.1
years; employment in industry — 12.2 years.

The connection between length of employment and participation in rationalization activity was even more clear-cut. Among
those who were constantly engaged in rationalization activity,
the overall length of employment reached 21 years, while employment in industry was 17.9 years. Among those who are engaged
in such activity irregularly, the overall period of employment was
19.2 years and employment in industry was 16.2 years. The
corresponding figures for individuals not participating in rationalization activity were 13.9 and 11.4 years respectively.

Workers with long periods of employment also participate
more actively in community activities. Length of employment
in industry is of greatest significance here. Individuals who
held elected positions in community work had 14.9 years of
work experience in industry, while those with permanent community assignments had 13.6 years, those with temporary community assignments — 13.1 years, and those not participating
in community work — 12.5 years.

The investigation in the Tatar Republic also corroborated the
influence of work experience on the production and political activities of workers in society. At the same time, it showed that
the length of employment is not the determining factor in these
activities, but only introduces certain modifications in indices
of social behavior to the extent that it instills habits of social
participation. Thus, the influence of length of employment on
participation in social and political activity, expressed in Chuprov
coefficients*, was 0.07 in Kazan and 0.08 in Almetevsk. Similar
indicators were found with respect to the influence of length of employment on attitudes toward the content of work — 0.07 (Kazan and
Almetevsk), on attitudes toward the amount of wages — 0.05 (Kazan)
and 0.06 (Almetevsk), and toward the opportunities to raise
one's skills — 0.06 (Kazan) and 0.07 (Almetevsk).

Thus, it is clear that it would be incorrect to exaggerate the

---

*The Chuprov coefficient used here and below by Shkaratan
is a measure of the degree of association between non-metric
(non-measurable) characteristics with a maximum value of 1.0.

influence of length of employment on the social cast of the working class in current conditions of a developed socialist society. The picture is completely different from what it was, for example, in the 1920-1930 period. At the same time, we should not ignore length of employment as an indicator of the acquisition of production and political experience in society.

*　　*　　*

Let us now examine some data characterizing the social features of groups of workers employed in socially heterogeneous labor. Since education is becoming a major factor in maintaining social differences in the working class, we begin with an analysis of social-group differences in this indicator.

The investigation of Leningrad machine-building personnel showed that unskilled workers are essentially characterized by a low educational level. It is typical that almost 60% of unskilled workers in manual, hand labor have no more than a six-year education, and their average educational level is 6.5 grades of school.

A completely different picture prevails for the group of skilled workers employed on machines and mechanisms. Their average educational level is 8.2 to 8.3 grades. Despite a considerable proportion of elderly workers in this group, approximately 20% of the total number are individuals with up to a 7th-grade education and with a complete secondary-school education*, while almost 50% have a 7th to 9th grade education. Another fact is noteworthy. Personnel in nonmanual labor, employed on jobs not requiring specialized education, now have an educational level close to that of workers in primarily manual labor, a situation that did not exist in industry 10 years ago, not to speak of the prewar period.

Personnel employed in highly skilled scientific and technical work, such as designers, as a rule now have a specialized

---

*This statement is not clear as it stands. Shkaratan may mean that 20% have 7 years or less, and another 20% have a complete secondary-school education (10 or 11 years). It may also mean that 20% have a 7th-grade or complete secondary-school education.

education, and for the most part it is a higher education.

In order to elucidate the trends in the increasing educational level of personnel in different occupational and skill groups, let us examine individuals in the same age group. What emerges is that in the age group from 18 to 24 — with an average age of 20.9 — the educational level is as follows: for unskilled workers in manual labor — 8.1 grades of school; for personnel in nonmanual labor of average skills (such as office workers, inspectors, etc.) — 9 grades; for personnel in skilled, primarily manual labor, employed on machines and mechanisms — 9.4 grades; for young people employed in skilled, primarily manual, hand labor — 10.3 grades. Thus, in the young age groups it is not the conventional division between mental work (in reality, low-skilled nonmanual labor) and primarily manual labor, but the degree of complexity of the labor which emerges as the principal factor affecting the distribution of the work force among different jobs according to educational levels.

It should be noted that the division into personnel in skilled manual labor and personnel in nonmanual labor not requiring a specialized education is increasingly based on natural factors rather than having a social character. Thus, a study of youngsters graduating from the 10th grade of Leningrad schools in the period 1963 to 1967 (7) showed that only 4.7% of the boys took jobs in nonmanual labor of the office-employee type, while 33.7% of the girls took such jobs. On the other hand, 62.6% of the boys who began to work after secondary school became skilled workers in manual labor while only 24.7% of the girls did so.

Thus, the division into workers and employees, without taking proper account of the type of work and the degree of its complexity, is increasingly becoming an anachronism.

The investigation of personnel of the Krasnaia zaria firm corroborated the above conclusions. Marked differences were observed in the educational levels of the different socio-occupational groups. But the average educational level of each group and of all personnel at each plant differed significantly depending on the type of urban settlement.

At the chief plant (Leningrad) the average educational level of all categories of personnel was 9.6 years of school, while in Pskov it was 9.3 years, in Porkhov — 8.4 years, and in Nevel — 8 years.

A curious tendency was revealed. In the lower socio-occupational groups the educational level was not to the advantage of Leningrad. Thus, among auxiliary workers it was as follows: at the chief factory of Krasnaia zaria — 6 grades; at the Pskov automatic telephone station factory — 7.1 grades; in Porkhov — 6.2 grades; and in Nevel — 6.5 grades. Among office employees included in the group of personnel in nonmanual labor of average skills, it was 8.8 grades in Leningrad, 9.3 grades in Pskov, and 10 grades in Porkhov and Nevel.

Then the picture changes. Among machine operators (i.e., personnel in skilled, primarily manual labor, employed on machines and mechanisms) the educational level was as follows: 8.2 grades in Leningrad, 8.4 in Pskov, 8 in Porkhov, and 8.1 in Nevel. Among metal craftsmen and assemblers (i.e., personnel in skilled, primarily manual, hand labor) it was 8.5 grades in Leningrad, 9.2 in Pskov, 8.1 in Porkhov, and 7.5 in Nevel. Among adjusters it was 8.2 grades in Leningrad, 8.3 in Pskov, 7.7 in Porkhov, and 6.5 in Nevel.

Let us now take personnel in mental work. Among economists the average period of schooling was 12.6 years in Leningrad, 12.3 in Pskov, 11.4 in Porkhov, and 10.9 in Nevel. Among designers the figures are 14.3 years of schooling in Leningrad and 12.9 in Pskov. This group was nonexistent, in effect, at other enterprises.

So that the comparison becomes obvious, we may note that personnel at the chief plant in Leningrad were the "oldest" group, with an average age of 36.1 years, while in Pskov and Porkhov the figure was 31.9 years, and in Nevel — 35 years.

Thus, as we move to the more skilled groups of personnel, the highest educational levels are found in Leningrad and Pskov. As for personnel in mental work, Leningrad shows the highest indicator. Moreover, the average age (among designers) is higher in Leningrad — 35.9 years, while in Pskov it is 28.9 years.

The data on age help us to understand that this tendency would be even more clear-cut if the average age of plant collectives as a whole and of the distinct socio-occupational groups were the same.

Lying behind what superficially appears to be a more or less equal educational level in Pskov (an average-sized city) and Nevel and Porkhov (small towns) in comparison to Leningrad, there are concealed certain peculiarities of social mobility in different types of urban settlements. Because of the more developed social structure of Leningrad and the multibranch structure of the city's economy, young people with higher educational attainments find greater opportunities available to them. Hence jobs requiring low skills are largely filled by workers with little schooling, and these workers are chiefly older people (averaging 44.3 years of age).

As we move from the large to the medium and then to the small city, the opportunities for choosing among jobs diminish, and the criteria used by young people reaching working age to evaluate these jobs are reinterpreted in accordance with the actual social structure of their community. The smaller the community, the greater the extent to which social contacts at work and in the community coincide, and therefore the greater the significance assumed by the totality of social traits of the specific individual's personality. The role of the work place, insofar as its regulated producing functions are concerned, becomes less significant in determining the individual's social status. Community activity, nonregulated work activity, leadership of the group at the place of residence, etc. — all these help a young person to compensate for the dissatisfaction associated with uninteresting work that does not correspond to his education. In a small city, with the spatial visibility of the social ties of individuals and groups, the solution to this problem becomes somewhat easier than in a large city.

As we move to the more skilled types of jobs we find a relative balance between the educational potential of the work force and the degree of complexity of labor at the work place. For this group the situation is approximately the same in all cities. As regards jobs requiring a higher education, as we move from the large city to the small one we observe an increasing shortage of labor, a situation which is directly the opposite of that pre-vailing for low-skilled groups. The complexity of the social structure inherent in a large city, the presence of a variety of higher educational institutions, and the possibility of advancing to jobs of any degree of complexity and responsibility yield clear advantages to enterprises located in such a city. Obvi-ously, it would be wrong to come to some kind of final conclu-sions on the basis of data applicable to a single firm. However, these preliminary observations should be considered in under-taking sociological investigations of the interaction of urban settlements and enterprises in the mechanism of the social structure of society.

A similar situation may be observed in the Tatar Republic (1967). The average educational level of executives of indus-trial and nonindustrial enterprises is 12.9 years of school in Kazan and Almetevsk, and 12.2 years in Menzelinsk. (8) At the same time, personnel in skilled manual labor have 8 to 9 grades of schooling, while personnel in highly skilled scientific and technical work have 14.3 and 14.4 years. Consequently, there is a certain gap between the rapid growth of education of executor-type personnel in industry and the less marked in-crease in the education of individuals performing executive functions.

The educational level of even unskilled workers is sufficiently high (6.5 grades of schooling) for them to advance to more com-plex types of work activity. It is characteristic that, according to data of the study of the causes of labor turnover in Leningrad (1963), 62.8% of auxiliary workers changed their occupations when they changed their places of employment. Departures from jobs associated with changes in social-group membership reach 30% of total labor turnover at some enterprises. This is promoted by the easy accessibility of occupational and general education in socialist society.

The division of workers into socio-occupational groups is also affected by the duration of vocational training. In Lenin-grad (1965) such training lasted about 4 months for unskilled and low-skilled workers, 7 months for personnel in skilled, pri-marily manual labor of the machine-operator type, and 13.3

months for highly skilled personnel required to perform a combination of mental and manual functions.

It should be emphasized that the principal means of transfer from one social group to another involves a change from a less skilled occupation to a more skilled occupation, not a rise in skill grade within a given occupation. Although average skill grades by groups also reflect socio-economic differences to a certain extent (the average skill grade of machine operators is 3.2 compared to 4.8 for adjusters and repair mechanics), an increase in skill grade is essentially a sign of the acquisition of work skills as age and duration of employment increase. According to K. Varshavskii's data, at the current rate of advancement in skill within a given occupation, the worker reaches the highest skill grade in 10 years, i.e., at the average age of 27 (the average age for beginning work is 17). (9) A qualitative leap in skills, leading to a change in social position in society, is associated with a change in occupation, which in turn depends to a decisive degree on the level of educational preparation.

Under the conditions of the current socialist economy, wages are the indicator which most adequately reflects the actual qualifications of the worker. But this is true only for groups performing work requiring the same physical exertion, where such factors as the importance of the branch of industry and the heaviness or danger of the work do not affect the wage level. Nonetheless, given these qualifications, it is perfectly clear that if we take the average figures by groups, the wage gap in our industry is on the order of 1:2, ranging from the lowest-paid to the highest-paid personnel. (10) Wages are typically the same for highly skilled personnel who combine mental and manual functions in their work, such as adjusters and repair mechanics, and for personnel in highly skilled mental work. A definite gap exists between the wages of organizers of production collectives and other groups. The former's level of pay is, on the average, almost half as much again as that of highly skilled groups of executors.

Let us now compare the wages of Leningrad machine-building personnel with the corresponding indices for different socio-occupational groups in the cities of the Tatar Republic.

Table 3

Average Wages of Surveyed Machine-Building Personnel in Leningrad, 1965, and Urban Population in Tatar Republic, 1967 (in rubles per month)

Groups of employed personnel	Cities							
	Leningrad		Kazan		Almetevsk		Menzelinsk	
	$\overline{X}$	σ	$\overline{X}$	σ	$\overline{X}$	σ	$\overline{X}$	σ
Personnel in unskilled manual labor and low-skilled nonmanual labor without special training	97.5	39.6	73.8	24.7	62.9	22.3	57.9	16.6
Personnel in skilled nonmanual labor without special education	83.6	31.1	75.7	20.0	77.4	25.3	67.1	18.5
Personnel in skilled, primarily manual labor, employed on machines and mechanisms	107.5	34.7	99.1	32.3	114.6	35.8	93.4	39.8
Personnel in skilled, primarily manual, hand labor	120.0	34.8	99.9	27.7	95.8	32.5	81.2	24.9
Personnel in highly skilled work combining mental and manual functions	129.0	37.3	97.9	27.6	115.6	36.5	119.9	42.4
Personnel in skilled mental work	109.8	36.8	111.0	37.8	111.7	36.5	106.6	47.5
Highly skilled scientific and technical personnel	127.0	36.6	156.9	68.9	146.3	57.9	187.4	37.5[a]
Executives of labor collectives, public and state organizations	172.9	59.8	164.3	45.5	178.3	58.4	141.8	50.3

(a) The data for this group in Menzelinsk are not representative.

Specific features of this republic's industrial structure, as of its economy as a whole, have produced a certain reordering in the wage sequence compared to what may be observed for this indicator in Leningrad machine-building. However, the basic principles remain unchanged (see Table 3). Skilled personnel in manual work in Kazan earn less than skilled personnel in mental work, but in Almetevsk, where highly skilled cadres of workers are concentrated in the oil industry, the picture is different. In this city the pay of skilled manual workers employed on machines and mechanisms is 2.9 rubles higher than that of personnel in skilled mental work. The wages of scientific and technical personnel are 25% higher than the wages of highly skilled workers. In the cities of the Tatar Republic as a whole, the overall ratio of highest to lowest pay of the socio-occupational groups is somewhat higher than 2:1. Thus, the wage gap in the Tatar Republic is somewhat greater than in Leningrad.

The attachment of an individual to a particular social group of the working class is clearly associated with the level of his social activity and the nature of his participation in production and community life (in rationalization activity, self-management, etc.).

Table 4 shows that the highest indicators among Leningrad machine-building personnel are exhibited by two social groups: executives of production collectives, and personnel who combine mental and manual functions in their work activities. In the first group, the proportion regularly participating in rationalization activity is 27.1%, the proportion of Party members is 54.4%, and the proportion carrying out community assignments is 84.2%. These figures confirm the fact that the mechanism of socialist democracy ensures the advancement to professional work in organization and management of individuals who are the best representatives of the working people, individuals who have extensive experience in life, in civic activity, and in production and technical affairs (their average age is 41.8, their average length of employment in industry — 17 years).

As for individuals in the second of these groups, they are characterized not only by high indicators of community and work

Table 4

Social Activity of Groups of Leningrad Machine-Building Personnel

Groups of employed personnel	Party membership (in %)		Participation in rationalization (in %)		Participation in community work (in %)		Number of persons
Unskilled personnel in manual labor	CPSU	3.7	regular	0.9	yes	35.1	115
	Komsomol	10.1	irregular	9.1	no	64.9	
	non-Party	86.2	none	90.0			
Personnel in nonmanual labor of medium skills	CPSU	7.8	regular	3.1	yes	54.5	353
	Komsomol	19.3	irregular	12.0	no	45.5	
	non-Party	72.9	none	84.9			
Personnel in skilled, primarily manual labor, employed on machines and mechanisms	CPSU	12.9	regular	4.6	yes	54.3	837
	Komsomol	27.3	irregular	20.8	no	45.7	
	non-Party	60.5	none	74.6			
Personnel in skilled, primarily manual, hand labor	CPSU	16.2	regular	10.8	yes	60.7	1,002
	Komsomol	21.2	irregular	34.7	no	39.3	
	non-Party	62.6	none	54.5			
Personnel in highly skilled work combining mental and manual functions	CPSU	23.4	regular	15.6	yes	79.2	67
	Komsomol	14.2	irregular	54.8	no	20.8	
	non-Party	62.4	none	29.6			
Personnel in skilled mental work	CPSU	19.6	regular	13.1	yes	82.4	287
	Komsomol	23.2	irregular	23.3	no	17.6	
	non-Party	57.2	none	63.6			
Highly skilled scientific and technical personnel	CPSU	19.8	regular	10.3	yes	70.4	135
	Komsomol	20.4	irregular	35.4	no	29.6	
	non-Party	59.8	none	54.3			
Organizers of production collectives	CPSU	54.4	regular	27.1	yes	84.2	92
	Komsomol	6.4	irregular	43.1	no	15.8	
	non-Party	39.2	none	29.8			

activity, but also by the highest degree of satisfaction with the content of their work (80% are satisfied, compared to 25.4% among unskilled workers, 60.9% among machine operators, and 63.3% among personnel in highly skilled mental work).

The data obtained in the other studies were no less significant. For example, the association between socio-occupational grouping and Party membership at the Pskov plant of automatic telephone stations was expressed in an index of T = 0.12, while in Kazan it was T = 0.15, in Almetevsk — T = 0.18, and in Menzelinsk — T = 0.22. Even with the obvious fluctuation of this index, it testifies to the existence of a significant association between these characteristics in all of the cities. In statistical terms the situation appears as follows. While 3.1% of unskilled workers at the Pskov factory were Party members, the proportion rose to 27.2% among highly skilled workers and to 65.5% among executive personnel. In Kazan the proportion of Party members in the corresponding groups was 3.7%, 20.0%, and 61.3% respectively, while in Almetevsk it was 3.8%, 35.2%, and 55.1% respectively, and in Menzelinsk — 3.8%, 33.3%, and 54.5% respectively.

The proportion of individuals participating in rationalization activity is strongly related to the degree of complexity and social importance of the work in all the plants surveyed.

In Almetevsk the picture is the following. Almost 4% of unskilled workers participate in rationalization activity, while among highly skilled personnel combining mental and physical work the figure is 32.4%, and among personnel in scientific and technical work it is 50%.

Thus, given all the deviations associated with the peculiarities of the type of production, the region, and the very procedures of the investigation, we may conclude that participation in inventive and rationalization activity is an important social characteristic of intraclass groups.

The data on participation in community work also corroborated the conclusions reached in the Leningrad investigation of machine-building personnel. Chuprov coefficients gave the following indices of association: T = 0.18 for Kazan, T = 0.19 for

Almetevsk, and T = 0.20 for Menzelinsk. It is interesting that the sequence in which the Chuprov coefficients rise is the same as it is for Party membership, i.e., the degree of association is strengthened as we move from the larger to the smaller city.

It would be premature, perhaps, on the basis of our investigation, to formulate very definite conclusions concerning the dependence of the social behavior of the different intraclass groups on the type of city. At first glance it appears that a large city, with its variety of official democratic institutions, still provides greater opportunities for the individual to participate in community activity in the formal organization of the enterprise as well as in the formal organization of the city.

However, this is not always the case in practice. Let us turn to the figures. The proportion of individuals participating in community activity among unskilled manual workers and personnel in nonmanual work without special training is 21.7% in Kazan, 21.1% in Almetevsk, and 26.3% in Menzelinsk. Among personnel in skilled, primarily manual labor, employed on machines and mechanisms, the proportion active in community activity is 35.4% in Kazan, 38.4% in Almetevsk, and 34.5% in Menzelinsk. The proportion participating in community work among personnel in skilled, primarily manual, hand labor is 37.3% in Kazan, 39.1% in Almetevsk, and 46.9% in Menzelinsk. Among highly skilled personnel combining mental and manual functions, this index stands at 56.7% in Kazan, 51.4% in Almetevsk, and 66.7% in Menzelinsk. Among scientific and technical personnel it is 87.1%, 90.9%, and 100% respectively. Executive personnel of organizations and enterprises participate in community activity to the extent of 93.5% in Kazan and 100% in Menzelinsk.

At first it was assumed that the reasons for these differences were to be found in the level of Party organizational work, but increasing familiarity with the status of this work in the communities convinced participants in the studies that it was being conducted quite successfully in all three cities. Apparently there are more profound causes at work. One of these, very likely, is that in a small city, with its visible social ties, existing systems of involving working people in community activity that rely on the direct observation of the Party committee and leadership, with their contacts with working people, are more successful than in a large city, where new and improved forms of regulating social activity should be introduced on the basis of constant probing of public opinion and scientifically substantiated programs of planning and managing this activity. Such programs, of course, should also be worked out in small and medium-sized cities, but the need for them is particularly urgent in large cities. Moreover, the social activity of an individual can be more readily performed in the cultural sphere in a large city. We now turn to an examination of indices of cultural level.

In all of our investigations we considered such cultural indices as the reading of newspapers and works of fiction, the possession of personal libraries, attendance at theaters, films and recreational evenings, and television viewing. We shall focus largely on the reading of newspapers and works of fiction, the possession of personal libraries, and theater attendance.

The regularity of newspaper reading is significantly associated with socio-occupational grouping. The Chuprov coefficient for this index does not fall below 0.16 in Leningrad, Pskov, and the cities of the Tatar Republic. As we move from the larger to the smaller city, we observe the same tendency for the Chuprov coefficient to increase as we noted for the indices of participation in community work and Party membership (T = 0.166 in Kazan, T = 0.171 in Almetevsk, T = 0.172 in Menzelinsk). Among Leningrad machine-building personnel, the proportions of individuals regularly reading newspapers are 55.5% of unskilled workers, 75-85% of skilled personnel, 71.8% of personnel in highly skilled scientific and technical work, and 85.4% of executives of production collectives. The proportion of those who do not read newspapers at all is extremely small in all groups — 1% to 3% — except among unskilled workers, where it reaches 15.6%.

A similar situation prevails in the Tatar Republic. In Kazan, 31.3% of unskilled workers regularly read newspapers, while 28.1% do not read them at all. Among skilled personnel, 55% are regular readers and 8% do not read them at all, while among

highly skilled workers the figures are 73.3% and 3.3% respectively, and among personnel in skilled mental work — 70% and
about 1%. Among personnel in highly skilled scientific and technical work, more than 77.6% read newspapers regularly, and
among executives the figure is 93.5%.

The data for Almetevsk and Menzelinsk do not differ essentially from those for Kazan. In Almetevsk the unskilled workers' group also stands apart, with 26.3% not reading newspapers
at all, while among skilled personnel in manual labor, employed
on machines and mechanisms, the proportion of nonreaders falls
to 2.3%; among the intelligentsia groups there are no such individuals. In Menzelinsk, 26.9% of unskilled personnel do not read
newspapers, while among skilled personnel in primarily manual,
hand labor the comparable indicator is only 7.4%, and among
personnel in mental work it falls to zero.

The situation is different with respect to the reading of fiction. The gap between groups is somewhat less, if we ignore
the qualitative aspect of the problem and consider only the
amount of reading. The index of association between socio-
occupational status and the reading of fiction ranges from T =
0.07 in Leningrad and Pskov to T = 0.13 in Kazan, T = 0.16 in
Menzelinsk, and T = 0.14 in Almetevsk. In other words, the
gaps between social groups are being reduced in connection
with the extensive development of social and cultural life.

The possession of personal libraries and theater attendance
are also significantly predetermined by socio-occupational status. The index of association between the latter and attendance
at theaters and concerts was T = 0.126 in Kazan, T = 0.117 in
Almetevsk, and T = 0.140 in Menzelinsk. The index of association between socio-occupational status and possession of personal libraries was T = 0.188 in Kazan, T = 0.181 in Almetevsk,
and T = 0.190 in Menzelinsk, as compared to T = 0.06-0.07 in
Leningrad and Pskov. These divergences may be explained in
part by group differences in living standards. However, a more
detailed analysis which we conducted in Leningrad convinced us
that there is not a close association between the wage level and
such indices of cultural consumption as theater and concert attendance, the possession of books, and the number of newspaper

subscriptions per family.

In fact, in some cases an inverse relationship prevailed. Thus, 80% to 85% of low-paid workers — with a modal wage of 68 rubles — attended theaters and concerts at least once a month, while among highly paid personnel — those with earnings of more than 200 rubles a month — only 58-59% did so. The number of newspaper subscriptions per family among workers earning less than 100 rubles per month was 1.2, while among those earning more than 150 rubles per month and more than 200 rubles per month it was 1.4-1.5. The same situation exists with respect to the number of books in the personal libraries of employed personnel. Newspapers and books have long ceased to be confined to selected strata of the population; they have become a necessary feature of the daily life of all industrial personnel. Low book prices in our country facilitate the acquisition of substantial home libraries (the average number of books in a home library is 75). The higher the wage level of an individual, the less frequently he attends such forms of mass culture as films. For example, only 1% of the workers with wages of 60 rubles per month did not attend films in the year of the investigation. Among personnel in the modal range of 100 to 150 rubles, the proportion of such individuals reaches 7%, and among highly paid personnel — 16%. The opposite kind of relationship may be observed in television viewing. Among workers with wages of 60 to 80 rubles per month, 23% regularly view all television programs, while the figure rises to 33% among those with wages of 100 to 150 rubles per month, and to 50% among those with wages in excess of 200 rubles per month. The conclusion which emerges from the data is that the general cultural level of all strata of the working class has risen.

The average level of income that has now been achieved makes it possible for all categories of working people to pursue their studies. Our data for Leningrad machine-building personnel do not reveal any clear association between income per family member and the extent to which individuals combine work with study. Average income per family member for those who are not studying (61.6 rubles) is only one ruble less than it is for those who combine work with study. Average income per family member for those who are combining work with study at secondary specialized schools was 67.3 rubles, while it was 65.7 rubles for those who are combining work with correspondence or evening study at higher educational institutions. It is interesting that the largest proportion of students who are combining work with study at a higher educational institution come from families with incomes of less than 30 rubles per family member. The proportion of families in this low-paid group that have children who combine work and study is 7.2%, which exceeds the analogous proportion in the group of highly paid families. The general tendency is that the largest proportion of those who combine work with study come from families with relatively low levels of income per family member, where one finds the greatest striving for advancement, and also from families with high educational attainments and cultural traditions regardless of their income level. At the same time, an association undoubtedly exists between income per family member and the frequency with which work and study are combined.

The data obtained from the survey of Leningrad machine-building personnel permit us to establish those indices and aspects of the behavior of working people that are affected by their living standards. For example, 2/3 of the low-paid category of personnel do not participate in the community life of the enterprise. The proportion of nonparticipants in community work among those in the modal wage interval (120 to 150 rubles) — which includes the largest number of working people — is 28%, and in the highly paid categories it falls to 8.4%.

A definite association exists between the wage level and the general cultural development of the worker. Only 1/3 of low-paid personnel read newspapers regularly, while in the modal wage interval (120 to 150 rubles) the figure is 85%. It should be noted that among highly paid personnel this percentage decreases rather than increases.

The supplementary earnings received by some enterprise personnel usually serve as a means of compensating for the decline in per capita income that is associated with an increase in the number of family members. Thus, average income per family member among employed personnel who had very small supplementary earnings, or had none at all, was 69 rubles, while those who received supplementary earnings of 10 to 13 rubles per month had an average income per family member of 66 rubles per month, and when supplementary earnings reached more than 50 rubles per month the average income per family member did not exceed 48 rubles. Comparing these data, as well as a considerable amount of other data, with indices of community activity permits us to establish a certain standard of income per capita which determines a kind of boundary in many aspects of the individual's behavior. In 1965-1967 this boundary was at the level of 65 to 75 rubles per family member. There was a tendency toward a reduced level of community activity among employed personnel whose income was below this standard. They devoted more attention to studies and to raising their qualifications, activities which operate to increase earnings only after an extended period of time.

Thus, the causes of divergences in cultural consumption must be sought not in the level of well-being but in the nature of labor, in the degree to which work is interesting, which predetermines the content of the consumption of cultural values and thereby also the structure of leisure. Let us briefly examine certain quantitative indices which provide greater support for the propositions presented here. We begin with the amount of reading of works of fiction.

Among unskilled personnel in Leningrad machine-building, we find that 25.5% do not read at all, 21.3% read less than one book per month, 32.8% read 1-2 books per month, and 20.4% read one or more books per week. Among personnel in skilled, primarily manual, hand labor the indices are noticeably higher: the proportion of those who do not read at all is close to 6%, while the proportion who read one or more books per week is 35%. It should be noted that the amount of reading done by personnel in highly skilled scientific and technical work and by executives of labor collectives is somewhat less. Among the former, 28.5% regularly read one or more books per week, while among the latter 29.9% do so. True, among highly skilled scientific and technical personnel, 0.7% do not read books at all, and among executives of labor collectives the figure is 7.3%.

In the case of the latter category this is explained, of course, not by a small need for the consumption of cultural values, but by the fact that they are overloaded with job responsibilities and community work.

The data for Pskov do not introduce any changes in the general picture. The proportion of those who do not read fiction at all is high only among unskilled workers — 39.5%. On the other hand, among skilled workers this proportion falls to 7% and among skilled personnel in mental work it is zero, while 3.4% of executives do not read works of fiction. Approximately the same relationships are found in the Tatar Republic, although the amount of reading in all socio-occupational groups there is considerably less than in Leningrad. Thus, the proportion of individuals reading one or more books per week was as follows: among unskilled workers — 9% in Kazan, 5% in Almetevsk, 15% in Menzelinsk; among skilled workers — 14% in Kazan, 18% in Almetevsk, 18% in Menzelinsk; among personnel in mental work — 15% to 25% in all cities. The proportion of unskilled workers not reading fiction in all three cities rises to 42-47%, while among skilled workers it is about 20%, and among personnel in mental work — about 5%.

In all cities in which the surveys were conducted most working people have personal libraries. However, there are substantial quantitative variations. Among unskilled workers in Leningrad, 26.9% do not have any books at all, 21.9% have 1-10 books, 26.9% have small libraries of up to 50 books, 15.6% have libraries of 50 to 100 books, 3.2% have 100 to 500 books, and 5.6% have libraries containing more than 500 books. What appears at first glance to be an unexpectedly high proportion having large libraries (more than 500 books) is explained by the fact that unskilled workers' families include a substantial number of graduates of secondary schools and members of higher socio-occupational groups. Among skilled workers in Leningrad machine-building, the proportion that do not have their own books falls to approximately 13%. As for owners of small libraries in this group, their proportion is the same as it is among unskilled workers. The proportion having libraries of 100 or more books — about 8% — is markedly greater than is the case with unskilled workers. In most instances the scientific and technical intelligentsia have libraries of 50 to 100 books (27.4%) and 100 to 500 books (33.5%). The indices for the professional executives' group are close to these. In Pskov the proportion of workers not having their own libraries is considerably higher. For example, in the unskilled group it rises to 53%, but the nature of the association between the possession and size of personal libraries, on the one hand, and socio-occupational status, on the other, is the same as in Leningrad. Nor do the data differ essentially for the Tatar Republic, although here we may observe their dependence on the type of city. Among unskilled workers in Kazan, 34.5% do not have their own books, 29% have 1-10 books, and 27% have 11 to 50 books. The other groups have considerably larger personal libraries. The situation is somewhat worse in Almetevsk. In this city, 48.4% of unskilled workers do not have their own books, 16.6% have 1-10 books, and 27.7% have 11 to 50 books. The indices are even lower in Menzelinsk, where 54.4% of this category of workers do not have any books at all, 25% own 1-10 books, 16.9% have libraries of 11 to 50 books, and the proportion having anything like substantial personal libraries is completely insignificant.

This is how the situation appears for the group of skilled workers employed on machines and mechanisms. In Kazan, 26.9% do not have any books, 25.9% have 1-10 books, and 33.6% have libraries of 11 to 50 books. The proportion of this group possessing libraries with 50 to 100 books is 9.7%, while 2.6% have libraries of 100 or more books. In Almetevsk and Menzelinsk the relationship between the indices is in favor of the latter: 46.1% and 34.5%, respectively, do not have any books, 16.2% and 28% have up to 10 books, 27.1% and 29.5% have up to 50 books. The inferior indices for Almetevsk in this instance are connected with specific peculiarities of the formation of workers' cadres. There is a large proportion of young workers in this group who have recently arrived in the city and who live in hostels or private apartments. The difference between cities is even greater in the case of the scientific and technical group of personnel. While in Kazan 14.1% of this group possess personal

libraries of more than 500 books and 29.4% have libraries of
100 to 500 books, in Almetevsk only 27.3% have libraries of
100 to 500 books, and owners of large libraries — as in Menzelinsk — are nonexistent.

As for theater attendance, analysis of the influence of type of
settlement on the amount of this activity is limited by objective
circumstances: there are no permanent Russian theaters in
Menzelinsk and Almetevsk. Therefore, a comparison of Leningrad, Kazan and Pskov is more appropriate. For all three cities
we use only one index: the proportion of individuals who — according to their own testimony — do not go to the theater. This
proportion is as follows: among unskilled workers in Leningrad
— 36.9%, in Pskov — 40.6%, in Kazan — 41.6%. Among skilled
workers the proportion is about 15% in Leningrad and Pskov,
and approximately 24% in Kazan. The great majority of the scientific and technical intelligentsia in Leningrad attend the theater with varying degrees of regularity. Only about 6% indicated
that they do not attend theatrical performances. In Pskov a
comparable answer was given by 20% of individuals in this kind
of work, and in Kazan — 15.2%.

Let us now examine some indices of well-being and daily life
for the principal socio-occupational groups. We begin with the
availability of housing for the working people. Differences in
this index among the groups are not very large. For example,
the average amount of housing space for executives of labor
collectives in Leningrad in 1965 (7.0 square meters per family
member) was only 0.9 square meters greater than for personnel in unskilled manual labor. A similar situation prevailed in
Pskov (1967). For all groups at the automatic telephone station
plant in that city, the amount of housing space per family member was 6.5 to 6.7 square meters. In Kazan the differences
were greater: 5.6 square meters for unskilled workers, about
6 square meters for skilled workers, 6.6 square meters for
highly skilled workers, 7.0 square meters for personnel in scientific and technical work, and, finally, 7.8 square meters for
executives of labor collectives.

If we convert the quantitative indices to Chuprov coefficients,
the association between socio-occupational position of employed

personnel and the provision of housing space may be expressed
as follows: T = 0.045 in Pskov, T = 0.093 in Kazan, T = 0.105
in Almetevsk, and T = 0.126 in Menzelinsk.

Thus, although an association exists, it is not strictly determined by socio-occupational status.

The data on housing conditions appear somewhat different if
we examine them from the standpoint of availability of separate
housing. The proportion of enterprise executives and personnel
in highly skilled scientific and technical work having separate
apartments and their own homes is $2-2\frac{1}{2}$ times that of unskilled
manual workers.

To measure the standard of living of workers, we used com-
binations of household goods as an index in all the investigations.
Following the proposal of the economist L. S. Bliakhman, the
full range of goods included were grouped into four categories
according to the availability of the goods in households:

1) dinner table, wardrobe, sofa, bicycle;

2) writing table, television set, radio, sewing machine, record player;

3) washing machine, refrigerator, accordion;

4) automobile, piano.

The results obtained by using this scale for Leningrad
machine-building personnel are presented in Table 5, which
was prepared by I. P. Trufanov. The possibility of drawing conclusions from this material is limited by the absence of value
indicators for the goods. Despite this, however, it is clear that
the proportion of the more complex goods and those that are
not prime necessities increases as we move from one socio-
occupational group to another. The conclusion, of course, is
not surprising, but it is corroborated here by clear facts.

It should be recalled that studies of household inventories
have been interrupted since 1930. It is interesting to note that
the minimum set of household goods that provides for daily
needs is now available to all groups, which was not the case in
the 1920s when S. G. Strumilin and his collaborators conducted
similar studies. (11) From the very beginning of our study we
have had to include the kinds of goods (television sets, washing
machines, refrigerators, etc.) that are the fruits of the mass

Table 5

Structure of Inventories of Household Goods,
Leningrad Machine–Building Personnel, 1965

Groups of employed personnel	Proportions of different sets of household goods (in %) (a)					Number of persons answering questions
	1st set	2nd set	3rd set	4th set	total	
Unskilled personnel in manual labor	44.2	41.7	11.8	2.3	100	125
Personnel in skilled, primarily manual labor, employed on machines and mechanisms	43.8	40.6	13.4	2.2	100	807
Personnel in skilled, primarily manual, hand labor	41.7	40.0	15.5	2.8	100	978
Personnel in nonmanual labor of medium skills	43.3	40.6	13.1	3.0	100	364
Highly skilled personnel combining mental and manual work	40.8	38.9	16.7	3.6	100	67
Personnel in skilled mental work	38.2	37.0	19.1	5.7	100	286
Personnel in highly skilled mental work	35.9	34.5	22.8	6.8	100	136
Executives of production collectives	37.3	37.3	19.8	5.6	100	254
Total	40.7	39.6	15.7	4.0	100	3,017

(a) The 100% stands for the total amount of household goods held by the surveyed representatives of the corresponding socio-occupational groups.

culture of the last two decades, particularly the last decade.
We can anticipate that the social groups differ not so much in
the amounts of household goods as in the qualitative and, therefore, value indices of these goods.

In concluding our general characterization of socio-
occupational groups of the working class, let us examine some
data concerning the size and structure of families.

Table 6 shows that small families — primarily two-generation
families — were typical among all social groups of Leningrad
machine-building personnel. During the years of the first five-
year plans there was a tendency for family size to decline
among skilled personnel, particularly among engineering and
technical personnel. Higher fertility was observed among
groups with lower social status and cultural level, groups with
lower living standards.

By the middle of the 1960s the situation had changed significantly. Comparatively large families prevailed precisely
among the highly paid and more skilled groups. These are the
families with larger numbers of dependents per family member having an independent source of income (for example, 1.0
among executives of collectives compared to 0.7-0.9 among
personnel in primarily manual labor and employees).

As Table 6 shows, the data on average income per family
member in contrast to the wage data reveals that the maximum
gap between the groups does not exceed 11.4 rubles.* This
means that the families of working people employed in the socialist economy represent collectives in which the low-paid are
generally the second and third members of the family. The
analysis of family social structure presented below also cor-
roborates the conclusion that the Soviet family consists, as a
rule, of representatives of different socio-occupational groups.

Thus, the material presented in Table 6 goes beyond simply
characterizing the social-production structure as such and testifies to the relatively high degree of social homogeneity of our
society.

In many ways the material obtained in subsequent investigations

---

*The correct figure, judging from Table 6, is 13.8.

Table 6

Family Characteristics of Different Groups of Employed Personnel
in Leningrad Machine-Building

Groups of employed personnel	Average family size		Average no. of individuals with independent source of income		No. of dependents per family member with independent source of income $(\bar{X}_1 - \bar{X}_2)$	Average income per family member (rubles per month)	
	$\bar{X}_1$	σ_1	$\bar{X}_2$	σ_2		$\bar{X}$	σ
Unskilled personnel in manual labor	2.9	1.2	2.2	1.1	0.7	60.8	23.5
Personnel in nonmanual labor of medium skills	3.2	1.2	2.3	0.9	0.9	62.3	21.3
Personnel in skilled, primarily manual labor, employed on machines and mechanisms	3.0	1.2	2.3	0.9	0.7	58.4	19.7
Personnel in skilled, primarily manual, hand labor	2.9	1.3	2.1	0.9	0.8	64.5	22.2
Personnel in highly skilled work combining mental and manual functions	3.4	1.3	2.5	1.0	0.9	62.6	20.0
Personnel in skilled mental work	3.0	1.2	2.3	1.1	0.7	67.2	21.8
Highly skilled scientific and technical personnel	3.2	1.3	2.4	1.0	0.8	72.2	19.3
Executives of production collectives	3.2	1.2	2.2*	0.9	1.0	71.1	22.7

*This figure is given as 2.9 in the Shkaratan volume, but it appears to be a misprint. Both the table and the discussion in the text cite the figure 1.0 as "number of dependents per family member with independent source of income" for executives. We assume that "average family size" (3.2) is shown correctly for executives in the table. Hence we have changed from 2.9 to 2.2 the figure for "average number of individuals with independent source of income."

confirmed the propositions we have just presented. Thus, in
Kazan the average size of family among unskilled workers was
3.4 persons, while among scientific and technical personnel it
was 3.7 persons and among executives of labor collectives it
was 3.6 persons. (12) Among unskilled workers the number of
dependents per family member was the same as among skilled
workers and scientific and technical personnel — 1.3 persons —
while among executives of labor collectives it was somewhat
higher — 1.4 persons.

In Kazan the average income per family member varied
markedly among the socio-occupational groups. It ranged from
58-59 rubles for skilled workers to 73.8 rubles for scientific
and technical personnel and 74.1 rubles for executives of labor
collectives. But this was connected with the fact that the study
covered the urban population as a whole, i.e., the category of
personnel in manual labor and low-skilled personnel in nonmanual labor included population groups employed in branches
with low wage levels (the service sectors, etc.), while the executives' category and that of scientific and technical personnel
included members of families employed in highly paid work in
scientific institutions and the administrative apparatus.

But as a whole the data for Kazan, while reflecting the differentiation which still exists in our society, also demonstrate its
steady movement toward social homogeneity.

We now attempt to summarize the features of the socio-
occupational groups we have been examining.

We have used the material gathered in the survey conducted
in the Tatar Republic to calculate Chuprov coefficients showing
the degree of association between socio-occupational status and
specific social characteristics. In Table 7 these coefficients
are ranked according to the data derived in Kazan. The highest
ranking characteristic is education, which emerges not only as
a factor bringing particular individuals into the corresponding
groups, but also as an attribute of the latter. Second place is
occupied by wages. Third — the possession of a personal library, i.e., an indicator of the cultural level. In fourth and fifth
place we have indicators of community activity. As for indicators

Table 7

Influence of Socio-Occupational Status on Intensity of Manifestation of Social Characteristics (in Chuprov Coefficients)

Social characteristics	Kazan	Almetevsk	Menzelinsk
1. Education	0.313	0.314	0.325
2. Wages	0.225	0.264	0.230
3. Possession of personal library	0.188	0.181	0.190
4. Participation in community work	0.180	0.188	0.197
5. Participation in rationalization or invention	0.180	0.146	0.124
6. Reading of newspapers	0.166	0.171	0.172
7. Party membership	0.145	0.180	0.216
8. Separate housing quarters	0.131	0.167	0.132
9. Theater attendance	0.126	0.117	0.140
10. Reading of fiction	0.125	0.142	0.158
11. Money income per family member per month	0.122	0.134	0.150
12. Age	0.114	0.108	0.212
13. Overall length of employment	0.097	0.103	0.129
14. Length of employment at enterprises in cities	0.093	0.092	0.105
15. Housing space per family member in meters	0.093	0.105	0.126
16. Satisfaction with content of work	0.077	0.080	0.092
17. Family size	0.064	0.096	0.103
18. Number of individuals with independent source of income	0.061	0.080	0.078

of well-being (income and housing space, in meters, per family member), it is evident from the table that they occupied a rather modest position. The table as a whole makes it possible to gauge the extent to which differences between socio-occupational groups in specific spheres of the vital activity of society have been eliminated. Moreover, the further we move from the production sphere the less manifest are these differences. In particular, we can state that in a typical region of the country such as the Tatar Republic the urban population is generally satisfied with the content of its labor activity, i.e., the functions it performs are adequate for the personal composition of the social groups. The indices of participation in nonregulated production activity, i.e., in rationalization, in community and political work, reveal a rather significant dependence on attachment to the corresponding group.

It is interesting that, of all the cultural indices, the one showing the closest association with socio-occupational group identification is the index of possession of personal libraries. And this is not accidental. Personal libraries testify to an active perception of culture: one must have a certain taste for books, one must obtain them, buy them, and in doing this one must change the structure of the family budget, etc.

The next most important cultural index, as one might expect, is the reading of newspapers, which also testifies to a certain social activity. This index stands at about the same level as such important characteristics as Party membership and participation in community work.

The two indices of association between length of employment and social status which are included in the table are characterized by more modest magnitudes. This means that at the present time the length of employment is not a significant characteristic either as a factor in differentiation or as an attribute of groups.

Table 7 also shows the dependence of the attributes of the socio-occupational groups on the type of urban settlement. The information summarized in this table is insufficient, of course, for a thorough analysis. However, we can formulate the following initial hypothesis: A more developed type of urban settlement

must make greater demands on the individual, i.e., it is as
though different types of urban settlements evaluate people differently according to their social potential. A city with a definite mode of life (and every city has a definite mode of life) im-
poses a certain socio-occupational selection. Since the socio-
occupational structure of the city of today determines the city
of tomorrow, this process of selection, which proceeds differently in different cities, determines the degree of progressive-
ness of different types of urban settlements. From this point of
view a large city that contains all the elements of present-day
socio-occupational structure and bears within it the germs of
the future socio-occupational structure of the population is a
more progressive city.

The extent to which a specific type of settlement approaches
the optimum type can be determined by the demands which the
city makes on individuals with respect to the performance of
the various socio-occupational roles. As an example, let us examine two series of indices, one of which characterizes the association between social status and age, while the other has to
do with the association between social status and income per
family member.

It is clear that the degree of manifestation of age characteristics as attributes* should decline as we move to the type of
city in which the opportunities for advancement are less strictly
predetermined by age. The fact is that, in this respect, first
place is occupied by a city in which the formation of occupational groups is still proceeding, a city in which these groups
have not yet been fully formed, the new industrial center of
Almetevsk. Kazan ranks second, and Menzelinsk — a city with
extremely limited opportunities for the advancement of youth —
ranks third. The corresponding Chuprov coefficient indices are
as follows: 0.108 in Almetevsk, 0.114 in Kazan, and 0.212 in
Menzelinsk.

---

*Shkaratan apparently means attributes of the socio-
occupational groups distinguished above. The concept of "attributes" or "attribute features" is elaborated by Shkaratan on
p. 20 above.

In evaluating the data on income per family member, we shall assume that increasing equality in income levels testifies to the declining differentiation between socio-occupational groups, to the merging of these groups, to the high degree of "openness" of these groups, and therefore that it coincides with the basic tendencies of the period of transition from socialism to communism. Given this interpretation, the calculated coefficients show that Kazan has the most advanced social relations and occupies first place, Almetevsk is second, and Menzelinsk is third.

The other indices presented in Table 7 can be analyzed in a similar manner. In general we may conclude that the type of settlement has a strong influence on the intensity of manifestation of the social characteristics of groups: the further the process of urbanization of the population has proceeded, the higher the demands made on the social potential of individuals included in the more advanced socio-occupational groups.

Thus, our investigations have corroborated the hypothesis that intraclass groups are formed on the basis of the still-persisting socio-economic heterogeneity of labor, and that as a result differences still exist among the members of society with respect to their role in the social organization of labor, their contribution to the development of the socialist economy and culture, the significance for society of their production activity, and that this is rooted in the unequal complexity and social value of labor.

One of the problems that is most difficult for economic science to solve involves the measurement of the complexity of labor, the reduction of complex labor to simple labor. The special examination of this problem was not one of our tasks. We shall only note that in the coefficients of reduction proposed by some writers (13), the starting point is the time or costs required for the reproduction of labor power of the given skill level (i.e., for general education, occupational training, the probation period in production). These proposals do not consider the influence of the whole complex of social circumstances which make it possible for an individual to become engaged in labor of a given level of complexity.

The availability of coefficients of reduction of labor would be highly useful for the analysis of intraclass differentiation, since it would permit us to measure the extent of differences in the complexity of labor of already established groups. Taken by themselves, of course, these coefficients cannot serve as criteria for the division of employed personnel into socially differentiated types, since in the formation of the latter a significant role is played by factors which cannot be reduced to a straightforward relationship of simple to complex labor. But it is fully possible and appropriate to determine the socio-economic role of social groups, which have been distinguished on the basis of combined characteristics, with the assistance of coefficients of reduction of labor.

In practice, of the various features which we have examined, the complexity of labor is characterized (directly) by the following: occupation, education, occupational training, skill, length of employment in the given occupation and in industry, and finally, wages.

The second important element in the social differentiation of classes under socialism is the degree of participation in the organization of production and in the management of social affairs. In this connection we considered job position [dolzhnost'], participation in social self-management, Party membership, and participation in invention and rationalization activity.

Both of these elements are closely connected and present a picture of the location of members of a class in socio-occupational groups. Of course, participation in social management and rationalization activity already break that hierarchical structure which is given by the formal status of the individual in the production system by virtue of his performance of regulated production duties. The whole system of socialism promotes the merging of social groups, their reduced differentiation and increased equality through the mechanism of socialist democracy.

The third essential element in intraclass differentiation is the position of the individual in the family and his patterns of association. This element is characterized by the following indices: social origin, social position of wife and adult children, friendship patterns by social background, and income per family member. The following section of the chapter is devoted to this element.*

Notes

1) See S. A. Kugel', Zakonomernosti izmeneniia sotsial'noi struktury obshchestva pri perekhode k kommunizmu, Moscow, 1963; V. S. Semenov, "The Working Class and Its Role in the Building of Communism," Stroitel'stvo kommunizma i razvitie obshchestvennykh otnoshenii, Moscow, 1966.

2) For a brief description of these surveys, see Chapter 1, section 5, and for the theoretical propositions on which they rest, see sections 1-4 of that chapter. [Editors' note: these sections have not been included in the present volume.]

3) We prepared the initial grouping jointly with the economists V. R. Polozov and G. F. Komarov on the basis of data from the occupational census, and in consultation with V. A. Iakovlev and L. I. Denisiuk of the Leningrad Statistical Administration (these groups are shown in Chapter 1, section 5).

4) This was done by relying on experts (employees of the former Leningrad Economic Council and of machine-building enterprises, as well as economists).

5) In the tables below, organizers of production collectives include, as a rule, heads of shops and departments, and executives of enterprises and combines. Exceptions are indicated in the notes to the corresponding tables.

6) Iu. E. Volkov, "The Organization of the Management of Society," Voprosy filosofii, 1965, No. 8, p. 17.

7) This study was done in 1968 by the Inter-Institutional Sociological Laboratory of the Institute of Ethnography of the USSR Academy of Sciences and the Leningrad Finance and Economics Institute.

8) The corresponding indicator in the study of Leningrad machine-building personnel was 13.6 years of schooling.

9) See K. Varshavskii, "Some Forms of Manifestation of the Law of Changes in Work at the Present Stage," Filosofskie

---

*See pp. 289-319 below.

nauki, 1965, No. 2.

10) Here and below we present wage data drawn from the 1965 to 1967 studies, i.e., before the increase in minimum wages and other measures which led to a marked rise in workers' pay in the 1968-1969 period.

11) See S. G. Strumilin, "On the Problem of the Birth Rate in Workers' Families," in his Problemy ekonomiki truda, Moscow, 1957.

12) These figures were taken from the findings of a sociological investigation, but they can be made more precise by relying on data of state statistics. The work was done by E. K. Vasil'ev (see his article "Ethno-Demographic Characteristics of Family Structure of the Population of Kazan in 1967: Materials of a Sociological Investigation," Sovetskaia etnografiia, 1968, No. 5).

13) See R. A. Batkaev and V. I. Markov, Differentsiatsiia zarabotnoi platy v promyshlennosti SSSR, Moscow, 1964, pp. 50-91; V. F. Maier, Zarabotnaia plata v period perekhoda k kommunizmu, pp. 67-90; E. I. Kapustin, Kachestvo truda i zarabotnaia plata, Moscow, 1964, pp. 116-178; Ia. I. Gomberg, Reduktsiia truda, Moscow, 1965, and other works.

7 The Distribution of Decision-Making Among the Rural Population of the USSR

IU. V. ARUTIUNIAN

Until recently all the existing differences between collective farmers, on the one hand, and workers and employees, on the other, were connected only with the existence of two forms of property. As a result, a serious displacement of factors took place. Differences between collective farmers, workers and employees are in fact significant, but one must realize what they stem from.

First of all, differences between town and countryside are superimposed upon differences caused by forms of property. As may be seen from material presented above, 2/3 of workers labor in cities. Urban conditions unquestionably affect people's life-styles, their cultural-daily life traits. In this regard, serious differences may be observed not only between workers and collective farmers but also between city workers and workers in the countryside. Furthermore, in comparing the populations of the collective-farm and state sectors, one should keep in mind the differences in the structures of their populations. For example, in the collective farm sector, as we have already pointed out, only 2.5% of people are engaged in mental labor, while in the state sector in the countryside approximately 1/4,

Our title. From Iu. V. Arutiunian, Sotsial'naia struktura sel'skogo naseleniia SSSR, "Mysl'" Publishing House, Moscow, 1971, pp. 101-111. Tables 1 and 2 below correspond to Tables 20 and 21 in the original. The title of the chapter from which this selection is drawn is "Socio-Economic Foundations of Group Differences."

and in cities 1/3, are so engaged. The differences between collective farmers, on the one hand, and workers and employees,
on the other, in this case are again caused not directly by the
form of property but by the backwardness of the occupational-
skill structure of collective farmers in comparison with that of
workers. Thus, in practice, class differences caused by the peculiarities of forms of property combine with differences between town and countryside, manual and mental labor, agriculture and industry. For an analysis to be really correct, we must
compare identical occupational-skill groups. In those cases in
which we want to ascertain the actual role of differences caused
directly by different forms of property, we must "cleanse" these
differences of other layers — in the first place, of layers caused
by an urban style of life.

Using the data of all-Union statistics, one can fill in the proposed scheme of the social structure of Soviet society only in
its general features. It is impossible to present a more concrete picture of how workers, employees, and collective farmers are distributed according to more specific social categories,
depending on the skill of manual or mental labor. It is even more
impossible to ascertain the extent to which the groups presented
in the scheme differ from one another in economic and cultural-
daily life terms. This would require mass data concerning the
material assets and cultural-daily life conditions of the different social strata of the population.

Since we do not have this data in general form, we can only
try out the proposed scheme on local material. Thus, the task
is to find out whether the distinguishing of the above-noted social groups is correct, whether these groups really differ from
each other, and to what extent.

First of all, what is their relation to property? Theoretically
we have already tried to show the advantage of the concept "utilization of property" (over "ownership of property"); we explained the need for analysis of relations of utilization of property in order to portray the real relations that occur between
people — between individuals, collectives, social groups,
classes — in regard to property. The empirical task which now
confronts us amounts in practice to measuring the degree of

utilization of property by classes and groups.

In the last ten years the conditions of the utilization of property in state and collective farm-cooperative enterprises have become significantly more similar in nature. This rapprochement has taken place as a result of the development of self-supporting relations in state farms, as well as because of certain changes in social and economic relations in collective farms, thanks to which the disposition of property has become more direct. Particularly significant shifts occurred after the March 1965 Plenum of the CPSU Central Committee, which provided a firm purchase plan for collective farms for a series of years, uniform prices for collective farms and state enterprises for agricultural technology, a lowering of income taxes on collective farms, their transfer to bank credit, etc. (1)

Although the rapprochement of the socio-economic positions of collective and state farms smoothed over the significant differences between them, it did not eliminate them by any means. They were expressed first of all in the different mechanisms for the sale of the produce of collective and state farms, the different sources of their distribution funds, and differences in the structure of management and self-management of these enterprises. For example, the state farms have trade unions that control the conditions of work and leisure of the workers; collective farms, on the other hand, have recently created their own organization to express their interests — the system of collective farm unions.

However, the traits noted, which are indicative of the general and the specific in the position of collective farms as cooperative organizations, relate only to their place in the social organization of labor on the scale of the entire society, as if in the system "society-enterprise." In this case a collective farm (and equally a state farm) is an object of management that uses property in specific conditions and possesses corresponding social and economic rights, social and economic power.

But what do a state and collective farm look like as subjects of management? This is an entirely different — internal, as it were — aspect of the problem. Here the question of the distribution of rights and power within a collective, among its members,

becomes central. In other words, one must explain how the
property already given for use is utilized in the system "collective — socio-occupational group — individual." Different variations are possible. In one case the growth of initiative and independence in disposing of collective farm property can be reduced to multiplication of the power of only the director of the
enterprise; in the other, the opposite is possible: greater rights
in the utilization of property can be equally distributed within
the collective.

Of late it has been widely held that the collective farm as a
cooperative organization provides greater scope for initiative
and independent activity in comparison with the state farm. In
principle this is true. But, one asks, whose initiative is it? Is
it reflected in every collective farmer, or does the right of disposition of property become concentrated among people who are
professionally prepared for leadership, and can one therefore
speak only about the different positions of directors of state enterprises and of collective farms but by no means about all
socio-occupational groups and every individual?

In order to answer this question it is necessary to face the essence of the phenomenon of collectivization of property. It is not
a one-time affair. Rather, it is a long process. From the legal
or, more precisely, the political act of collectivization to actual
collectivization there is a whole period, perhaps even epoch, of
historical development that only begins with the immediate act
of collectivization. The revolution in our country eliminated the
order under which property was separated from work and created the conditions for their unification. But such a unification
is possible only through a long evolution and a series of intermediate socio-economic forms. The criterion for the unification
of the means of production and labor power, materialized and
living labor, is the degree of the realization by the producer
himself of the functions of management or, in other words, of
the disposition of collectivized property.

The effectiveness of realization of the function of disposition
depends to some extent on the concrete form of the socio-
economic organization of the enterprise. In this sense there is
a definite difference between collective farms and state enterprises

as regards the organization and mechanism of management. In collective farms this mechanism is really better adapted for attracting the individual to management and for control over the activity of the administration on the part of the collective farmers. Election of the chairman of the collective farm and, in connection with the new regulation, the possibility of choosing a brigade leader, regular general meetings or meetings of those entrusted with broad functions, management activity, brigade councils, and production meetings make it easier for each collective farmer to influence decisions on general collective matters and actually to participate in the disposition of property. (A corresponding mechanism, but in a somewhat modified form, exists also in state enterprises.) However, empirical studies show that in practice this mechanism by itself does not ensure sufficiently effective participation of each person in the disposition of property. (2)

The reason for this is that realization of the functions of disposition of property (in the conditions of the uniform socialist system that has emerged) depends not only on concrete forms of organization of production but also on the producer himself. The collective farms and state enterprises have different systems of personification of social relations. But the result is approximately the same, since there is no significant difference in "those who are managed." Lenin spoke of how every cook will govern. But it would be a vulgarization and naive to interpret this literally. A cook who is able to take part in the direction of a complicated social or technical organism cannot remain the same cook.

Realization of the social function of disposition of property directly by society and by every member of that society is only possible if the population has a high educational level, augmented by rich social experience. As long as this is not the case, professionally prepared leaders specially designated for the purpose (the so-called administrative intelligentsia) perform, and cannot help but perform, the function of disposition regardless of the concrete system of social institutions. One can judge the validity of this conclusion through analysis of the activity of concrete institutions responsible for the internal management of

collective and state farms. Such types of research are well
known. One can approach this problem also from the other
side — by finding out from the collective farmers and the workers themselves how much they feel that they are the masters of
the enterprise, what their role is in decisions regarding the collective's current affairs. Such an approach may not give an exact picture of the concrete activity of people and institutions,
but it will give something more: the degree of awareness (be it
subjective) of a person of his social role as a co-owner of a
given form of collectivized property. In reality this is the subjective perception of the degree of actual collectivization of
property.

A survey which we conducted in the farmlands of Kalinin Region, Krasnodar Territory, and the Tatar ASSR produced a picture which coincides in principle in all three cases. The process of unification of labor power with the means of production
has progressed quite far. Despite the increasing complexity of
production and the rapid increase in the volume of specialized
information requiring technical knowledge, more than half the
working people in rural areas have a sense that they influence
the affairs of the collective. However, notwithstanding existing
opinions concerning the advantages of the collective farm for
the expression of the will and influence of rank-and-file working people, these data testify to the fact that collective farmers
influence decisions on "important questions in the collective"
to a lesser extent than workers. In all cases the proportion exercising influence is greater in state farms, and it is particularly high in industrial enterprises and other establishments.
In Kalinin Region, 63% of those working in the collective farms,
54% in state farms, and 29% in enterprises and institutions "do
not influence" the decisions of the collective. The situation was
about the same in Krasnodar Territory and the Tatar ASSR. (3)

How is one to explain such a seemingly persistent lagging behind of the most self-governing cooperative form? The answer
to this question emerges upon analysis of the participation of
socio-occupational groups in the disposition of property. The
group engaged in unskilled labor — common laborers, cattle-
breeders — has little influence on production affairs, and this

is natural, if only because of insufficient education. The greater people's skill and the more they understand today's complicated production, the greater is their responsibility for the fate of the collective and the more active is their societal role. In essence, they influence production affairs in accordance with their responsibilities, "according to their jobs." In practice, naturally, all higher-level managerial personnel and specialists in collective and state farms influence "decisions on important problems in the collective." Middle-level managerial personnel and specialists exert influence in a majority of cases, machine operators in approximately half the cases, etc. (see Table 1).

These data make understandable the relatively weak participation of collective farmers in management and in the disposition of "their own property." After all, the socio-occupational structure of collective farms is less developed than that of state farms, not to mention that of the nonagricultural branches of the state sector. The collective farms have fewer skilled workers and, most important, fewer intelligentsia functioning in managerial, disposing roles. True, the Kuban is an exception. In the collective farms of Krasnodar Territory, as opposed to Kalinin Region and the Tatar ASSR, somewhat more people influence the collective's affairs than in the state farms (see Table 1). But the fact is that the Kuban is one of the few regions in the country where the socio-occupational structure in collective farms is more complex than in state farms. Thus, this exception confirms the rule: under Soviet conditions it is not the form of property directly, nor the social type of enterprise, but the socio-occupational structure of working people that determines the degree of self-government and the actual disposition of property.

Since a large proportion of collective farmers do not have any skill whatever, nor enough education, all of the constantly expanding rights of collective farms are first of all personified in managerial personnel and specialists who must combine the interests of society (the state) with the interests of the collective, of socio-occupational groups, and of individuals within the collective. It stands to reason that not being individual owners of property, they are limited also in their rights to dispose of it.

Table 1

Percentage of People Who Feel They Have No Influence
on the Affairs of Their Work Collectives
(by socio-occupational group)

Socio-occupational groups	Absolute number of respondents		Percent not having any influence			
	Actual	Weighted	In collective farms	In state farms	Other enterprises	Total
Krasnodar Territory						
Higher-level managerial personnel and specialists (A$_1$)	130	213	10	9	n.a.*	9
Middle-level managerial personnel and specialists (A$_2$)	148	243	28	18	24	21
Employees (B)	135	146	48	33	50	44
Machine operators (C)	414	637	45	61	32	50
Skilled manual workers (D$_1$)	117	767	48	66	67	55
Low-skilled and unskilled manual workers (D$_{2-3}$)	536	3,593	59	74	67	65
Total	1,480	5,599	53	66	43	57
Kalinin Region						
Higher-level managerial personnel and specialists (A$_1$)	111	297	n.a.*	8	n.a.*	9
Middle-level managerial personnel and specialists (A$_2$)	162	283	12	13	13	13
Employees (B)	150	321	19	39	35	31
Machine operators (C)	191	642	53	51	36	44
Skilled manual workers (D$_1$)	83	492	67	61	32	57
Low-skilled and unskilled manual workers (D$_{2-3}$)	478	3,606	65	55	n.a.*	58
Total	1,175	5,641	63	54	29	51

Table 1 (continued)

Socio-occupational groups	Absolute number of respondents		Percent not having any influence			
	Actual	Weighted	In collective farms	In state farms	Other enterprises	Total
Tatar ASSR						
Higher-level managerial personnel and specialists (A$_1$)	225	478	13	n.a.*	20	12
Middle-level managerial personnel and specialists (A$_2$)	164	258	17	36	n.a.*	20
Employees (B)	220	286	33	48	37	38
Machine operators (C)	444	785	54	45	45	50
Skilled manual workers (D$_1$)	117	313	64	51	58	58
Low-skilled and unskilled manual workers (D$_{2-3}$)	943	3,046	69	72	68	69
Total	2,113	5,166	63	55	50	56

* — not available.

In the first place, activity involving the disposition of property is regulated in all its aspects by general state norms and it proceeds within the framework of plan predeterminations; second, it is controlled from the top (by higher-level organizations) as well as from below (by those directed); third, as society develops and the population's culture grows, nonprofessional management is expanding, along with professional management, and participation in it is being constantly activated to the degree that the social experience of the masses is growing. The social task of the day comes down to the need for further democratization of the functions involved in the disposition of property. The 24th

Congress of the CPSU called for "wider involvement of the working masses in management of economic affairs" (4) and placed
particular stress on the crucial significance of the economic
education of the broad masses.

It is natural that even when the entire population will participate
actively in the direction of production and societal affairs, the
specific function of management and the people who perform it
will not disappear. But as society develops, their activity, increasingly controlled from below, will be transformed into
administrative-technological activity in accordance with the
most rational fulfillment of societal directives. In these conditions every individual becomes a disposer of societal property
and is conscious of himself as such. The goal of democratizing
the function of disposition leads to efforts to achieve a union of
collective and general state interests not on the level of leaders
but on the lower rungs, to give a personal character to societal
interests and a societal character to personal ones. Many creative efforts are promoting this. For example, one can point to
the creation of nonassigned units and brigades that confirm in
every toiler the sense of being a master, and that are intended
to make the individual feel the direct dependence of reward on
his own initiative and labor. But regardless of the results
achieved in this direction, the process of unification of the
means of production and the work force, as we have already noted,
is inseparable from the development of the work force itself.

It is not only the socio-occupational structure of the labor
force, but also such changes in it as the broadening of horizons
and the growth of education of the working people, that actively
influence their social-productive activity and involve them in
the disposition of property. It is evident from Table 1, for example, that even within the same socio-occupational groups,
workers in Kalinin Region without a specialty influence the collective's affairs less in collective farms than they do in state
farms, while the opposite is true in Krasnodar Territory and
the Tatar ASSR. And this is not accidental. It turns out that
because of specific conditions (the relative well-being of
the Kuban collective farms in comparison with the state
farms, the less active migration from the Tatar collective

Table 2

Percentage of People Who Feel They Have No
Influence on Decisions Concerning Important
Problems in the Collective (a)
(in % of each socio-occupational group)

Groups	Krasnodar Territory		Kalinin Region		Tatar ASSR	
	without education	with education	without education	with education	without education	with education
A$_1$	20	6	14	5	12	18
A$_2$	20	25	11	9	31	23
B	44	19	29	35	56	41
C	52	18	52	48	48	50
D$_1$	66	56	62	49	62	55
D$_2$	69	60	59	44	68	68

(a) The polar groups by education are compared. The concept
of what is considered educated changes from group to group, of
course. For workers without any specialty, for example, persons who have finished at least 7 grades are treated as those
with education; illiterates and semiliterates — as those without
education; among higher-level specialists, only those with higher
or specialized secondary education are regarded as educated,
and so on.

farms), the level of education of workers without a specialty in
the Kuban and the Tatar ASSR is higher than in Kalinin Region.
In Kalinin Region, among workers without specialties in the collective farms there are significantly more semiliterates (30%)
than among those in the state farms (19%); in Krasnodar Territory and the Tatar ASSR the opposite is true (in the collective
farms — 15%, in the state farms — 17-20%). Thus, as a result
of differing preparation, the same socio-occupational group differs in its social influence and, according to its own potential,

will more effectively use the form of a collective farm in one case and the form of the state enterprise in another. As they say, "It's not the job that makes the man, but the man who makes the job." The data in Table 2 also testify to the particular significance of education for the participation of the working masses in management.

Almost all cases in Table 2 show a close link between education and the social productivity of an individual. But there are also exceptions. Among machine operators of the Tatar ASSR, the educated include a great many youth, and by virtue of their youth they are not particularly influential in the collective's affairs. (More mature age is, in some measure, evidence of greater social experience. The more the experience, the more significant the influence in the collective.) Therefore, if one compares the same machine operators within the same age group, the influence of education shows itself in its pure form and the data again confirm the general tendency. In the Tatar ASSR, among machine operators older than 34 years, 41% of those who have up to 4 grades of schooling exert influence on the collective's affairs, 49% of those with up to 4-6 grades do so, and 54% of those with 7 grades and more do so.

If the actual disposition of property, actual administration, is only slightly dependent on whether the enterprise is a state or cooperative type, and is determined by people's functions, their occupations, skills and education, then is not any change of societal organization pointless? Is it not enough to perfect production relations only indirectly — through culture and people's skills? Such an assumption, however, would be premature. The fact that our comparison involves only one Soviet type of societal production makes for exceptional limitations. The available material allows one only to state the hypothesis that, at the present time in the USSR, differences in the social and branch organization of production are not significant enough to influence by themselves the degree of the actual disposition of property, of its actual socialization. The degree of democratization of the function of disposition of property in our rural areas depends primarily on the socio-occupational structure of the population, its culture and education.

Notes

1) The material position of collective farmers and of those who work on state farms is also becoming equalized. As of July 1966, a guaranteed monetary payment was introduced in the collective farms according to the norms and wage rates of the state farms. The pension benefits of collective farmers and workers are coming closer together. Pensions were introduced for collective farmers in 1964. These pensions have been increasing significantly since September 1967, and since July 1971 (in accordance with the Directives of the Ninth Five-Year Plan) the system for computing pensions for workers and employees is being extended to collective farmers.

2) See Iu. A. Khagurov, Nekotorye sotsial'nye aspekty vnutri-kolkhoznogo upravleniia, Moscow, 1970, pp. 15, 16, and passim.

3) In Krasnodar Territory the proportion of those "having no influence" in collective farms is 53%, in state farms — 63%, in enterprises and institutions — 43%. In the Tatar ASSR, the corresponding figures for the collective farms and state farms are 62.5% and 54.7%.

4) Direktivy XXIV s'ezda KPSS po piatiletnemu planu razvitiia narodnogo khoziaistva SSSR na 1971-1975 gody, Moscow, 1971, p. 10.

8 Culture and the Social Psychology of the Soviet Rural Population

IU. V. ARUTIUNIAN

Differences in level of education influence an individual's entire cultural profile in the broad sense of this word — his world view, his range of interests, and even his psychology. Education exerts not only a direct influence in giving rise to cultural needs, but also an indirect one in opening up access to more skilled, more highly paid work and, thereby, widening material opportunities for the "appropriation" of culture.

Naturally, the intelligentsia, a majority of whom have received higher or secondary specialized education, are more easily and readily drawn to the achievements of culture than, let us say, those engaged in unskilled work who primarily have an elementary education. Moreover, higher income makes culture more accessible to the intelligentsia, i.e., spiritual demands are accompanied by the material means necessary for the satisfaction of these demands; the families of members of the intelligentsia have more cultural articles — television sets, record players, books, and so on (see Table 1).

It stands to reason that the possession of cultural articles is not the same in different places. The majority of districts are not in as good a position as Moscow Region (see Table 2).

But the tendencies are everywhere the same: differences between socio-occupational groups in the cases given in the tables,

Our title. Translated from Iu. V. Arutiunian, Sotsial'naia struktura sel'skogo naseleniia SSSR, Moscow, "Mysl'" Publishing House, 1971, pp. 173-189. Tables 1-13 correspond to Tables 46-58 in the original.

Table 1

Proportion of Individuals Possessing Means
of Culture by Social Status,
Lukhovitskii District of Moscow Region (in %)*

Possession of articles of culture in the family	Collective farms				State farms				Enterprises and institutions			
	A	B	C	D	A	B	C	D	A	B	C	D
Library	50	20	38	20	58	17	31	24	61	26	23	10
Subscribe to at least two newspapers	79	45	53	39	77	50	62	14	85	76	59	29
Radios	86	85	75	84	87	67	74	62	94	88	95	55
Television sets	79	45	38	25	81	70	88	46	73	65	68	41

*Arutiunian uses A to designate the intelligentsia, B — employees, C — machine operators, D — low-skilled and unskilled workers.

as well as in all others, are significantly sharper than between sectors. As Table 1 shows, the bulk of intelligentsia families in the villages of Moscow Region have television sets, radios and libraries, and they subscribe to several publications. Among those engaged in unskilled manual labor, such families are in the minority.

It is logical to assume that, thanks to a high level of education and a comparatively rich supply of cultural articles, the more skilled socio-occupational groups acquire cultural habits more easily, become accustomed to newspapers, books, movies, television, and radio.

One can get an idea from the materials of the survey how the process of involvement of the rural population in contemporary culture is proceeding. The survey revealed who continually listens to the radio, reads newspapers and books, watches television, goes to the cinema. As a result we obtained a distribution

Table 2

Proportion of Owners of Television Sets and Radios
in Socio-Occupational Groups (in %)

Socio-occupational groups	Krasnodar Territory		Kalinin Region	
	television sets	radios	television sets	radios
Intelligentsia A_1*	46	69	61	66
Intelligentsia A_2**	41	70	44	77
Employees	41	67	39	75
Machine operators	35	74	42	72
Low-skilled and unskilled workers	23	63	36	59
Total	27	65	36	59
Including:				
Collective farms	28	70	27	66
State farms	25	62	30	64
Enterprises, institutions, etc.	38	68	44	73

*Arutiunian's designation for higher-level managerial personnel and specialists.
**Middle-level managerial personnel and specialists.

which, with all its fluctuations by districts, most definitely reveals certain general tendencies (see Table 3).

Analysis of Table 3 allows one to draw several conclusions:

1) First of all, there is the deep penetration of contemporary culture into the very midst of the rural population. Indeed, the overwhelming majority of the population has acquired the habits of regularly listening to radio programs and reading newspapers. The rural inhabitant has already become comparable to the

Table 3

Active Cultural Habits of the Rural Population
by Social Status (in %)

Socio-occupational groups	Read news-papers	Listen to radio	Watch tele-vision	Attend movies	Read fiction
Krasnodar Territory					
Intelligentsia A_1	87	78	61	49	64
Intelligentsia A_2	80	70	40	51	53
Employees	69	71	46	49	42
Machine operators	72	68	36	47	38
Low-skilled and unskilled manual workers	51	61	26	42	26
Total	56	63	29	43	30
Including:					
Collective farms	58	69	33	45	30
State farms	52	58	25	42	28
Enterprises, institutions, etc.	68	67	40	42	46
Kalinin Region					
Intelligentsia A_1	79	79	54	34	51
Intelligentsia A_2	80	80	45	34	43
Employees	71	76	35	37	
Machine operators	76	75	41	38	33
Low-skilled and unskilled manual workers	46	62	26	11	10
Total	54	68	31	18	19
Including:					
Collective farms	49	65	25	10	11
State farms	49	65	27	14	17
Enterprises, institutions, etc.	68	79	44	35	34

urban inhabitant with respect to these attributes of culture. Statistical data also show this: at the present time there are the same number of newspapers, radio transmission points, and movie performances for each rural inhabitant as there are for each urban inhabitant. The extent of dissemination of cultural habits fluctuates by districts depending on the degree of their industrialization and urbanization. The villages of Moscow Region make the best showing.

2) In degree of penetration among the masses, the means of communication fall into a definite order. Most widely diffused is the radio, which has already become a tradition for the Soviet countryside. After the radio come newspapers, the cinema, books and television. The radio and, to some extent, newspapers have no competitors and are gradually pushing out all unofficial, informal sources of information. There is a certain division of labor between the radio and newspapers, on the one hand, and the movies, television and books, on the other; newspapers and the radio satisfy the population's rational needs while the movies, television and books tend more to satisfy its emotional-aesthetic needs. While the newspapers and the radio reach practically every inhabitant, this cannot be said for books and television at present. The emotional-aesthetic vacuum is being filled to some extent by outdated forms of culture.

3) Substantial differences exist in the dissemination of, and preference for, particular aspects of culture among the various socio-occupational groups. Most "democratic" is the radio, which addresses itself equally to the intelligentsia, employees, machine operators, and common laborers. Newspapers are a bit "choosy" — they are to a greater extent the property of the rural intelligentsia. This is all the more true if one speaks of the female portion of the population. In general, the overwhelming majority of the rural intelligentsia regularly read newspapers, while less than half of the common laborers do so. Books are particularly "selective." While about 50% of the intelligentsia are in the habit of reading, approximately 10-20% of common laborers regularly read books.

Thus, the depth of penetration of information among socio-occupational groups varies. Among the rural intelligentsia this

Table 4

Activities in Time Free from Work (in %)

What do you do most of all in time free from work?	Krasnodar Territory					Kalinin Region				
	Socio-occupational groups*									
	A_1	A_2	B	C	D	A_1	A_2	B	C	D
Housework, spend time with children	37	59	74	64	77	54	73	70	55	76
Watch television, listen to the radio	42	28	30	25	17	51	38	31	39	24
Read	62	39	33	38	23	53	40	31	32	17
Go to the movies, to dances	39	36	38	36	29	41	35	29	29	12
Simply rest	8	8	11	13	12	9	12	9	21	28
Play dominoes, cards	6	6	6	13	8	14	11	13	20	7
Engage in sports, hunting, fishing	12	16	10	14	4	29	9	15	32	6
Study, engage in self-education	22	16	8	4	3	35	12	9	6	3
Participate in amateur activities	9	5	3	4	3	4	3	5	6	3

*See Tables 1 and 2 for the socio-occupational groups designated by Arutiunian as A_1, A_2, B, C, and D.

penetration is roughly twice as great as among those engaged in manual unskilled labor. Differences are also observable between sectors of the economy, and to a certain extent this is also connected with the more developed socio-occupational structure of the state sector in comparison to the collective farm-cooperative one.

The varying degrees of dissemination of cultural habits among socio-occupational groups may also be observed in the distribution of free time. As Table 4 shows, the lower the skill of working people, the more time they spend in housework and the less they read or study.

Differences between socio-occupational groups express themselves not only in the periodicity and regularity, let us say, of reading, etc., but also in the quality of the preferred articles of culture. It is no accident that members of the intelligentsia, more often than people engaged in manual labor, respond to the question concerning what books they prefer to read by indicating fiction of primarily psychological content, production literature, and social-political literature (see Table 5).

Cultural habits derive from several variables: above all, education, availability of free time, and social role. A rural member of the intelligentsia not only has the opportunity, thanks to his high level of education, to read books and newspapers but is forced to do so in order to fulfill his productive functions.

Demographic traits — sex and age — also influence the spread of cultural habits. As the materials of empirical sociological studies show, young people (particularly those who are 18 to 22) are not only the most educated but also the most informed segment of the village population. People of different ages use radios, newspapers and television more or less to the same extent, but where those attributes of culture that bear a significant emotional-aesthetic impact or demand relatively greater training are concerned, the difference between age groups is very noticeable. Thus, books and the cinema are primarily the property of young people (see Table 6).

As can be seen, at least half of young people regularly read books and go to the movies, while in the older age group (over 50 years of age) no more than 10-15% are regular movie-goers and readers. Rural youth is distinguished by its "contemporary tastes," although the tie with past peasant culture is quite strong. The researchers of Orlov Region's rural youth note that, along with works of art about our heroic past and war memoirs, books with a certain amount of daily-life drama are in demand among rural inhabitants, particularly the older ones. (1)

Young people named as their favorite writers M. Sholokhov (23% of the respondents), N. Ostrovsky (22%), L. Tolstoy, M. Gorky, A. Fadeev, and Iu. German, which testifies to the

Table 5

Literary Tastes by Social Status (Data for Krasnodar Territory)
(% of respondents)

Question: "What type of literature do you read most?"	About love and friendship	About adventures	About war and military events	Other fiction	Production literature	Social-political literature
Socio-occupational groups						
Higher-level managerial personnel	12	18	32	41	12	29
Higher-level specialists	28	21	26	51	47	24
Middle-level managerial personnel	29	25	41	23	16	13
Middle-level specialists	35	24	35	41	28	10
Employees	30	28	33	25	12	9
Machine operators	19	28	38	17	15	9
Skilled manual laborers	27	17	38	19	4	6
Low-skilled manual laborers	19	13	15	16	7	9
Common and other unskilled laborers	22	18	28	12	4	3
Total	22	18	27	17	8	7
Including:						
Collective farms	21	20	33	13	7	5
State farms	20	15	22	19	7	8

Table 6

Active Cultural Habits of the Rural Population by Age Groups (in %)

Age groups	Krasnodar Territory					Kalinin Region					Tatar ASSR				
	Read news-papers	Listen to radio	Watch tele-vision	Attend movies	Read fic-tion	Read news-papers	Listen to radio	Watch tele-vision	Attend movies	Read fic-tion	Read news-papers	Listen to radio	Watch tele-vision	Attend movies	Read fic-tion
16-17	48	56	22	73	45	46	63	35	88	50	72	79	26	80	61
18-22	71	74	31	78	67	78	73	29	62	52	74	84	15	71	64
23-27	62	66	28	59	38	70	65	45	50	36	69	68	11	46	29
28-34	65	61	33	39	33	75	79	45	25	25	62	72	16	35	26
35-49	60	64	31	40	28	58	68	34	12	20	54	71	13	23	14
50-59	34	63	25	35	16	41	66	24	8	5	31	58	10	12	9
60 and over	30	49	10	21	15	37	60	19	5	9	18	51	6	6	6
Total	56	63	29	43	30	54	68	31	18	19	55	70	13	32	22
Including:															
Men	68	66	30	44	31	74	75	35	22	24	65	73	13	38	24
Women	46	60	28	42	29.5	42	63	29	14	15	40	64	12	23	19

correspondence of rural youth's artistic tastes to the literary
examples most diffused in their milieu through schools and the
system of propaganda. The majority of rural — as opposed to
urban — boys and girls prefer prose to poetry; only very few
are admirers of Russian and contemporary Soviet poetry. The
researchers perceive in this a tradition: "The habit of being restrained in public display of emotions is more characteristic of
the older inhabitants of the village, but to some extent it is also
reflected in the behavior of youth. Poetry is perceived by some
of them as, first, overly abstract and, second, as overly expres-
sive of people's inner motives, which are best kept hidden from
the eyes of strangers." (2)

So far as art is concerned, rural inhabitants generally prefer
works distinguished by a bright richness of colors and clarity
of lines and images. The researchers relate these tastes to the
effort to decorate residences with posters. Among rural youth,
acquainted with art chiefly from reproductions, more exacting
aesthetic tastes are formed. (3)

Differences in cultural habits between men and women (reading, amusements, etc.), just like differences in education, have
already been significantly reduced in the younger age groups
and, independently of age, among the intelligentsia (see Table 7).

The data presented may arouse doubts concerning the propositions advanced above concerning the reasons for significant
cultural differences between socio-occupational groups: Are not
these differences connected with the demographic traits of the
groups? These doubts turn out to be baseless. In the villages
of Moscow Region that we studied, the average age of a member
of the intelligentsia was 41, of an employee — 38, of a machine-
operator — 35, of a common laborer — 44. Thus, one cannot explain the more progressive cultural habits of the intelligentsia
by their age level. As regards sex composition, a bias is observable only in the group of machine-operators, which is almost entirely made up of men. Demographic differences emerge
not between groups but within them — i.e., the younger age
groups of particular occupational groups have relatively progressive cultural habits.

The following question arises: To what extent are differences

Table 7

Cultural Habits of Men and Women in the Villages of N. Maslovo
and Grigorievskoe and the Rural Settlement of Gazoprovod,
Lukhovitskii District of Moscow Region
(% of respondents)

| Socio-occupational groups | Number of respondents | Men | | | | Women | | | |
		Listen to radio	Read newspapers	Watch television	Read fiction	Listen to radio	Read newspapers	Watch television	Read fiction
Intelligentsia (A)	71	77	93	64	88	81	86	45	96
Employees (B)	66	81	88	37	78	80	84	67	83
Machine operators (C) and other skilled manual laborers	68	81	85	60	78	—	—	—	—
Unskilled manual laborers (D)	196	82	82	57	67	65	50	39	47

in the penetration of information reflected in the life orientations
and mentality of different socio-occupational and demographic
groups? Analysis of the system of social-psychological orientations allows us to answer this question to some extent. A question was posed to respondents in Moscow Region: "What, in your
opinion, does it mean to live well?" Of the 11 versions of answers, the most frequently chosen were: "To have a happy family life," "To have material security," "To live comfortably,"
"To have good, interesting work." Each of these orientations
received more than half the votes and was clearly defined as an
enduring orientation. Once again differences were found between
socio-occupational groups. For people engaged in mental labor,
orientation toward work and family turned out to be most important;

Table 8

Life Ideals in the Villages of Lukhovitskii District
of Moscow Region
(% of respondents in each group)

Question: "What, in your opinion, does it mean to live well?"	A		B		C*	D	
	Men	Women	Men	Women	Men	Men	Women
Number of respondents	59	50	29	83	140	122	232
Answers:							
"To have good, interesting work"	71	78	76	69	63	53	47
"To have a happy family life"	68	72	76	62	58	51	54
"To have material security, to live comfortably"	43	50	55	43	65	67	62
"To live with a clean conscience"	35	44	3	4	16	18	17

*This occupational category included only men.

for those engaged in manual labor, orientation to material well-being came first and only then, orientation to family. Such a distribution correlates with data concerning payment for labor. Evidently those engaged in manual labor, particularly in un-skilled manual labor, feel the need for material well-being more strongly. The "higher," more "spiritual" types of value orien-tations of the rural intelligentsia show up also in the relative frequency of such versions of the answer as "To live with a clean conscience" (30-40% of the selections by the intelligentsia) and "Freedom of thought and action" (about 10%). Among the re-maining groups of the rural population these selections were practically not made at all.

In this area, as in several previous ones, a certain difference appears in the life orientations of men and women (see Table 8).

In contrast to men, women (if one takes the largest category for the countryside, those engaged in unskilled labor) have a

Table 9

Life Ideals of Men by Age,
Lukhovitskii District of Moscow Region
(% of respondents in each age group)

Question: "What, in your opinion, does it mean to live well?"	Up to 30 years of age	31–35	36–40	41–50	51 and over
Number of respondents	37	32	43	39	56
Answers:					
"To have interesting work"	65	53	55	62	65
"To have a happy family life"	73	63	70	70	56
"To have material security, to live comfortably"	60	66	74	74	70
"To live with a clean conscience"	38	22	21	13	15
"To enjoy freedom of thought and action"	11	–	7	–	–

more enduring orientation toward the family than toward work. Certain specific characteristics were found in the value orientations of youth (see Table 9).

Young people under 30 years of age are the only age group of the rural population for whom material well-being ranks below interesting work and family as a value.

On the whole, one can speak of significant changes in the psychology of the rural inhabitant. An enduring material interest does not oppose but complements orientations toward work and family. The fact that only 10% of the respondents gave preference to the answer "To live in wealth" (as against 60% choosing "To have material security, to live comfortably") shows that such an interpretation is correct. Thus, the question is one of the material well-being necessary for the satisfaction of needs within reasonable limits. An analogous picture was found in the

Table 10

Moral Ideas of Men by Social Status, According to
Materials of the Villages Studied in Lukhovitskii
District of Moscow Region
("selections" in % of respondents)

Selected answers	A	B	C	D
If the possibility presents itself, it is better for a wife to engage only in housework and the up-bringing of children	9	30	31	20
In the upbringing of children it is permissible to employ physical punishment	26	22	30	30
Marriages that are mixed in terms of nationality are undesirable, or no definite opinion concerning this question	10	0	8	18

study of rural inhabitants' moral orientations.

In order to reveal certain orientations and other traits characterizing personality, we posed questions to those interviewed
concerning attitudes toward women, views on the upbringing of
children, attitudes toward other nationalities, etc. The data of
the survey are presented in Table 10.

Judging by their answers, most of the rural population has already almost abandoned many conservative habits of the traditional peasant way of life. One cannot even say that people engaged in unskilled labor lag significantly behind the rural intelligentsia in this respect. True, among the intelligentsia, certain
habits of the past are becoming outmoded relatively faster. For
example, only 9% of the male intelligentsia favored a wife's
"occupying herself with housework if the material possibility
for this presents itself"; among women, only 5% favored the lot

Table 11

Changes in the Moral Ideas of Men Depending on Age,
According to Materials of the Villages Studied in
Lukhovitskii District of Moscow Region
("selections" in % of respondents)

Selected answers	Age groups				
	Up to 30	31–35	36–40	41–50	51–60
If the possibility presents itself, it is better for a wife to engage only in housework and the up-bringing of children	14	25	28	42	26
In the upbringing of children it is permissible to employ physical punishment	28	50	30	24	25
Marriages that are mixed in terms of nationality are undesirable, or no definite opinion concerning this question	3	3	2	14	20

of a housewife. In other groups of the rural population, the
choice "wife-housewife" enjoyed somewhat greater popularity
(20-30%). According to many other indications of moral orientations, however, the more advanced position of the intelligentsia is less definitely pronounced. For the most part, the norms
of socialist society in human relations prevail equally in all social strata. In the case in question, differences were found that
point to the more progressive personality structure of young
people. A smaller proportion favored limiting the functions of
women to housework, regarded the physical punishment of children as permissible, felt the undesirability of mixed inter-
nationality marriages, etc. (see Table 11).

Table 12

Percent of Religious Believers by Social Groups

Socio-occupational groups	Krasnodar Territory	Kalinin Region	Tatar ASSR	Moscow Region		
				Both sexes	Men	Women
Intelligentsia A_1	5	12	3 }	7	7	7
Intelligentsia A_2	5	3	4 }			
Employees	9	3	9	24	12	29
Machine operators	4	5	7	12	12	—
Low-skilled and unskilled laborers	14	21	35	48	27	60
Total	12	16	31	32	16	45
Including:						
Collective farms	13	23	33	44	28	62
State farms	12	15	23	25	10	39
Enterprises, institutions, etc.	10	5	n.a.*	22	8	35

* — not available.

On the whole, these data testify to a significant psychological change in the concepts of the rural inhabitant (4); in the 1920s (as the study of those years shows) he still related in a "proprietary manner" to his wife and children, etc. (5)

Thus, differences between groups in material position and education are more clearly expressed than differences in the realm of ordinary consciousness, psychology, and morality. This by no means signifies the full identity of the social-psychological profile of the various population groups. Differences

Table 13

Percent of Religious Believers by Sex-Age Groups,
According to Material from Lukhovitskii District
of Moscow Region

Age	Men		Women	
	Number	%	Number	%
30 years	39	5	51	16
31-35	31	13	28	47
36-40	44	12	30	40
41-50	36	17	68	45
51-60	40	22	48	65
61 and over	15	20	–	–

in the realm of spiritual life, for example, are very clear in regard to religion (see Table 12).

While there are practically no religious believers among the intelligentsia, in the groups engaged in less-skilled work — mental as well as manual — their proportion consistently rises and, according to the data derived from the study of villages in Moscow Region, reaches 27% among male common laborers and 60% among female common laborers. The percentage of believers rises with age. Within this general relation, the relation between male and female believers remains almost unchanged (see Table 13). One should not exaggerate the significance of these data, however. It is necessary to keep in mind that the influence of communist ideology is so great in our country that religiosity is combined, very often in a fantastic way, with principles of communist ideology and morality in people's ordinary consciousness. (6)

The absence of a strict, simple connection between social position and social psychology is the result of many factors, the primary one being the common social origins of the various categories of the village's working people. As our study shows, the overwhelming majority of the rural intelligentsia is formed from the same social sources as are other categories of working people in the village. This results in a unity of upbringing and, consequently, of norms and ideas. The common ideological and cultural principles systematically disseminated through all the channels of information, and the unity of communist ideology and morality, also have an influence on the unification of the social-psychological profile.

Notes

1) See Sel'skaia molodezh'. Sotsiologicheskii ocherk, Moscow, 1970, pp. 84-85.

2) Ibid., p. 94.

3) Ibid., pp. 101-102.

4) We purposely did not touch on the relation of the rural inhabitant to work since this side of his social-psychological profile is described by N. M. Blinov on the basis of the materials of this study (see Vestnik Moskovskogo Universiteta, Filosofiia, seriia 8, 1967, pp. 3-11).

5) See Iu. V. Arutiunian, "The Results of Sociological Studies of the Village in the Twenties," Voprosy istorii KPSS, 1966, No. 3.

6) Characteristic data have been obtained by V. I. Lebedev who, studying the Movement for Communist Labor in the village in Penza Region, found that 9.8% of the participants in this movement are religious believers but "see the meaning of their lives in the struggle for the building of communism" (Voprosy formirovaniia nauchno-ateisticheskikh vzgliadov, Moscow, 1964, pp. 50-52).

9 Some Social Consequences of a City-Building Experiment

M. V. TIMIASHEVSKAIA

From the sociologist's point of view, a city is a complicated system composed of a plethora of interconnected and interdependent elements. People and organizations of people, buildings and transportation, communications, industry and trade, communication systems of various types — all these elements of a city can be subdivided into two interdependent subsystems: the material-spatial environment of objects, and social structures and processes.

In creating new cities — i.e., in participating in the creation of conditions for society's material life — we at the same time create the conditions for the realization of social processes.

In using the expression "social consequences," we have in mind the most significant results of people's activity that find expression in the formation of new types of relations between people, their groups, strata, classes. The social consequences of the rise and development of new city-building complexes in the conditions of socialism may be found in the formation of new progressive communist relations. In order to confirm this hypothesis, it is necessary to analyze the closeness and character of social contacts between people and their groups, having chosen an object of research that is typical for socialist society. "The concept of typification is an expression of general concepts, of manifestations of the social essence of things, an

From Akademiia Nauk SSSR, Institut mezhdunarodnogo rabochego dvizheniia, Urbanizatsiia i rabochii klass v usloviiakh nauchno-tekhnicheskoi revoliutsii, Moscow, 1970, pp. 283-298.

essence that is by no means defined by the average dimensions of an indicator." (1) It not infrequently happens that particular facts that are not prevalent today may be typical tomorrow. It is precisely such facts that express most fully the essence of a given social force.

Governed by these considerations (though not only by these), we chose as our general object of study Akademgorodok, which is under the Siberian Division of the USSR Academy of Sciences near Novosibirsk. This is a new industrial-residential complex. In the course of planning and building Akademgorodok, the task of creating a material base for the valuable activity of scholars, of creating the most favorable residential and cultural-living conditions for the population, was carried out, i.e., a rough draft of tomorrow's contours was realized.

Built 25 kilometers from the city of Novosibirsk in a most picturesque forest location, Akademgorodok combines the conveniences of a well-situated town with immediate proximity to nature. Shores covered by a pine forest, sandy beaches, an enormous aquatorium of a reservoir and the valley of the little river Zyrianka — the Golden Valley — all these are greatly loved by the local population.

For today's world Akademgorodok serves to some extent as an example of the implementation of a series of contemporary requirements of Soviet city-building science. Its territory is clearly divided into four zones: the settlement (residential) zone, a zone of scientific research institutes, a communal storage zone, and a recreation zone. The compactness of the planning was such that a significant number of the employed practically use no transportation. The architectural-planning decisions for Akademgorodok led to the award of a state prize in 1967.

Some 86% of the population answered affirmatively to the question "Are you satisfied with life in Akademgorodok?"

The structure of the time budget of the town's population, since it is close to that projected for the future, also permits us to examine the town as a singular architectural-planning and social experiment stretching into the future. This experiment is of even greater interest in that we examine it not as a unique city-building experiment and not as some kind of episodic fact.

In connection with the process of converting science into a direct productive force, the share and significance of scientific work in the great mass of societal labor will grow. (2) Education is becoming one of the indicators of national wealth. The concentration of ever-expanding scientific research in special cities will inexorably demand the repetition of this precedent. And if one looks not from the perspective of today but glances a little ahead, one can discover that in the composition of the city's cadres, in the principles of interconnection of places of work and residential complexes, there will be increasingly common features between city-scientific centers and industrial towns. (3) And this will be in accord with the regularities of the urbanization process.

Characteristic of Akademgorodok as a single functional-spatial system, as an "organic social whole," are certain definite social relations, needs, and requirements of quite concrete social groups.

The limited spheres of activity in Akademgorodok (4) made it possible to classify the universe of the employed population into 4 social groups. These groups differed with respect to the following objective and distinguishable — i.e., "informal" — features; (a) attachment to one of the spheres of activity; (b) occupational position; (c) level of education; and (d) size of income per family member. Placing members of the sample universe higher or lower according to the features chosen, we obtained a scheme that provides a realistic idea of the social structure of Akademgorodok. (5)

The classification is based on occupational-skill and economic characteristics that reflect a connection inherent in socialism: work — social status — degree of use of property. (6) Consequently, the social structure of Akademgorodok's population consists of four basic social groups: Group I, which includes Doctors of Science and Candidates of Science who occupy leading posts and have a per capita family income of 110 rubles or more; Group II, which includes people with higher education, scientific workers, doctors, lawyers, etc., with a per capita family income of 70 rubles or more; Group III, which includes middle-level technical personnel who have a complete secondary

Classification Scheme of Social Groups in Akademgorodok

Social groups and their relative magnitude, in % \ Spheres of activity and their relative magnitude, in %	Science 51.5%	Construction 28.4%	Services 12.3%	Health, education, state apparatus 7.8%
I 10.5%	Directors of institutes, scientific institutions and subdivisions; senior research workers	Directors of trusts, enterprises, leading designers, chief specialists	Head of Workers' Supply Department	Directors of institutions, school directors, hospital directors, chief physicians, leading party workers
II 47.1%	Junior research workers, senior faculty; engineers of research institutes	Heads of shops and sections; engineering-technical personnel	Heads of stores, ateliers, hotels, chief specialists of personal service enterprises	Physicians, teachers, lawyers, heads of institutions for children, accountants, etc.
III 22.4%	Technicians, senior and other laboratory workers	Middle-level technical personnel, foremen, workers	Employees, senior and other sales personnel, receptionists, communications workers	Senior and other nurses, kindergarten teachers
IV 20.0%	Junior service personnel; low-skilled workers	Junior service personnel; low-skilled workers	Junior service personnel; low-skilled workers	Junior service personnel; low-skilled workers

Table 1

Availability of Cultural-Household Articles for
Akademgorodok's Population

Cultural-household articles	% possessing these articles
1. Radio	90.9
2. Sewing machine	82.5
3. Washing machine	81.1
4. Refrigerator	71.3
5. Television set	68.7
6. Library (more than 100 books)	52.2
7. Bicycle, motorcycle or motorscooter	51.9
8. Vacuum cleaner	30.9
9. Piano, accordion	22.1
10. Automobile or motorboat	11.4

education and a per capita family income of 40 rubles or more;
and Group IV, which includes people with less than secondary
education, low qualifications, and a per capita family income of
40 rubles or less.

The extent and nature of the provision of these social groups
with cultural-household articles, with a "cultural-household in-
ventory" (7), seems to us to be one of the most important envi-
ronmental elements influencing the formation and establishment
of social interrelations. On the whole, in Akademgorodok the
level of provision is rather high (see Table 1).

The high degree to which radios, washing machines, sewing
machines, television sets and refrigerators have been provided
does not exclude differentiation among social groups delineated
by differences in social status, level of education, and per capita income. Thus, in Group I the provision level for almost the
entire set of articles is higher than in other social groups. If
this level is taken as the optimal variant of the contemporary
standard of living providing for the satisfaction of man's basic

Table 2

Availability of Cultural-Household Articles
by Basic Social Groups (in %)

Cultural-household Articles	% possessing these articles			
	Group I	Group II	Group III	Group IV
1. Radio	100	96	91	87
2. Sewing machine	75	80	90	80
3. Washing machine	90	75	88	75
4. Refrigerator	85	78	65	52
5. Television set	68	60	65	80
6. Library (more than 100 books)	90	80	38	25
7. Bicycle, motorcycle or motorscooter	50	42	70	40
8. Vacuum cleaner	68	34	30	10
9. Piano, accordion	45	30	20	8
10. Automobile or motorboat	22	10	8	8

needs, then the nature of provision in Group II will be analogous
[sic] to the nature of provision in Group I (see Table 2).

The nature of provision with cultural-household articles is
somewhat different in Groups III and IV. Here preference is
given to sewing machines, television sets and motorcycles, and
not to libraries, pianos or refrigerators. The differential possession of things reflects the differentiation of social behavior
and is also one of the features that characterizes the conditions
for formation of people's corresponding needs and aspirations.

Now let us look directly at the question of the nature of people's relations in Akademgorodok. Since the inquiry was conducted according to a territorial parameter, we studied relations in the residential sphere. Analysis of personal contacts
in this sphere can have practical significance in the creation of
social and spatial conditions in which new, progressive forms
of contact would receive scope for development. Having analyzed

Table 3

Preferred Meetings in Free Time

With whom do you meet most often in your free time?	Distribution of answers, in %
Fellow workers	31.9
People who share recreation and hobby	11.9
Relatives	27.0
Neighbors	19.7
Childhood friends	5.5
Others	4.0

the nature and closeness of personal contacts in Akademgorodok, we concluded that contacts according to interests are most typical there (see Table 3). Let us examine the nature of deviations from these averaged figures depending on a series of variables. Young people up to 24 years of age have essentially the same distribution of preferences in personal contacts. However, their contacts with neighbors living in the same house are considerably weaker (10%), and their meetings with childhood friends are more widespread (20%). The importance of kinship ties increases in the older age groups (see Table 4).

The social status of the individuals surveyed has an influence on changes in the nature of preferred meetings in free time.

Table 4

Percentage of Meetings with Relatives, by Age of Respondent

Up to 18 years	From 18 to 24	From 25 to 29	From 30 to 39	From 40 to 49	From 50 to 59	From 60 to 69	70 and over
14%	20%	28%	27%	24%	36%	38%	47%

Table 5

Preferred Meetings in Free Time Depending on
Social Group Membership (in %)

Nature of contacts	Social groups			
	I	II	III	IV
Fellow workers	54.9	37.3	30.4	24.8
People who share recreation	17.0	16.2	11.5	6.7
Relatives	16.9	22.5	31.2	34.5
Neighbors	6.4	15.0	19.0	28.1
Childhood friends	2.4	4.6	4.5	4.1
Others	2.4	4.4	2.9	1.8
Total	100.0	100.0	100.0	100.0

Thus, some 80-90% of pensioners, housewives and others outside the labor force prefer to meet in their free time with relatives and neighbors who live in their houses, while students and
pupils prefer being with fellow students and childhood friends.
The attitude of the working population to the choice of meetings
in free time is quite differentiated. Those in Group I meet more
often with fellow workers (54.9%), with people who share their
recreation (17.0%), and with relatives (16.9%). Here socializing
according to interests is clearly preferred (see Table 5). Working individuals in Group IV meet in their free time primarily
with relatives, neighbors, and only secondarily with fellow workers and people who share their recreation.

Thus, in Akademgorodok, as social status, level of education
and material well-being rise, the role of contacts according to
interests grows stronger and ties with mere neighbors grow
weaker. Territorial propinquity by itself has little impact on
the initiation and consolidation of social contacts between people. Neighborly relations arise here principally on the basis of
mutual economic aid. Of the contacts in Group I, 39% are based

Table 6

Neighbors Preferred Depending on Membership
in Social Group (in %)

What people would you want to have as your neighbors?	Social groups			
	I	II	III	IV
People with a similar occupation	18.6	15.2	10.4	10.2
People of your own age	17.7	21.9	31.8	25.5
People at a similar cultural level	25.5	25.2	19.4	8.7
People similar in level of education	11.9	15.2	10.1	4.6

on economic mutual aid, while in Group II they are 53.2%, in
III — 53.3%, and in IV — 59.3%. The social contacts among
neighbors, if they are of such a character, are not very stable
in comparison with social contacts according to interests, and
they decline in accordance with the degree of growth of material well-being. Analysis of a question concerning neighbors
preferred showed that for people in Groups I and II the main
criteria in choosing neighbors are their cultural level and general level of education. The importance of these criteria decreases for Groups III and IV, and the variable age occupies
first place (see Table 6).

   People's preferences for neighbors, expressed hypothetically,
are reflected in life. If one looks at the actual frequency with
which people visit neighbors, one can see that visiting neighbors
is least frequent in Group I and that it becomes more frequent
as one moves to Group IV. Thus, 6.8% of Group I visit their
neighbors every day or almost every day, while 11.8% of Group
II, 16.5% of Group III, and 26.2% of Group IV do so. What are
the obstacles today to the strengthening of social contacts in the
residential sphere? A lack of free time is cited first of all by
those surveyed. However, on the basis of their observations,
our interviewers gained the impression that "lack of free time"
is a formula that more often hides a lack of common interest,

a lack of any point to social contacts with those who are merely
neighbors. Of those studied, 28% directly name a lack of common interests as an impediment to socializing by residents;
11% see the reason in the absence of facilities for getting together with neighbors.

Participation in civic activity at one's place of residence
plays a completely insignificant role in Akademgorodok. Sixty
percent do not take part at all in any collective forms of activity
at their place of residence; 21.5% occasionally participate in
voluntary Sundays, or once or twice a year carry out some re-
quest of their Housing Operation Office, 19% answered that they
take part in civic work at their housing complex and consider
the housing complex their collective. Who are these latter people? Primarily the employed of Group IV, then members of
Group III and pensioners, and only then representatives of the
other groups of the population. This means that a collective
based on place of residence does exist. It is possible that under
other conditions, for example, in Uzbekistan, such factors as a
climate favorable to contacts between neighbors, collectivist
traditions, and so forth, can be the prerequisites for the future
existence of social collectives according to place of residence. (8)
In the conditions of a science-city we did not discover factors
that suggested a broadening and development of this type of activity in the future.

Nonetheless it would be a mistake to ignore civic activity by
place of residence, since it is one of the integrating elements
of societal life and, at the same time, it determines what the
real needs are for suitable facilities in the residential sphere.
Here, apparently, an experiment is necessary. If the facilities
envisaged and allotted for the existing volume of civic work will
promote its expansion, or at least its stabilization, at the present level, then the future projection of such facilities makes
sense for the government. Analysis of our study's materials
suggests that it would be premature to count on facilities for
civic activity in the residential sphere "for all"; "...attempts
'to prescribe,' mainly through the planning structure, the direction
of development of a particular type of social behavior can only lead
to a loss of control over this process in the interests of society." (9)

Table 7

Need for Collective Facilities by Size
of Per Capita Family Income

Income per capita, rubles per month	Up to 30 rubles	31-50	51-70	71-90	91-110	111-130	131-150	151 and more
In favor of collective facilities, in %	68.0	70.0	70.0	72.7	68.0	59.5	55.0	56.0

Let us consider briefly some points in the analysis of collective principles that came up in the cultural-household study by residence in Akademgorodok.

An absolute majority responded positively to the question: "Do you consider it desirable to plan for collective facilities in a residential house, in addition to individual apartments?" The level of material well-being has a decisive influence on the size and nature of needs for collective facilities. The higher it is, the less people feel a need for the collectivization of daily life (see Table 7).

It is clear from Table 7 that as income increases there is a growing indifference to collective facilities for daily living. Those who have a television set, washing machine, and other cultural-household articles are in favor of their collective use to a significantly lesser extent than those who do not have them (see Table 8).

As the norms of living space per person increase, the demand for various kinds of collective facilities falls somewhat. An exception are those facilities that ensure the pursuit of an interest: photography laboratories, amateur workshops, rooms for physical culture (see Table 9).

Thus, raising the level of material provision leads (in Akademgorodok's conditions) to a lowering of aspirations for a socialized, collective daily life. However, the appearance of

Table 8

Need for Collective Use of Some Cultural-Household Articles
Depending on Their Private Possession (in %)

	Television		Washing machine		Refrigerator		Vacuum cleaner	
	Neces-sary	Not nec-essary	Neces-sary	Not nec-essary	Neces-sary	Not nec-essary	Neces-sary	Not nec-essary
Television								
Have	9.6	90.4						
Do not have	28.4	71.6						
Washing machine								
Have			4.8	95.2				
Do not have			14.7	85.3				
Refrigerator								
Have					3.9	96.1		
Do not have					16.6	83.4		
Vacuum cleaner								
Have							9.2	90.8
Do not have							22.2	77.8

Table 9

Need for Collective Facilities Depending upon Whether
Living Conditions Are Satisfactory or Unsatisfactory
(in % of Respondents in Each Category)

Types of facilities	Satisfactory living conditions (9 square meters or more per person)	Unsatisfactory living conditions (less than 9 square meters per person)
1. Room for temporary child care	40	50
2. Library with reading room	40	50
3. Health and physical culture room	46	44
4. Room for family evenings	34	56
5. Facilities for washing and drying	38	52
6. Facilities for food storage	50	40
7. Hobby workshops	48	43
8. Photography laboratory	49	41
9. Facilities for storage of nonseasonal items	41	49

such tendencies still does not mean the disappearance of demand for collective facilities either in the near or more distant
future. Insofar as the level of material provision under the conditions of socialism is differentiated and will remain differentiated in the foreseeable future, there is and will be an objective
need for socialization of the use of cultural-household articles
in consideration of those groups of the population that need them.
In Akademgorodok, the proportion desiring collective facilities
to meet their needs is 50-60% (see Table 9). Where household-
daily life facilities are concerned, the degree of preference
rises as one goes from Group I to Group IV. And vice versa,

where facilities that promote the pursuit of an interest are concerned, the degree of preference goes up as one goes from Group IV to Group I.

Integrated sociological analysis of the nature of personal contacts in the residential sphere, of collective principles in everyday life, and of residential patterns that in effect follow the principle of membership of the responsible apartment-renter in one of four social groups, allows us to conclude that membership in a social group, level of education, and level of per capita family income are the basic criteria of social differentiation in Akademgorodok, and that they also predetermine the differentiation of contacts and needs not only for today but in the future.

Akademgorodok, as a system assuring the very best conditions for work, daily life, and recreation, at the same time promotes the stabilization and consolidation of social differentiation — not so much spatially as in the sphere of social relations. Herein, in our view, are the basic social consequences of a social city-building experiment such as Akademgorodok. The local character of clearly manifested differentiating tendencies also explains the fact that similar social processes are not perceptible for society as a whole. It is possible that the widespread diffusion of such city-building formations as Akademgorodok will lead to the emergence of contradictions between the idea of building a communist society and the actual formation of relations that do not correspond to the communist mode of life.

Analysis of the formation of relationships arising in the residential sphere in Akademgorodok shows that another tendency also exists — an integrating one that expresses itself in people's striving to have social contact with one another not simply because the object of such social contact lives next door but because there is a common interest. It is possible that this very sphere of "common interest" could become a real basis for the creation of a material-spatial environment that would correspond to it, as a condition for the general integration of socialist society.

Searching for means by which to strengthen the ties between man and society, to strengthen the ties between social groups,

to control differentiating and integrating tendencies in social
development — in this we see the ultimate goal of sociological
research. In the same way, collectivization of the sphere of
daily life, to the extent that the needs of various societal groups
require it, is an objective necessity in socialist conditions when
a leisure-goods and household-goods industry and the material
base of communist society, of communist social relations, are
only in the process of being created. And here we share the
point of view of G. A. Gradov, who is convinced that "collectivization is a prerequisite and condition for the application of
highly productive technology (high productivity)." (10) Without
this neither technological progress in the field of cultural-
household services nor progress in the formation of the world-
view of the communist man of tomorrow is possible.

Notes

1) P. P. Maslov, "Statistics and Its Role in Concrete Sociological Research," in Voprosy organizatsii i metodiki konkretno-
sotsiologicheskikh issledovanii, Rosvuzizdat, 1963, p. 47.

2) N. Aitov, "Social Aspects of Obtaining an Education in the
USSR," in Sotsial'nye issledovaniia, Vyp. 2, 1968, pp. 187-188.

3) A. S. Peremyslov, Koeffitsient budushchego, Novosibirsk,
1968, pp. 193-196.

4) Main spheres of activity in Akademgorodok: (1) science,
(2) construction, (3) services, (4) education, health, and government apparatus, combined into one group in view of their small
numbers.

5) The classification scheme for social groups in Akademgorodok was worked out together with Zh. K. Arkhangel'skii,
a researcher at the Institute of Economics of the Siberian Division of the USSR Academy of Sciences.

6) See Iu. V. Arutiunian, Opyt sotsiologicheskogo issledovaniia
sela, Moscow State University Publishing House, Moscow, 1968,
p. 40.

7) The term is S. G. Strumilin's.

8) M. A. Budagova, "Creation of a Neighbors' Collective on
the Basis of a Primary Residential Formation," Stroitel'stvo

i arkhitektura Uzbekistana, 1968, No. 9.

9) L. B. Kogan, "On the Role of Sociological Factors in the Formation of a City's Material-Spatial Environment," in Nauchnye prognozy razvitiia i formirovaniia sovetskikh gorodov na baze sotsial'nogo i nauchno-tekhnicheskogo progressa, Collection 2, Moscow, 1969, p. 10.

10) G. A. Gradov, "Searching for Promising Future Types of Residential Complexes," Arkhitektura SSSR, 1968, No. 2.

10 Orientations Toward Occupations

V. V. VODZINSKAIA

Orientations toward occupations are one of the forms of an individual's value orientations. In other words, a person has a more or less fixed relation to occupations that has been formed on the basis of a certain amount of knowledge of them (their content, the economic demand for them, where to acquire training for them, etc.), a positive or negative emotional perception of everything connected with them, and a stock-taking of one's own physical, mental, and material capacities.

We devoted an experimental survey of a sample of 1965 graduates of several Leningrad secondary schools to the study of value orientations toward occupations. (1)

Two groups of graduates — an experimental group and a control group matched according to sex, social origins, per capita family income, and parental level of education — were asked to rate 80 occupations representative of the basic areas of labor activity (2) on a point scale (from 1 to 10) according to four criteria (value characteristics of the occupations): possibilities for creativity (C), possibilities for growth — raising skills in the broadest sense of the word (G), level of wages (W), and social prestige — the authority of an occupation in public opinion (P).

From V. A. Iadov, ed., Molodezh' i trud, Moscow, "Molodaia gvardiia" Publishing House, 1970, pp. 79-82, 84-101; and G. V. Osipov and Ia. Shchepanskii, eds., Sotsial'nye problemy truda i proizvodstva, Moscow, "Mysl'" Publishing House, 1969, pp. 47-53. Pages 153-155 and 168-186 were taken from the Iadov volume, while pages 155-168 were extracted from Osipov and Shchepanskii.

These evaluation criteria are the basic components of the concept "attractiveness of an occupation." As the pilot surveys and interviews with boys and girls on the eve of their graduation from secondary school made clear, it is these characteristics that are decisive in the choice of an occupation. Thus, the views of the graduates themselves determined the choice of the evaluation criteria.

The experimental group (N = 100) was asked to rate all the occupations according to each of the four criteria in turn (according to C, G, W, P) and, on the basis of these evaluations, to arrange the list of occupations according to a fifth criterion — their general attractiveness, as if making a selection for themselves (S). Before the experimental group carried out the assignment there was a detailed discussion on the importance of choosing a particular type of work activity by considering many objective and subjective aspects of the matter, among which the attractiveness of an occupation from various points of view plays an important role.

The control group (N = 524), composed of five subgroups (100 people each, on the average), rated the same list of occupations only according to one of the four criteria or according to overall attractiveness. There was no preliminary talk in the subgroups. The students received the short assignment of rating the occupations on a point scale according to one or another criterion so as to clarify the degree of their knowledge of occupations. They were deliberately not reminded of the possibility of other evaluation criteria.

The purpose of proceeding in this way was to "extract" orientations regarding occupations in a projective — that is, imaginary — situation, but at different levels of proximity to a real situation: in an abstract projective situation — in the rating of a list of occupations only according to one of the value characteristics (in the control subgroups); in a projective situation but with a successive "weighing" of each occupation from the point of view of such characteristics as social prestige, the creative character of the work, possibilities for growth and level of wages, in order finally to make an evaluation-selection (in the experimental group). In addition, we had the opportunity to "extract" orientations in a projective situation maximally close to a real one. This occurred in the filling out of the "Graduate's Questionnaire," when occupations were evaluated by their attractiveness in connection with concrete questions concerning personal plans and motives for choosing a particular occupation only a month before graduation from secondary school (a mass survey).* The juxtaposition of information obtained in the experimental survey with the materials from polls of graduates in 1964 and 1965 allows us to make judgments concerning social-psychological and value orientations in relation to occupations that boys and girls of 17 to 18 have close to the moment when they make a decision concerning the choice of a definite sphere of work.

———————

Diagram 1 presents the distribution of the average ratings (3) of the 80 occupations given by the experimental group of students according to the four criteria in sequence and according to overall attractiveness. As the diagram shows, different occupations are variously rated according to one or another characteristic. For example, worker occupations in industry, transportation, construction, agriculture and the service sector generally are evaluated higher according to wage level than according to their other characteristics. Of the worker occupations, automatic equipment setter and shipbuilder received the highest rating in possibilities for creativity; automatic equipment operator and chemical worker in possibilities for growth; miner and shipbuilder in social prestige.

Occupations that require higher education (the so-called intelligentsia occupations) are highly evaluated. Moroever, their ratings on all the criteria are very close to each other. The ratings of this group of occupations by possibilities for creativity

———————

*This 1965 survey that Vodzinskaia refers to here encompassed graduates of urban and rural schools in Leningrad Region (N = 783) and is to be distinguished from the samples described above.

and social prestige stand out somewhat. The occupations of physicist (C-9; P-9.3), chemist (C-8.9; P-8.9), and worker in literature and art (C-8.8; P-8.3) received the highest ratings. Occupations in the service sector and in agriculture, irrespective of skill level, were unpopular among the Leningrad students. In this respect, the occupation of housing-maintenance worker is significant; it received the lowest ratings from all points of view (G-2.0; P-2.2; C-2.3; W-3.2).

The curve of average ratings according to overall attractiveness of the occupations (S) stands out in Diagram 1. It turned out to be lower than all the rest because the ratings according to overall attractiveness were distributed by the students extremely stingily. After all, the question was not one of evaluation from the standpoint of "so far as I know" or "as is customarily considered" but of rating occupations in terms of personal choice. The following occupations were highest and lowest in the list of occupations rated according to the final evaluation (the evaluation-selection "S"):

1. Physicist
2. Radio engineer
3. Medical scientist
4. Geological engineer
5. Mathematician
6. Chemist
7. Radio technician
8. Pilot
9. Chemical engineer
10. Biologist
11. Physician
12. Worker in literature and art
. . . .
55. Lathe operator
. . . .
62. Milling-machine operator
. . . .
75. Salesclerk
76. Clerical worker, bookkeeper, accountant
77. Housepainter, mason, plasterer

78. Agricultural worker
79. Printer
80. Housing-maintenance worker

It is characteristic that the "peaks" and "valleys" of all the curves on the diagram (including also the summary "S") basically coincide. This confirms the fact that each of these four value characteristics of an occupation — creativity, growth, prestige, wages — has significance for its overall rating according to attractiveness and influences the magnitude of that rating.

But is the degree of influence the same? Which one of the values are students primarily oriented toward in choosing an occupation?

Let us try to determine the content of school graduates' orientations by considering the ordering of the four characteristics of occupations which we conditionally accept as a type of system of value orientations regarding occupational activity.

In the group of worker occupations, miner and steel founder are rated highest according to level of wages (7.8). However, according to overall attractiveness or, more precisely, according to evaluation-selection, the highest ratings in the group of worker occupations were received by shipbuilder, and operator and setter of automatic equipment.

Along with the occupations of miner and steel founder, the occupations of pilot, mathematician, physicist, and geologist are rated equally high by the graduates according to level of wages (from 7.8 to 8.4 points). But despite the coincidence of ratings according to wages, the evaluations according to overall attractiveness differ significantly. Thus, the occupation of miner received 2.2; steel founder — 2.1; pilot — 5.7; geologist — 5.6; mathematician — 6.0; physicist — 6.7.

The examples given bear witness to the fact that it is not wages but another criterion that, in the opinion of the graduates, determines the attractiveness of the occupations enumerated. Obviously, that characteristic of an occupation which has more weight in the whole value structure of a young person selecting a first occupation has the decisive influence on his evaluation-selection. We believe that this explains the lack of correspondence between the ratings according to wages and those according

Distribution of Average Ratings of
Group of Students According to Cri-
Wages (W), Growth (G), and

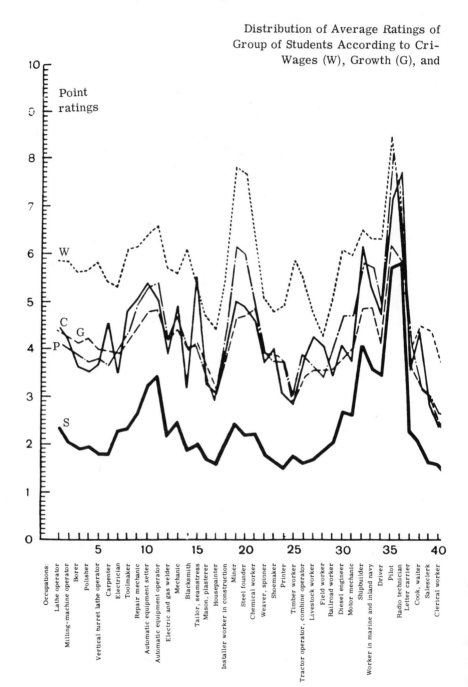

Occupations by the Experimental
teria of: Creativity (C), Prestige (P),
Evaluation-Selection (S)

Diagram 1

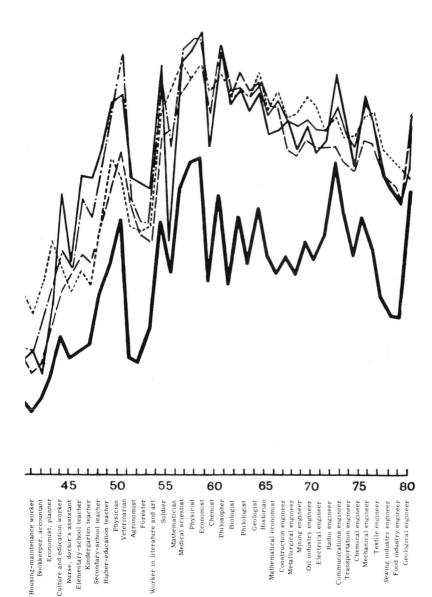

Table 1

Degree of Relationship (Correlation Coefficient r)
Between Ratings According to Attractiveness and Some
Characteristics of Occupations (Experimental Group)

Characteristics of occupations	r	S_r
Possibility for creativity	0.862	0.03
Possibility for growth	0.821	0.04
Social prestige	0.810	0.04
Wages	0.622	0.07

S_r is the standard error of the correlation coefficient.

to attractiveness in the examples.

The high rating of the occupations of shipbuilder and automatic equipment setter according to attractiveness corresponds to a higher rating (in comparison with the occupations of miner and steel founder) according to possibilities for creativity. The same tendency is found upon examination of the average ratings of those occupations most highly rated according to attractiveness: the ratings according to creativity occupy the upper limits. All this provides a basis for supposing that the attractiveness of an occupation is determined above all by the creative character of the work. This assumption is confirmed by a comparison of the degree of relationship between the overall attractiveness and each separate value characteristic of the occupations (see Table 1).

The distribution of coefficients of correlation given in Table 1 shows that the average ratings of occupations according to possibilities for creativity are chiefly responsible for the connection with the evaluations-selections according to general attractiveness.

Thus, in the system of value orientations of the experimental group toward occupational activity, orientation toward the creative character of work occupies first place.

Table 2

Distribution of Average Ratings of Occupations According to Possibilities for
Creativity (C), Growth (G), Wages (W), Social Prestige (P), and Overall Attractiveness

Occupations grouped according to occupational sectors and skill level	Average ratings according to the criteria:				
	C	G	W	P	Attractiveness
Industry	3.90 (a)	5.08	4.44	5.43	4.01
	6.69 (a)	7.90	7.39	7.93	6.57
Agriculture	3.63	3.80	3.37	4.72	2.84
	4.18	5.86	5.39	6.36	4.05
Transport and communications	3.95	4.78	4.46	5.79	4.40
	6.58	7.75	7.30	7.94	7.00
Construction	3.43	3.70	3.52	4.87	2.97
	6.55	7.49	7.47	8.28	6.16
Service sector	3.30	3.10	2.34	3.78	2.50
	4.76	5.77	5.62	6.56	3.82
Education, health	5.07	4.98	4.81	6.50	3.62
	7.18	7.16	7.29	8.40	6.22
Science	8.67 (b)	8.71	8.60	9.03	7.43
	7.31 (b)	7.32	7.30	7.92	6.31

(a) The upper row gives the average ratings of unskilled and semi-skilled occupations; the lower, of highly-skilled ones (occupations acquired as a result of higher education).
(b) The upper row gives the average ratings of occupations in the physical-mathematical and natural sciences; the lower, in the humanities and social sciences.
Note: The mean square deviation (S^2) of the average ratings does not exceed 1.7.

Let us examine the results of the survey of the <u>control</u> group
of students who evaluated the same occupations only according
to one of the four characteristics or according to overall attractiveness.

In accordance with the conditions and organization of the experiment, the control group evaluated occupations "in general,
and not for purposes of making a selection." One can therefore
consider the opinion of the 11th graders of the control group as
a manifestation of public opinion on the level of school youth's
social consciousness (see Table 2).

As Table 2 shows, occupations in all spheres of activity received the highest ratings according to social prestige. Particularly highly evaluated from this point of view are the occupations of scientific workers in the physical-mathematical and
natural sciences. This group of occupations is distinguished by
its high ratings according to other criteria as well. Occupations
in education and public health are second. Occupations in industry, transport, and communications occupy third place. These
groups of occupations are very close to each other in their ratings.

The differences between the ratings of higher- and lower-
skilled occupations are significant. This difference is particularly great in the construction sector. Occupations in the service sector and in agriculture have the lowest ratings irrespective of skill levels.

The information obtained in the control group showed that the
<u>social prestige</u> of an occupation, its authority in society, is pri-
mary among such value characteristics as the possibility for
creativity and growth, social prestige, and wages. The remaining characteristics were distributed in the following sequence:
possibility for growth, wages, possibility for creativity.

It is significant that in comparing the ratings according to
each of the four criteria with the ratings according to attractiveness, the connection shown in Table 3 was established.

As can be seen, the degree of relationship of all evaluation
criteria with overall attractiveness is high. Occupational prestige occupies first place.

The data presented permit us to assume that in evaluating

Table 3

Degree of Relationship (Correlation Coefficient r)
Between Ratings According to Attractiveness and Some
Characteristics of Occupations (Control Group)

Characteristics of occupations	r	S_r
Social prestige	0.960	0.02
Possibilities for growth	0.947	0.02
Possibilities for creativity	0.872	0.03
Wages	0.814	0.04

occupations according to overall attractiveness, the majority of
students in the control subgroups were guided by their evaluation of occupations from the standpoint of their prestige in public opinion. In this respect it is also no accident that the average ratings by social prestige are closest to the ratings of occupations by possibilities for growth — raising of skills in the
broad sense of the word. In the opinion of the students surveyed,
these values are connected with each other very closely (in both
the experimental and the control groups the correlation coefficients between "P" and "G" are almost equal to 1.00): the higher
the social prestige of an occupation, the more prospects for
growth it has.

   Thus, when it is not yet a question of personal selection of an
occupation but only of its evaluation, the graduates put criteria
of a high order foremost (let us call them such provisionally so
as to distinguish them from other criteria). In this situation the
opinion expressed corresponds to the general norms accepted in
our society. Orientations of a high order are "at work." (4)

   Let us compare the data obtained in the experimental and control groups (see Table 4).

   The distribution of correlation coefficients presented in Table
4 supports the existence of a high degree of relationship between
the average ratings of occupations in the two groups according to all
the value characteristics and according to overall attractiveness.

Table 4

Degree of Relationship Between Ratings of
Occupations in the Experimental Group
and Those in the Control Group

Characteristics of occupations	Correlation coefficient r
Social prestige	0.959
Possibilities for creativity	0.953
Overall attractiveness of occupation	0.950
Possibilities for growth	0.942
Wages	0.926

The following comparison of information showed that differences also exist within the overall similarity of ratings. In the
first place, the ratings of occupations according to social prestige are lower in the experimental group, but the ratings according to the possibilities for creativity and wages are higher. Second, evaluations according to overall attractiveness are signifi -
cantly higher in the control subgroup than in the experimental
group, which rated occupations according to attractiveness after
considering them from the standpoint of concrete value characteristics. Based on the average ratings given by students in
both groups, the value characteristics of occupations order themselves in the following sequence:

Experimental Group	Control Group
1. Possibilities for creativity	1. Social prestige of occupation
2. Wages	2. Possibilities for growth
3. Social prestige of occupation	3. Wages
4. Possibilities for growth	4. Possibilities for creativity

How can one explain such a lack of correspondence?
To reach any kind of categorical conclusions on the basis of
the given experiment does not seem possible to us, but one thing
is certain: depending on the goals of behavior, an entirely different value orientation comes to the fore. As the situation approaches

a real one, social-psychological orientations of another sort come into play in comparison with a more "abstract" situation.

The characteristic feature in our case is not that students simultaneously evaluating occupations from different points of view on the average gave them higher ratings according to possibilities for creativity and social prestige, but that in the evaluation of occupations according to overall attractiveness, particular characteristics of each occupation were taken into account separately and in comparison with others. The value of an occupation was consciously "weighed" (insofar as the conditions and organization of the experiment permitted) according to several parameters and from the standpoint of personal traits.

Information of this type is particularly valuable if one considers that it was obtained from 11th-grade graduates three months before their graduation from secondary school, that is, not long before they were obliged in one way or another to select a particular type of work and at a time when they were ready, to one degree or another, to make a decision.

A good control for these data would be the study of orientations of a similar type in a real situation — at the moment when graduates are looking for jobs. In this connection let us recall the distribution of motives for occupational choice on the eve of graduation from secondary school. As a motive determining the choice of a particular occupation, the majority of boys and girls advanced interest in the content of work, having in mind above all the possibility for creativity. Analogous data have been obtained in studying the motives for occupational choice of young workers in Leningrad industry. The content and nature of work are the leading motives determining choice and change of occupation, evaluation of the occupation selected, and degree of satisfaction with it.

Thus, orientation toward the creative character of work is of decisive significance in the system of value orientations associated with the choice of an occupation.

Juxtaposition of the information obtained from the survey of the experimental group of students and the mass survey using the "Graduate's Questionnaire" showed that the "contentful"

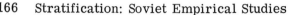

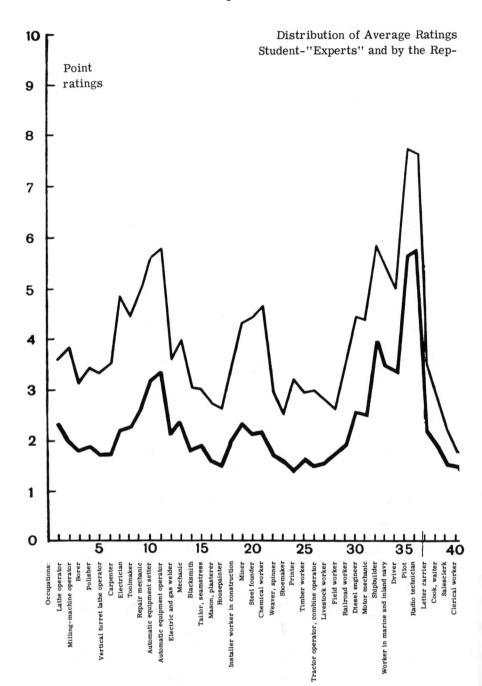

Distribution of Average Ratings
Student-"Experts" and by the Rep-

Point
ratings

Diagram 2

of Occupations Given by the
resentatives of the Mass Survey

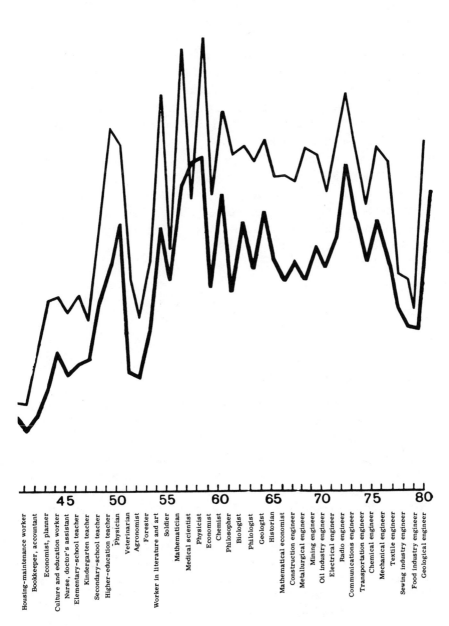

evaluations of each occupation according to four of its characteristics (creativity, growth, prestige, wages) coincide with the
direction of evaluation according to overall attractiveness given
by the graduates in the general survey (see Diagram 2).

As Diagram 2 shows, the "contentful" curve repeats the curve
of evaluations according to overall attractiveness. The similarity of the distribution of evaluations permits us to accept the experimental group of students as judges-experts, and to use their
evaluations as expert ones for interpretation of the content of
the concept "attractiveness of an occupation" as viewed by
secondary-school graduates. (5)

Moreover, on the basis of the indices of the correlation between the evaluations of the attractiveness of a particular occupation and its separate characteristics, one can affirm that, according to the students themselves, the concept of the attractiveness of an occupation includes, in the following order, the value
characteristics we have examined:

1. Creativity
2. Growth
3. Social prestige
4. Wages

Our study's analysis of the structure of secondary-school
graduates' value orientations depending on their sex, geographic
distribution, social origins, parental level of education, and the
material position of their families demonstrated the influence
of these factors on occupational orientation. Furthermore, this
dependence manifested itself in a very distinctive way: the hierarchy of values — creativity, occupational growth, social prestige, wages — remained the same for all the groups, but the
"assortment" of occupations in which the students locate these
value characteristics turned out to be varied.

Let us examine the influence of sex in the evaluation of occupations according to several value characteristics. This demographic trait, a significant social variable, predetermined the
differentiation of attitudes toward occupations (see Table 5). (6)

Table 5

Distribution of Occupations on the Scales of Attractiveness
(Preferred Selection) (S), Creativity (C), and Social Prestige (P)
According to the Evaluations of Boy and Girl Graduates
of Leningrad's Secondary Schools (N = 124)

| | | Ranks of 40 occupations according to the criteria of attractiveness (S), creativity (C), and prestige (P) | | | | | |
| | Occupations | Boys | | | Girls | | |
		S	C	P	S	C	P
1.	Physicist	1	1	3	2	2	1
2.	Mathematician	2	4	1	6	4	2
3.	Radio engineer	3	2	6	5	9	14
4.	Radio technician	4	5	10	9	13	17
5.	Scientific worker	5	3	2	3	3	3
6.	Pilot	6	14	5	4	16	4
7.	Chemical engineer	7	7	8	10	10	9
8.	Mechanical engineer	8	10	12	14	15	15
9.	Geologist	9	11	11	7	6	8
10.	Physician	10	8	7	1	7	5
11.	Higher-education teacher	11	12	9	12	11	7
12.	Philosopher	12	9	13	18	5	11
13.	Construction engineer	13	13	15	12	12	16
14.	Metallurgical engineer	14	16	14	15	17	13
15.	Philologist	15	15	17	11	8	12
16.	Driver	16	31	27	20	27	25
17.	Worker in literature and art	17	6	4	8	1	6
18.	Locksmith	18	20	22	35	30	33
19.	Shipbuilder	19	16	20	17	20	21
20.	Automatic equipment setter	20	19	21	27	30	30
21.	Automatic equipment operator	21	21	24	24	29	28
22.	Mechanic	22	21	25	30	30	32
23.	Secondary-school teacher	23	18	16	13	14	10
24.	Steel founder	24	26	18	30	28	23

Table 5 (continued)

| Occupations | Ranks of 40 occupations according to the criteria of attractiveness (S), creativity (C), and prestige (P) | | | | | |
| | Boys | | | Girls | | |
	S	C	P	S	C	P
25. Chemical worker	25	29	31	28	32	26
26. Lathe operator	26	30	26	29	31	29
27. Railroad worker	27	33	32	28	35	30
28. Agronomist	28	21	30	27	19	20
29. Installation worker in construction	29	30	31	28	33	31
30. Tractor operator, combine operator	30	32	31	37	32	30
31. Culture and education worker	31	29	28	21	20	24
32. Cook, waiter	32	32	36	32	24	33
33. Kindergarten teacher	33	28	23	20	18	19
34. Livestock worker	34	33	34	31	28	36
35. Housepainter	35	37	37	37	38	37
36. Field worker	36	36	36	35	29	34
37. Tailor, seamstress	37	27	34	32	23	30
38. Clerical worker	38	40	40	38	39	39
39. Housing-maintenance worker	39	38	39	40	40	40
40. Salesclerk	40	39	35	35	36	38

Table 5 shows that the occupations which boys and girls rated among the highest 10 according to the criterion of overall attractiveness (S) were almost identical. The only differences were that boys also included the occupation of mechanical engineer while the girls included workers in literature and art; and that the occupation of physician was first for girls but tenth for boys. These two facts would seem to have laid the foundation for further divergences (see Table 6).

It is obvious that the occupations in Table 6 were sharply

Table 6

Divergence in the Evaluations of Several Occupations
According to the Criterion of Attractiveness (S)
Given by Boys and Girls (N = 124)

Occupations	Ranks of occupations on the scale of attractiveness (within the limits of 1-40)				Range of differences (number of places) (b)
	Boys		Girls		
	S	E (a)	S	E (a)	
1. Locksmith	18	2.670	35	1.905	−17
2. Mechanic	22	2.661	30	2.381	− 8
3. Tractor operator, combine operator	30	1.920	37	1.760	− 7
4. Steel founder	24	2.512	30	1.783	− 6
5. Mechanical engineer	8	2.866	14	3.257	− 6
6. Kindergarten teacher	33	1.201	20	2.862	+13
7. Secondary-school teacher	23	2.501	13	2.619	+13
8. Physician	10	3.102	1	3.094	+10
9. Culture and education worker	31	2.298	21	2.383	+10
10. Worker in literature and art	17	3.082	8	2.397	+ 9

(a) E is a statistical evaluation of entropy that demonstrates the degree of uniformity of the ratings. Complete uniformity exists when E = 0, that is, when all the respondents rate an occupation identically according to the given criterion.

(b) The plus sign indicates a preferred relation to the occupations by girls, and a minus sign indicates the same for boys.

Table 7

Distribution of First Ten Places Among Occupations Evaluated by Graduates of Urban and Rural Schools of Leningrad Region According to the Criterion "Attractiveness of Occupation" (N = 200)

Boys		Girls	
Leningrad	Rural areas	Leningrad	Rural areas
1. Physicist	1. Pilot	1. Worker in literature and art	1. Pilot
2. Mathematician	2. Driver	2. Physicist	2. Mathematician
3. Radio engineer	3. Radio engineer	3. Mathematician	3. Medical scientist
4. Radio technician	4. Mechanical engineer	4. Pilot	4. Physician
5. Medical scientist	5. Radio technician	5. Medical scientist	5. Chemical engineer
6. Pilot	6. Physicist	6. Philologist	6. Philologist
7. Chemical engineer	7. Mathematician	7. University teacher	7. Geologist
8. Mechanical engineer	8. Tractor operator, combine operator	8. Geologist	8. Worker in literature and art
9. Geologist	9. Construction worker	9. Physician	9. Radio engineer
10. Physician	10. Chemical engineer	10. Philosopher	10. Mechanical engineer

divided by the students into "masculine" and "feminine" ones.

Boys and girls unanimously gave the lowest ratings on the scale of attractiveness in the list of 40 occupations to occupations in the service, construction, and agricultural sectors. The boys' list of unattractive occupations includes "feminine" occupations (for example, kindergarten teacher) and the girls' list includes "masculine" occupations (for example, locksmith).

The fact that boys and girls to an equal extent give highest preference (the first ten places) to occupations in scientific and engineering work testifies to an identical direction of interests and an awareness of equal opportunities in occupational choice independent of sex. It also indicates a broadening of the sphere of women's occupational interests. The differences in the evaluations point to that degree of connection that does exist between orientations toward particular occupations and students' sex.

Let us examine the relationship between evaluations of occupations according to the criterion of attractiveness and the territorial distribution of youth. (7)

As can be seen in Table 7, rural boys and girls have significantly more similar tastes than do urban youth. The group of occupations attractive to male graduates of rural schools as opposed to urban boys is "diluted" by occupations peculiar to rural areas. The occupation of pilot, which in general enjoys great popularity, is placed first by the rural youth in our sample. But the picture would be incomplete if we were to limit ourselves to an examination of only the first ten occupations.

Diagram 3 shows the distribution of 38 occupations according to the evaluations of 200 boy graduates of Leningrad and of the rural schools of Leningrad Region. The influence of local conditions is obvious. It is also obvious, however, that the occupations of agronomist, field worker, livestock-tender — i.e., agricultural occupations — are still not very highly evaluated by rural youth.

It is interesting to compare our data with information obtained in a study in Novosibirsk Region. The hierarchy of occupations on the scale of attractiveness according to the evaluations of the graduates of the city of Novosibirsk tends to be closer to the hierarchy of occupations according to rural graduates of

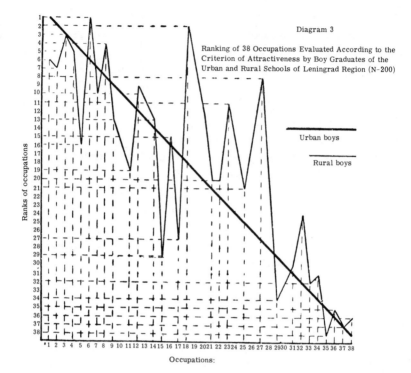

Ranks of occupations

Occupations:

Diagram 3

Ranking of 38 Occupations Evaluated According to the
Criterion of Attractiveness by Boy Graduates of the
Urban and Rural Schools of Leningrad Region (N-200)

Urban boys

Rural boys

Rank list of occupations according to the ratings
of boy graduates of Leningrad urban schools

1. Physicist
2. Mathematician
3. Radio engineer
4. Radio technician
5. Medical scientist
6. Pilot
7. Chemical engineer
8. Mechanical engineer
9. Geologist
10. Physician
11. University teacher
12. Philosopher
13. Construction engineer
14. Metallurgical engineer
15. Philologist
16. Worker in literature and art
17. Secondary-school teacher
18. Driver
19. Locksmith

20. Mechanic
21. Steel founder
22. Chemical worker
23. Lathe operator
24. Railroad worker
25. Agronomist
26. Installation worker in construction
27. Tractor operator, combine operator
28. Culture and education worker
29. Cook, waiter
30. Kindergarten teacher
31. Field worker
32. Mason, plasterer
33. Housepainter
34. Livestock worker
35. Tailor, seamstress
36. Clerical worker
37. Housing-maintenance worker
38. Salesclerk

Leningrad Region. Such occupations as medical scientist, philologist, philosopher, secondary-school teacher, and several
others are rated as low by Novosibirsk boys as by boys from
the rural schools of Leningrad Region. As far as the male graduates of the rural schools of the Novosibirsk and Leningrad Regions are concerned, their evaluations are very similar: the
occupations of driver, tractor operator, and combine operator
are almost equally attractive, while scientific workers in the
humanities received comparatively low ratings. Boys from
Novosibirsk Region evaluate occupations in agriculture somewhat higher than do boys from Leningrad Region. The latter,
however, consider occupations in industry — locksmith, lathe
operator, mechanic — more attractive.

The opinions of girls from these two regions differ significantly. In general, one can say that girls from Leningrad Region evaluate more skilled occupations higher than do girls
from Novosibirsk Region.

As the examples show, male-female differences in evaluation
of occupations in terms of their attractiveness are greatly supplemented by regional differences in evaluation. (8)

Comparison of the ranks of occupations on the scale of creative possibilities (C) showed that boys and girls unanimously
give the first ten places to scholarly occupations in the fields
of physics, medicine, mathematics, philosophy, to radio engineers, chemists, workers in literature and art, and to the occupation of physician. Boys and girls gave a negative evaluation,
according to the criterion of creative possibilities, of housing-
maintenance worker, clerk, salesclerk, housepainter, etc. However, for some groups of occupations, the opinions of boys and
girls differed (see Table 8).

The data in Table 8 eloquently testify to the presence of definite stereotypes in the perception of "masculine" and "feminine" work.

Let us "key in" to the hierarchy of occupations on the scale
of creative possibilities still another variable — social origins.
Diagrams 4 and 5 show the distribution of the average ratings
of 40 occupations given by the children of industrial workers
(N = 80), engineering-technical personnel (N = 68), and scientific

Diagram 4

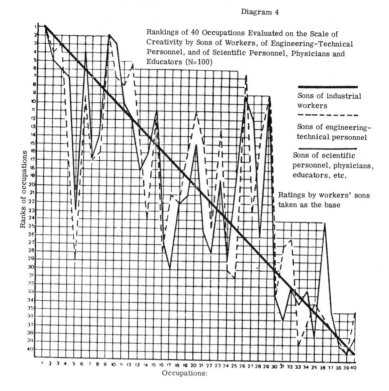

Rankings of 40 Occupations Evaluated on the Scale of
Creativity by Sons of Workers, of Engineering-Technical
Personnel, and of Scientific Personnel, Physicians and
Educators (N=100)

▬▬▬▬ Sons of industrial
        workers

▬ ▬ ▬ ▬ Sons of engineering-
        technical personnel

▬▬▬▬ Sons of scientific
        personnel, physicians,
        educators, etc.

Ratings by workers' sons
taken as the base

Occupations:

Rank list of occupations according to the ratings of workers' sons

1. Physicist
2. Radio engineer
3. Worker in literature and art
4. Radio technician
5. Shipbuilder
6. Physician
7. Mechanical engineer
8. Construction engineer
9. Mathematician
10. Medical scientist
11. Pilot
12. University teacher
13. Chemical engineer
14. Automatic equipment setter
15. Geologist
16. Lathe operator
17. Tailor, seamstress
18. Metallurgical engineer
19. Mechanic
20. Secondary-school teacher
21. Locksmith
22. Driver
23. Culture and education worker
24. Steel founder
25. Automatic equipment operator
26. Philosopher
27. Agronomist
28. Kindergarten teacher
29. Philologist
30. Installation worker in construction
31. Chemical worker
32. Cook, waiter
33. Tractor operator, combine operator
34. Railroad worker
35. Housepainter
36. Field worker
37. Livestock worker
38. Salesclerk
39. Clerical worker
40. Housing-maintenance worker

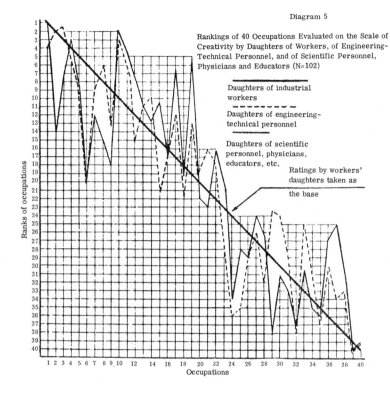

Diagram 5

Rankings of 40 Occupations Evaluated on the Scale of Creativity by Daughters of Workers, of Engineering-Technical Personnel, and of Scientific Personnel, Physicians and Educators (N=102)

Daughters of industrial workers

Daughters of engineering-technical personnel

Daughters of scientific personnel, physicians, educators, etc.

Ratings by workers' daughters taken as the base

Rank list of occupations according to the ratings of workers' daughters

1. Physicist
2. Worker in literature and art
3. Physician
4. Medical scientist
5. University teacher
6. Kindergarten teacher
7. Chemical engineer
8. Construction engineer
9. Radio technician
10. Geologist
11. Mathematician
12. Radio technician
13. Secondary-school teacher
14. Pilot
15. Mechanical engineer
16. Metallurgical engineer
17. Philosopher
18. Tailor, seamstress
19. Philologist
20. Agronomist

21. Culture and education worker
22. Shipbuilder
23. Cook, waiter
24. Lathe operator
25. Chemical worker
26. Livestock worker
27. Driver
28. Steel founder
29. Mechanic
30. Locksmith
31. Field worker
32. Housepainter
33. Automatic equipment setter
34. Tractor operator, combine operator
35. Installation worker in construction
36. Automatic equipment operator
37. Salesclerk
38. Railroad worker
39. Housing-maintenance worker
40. Clerical worker

Table 8

Divergence in the Ratings of Several Occupations According
to the Criterion of Creative Possibilities (C) Given by Boy
and Girl Graduates of Leningrad Schools (N = 124)

Num-ber	Occupations	Ranks of occupations within the limits of 1-40 on the criterion of creativity				Range of differences (number of places)
		Boys		Girls		
		C	E	C	E	
1.	Automatic equipment setter	19	2.464	30	2.254	−11
2.	Repair mechanic	20	2.408	30	2.437	−10
3.	Mechanic	21	2.806	30	2.559	− 9
4.	Radio technician	5	2.928	13	2.785	− 8
5.	Radio engineer	2	2.916	9	2.680	− 7
6.	Kindergarten teacher	28	2.709	18	2.564	+10
7.	Culture and education worker	29	2.709	20	2.588	+ 9
8.	Philologist	15	2.474	8	2.523	+ 7
9.	Field worker	36	2.660	29	2.550	+ 7
10.	Livestock worker	33	2.690	28	2.678	+ 5

personnel, physicians and educators (N = 54). (9)

The tendency toward a high evaluation of occupations involving
so-called intelligentsia labor according to the criterion of creativity is present in all socio-occupational groups both for boys
and girls. But there are also differences. For example, the sons
of scientific personnel, physicians, and teachers evaluate the
occupations of their own group higher than do others. Their
evaluations of the creative possibilities of engineering occupations are close to the evaluations given by boys from engineers'
families and are somewhat lower than the evaluations of workers'

children. Boys from engineers' families evaluate such occupations as higher-education and secondary-school teacher, culture
and education worker, tailor, seamstress, cook, and waiter higher than do the children of workers and of scientific personnel.
On the criterion of creativity, worker occupations are rated
most highly by workers' children. Their evaluations of worker
occupations are comparatively close to their evaluations of engineering occupations. Girls rate worker occupations lower on
the whole than do boys, but the trend in evaluations is about the
same. Girls from families of scientific personnel, physicians,
and teachers gave the highest ratings on the scale of creativity
to workers in literature and art and also to geologists, philolo-
gists, and philosophers. In comparison with this group, girls
from the families of engineering-technical personnel evaluate
the occupations of physician, construction engineer, pilot, mechanic, and automatic equipment setter significantly higher.
Just as boys' opinions differed regarding the occupation of field-
worker, so girls evaluate variously the creative possibilities of
the occupation of salesclerk.

Thus, one can attribute divergences in the evaluation of occupations according to the criterion of creativity by students from
different socio-occupational groups to the influence of contact
in the family with representatives of particular occupations, to
the influence of the psychological atmosphere in which a conception of one's parents' occupation and an orientation toward
it are formed. This influence is more definitely expressed in
the families of workers and scientific personnel, physicians,
and teachers than in the group of children of engineering-
technical personnel. It is evident that in some cases the specific nature of engineering work, and in others the absence of
firm boundaries to it, limit to a certain extent the possibilities
for full information concerning an engineer's work, and the children do not form a completely clear orientation toward their
parents' occupation as regards a particular value characteristic
(for example, creativity).

Contact with representatives of an occupation, the social environment, and the psychological atmosphere in the families of
specialists in various occupations are the leading factors that

form value orientations in relation to occupations. The students themselves write about this. In answer to the open-ended question "What help do you need in the choice of an occupation?" 72% of the graduates surveyed noted in one form or another the need for wider contact with representatives of various occupations as one of the most effective means of obtaining information.

In examining the hierarchy of occupations on the scale of prestige (see Table 5), the following items attract attention. In the first place, the same groups of occupations — scientific personnel in the field of physical-mathematical and natural sciences, radio and chemical engineers, physicians, and workers in literature and art — basically occupy the highest places for boys and girls. The occupation of pilot was also included among the highest rated on the criterion of prestige. Second, the group of occupations for which the opinions of boys and girls diverge has grown. Third, social origins showed a stronger influence on the hierarchy of occupations by the criterion of prestige than in the evaluations by other criteria (the correlation coefficient for boys equals 0.910, for girls — 0.842). For boys from worker families, for example, the prestige of higher-skilled occupations (engineer, higher-education teacher, physician, etc.) is on the average 12 points higher than it is for the children of engineers and scientific personnel. And vice versa, the prestige of worker occupations in all sectors of the economy is on the average 8 points lower. Boys and girls from intelligentsia families assign the highest prestige to occupations in the realm of scientific activity.

Parental level of education also affected the evaluations of the prestige of occupations. Here there was a closer connection between the ratings and the educational level of the mother (the degree of association $\mathsf{y} = 0.872$ for girls and 0.706 for boys). Girls whose parents have seven grades of education or less evaluate unskilled and semi-skilled occupations in all the service areas and in agriculture higher on the criterion of prestige than do representatives of other groups. For boys whose parents have an education of seven grades or less, the degree of prestige of worker occupations is lower than for boys whose parents have higher

Table 9

Divergence in the Ratings of Several Occupations According
to the Criterion of Prestige by Per Capita Family Income,
Boy and Girl Graduates of Leningrad Schools

Occupations	Ranks of occupations (within the limits of 1-40) according to the criterion of prestige (P)		Range of differences (number of places on the scale)
	Per capita family income of graduates		
	50 rubles or less	More than 80 rubles	
Boys			
1. Pilot	5	14	− 9
2. Worker in literature and art	6	12	− 6
3. Chemical engineer	7	15	− 8
4. Driver	9	20	−11
5. Installation worker in construction	10	26	−16
6. Steel founder	11	23	−12
7. Higher-education teacher	12	6	+ 6
8. Philosopher	12	6	+ 6
9. Philologist	17	8	+ 9
10. Secondary-school teacher	13	4	+ 9
Girls			
1. Physician	8	12	− 4
2. Secondary-school teacher	8	13	− 5
3. Kindergarten teacher	15	21	− 6
4. Pilot	5	11	− 6
5. Chemical engineer	11	5	+ 6
6. Philologist	12	8	+ 4
7. Lathe operator, plasterer	29	25	+ 4
8. Locksmith	30	24	+ 6
9. Metallurgical engineer	21	11	+10
10. Radio engineer	17	8	+ 9

education. One can assume that girls are subject to the influence of their families to a greater extent than are boys.

While we did not find a clear relationship between the ratings of occupations by the criteria of attractiveness and creative possibilities, on the one hand, and family material position, on the other, in the analysis of the hierarchy of prestige of occupations a significant degree of relationship with this social trait was manifest: the degree of association ч = .890 for boys and 0.702 for girls (see Table 9).

As we see, for boys and girls the hierarchy of prestige of occupations varies depending on family material position. Within this general relation, the different selection of occupations shows that their prestige is determined by different values.

Until now we have examined the category of prestige as one of the value characteristics of an occupation. But as has already been said, the concept of social prestige is a synthesized concept. Equivalent to the concept of the "authority" of an occupation in public opinion, it includes as component elements: the popularity and attractiveness, social significance, and other value characteristics of an occupation. Moreover, certain value orientations are criteria of prestige. They are the ones that determine the "prestige" hierarchy of occupations in the final analysis. But this is only one aspect of the concept of the prestige of an occupation.

Another aspect consists in the fact that the prestige of an occupation designates a complicated social phenomenon, the result of objective processes. The rise or fall of the prestige of an occupation in public opinion is determined by changes that occur, first, in the content and conditions of work and, second, in the degree of social significance of one or another occupation.

American sociologists, for example, regard the study of occupational prestige as a method of studying social stratification. It is precisely in this sense that the criterion of prestige is used in the comparative research of foreign sociologists.

For example, Bernard Barber considers that "occupational position is the best single indicator of social stratificational position in contemporary American society." (10)

Another American sociologist, Kahl, writes: "...in our

industrial culture, skill (ability plus education and training), authority, income, and prestige are a single meaningful complex.... There is no point in wasting a lot of ingenuity trying to figure out which is most important: the significant fact is that the public sees them as fitting together." (11)

The affirmations of these and a series of other authors evoke an objection of principle. In capitalist conditions, does the concept "occupation" really include the main characteristic of stratification by social position, i.e., relationship to ownership of the means of production and degree of possession of power? Under capitalism it is not occupation as such that serves as the main criterion of social position but differences between the possessors of the means of production and those who sell their labor to the owner of the means of production. Not every occupation in capitalist conditions can be an indicator of social position, and consequently occupation cannot be a sufficient criterion in the study of social stratification.

Under socialism the liquidation of private property has created new criteria for the evaluation of social position. Attitude toward work in one's occupation and the results of one's labor are becoming the basic indicators of a Soviet person's social position.

By studying the prestige of occupations in our society, one can judge the degree of social differentiation and social homogeneity of society. As a real element of consciousness, evaluation of occupations by the criterion of prestige provides information concerning the system of values and value orientations prevalent in society. The hierarchy of prestige of occupations singles out particular value characteristics to which are ascribed specific weights. Finally, through the prestige of occupations it is possible not only to determine the place of an occupation in public opinion but also to trace the social changes that have occurred in a particular historical period.

Thus, subjective evaluations of occupations according to particular value criteria and prestige are nothing more than the reflection of real relationships transformed in people's minds. Changes in the hierarchy of prestige of occupations are the result of objective regularities of societal development.

In the hierarchy of occupations we studied in relation to a series of social characteristics, basically the same occupations — occupations in the sphere of scientific research and engineering work — received the highest ratings. This testifies to the high degree of young people's community of interests, strivings, and opportunities independent of differences in sex, social origins, geographic distribution, etc. This is, so to speak, the "upper layer," in which value orientations and the prestige of occupations, determined by the most general social factors, are an indicator of the level of social consciousness and of an individual's (group's, class') acquisition of social experience.

The second "layer" showed a peculiar differentiation of the hierarchy of occupations depending on a series of social characteristics (sex, geographic distribution, social origins, family material position, and parental level of education). In this case, value orientations and the prestige of occupations, determined by more specific factors, are an indicator of the social differences characteristic of the contemporary level of our society's development and, at the same time, a manifestation of individual selectiveness in occupational orientations.

The practical conclusion from this analysis, above all, is that those engaged in educational work involving occupational orientations and vocational counseling must have an idea of what youth knows of occupational reality in embarking on an independent working life. In order to help a young person who is choosing an occupation to find the optimal correspondence of his or her personal qualities and intentions with a future activity within the framework of real societal needs (this is the basic task of work on occupational orientations), it is important to take into account existing orientations toward occupations and their prestige in public opinion.

Notes

1) The sample consisted of 624 people (279 boys and 345 girls), graduates of five Leningrad secondary schools located in various districts of the city.

2) The list of occupations from the Novosibirsk "Graduates'

Questionnaire" is used with the addition of occupations typical for Leningrad. See V. N. Shubkin, Kolichestvennye metody v sotsiologicheskikh issledovaniiakh, Nauchnye trudy Novosibirskogo gosudarstvennogo universiteta, Novosibirsk, 1964.

3) The average evaluation of each occupation is computed according to the formula $X = \dfrac{n_i \, i}{N}$, where n_i is the number of graduates who rated the given occupation by a point equal to i (varies from 1 to 10); N is the total number of graduates rating the occupation.

4) Just as human needs differ in their order, so orientations produced by particular needs and the corresponding conditions for their realization can be ranked from their lowest level to their highest.

5) These conclusions have methodological significance. The coincidence of the character of the evaluations confirms the necessity of choosing experts for the "measurement" of the opinion of the universe of students from the same milieu. It is rational to use the opinion of labor experts (to whom, for example, the Novosibirsk sociologists turned) in the given case only as a standard in place of the nonexistent official classification of occupations according to degree of creativity and other characteristics, but not for determining the attractiveness of an occupation from schoolchildren's point of view.

6) For simplicity of comparison, the listing of 40 occupations is presented according to the absolute number of points given occupations from the point of view of "attractiveness" (S) in the group of boys.

7) Data of the 1965 mass survey using the "Graduates' Questionnaire" are cited. Along with other questions, the students of the 10th and 11th grades of the schools of Leningrad and Leningrad Region rated a list of occupations according to the criterion of attractiveness.

8) Analogous data are cited by the Novosibirsk sociologists. See Kolichestvennye metody v sotsiologicheskikh issledovaniiakh, Novosibirsk, 1964, p. 234, and Sotsiologicheskie issledovaniia. Voprosy metodologii i metodiki, Novosibirsk, 1966, p. 247.

9) Since in the given case we are analyzing materials of the

experimental survey of the graduates of five secondary schools of Leningrad, we must limit ourselves to examining only three socio-occupational groups whose representation in our sample is comparatively adequate. We will interpret the results as an indicator of the family's influence on attitudes toward occupations according to the criterion of "creativity." In Diagrams 4 and 5 the curve of evaluations of occupations by the children of workers is taken as the average.

10) B. Barber, Social Stratification. A Comparative Analysis of Structure and Process, New York, 1957, p. 184.

11) J. A. Kahl, The American Class Structure, New York, 1957, p. 75.

11 The Influence of Social Origins on the Occupational Values of Graduating Secondary-School Students

M. KH. TITMA

We examined social origins in terms of the occupations of the father and mother, setting three tasks for ourselves: (1) to find a basis for a more detailed division of society than its class structure, and to establish criteria for delimiting social groups; (2) to ascertain whether it is valid to regard the father's occupation as the sole criterion of social origins, or whether this leads to distortions in describing social reality; (3) to study the influence of social origins on the graduating student's assimilation of particular occupational values. (1)

Our sociological literature contains no established procedures for breaking down society into smaller social groups. For our empirical investigation we provisionally distinguished only certain social groups, making no claims to encompass all those possible. In accordance with our objectives, while taking into account the standard division of society into two classes (the working class and the peasantry) plus the intelligentsia, we distinguished ten social groups.

Since we did not have any established criteria for delimiting social groups in our society, we took our empirical observations as a starting point. Our reasoning in setting up the groups as we did differed from that of most investigators. Most studies

From Uchenye zapiski Tartuskogo gosudarstvennogo universiteta, Trudy po filosofii, XV, Tartu, 1970, pp. 169-197. The findings presented in this article are based on a survey conducted in May 1966, of a 50% stratified random sample (N = 2,250) of graduating students of daytime secondary schools in the Estonian SSR with instruction in Estonian.

try to include the social origins of all respondents, setting up a classification in which everyone can find a "column" where his own parents belong. But posing the problem in this manner quite frequently obscures the main objective of the classification: to study real social groups, each with its own unique features which distinguish it from all others. Such a classification, while it does encompass everyone, is too formalistic and is inadequate to describe real social groups. To avoid this sort of formalism, we deliberately did not attempt a complete stratification analysis of our society; instead, we made a provisional classification that encompassed only a restricted number of social groups.

Since the peasantry (collective farmers) is very difficult to differentiate, we did not subdivide it into smaller groups. (2) Four hundred ninety-eight of the students' fathers and 588 of their mothers were collective farmers.

Drawing on the practice of other investigators, we can divide the working class into several social groups (3):

Workers in enterprises with less than 50 workers. Labor in such enterprises is usually of a craft nature and is less organized than elsewhere. Social contacts are more personal, and social roles are not so clearly defined as in large-scale industry. In Estonia it is still necessary to take into account the class base of this particular social group (peasantry, petty bourgeoisie, and individual handicraft workers). There were 105 men and 102 women in this group.

Workers in enterprises with more than 50 workers. This group was composed primarily of workers in large-scale industry. The features distinguishing this group from the preceding group have been outlined above. There were more men (520) in this group than in any of the others; there were 330 women.

Trade workers. In the public mind a number of unhealthy notions have grown up around this group. Public opinion at certain levels considers it almost a normal phenomenon for trade workers to engage in petty pilfering, and it is only cases of excessive misappropriation that arouse indignation. A large percentage of such offenses among trade workers are clearly linked with the objective conditions of their occupations (low wages combined with the opportunity to pilfer). Both the social status and the specific activity of this group warrant setting it off as a separate group distinct from industrial workers. The group contained a total of 101 men and 222 women.

Office employees of enterprises and institutions. This group probably resembles the "white collar workers" in American society to some extent, but it does not, of course, take in all the occupations included in that group in the USA. (4) There were 329 men and 396 women in this group. To a certain degree it is an intermediate group between the workers and the intelligentsia, and is quite heterogeneous.

Medical personnel were also an intermediate group in our investigation. Though it was initially set up for physicians alone, this group became a heterogeneous one when we began including anyone who worked in a medical institution (from the orderlies to the physicians). Our inclusion of the entire range of medical employees influenced the sex composition of this group: 32 men and 129 women.

The technical intelligentsia included 89 men and 20 women.

The intelligentsia in the humanities. As might be expected, this group contained more women (109) than men (87).

Scientific workers are also unique not only as regards their sphere of activity but also with respect to their social position. As a result, they show specific differences from other groups of the intelligentsia. For this reason we distinguished scientific workers as a special group. In our study this group was small, consisting of 33 men and 14 women.

Leaders in trade unions, soviets, and other organizations. We assumed that this group would display certain features peculiar to its unique social position. The group consisted of 35 men and 14 women.

On the whole, differences among the intelligentsia groups were studied in greater detail. (5) These differences were selected as a basis for studying the dissimilar influences of groups within the same stratum. This made it possible to investigate the influence of the particular way in which occupational values operate, of the actual performance of occupational activity, and of the way in which certain factors are reflected subjectively in the consciousness of the parents. It also enabled us to study the child's assimilation of particular occupational values.

The influence of other factors also had to be taken into account in analyzing our data. Such additional factors may lie at the root of certain differences between social groups, especially as regards the collective farm peasantry. One factor that is likely to be a source of disparity between this group and the others is the quality of schooling (the rural school still lags behind the urban school in the composition of its teaching staff and in the amount and quality of its equipment).

The influence of other factors on the graduating student's assimilation of particular occupational values is more difficult to interpret from the empirical data. The student receives information about these values from various channels, although of course the possibilities these channels have for exercising influence and their impact will vary considerably from case to case.

What kind of social policy is pursued with respect to a particular value? The situation here is one of effective competition between different channels. The most easily analyzed situation occurs when the main channels act in concert. If this is the case, then empirically observed differences in the influence of social origins on the student's assimilation of a value will reflect differences in the effective impact of various social groups on the student. The same holds true when a particular value is assimilated solely through the channels of social origins. This is clearly the case with respect to occupational values (6) bearing on the specific conditions of a particular occupation.

It is much more difficult to determine the influence of social origins in cases where official social policy, acting through formal channels (government-controlled social institutions), operates counter to the influence of specific social groups. In such a situation it is very difficult to establish the direction and impact of social origins on the shaping of an occupational value; we can arrive at an analysis of the problem only by indirect means.

In order to put our empirical data into better relief, we shall employ a quantitative rating scale for all the values we have examined, multiplying the percentage of respondents rating a value as "very important" by +1, "moderately important" by 0, and "unimportant" by −1. If the students gave a particular value a predominantly positive rating (i.e., indicating that for them it was a very important requirement), then our calculation yielded a mean with a plus sign; if the rating was predominantly negative (signifying that it was an unimportant requirement), we obtained a mean with a minus sign. Through the use of this weighted mean (percentage), the influence of different social groups on the shaping of an individual's occupational values can be compared on a more general level. This also makes it easier to perceive the importance of breaking down society into smaller groups than classes.(7)

Our material does not lend itself easily to a determination of the influence of the mother and father on the shaping of occupational values within social groups. For purposes of such an analysis, we present the family composition of our students in Table 1. We find the most socially homogeneous families (those in which the mother and father come from the same social group) among collective farmers (76.9% of the fathers and 65.1% of the mothers are married to other collective farmers), followed by office employees (44.4% and 37%, respectively), medical personnel (53.1% and 13.2%), and the intelligentsia in the humanities (40.2% and 32.1%). When the family is homogeneous (the mother and father come from the same social group), it is impossible to determine any differences between the maternal and paternal influences, for the data themselves show no differences. Unequal maternal and paternal influences are discernible only when the families are heterogeneous (when the father has one occupation and the mother another). Variations on a graph or diagram can show a predominance of one parent's influence; only the extreme points of a curve enable us to state that in this social group the mother or the father clearly predominates and that there is no evidence of the influence of a father or mother of another occupation. It is more difficult to detect unequivocal differences between fathers and mothers if their influence is not represented by extreme points on the curve. In such a case it is necessary to undertake an analysis of the family composition of these groups of parents. One must determine whether these variations in the graph are a manifestation of the influence of other social groups, i.e., of the husband or wife of the parent in question.

Extent of Status Homogamy
Graduating Secondary-School

Occupation of father \ Occupation of mother	0	1	2	3	4
0 parental occupation not stated	40.2%(c) 107 (a) 29.8% (b)	12.9% 76 21.2	18.6% 19 5.3	12.6% 28 7.8	11.2% 37 10.3
1 agricultural personnel	12.8 34 6.8%	65.1 383 76.9	8.8 9 1.8	4.1 9 1.8	4.2 14 2.8
2 workers in enterprises with up to 50 workers	4.5 12 11.4%	3.1 18 17.1	23.5 24 22.9	7.2 16 15.2	5.2 17 16.2
3 workers in trade and public catering	3.0 8 7.9%	0.5 3 3.0	4.9 5 5.0	17.1 38 37.6	2.7 9 8.9
4 workers in enterprises with more than 50 workers	17.3 46 8.8%	8.3 49 9.4	24.5 25 4.8	25.7 57 11.0	60.6 200 38.5
5 technical intelligentsia (engineers)	1.9 5 5.6%	0.7 4 4.5	4.9 5 5.6	5.4 12 13.5	3.9 13 14.6
6 office employees in offices and institutions	10.9 29 8.8%	5.3 31 9.4	9.8 10 3.0	18.9 42 12.8	7.3 24 7.3
7 medical personnel	0.4 1 3.1%	0.2 1 3.1	1.0 1 3.1	0.9 2 6.3	0.3 1 3.1
8 intelligentsia in the humanities (teachers, journalists, etc.)	2.6 7 8.0%	0.2 1 1.1	2.9 3 3.4	2.7 6 6.9	1.5 5 5.7
9 leaders in trade unions, soviets, and other organizations	0.4 1 2.9%	0.5 3 8.6	0.0 0 0.0	2.3 5 14.3	1.2 4 11.4
10 scientific workers	2.6 7 21.2%	0.2 1 3.0	0.0 0 0.0	0.5 1 3.0	0.3 1 3.0
11 occupations not in above categories	3.4 9 14.5%	3.1 18 29.0	1.0 1 1.6	2.7 6 9.7	1.5 5 8.1
Total	100.0% 266	100.0% 588	100.0% 102	100.0% 222	100.0% 330

(a) Number of marriages between fathers in given category and mothers in given category.
(b) Percentage of fathers in given category married to mothers in given category.
(c) Percentage of mothers in given category married to fathers in given category.

Table 1

Among Parents of a Sample of
Students, Estonian SSR, 1966*

Each cell lists: column % (rotated), count, row %.

	5	6	7	8	9	10	11	Total
	0.0% · 0 · 0.0	12.9% · 51 · 14.2	16.3% · 21 · 5.8	11.0% · 12 · 3.3	28.6% · 4 · 1.1	0.0% · 0 · 0.0	6.6% · 4 · 1.1	359 · 100.0%
	0.0 · 0 · 0.0	4.8 · 19 · 3.8	7.0 · 9 · 1.8	5.5 · 6 · 1.2	0.0 · 0 · 0.0	0.0 · 0 · 0.0	24.6 · 15 · 3.0	498 · 100.0%
	5.0 · 1 · 0.9	1.8 · 7 · 6.7	0.8 · 1 · 0.9	2.8 · 3 · 2.9	0.0 · 0 · 0.0	0.0 · 0 · 0.0	9.8 · 6 · 5.7	105 · 100.0%
	5.0 · 1 · 1.0	4.8 · 19 · 18.8	3.9 · 5 · 5.0	7.3 · 8 · 7.9	14.3 · 2 · 2.0	0.0 · 0 · 0.0	4.9 · 3 · 3.0	101 · 100.0%
	15.0 · 3 · 0.6	19.7 · 78 · 15.0	28.7 · 37 · 7.1	9.2 · 10 · 1.9	7.1 · 1 · 0.2	0.0 · 0 · 0.0	23.0 · 14 · 2.7	520 · 100.0%
	30.0 · 6 · 6.7	6.1 · 24 · 27.0	7.0 · 9 · 10.1	6.4 · 7 · 7.9	7.1 · 1 · 1.1	7.1 · 1 · 1.1	3.3 · 2 · 2.2	89 · 100.0%
	15.0 · 3 · 0.9	37.0 · 146 · 44.4	15.5 · 20 · 6.1	11.9 · 13 · 4.0	21.4 · 3 · 0.9	14.3 · 2 · 0.6	9.8 · 6 · 1.8	329 · 100.0%
	5.0 · 1 · 3.1	1.3 · 5 · 15.6	13.2 · 17 · 53.1	1.8 · 2 · 6.3	0.0 · 0 · 0.0	7.1 · 1 · 3.1	0.0 · 0 · 0.0	32 · 100.0%
	20.0 · 4 · 4.6	5.1 · 20 · 23.0	3.1 · 4 · 4.6	32.1 · 35 · 40.2	0.0 · 0 · 0.0	7.1 · 1 · 1.1	1.6 · 1 · 1.1	87 · 100.0%
	0.0 · 0 · 0.0	3.5 · 14 · 40.0	0.0 · 0 · 0.0	4.6 · 5 · 14.3	14.3 · 2 · 5.7	7.1 · 1 · 2.9	0.0 · 0 · 0.0	35 · 100.0%
	5.0 · 1 · 3.0	1.5 · 6 · 18.2	0.8 · 1 · 3.0	6.4 · 7 · 21.2	0.0 · 0 · 0.0	57.1 · 8 · 24.2	0.0 · 0 · 0.0	33 · 100.0%
	0.0 · 0 · 0.0	1.5 · 6 · 9.7	3.9 · 5 · 8.1	0.9 · 1 · 1.6	7.1 · 1 · 1.6	0.0 · 0 · 0.0	16.4 · 10 · 16.1	62 · 100.0%
Total	100.0% · 20	100.0% · 395	100.0% · 129	100.0% · 109	100.0% · 14	100.0% · 14	100.0% · 61	2,250

*We have corrected a number of computational and typographical
errors in the original table.

In order to discover differences in the influence exerted by
families from different social groups, we shall analyze Graphs
1-4. The graphs show weighted means (percentages) representing the influence of social origins on the students' assimilation
of the first set of occupational values* and a value closely associated with them, "being useful to the national economy." (8)
All these values are the subject of vigorous propaganda (overt
and indirect) on the part of the school, the mass media, and
other formal institutions. Hence, in this case the family acts
as a mediating factor that counterbalances the influence of other
channels of information on the children. This counterbalancing
function is usually exercised both by evaluating particular information and by establishing the prestige of the channel. In
reading the graphs, therefore, one must take into account that
the designations used in our questionnaire may take on a completely different meaning for the students than they have in propaganda, and that they may not have been conceptualized and in-
ternalized at all by the students.

1. "Constant opportunities for self-fulfillment and development of one's mental outlook" represents the value of self-
fulfillment being inculcated vigorously by the school, mass media, and other formal institutions that transmit this value in society. The family may either support this policy or remain indifferent to it. As may be seen from Graph 1, the differences
in the influence exerted by the subject's social origins, both
from the mother's and father's side, are insignificant (the
graph shows only minor fluctuations). Among fathers the most
atypical category as regards transmission of this value is the
group of scientists. Compared to other children, the children of scientists clearly have better opportunities for self-
fulfillment. A deficiency of such opportunities does not develop
in these families, and hence official social policy, carried
on through other channels, is not supported in such an environment as strongly as in the other social groups. The result is that this criterion is less active in shaping the choice

---

*Titma's first set of occupational values includes: self-
fulfillment, creativity, the use of one's personal abilities.

Graph 1

Students' Ratings of "Self-Fulfillment" as a Value
in Occupational Choice, by Parents' Occupations

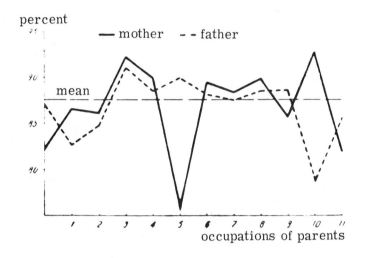

Note: 0 — parental occupation not stated; 1 — agricultural personnel; 2 — workers in enterprises with up to 50 workers; 3 — workers in trade and public catering; 4 — workers in enterprises with more than 50 workers; 5 — technical intelligentsia (engineers); 6 — office employees in enterprises and institutions; 7 — medical personnel; 8 — intelligentsia in the humanities (teachers, journalists, etc.); 9 — leaders in trade unions, soviets, and other organizations; 10 — scientific workers; 11 — occupations not in above categories.

Editors' note: We have reversed the apparently mistaken designations for "mother" and "father" in the original to make them correspond to Titma's discussion in the text. Titma's method of deriving the ratings shown here and in the graphs and diagrams that follow is given on pages 190-191 above.

of occupation by children of scientists.

2. <u>Creativity</u> is less intensely disseminated as a value by the schools and the mass media. Because of its association with self-affirmation, it is not so easily assimilated as the preceding value. The students generally associated this value with a particular type of activity (intellectual activity), though they sometimes have a confused notion of such activity. This value is usually not given explicit individual attention in school, for in that setting instruction is aimed at the entire group and the meaning of creativity is not singled out for special emphasis. Quite often it is the social environment, where the social group plays an important role, from which the child gains an understanding of the meaning of creativity.

Our data on the influence of the social group on the assimilation of creativity as a value in one's occupation are presented in Graph 2. The curves for the mother and father fluctuate considerably, thus showing that social origins are clearly influential in the student's assimilation of this value.

Students who rated creativity as "very important" comprised from 42.6% to 78.6% of all the children in the social groups as defined by the mother's occupation, and from 47.8% to 68% of children in the social groups as defined by the father's occupation. The corresponding weighted means ranged from 32.8 to 71.4 and from 39.8 to 63.2. This wide variation in the figures bears out the hypothesis that society must be broken down into smaller groups than classes, for such groups do indeed differ significantly with respect to the role they play in transmitting occupational values. "Creativity" is most thoroughly assimilated in families of the non-technical intelligentsia, scientists, and medical personnel; it is assimilated much less thoroughly in families of the technical intelligentsia than in other groups of the intelligentsia. The influence exerted by office employees and workers in large-scale industry on the transmission of this occupational value is at about the same level as that exerted by the technical intelligentsia. The percentages reflecting their influence are the lowest points on Graph 2, if one disregards the groups made up of parents whose occupation was not stated by the students and of parents who belong to social groups not

Graph 2

Students' Ratings of "Creativity" as a Value in
Occupational Choice, by Parents' Occupations

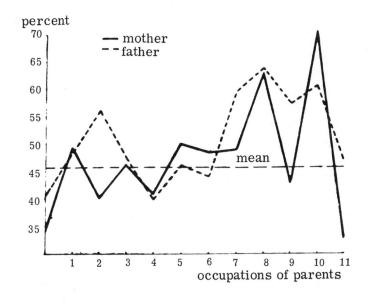

included in the study. In investigating the transmission of creativity as a value, one is struck by the considerable difference
between the influence of workers in small enterprises and in
large enterprises on the transmission of creativity as a value
(their weighted means were 56.2 and 39.8, respectively; and
64.7% and 47.8% of children whose fathers worked in small and
large enterprises, respectively, considered creativity to be
"very important"). This difference can be attributed to the content of work in the two social groups in question. The labor performed by a (male) worker in a small enterprise in Estonia
(small workshops, repair shops, etc., where the work is basically

of a craft nature) has retained its individuality and creative character. In large-scale industry, on the other hand, the nature of the work is such that there are strictly regulated limits to the worker's exercise of his own individuality. In this sense, it is also quite consistent that the influence of the technical intelligentsia is more on a par with that of workers in large-scale industry than it is with other groups of the intelligentsia. Large-scale industry, with its job atmosphere, does not promote group consciousness of creativity among its workers or among the technical intelligentsia. (9)

It is interesting that the students who failed to state the occupation of their father or mother, as well as those whose parents' occupations were not included in our categories (the students wrote them in), rated creativity lowest of all. Graph 2 quite clearly reveals a difference between maternal and paternal influence on the child's assimilation of creativity as a value.

It is obvious that the greatest variations in the curve representing maternal influence (low points of 32.8 and 34.2 and high points of 71.4 and 63.3) on the transmission of this value can only be due to the fact that the mother has a greater influence than the father. The paternal and maternal influences are clearly contradictory among workers in small enterprises. An analysis of mixed families shows clearly that in such families the parent from this group dominated (of the mothers from this group, 24.5% were married to workers in large enterprises, 18.6% were married to men whose occupations were not stated by the students, and 9.8% were married to office employees). Only one of these groups (paternally defined) was slightly less effective in transmitting this value than mothers working in small enterprises. Of the fathers in this group, 16.2% were married to workers in large enterprises, 17.1% were married to collective farmers, 15.2% were married to trade workers, and 11.4% were married to women whose occupation was not stated by the students. All these groups (maternally defined) were considerably less influential in their children's assimilation of creativity as a value. (10) Such great differences between the paternal and maternal influences in this particular social group are due to the differences in the nature of the work. Women in small

enterprises are primarily engaged in subsidiary work, and
hence their labor is not creative in nature.

The differences between mothers and fathers who are medical workers in transmitting creativity as a value may be due to
the social heterogeneity of the female members of this group
(ranging from physicians to attendants). It is difficult to account
for the differences in maternal and paternal influences among
scientists and trade-union and organizational leaders. It is
quite obvious that in mixed families both fathers and mothers
working in the humanities are more effective in inculcating creativity as a value in their children. The differences in groups
of students who failed to state the occupation of their parents
or who wrote them in on our list may be due to the heterogeneity
of the social groups to which their mothers and fathers belong.
On the whole, Graph 2 clearly shows that in different social
groups the father and mother have unequal influence on the
child's assimilation of creativity as a value.

3. The fruitfulness of an analysis of social groups as channels for transmitting values is also evident from Graph 3 (the
curve of maternal influence ranges from 65 to 100, and that of
paternal influence from 65.7 to 87.5). On the whole, the children
of the intelligentsia better assimilate this value [the use of one's
personal abilities]*. The sole exception is the children of the
technical intelligentsia. Among the children of workers, the
children of trade workers differ most noticeably from the other
groups. One would have to test the possibility that they assimilate this value because of deficient opportunities for its realization in the occupational activity of their families; or that they
interpret "abilities" to mean "clever manipulation" and "skill-
ful tricks." The latter interpretation is rather prevalent among
trade workers. The peculiar ratings given by children of medical personnel is due to the nature of their parents' work. The
individual character of their jobs reinforces the role of personal
abilities as a value among medical personnel.

There are also quite considerable differences between paternal

---

*The material below makes it clear that this is the value
Titma has in mind here.

Graph 3

Students' Ratings of "The Use of One's Personal
Abilities" as a Value in Occupational Choice,
by Parents' Occupations

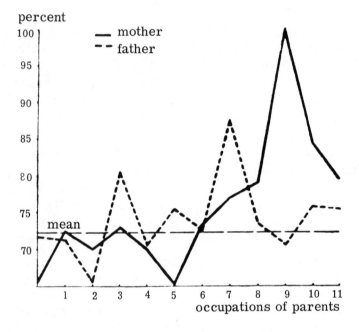

Note: see notes to Graph 1.

and maternal influences within the same social group. We shall
only point out the fact that mothers have a greater influence on
the internalization of this value in the families of trade-union
and organizational leaders (100%, i.e., all their children consider the use of one's personal abilities to be "very important"),
while mothers from the technical intelligentsia are least effective in inculcating this value (a mean of 65). Families in which
the father is a medical worker, engineer or trade worker more

thoroughly assimilate "the use of one's personal abilities" as
a criterion for evaluating an occupation. Here, too, the paternal and maternal influences are contradictory, and the father's
occupation cannot be the sole criterion of social origins.

4. As we have already noted, usefulness to the national economy is utilized in our social policy as one of the primary means
to regulate choice of occupation. This fact must be taken into
account in interpreting our data, and a low degree of assimilation of this value by the children of any social group must be
attributed to the failure of their environment to effectively
transmit this criterion. In the case of Estonia, this situation
may also reflect a political attitude toward Soviet power. The
influence of social origins on the transmission of this value is
substantial (this criterion for choosing an occupation was rated
"very important" by 33.3% to 55.8% of the students in the various social groups, paternally defined, and by 32.8% to 58.8%,
maternally defined; the same criterion was rated "unimportant" by 4.2% to 21.9% of students in the groups, paternally defined, and by 3.9% to 21.1%, maternally defined). The variations
of the weighted means may be seen in Graph 4. On the whole,
the intelligentsia are clearly less effective in inculcating this
value as a criterion for choosing an occupation, while collective
farmers and trade workers more readily accept it as a criterion for their children's choice of career. Then comes the
group of workers. Workers in small enterprises are more effective in passing this value on to their children.

Among the intelligentsia it is perfectly clear why children of
trade-union and organizational leaders should rate this value
high. The technical intelligentsia also instill in their children
the idea that one's usefulness to the national economy should
be a criterion for choosing an occupation. The groups that are
least inclined to pass this value on to their children are fathers
who are medical workers (the influence of mothers in that group
is not amenable to analysis because of the group's heterogeneous social makeup), scientists, and the intelligentsia in the
humanities. The varying degrees to which different social
groups inculcate in their children the value of usefulness to the
national economy as a guide for choosing an occupation cannot

Graph 4

Students' Ratings of "Usefulness to the National
Economy" as a Value in Occupational Choice,
by Parents' Occupations

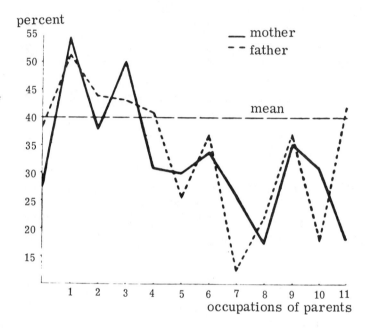

Note: see notes to Graph 1.

be wholly explained by reference to the political overtones of
this standard of behavior, although they certainly are present.
A negative attitude might also stem from the fact that in the
public mind certain occupations are simply not associated with
the national economy and that any consideration of usefulness
to the national economy inevitably runs counter to the prestige
of these occupations. Our data show the students' understanding
of, and corresponding rejection or acceptance of, usefulness to

the national economy as a criterion for choosing an occupation. That this value should directly influence a person's choice of occupation is unacceptable to the intelligentsia, and they oppose the assimilation of this value by their children. The same attitude is also responsible for the relatively poor assimilation of this value by the children of workers in large-scale industry, even though they come from the most developed section of the working class and should, given their political point of view, assign the most positive rating to this criterion for choosing an occupation. The high degree of assimilation of this criterion in families in which the upbringing is not so consciously directed and the influence of the school and other formal institutions is unquestionably stronger bears out our view that this value cannot be considered as the main criterion in the selection of one's occupation.

The poor transmission of this value may stem, to some extent, from the intelligentsia's subjective perception that social policy does not (relatively speaking) value the labor of some segments of the intelligentsia as highly as the labor of other strata of the population (the remuneration for one's labor, the power, position and prestige of an occupation are perceived relative to other occupations, and if one person receives 60 rubles for cleaning an apartment and another person gets 65 rubles as a scientific assistant in a museum, this state of affairs will inevitably have a negative social-psychological effect). A comparison of the curves of maternal and paternal influence reveals some rather significant differences. Unfortunately, we are unable to analyze the answers of those who failed to note their parents' occupations or of those who wrote in occupations not included on the list, although the differences were most striking in these groups. It is very difficult to determine in which families the father or the mother exercises a stronger influence on the assimilation of the value in question. In the intelligentsia groups, parental influence obviously does not contribute to the assimilation of this value. We can conclude that mothers who work in the humanities most strongly counteract the assimilation of "usefulness to the national economy" as a criterion in their children's choice of occupation (35.8% of the children of such mothers rated usefulness to the national economy as "very important," while 21.1% rated it as "unimportant).* Fathers who are medical workers have almost the same sort of influence (34.4% of their children rated usefulness to the national economy as "very important," and 21.9% as "unimportant").

Though it is difficult to detect any clear differences in the other social groups, it is apparent that mothers who are collective farmers or trade personnel are more effective in inculcating this value as a criterion in their children's choice of occupation than are fathers in these same groups. Male workers, on the other hand, do more to promote assimilation of this value by their children than female workers.

On the whole, Graph 4 and the previous ones clearly bear out the hypothesis that there are substantial differences between maternal and paternal influences and that it is erroneous to interpret social origins in terms of the father alone.

Our analysis of the first set of values has clearly demonstrated the fruitfulness, for a sociological analysis, of using a classification with smaller social groups. From this point on we will concentrate our attention on analysis of the differences in paternal and maternal influences within the same social group on the transmission of occupational values to children.

In interpreting the data on the group of values which act as the external functional expressions of a person's occupation, one must take into account that these values have evolved historically and that they have been assimilated to varying degrees by different social groups as the groups themselves developed. The more important influence on the transmission of these values in society is that exercised by a person's social origins. This influence is reinforced by social policy, which in most cases has been negatively oriented toward values associated with remuneration for occupational activity. On the other hand, it is true that there has been a concentrated emphasis on remuneration as a value and that it has been used as an incentive to work, particularly in occupations where work clearly lacks creative aspects.

---

*The average rating implied by these figures is 14.7. The corresponding figure in Graph 4 appears to be about 3 points higher.

5. The first value in this set that we shall examine is <u>material</u> <u>remuneration</u> for a person's occupational activity. Our society has no clear-cut and unified policy with respect to this value. Recent propaganda has emphasized material incentives for occupational activity, but schools still foster a negative attitude toward this aspect of one's occupation.

Diagram 1 shows the family's influence on the assimilation of this value. As one can see from the diagram, social origins exercise a considerable influence on the transmission of the value of material remuneration for labor (the weighted mean ranges from 34.43 to −7.14). Children of the intelligentsia rate material remuneration higher than children of other groups (the only exceptions are children of scientists and personnel in leadership positions). The children of scientists, collective farmers, and personnel in leadership positions stand out distinctly from the rest: they rate material remuneration for one's work very low as a criterion for choosing an occupation. The fact that these groups enjoy the greatest material security of any groups in Estonia points up the significance of material incentives for occupational activity and their function as a criterion in choosing an occupation. Children from these groups have greater freedom in choosing an occupation than less well-off youth. The limitations placed upon that choice are not only objective; they are also manifested in an individual's subjective criteria determining his choice of occupation (e.g., the significance of material remuneration as a criterion in that choice). Material remuneration is most important to the children of the technical intelligentsia, the intelligentsia working in the humanities, and medical personnel. Nominal wages in these social groups are certainly not lower than those earned by workers, and are actually much higher than the wages of trade workers and office employees. A social-psychological effect of wages is at work here: a person's subjective perception of his own wages relative to the wages prevailing in other social groups causes a general feeling of inadequacy with respect to this aspect of occupational remuneration. This feeling in turn creates in the group consciousness an exaggerated notion of the importance of material incentives in one's occupation.

Diagram 1

Students' Ratings of "Material Remuneration"
as a Value in Occupational Choice,
by Parents' Occupations

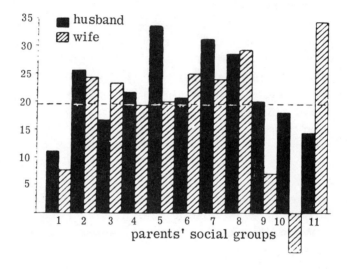

Note: 1 — agricultural personnel; 2 — workers in enterprises with up to 50 workers; 3 — workers in trade and public
catering; 4 — workers in enterprises with more than 50 workers; 5 — technical intelligentsia (engineers); 6 — office employees in enterprises and institutions; 7 — medical personnel;
8 — intelligentsia in the humanities (teachers, journalists, etc.);
9 — leaders in trade unions, soviets, and other organizations;
10 — scientific workers; 11 — occupations not in above categories.

There are considerable differences between paternal and maternal influence among the children of scientists, personnel in leadership positions, the technical intelligentsia, and children who wrote in their father's occupation. The import of all these differences in Diagram 1 is that the mother transmits this value less effectively. This phenomenon may be due to the fact that she does not perceive such a sharp discrepancy in material remuneration and is content with a lower level of remuneration.

Female trade workers are much more effective in transmitting this value to their children than are fathers of this group. The difference in this case stems from the fact that the mothers are primarily sales clerks, while the fathers work in warehouses, offices, etc. The mother's wages are low, and hence material remuneration takes on greater importance for her children.

Here, for the first time, we can note a peculiar phenomenon: children with mothers in the intelligentsia rate material remuneration significantly lower than do children with fathers in the corresponding groups of the intelligentsia. For scientists, the figures are −7.14 for mothers and 18.18 for fathers; for personnel in leadership positions, 7.14 and 20.0; for the technical intelligentsia, 20.0 and 33.7; and for medical workers, 24.0 and 31.3. It is only the intelligentsia in the humanities that show no differences (for mothers the figure is 29.4 and for fathers it is 28.7). Mothers from the intelligentsia are clearly less apt to instill in their children the notion that material remuneration for one's labor should be an occupational value.

6. The value of one's future security is closely associated with the desire for material remuneration. An individual's assimilation of this value is determined by the social group to which he belongs, for there is no active social policy conducted with regard to this value. The influence of social origins on the transmission of this value is greater than in the case of any other value we have analyzed (5.3% to 26.2% of students from paternally-defined social groups and 0% to 28.5% from maternally-defined groups rated this value "very important," while 20% to 35% and 5.7% to 50%, respectively, rated it "unimportant"). Students from families of workers in small

enterprises, medical personnel, and workers in large-scale industry are most uneasy about their future. Students from families of personnel in leadership positions, scientists, and the intelligentsia in the humanities, on the other hand, assimilate this value least. The assimilation of this value corresponds in some measure to the way material remuneration was rated by students from these same social groups. Only the intelligentsia groups showed a shift toward a more negative evaluation. Here it is the level of the individual's security rather than his relative material remuneration that is at work. That level is clearly lowest among children of workers in small enterprises. This consideration also accounts for the shift in the way children of the intelligentsia in the humanities rated this value, since their parents enjoy a rather high degree of material security. In other words, we are correct in interpreting this value as dependent upon the individual's security in society (socially, rather than individually). In only one group — the children of workers in small-scale production — were there more students rating security for the future "very important" than there were students giving that value a negative rating. The differences between the groups show that the role of this value as a criterion for choosing an occupation is tending to diminish and freedom in one's choice of a career is tending to increase, for this value expresses limitations on a person's freedom. One must take into account that this value is to some extent a reflection of the petty bourgeois ideology of a tranquil life.

The influence of the father and mother on the transmission of a secure future as a cultural standard differ considerably. Mothers from all intelligentsia groups instill this value in their children to a lesser degree than do fathers from that category or mothers from other social groups (among personnel in leadership positions, the weighted mean for the group as defined paternally was −28.6, and for the group as defined maternally, −50; for scientists, the respective figures were −18.2 and −28.6; for the intelligentsia in the humanities, −11.5 and −18.4; for the technical intelligentsia, −6.7 and −15; and for medical workers, 0 and −7.8). The situation is reversed for all other groups except collective farmers: the mothers are more

instrumental in the assimilation of this value. No matter what
the influence of the family — no matter whether it encourages
acceptance or rejection of this particular value — it is the
mother in all the social groups who has the greater influence
on the child's assimilation or failure to assimilate the value.
As may be seen from the diagram*, mothers account for both
the highest and lowest columns — i.e., the most positive and
most negative ratings of this value (the groups composed of
workers in small enterprises and the group made up of personnel in leadership positions, respectively).

7. The value of recognition by people in one's immediate social
environment was rated roughly the same by children of all social
groups from the working class and the peasantry (see Diagram 3).
Among these groups the only real anomaly is the group of mothers
who are trade workers: their greater influence on their children
with respect to this value may be due to their own social position (most of these women are sales clerks). As a group, they
are oversensitive to how their own work is judged by the people around them (the problem of a sales person's honesty), and
they probably pass this on to their children. On the whole,
these groups rank as follows in transmitting this value to their
children (in ascending order): collective farmers, workers,
trade workers and office employees. The relative uniformity
in the way this value was rated by children in these social
groups stems from the fact that a person in their parents' occupations is not so easily judged by his individual work or the
particular product of his work. As a result, not only does this
value come to function as an external regulator of the behavior
of these social groups, but it also creates the corresponding
subjective attitude that this deficiency does not actually exist.
Recognition by those in one's immediate social environment is
more important for children of the intelligentsia than for those
of other groups. Such an attitude is to be expected since this
value is of greater importance both in their parents' practical
activity and in their subjective perception of that activity.

---

*Diagram 2 has been omitted. Unfortunately, it appears to
have been incorrectly presented in the original.

Children of scientists rate this criterion highest of all (58.7% of this group as defined paternally and 61.5% as defined maternally rated the value "very important," while 9.8% and 0%, respectively, rated it "unimportant"). Social recognition is important for the scientist because it is precisely this value that serves as his main gauge both within and outside his profession. Children of the technical and non-technical intelligentsia are also more likely than others to use this guideline in choosing a career. The children of medical personnel, however, rate this value clearly lower than do children of other groups in the intelligentsia. This rating, when influenced by the mother, is a consequence of the social composition of this particular group, which is quite similar to social groups not belonging to the intelligentsia. The father's influence in this direction can be explained by the physician's position in our society and in his work (he is surrounded by people who consider him a highly qualified specialist, a man capable of saving a human life: "Doctor"). For this reason, a physician does not experience any deficiency in the respect offered him by other people, and hence no such deficiency is felt within his family.

Diagram 3 shows the extremely high degree of similarity between fathers and mothers in transmitting this value to their children. Female trade workers and the intelligentsia in the humanities are the only groups marked by significant differences in paternal and maternal influence on the assimilation of this value. In the case of trade workers it is the mothers, and among the non-technical intelligentsia it is the fathers, who are more effective in transmitting the value of social esteem. Most mothers from the intelligentsia in the humanities work as teachers, while the fathers are generally active in other professions (lawyers, journalists, etc.). The fathers' occupations are more individual, and a person is judged by the product of his work; this circumstance is most likely to account for their greater influence within the family on their children's assimilation of this value. The mechanism of assimilation is similar to the one at work in the families of female trade workers.

All the differences evident in Diagram 3 demonstrate the influence of social origins, an influence that depends upon how the

Diagram 3

Students' Ratings of "Recognition by People in One's
Immediate Social Environment" as a Value in
Occupational Choice, by Parents' Occupations

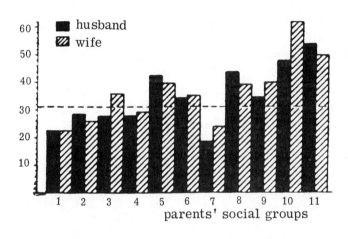

parents' social groups

Note: see note to Diagram 1.

guideline in question is manifested in the parents' occupational
activity. If a given value is insufficiently operative, its importance for the children is greater; if, on the other hand, it is
totally absent, or if the need it represents is adequately fulfilled, its importance tends to be diminished.

8. The fourth of the values falling under the heading of external rewards that we shall study is the attainment of social
prominence through one's occupational activity (Diagram 4).
The attainment of prominent status is occasionally associated
with careerism in the field of politics. The variations due to
social origins are quite considerable (the percentage of students
rating this value "very important" ranged from 0% to 13.6% in
the paternally-defined social groups and from 5% to 11.3% in
the maternally-defined groups; the corresponding figures for a

rating of "moderately important" were 24.7% to 52.7% and 24.8% to 55%; and they ranged from 32.4% to 65% and from 31.6% to 61.2% for "unimportant").

The children of medical personnel stand out conspicuously in their negative appraisal of this value. Not a single child whose father was in this group felt that it was "very important" that he achieve social prominence, and 65% considered that it was "unimportant" in one's profession. Similarly, children whose mothers were medical personnel rated this value lower than did children of similar social origins. Their negative appraisal is apparently due to the rewards that medical personnel receive in society. A physician's professional activity is generally not rewarded by any change in his social status. Professional success does not lead to a change in his position in society (physicians lack the sort of changing status scale that is characteristic of lawyers, for instance; scales of prestige and status are only marginally active in the medical profession). The role of this guideline in the parents' occupation determines how they influence their children and, consequently, the importance of this criterion in the child's own occupational choice.

Diagram 4 clearly reflects the influence of rewards for occupational activity in the various social groups. The children of industrial workers and collective farmers are considerably less inclined to base their occupational choice on this particular value. Their attitude stems from the fact that this type of reward is less frequently operative in their parents' occupations. The sole exception among workers is trade workers, whose influence on their children is contradictory. They have the highest percentage of children rating the attainment of prominent status as "very important" (13.6% of the paternally-defined group and 11.3% of the maternally-defined group); at the same time, however, they also are one of the groups with the highest percentage of negative ratings (56.4% of the paternally-defined group and 48.4% of the maternally-defined group). This phenomenon may be due to the low social prestige of this group, a status that has a contradictory effect on the children. On the one hand, the child experiences a deficiency in this value and, consequently, he internalizes it to a high degree; on the other

Diagram 4

Students' Ratings of "Attainment of Social Prominence"
as a Value in Occupational Choice,
by Parents' Occupations

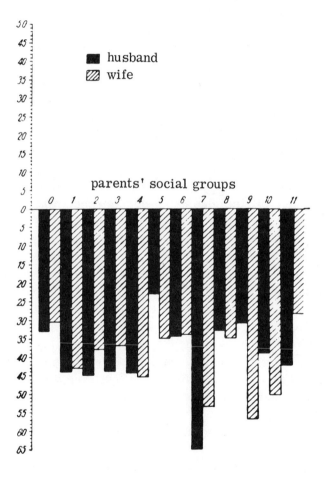

Note: see note to Diagram 1. 0 designates cases in which
parental occupation was not stated.

hand, he might also develop a defensive reaction and reject the value altogether ("I don't care what they think").

In various groups of the intelligentsia (those working in technical fields and in the humanities, plus those in leadership positions), this value serves as an important guideline. Consequently, it is also transmitted to the children from these groups. The children of the technical intelligentsia gave the highest ratings to the idea that a person should be able to attain social prominence through his job (35.6% in this group, paternally defined, and 40%, maternally defined, stated that this value was "very important"). In their parents' occupations, distinctions due to social status are no greater than those that exist among, for instance, the intelligentsia in the humanities or among those in leadership positions. Hence our data suggest that the technical intelligentsia sense the greatest deficiency (whether real or imagined) in the realization of this value, i.e., that status mobility is a problem in their families.

On the whole, social origins do influence a child's assimilation of the value of attaining social prominence. As the preceding analysis demonstrates, the degree to which this value is transmitted to the child depends primarily on the degree to which it is operative in the parent's own occupation.

Diagram 4 shows a regular pattern in the differences between paternal and maternal transmission of this value to the children. In all groups of the intelligentsia, the fathers instill this value in the children more effectively than do the mothers (as we have pointed out, female medical personnel are a heterogeneous group). In fact, of all social groups in the study, mothers from the intelligentsia are least effective in instilling this value (except for male medical personnel), while fathers from the intelligentsia are the most effective of all parents in inculcating it in their children. It is very difficult to account for the contradictions between paternal and maternal influence among the intelligentsia; the problem requires further study. The most likely explanation is that females in these fields perform jobs in which a person's performance is not rewarded by changes in his social status. There are very few women in leadership positions (directors, executives, managers, etc.).

9. The <u>opportunity to lead other people</u> was rated most negatively by our students as a criterion for occupational choice
(see Diagram 5). This value can be interpreted in two ways:
as the aspiration for power (love of power) or as the desire to
engage in a particular type of activity (leadership). These differing interpretations have been equated in the public mind, and
the overall view of this value is a negative one. It is conceiv-
able that opinions regarding this value might reflect some sort
of "residue" of a traditional attitude held by the intelligentsia
with regard to power in bourgeois society, when a part of the
intelligentsia concealed a deficiency in its own power by reject-
ing this value altogether. We believe, for instance, that it is
precisely these "residual" attitudes that account for the extremely negative ratings assigned to the value of leadership
over other people by children of scientists. While this value
was rated "very important" by anywhere from 2.6% to 11.5% of
children of the different social groups, paternally defined,
"moderately important" by 19.5% to 33.4%, and "unimportant"
by 48.6% to 75.2%, the figures for children of scientists were
2.6%, 19.5%, and 75.2% respectively. If the children of scientists were excluded, the range of percentages (of children who
considered the value "very important," "moderately important,"
and "unimportant") would be only half as great. Although the
variations in Diagram 5 are not very great, children of the intelligentsia give appreciably more negative ratings to the possibility of exercising leadership over others as a criterion for
choosing an occupation. Their ratings reflect the commonly
held negative attitude toward ambition and, at the same time,
they are an indication of how this specific attitude has developed into a negative appraisal of leadership activity in general.
Because of the nature of their parents' jobs, children of the intelligentsia do not develop a sense of the importance of leadership as a criterion in their choice of a career. Although in social groups where there is the greatest exercise of leadership
over other people (personnel in leadership positions and the intelligentsia in the humanities): fathers do encourage the assimilation of this criterion (11.4% and 10.3%, respectively, of children
from these two groups rated this value as "very important"),

Diagram 5

Students' Ratings of "Opportunity to Lead Other People"
as a Value in Occupational Choice,
by Parents' Occupations

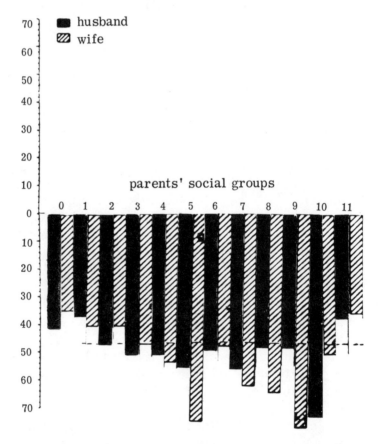

Note: The original diagram shows these ratings as positive
values. We have changed the diagram to correspond to Titma's
discussion in the text — which makes clear that the ratings
should appear as negative values (as in Diagram 4). 0 designates cases in which parental occupation was not stated.

this does not warrant assertions to the contrary. The discrepancy between maternal and paternal influences among the intelligentsia indicates that the practice of providing rewards for professional activity has some effect. The differences expressed in weighted means are as follows: for the technical intelligentsia, -52.8 for children in the group paternally defined versus -75 maternally defined; for the intelligentsia in the humanities, -48.3 versus -64.2; and for medical personnel, -56.2 versus -61.2. The sole exception is the scientists: -72.7 for the paternally-defined group as opposed to -50.0 for the maternally-defined group. This obvious disparity confirms our hypothesis that the roots of such influence must be sought in the actual operation of the system of rewards in a person's own occupation. There are considerably fewer women than men in leadership positions. Consequently, this criterion is less overtly manifest in the mother's occupational activity, and this in turn results in a less thorough transmission of this value to the children.

Characteristic Differences Between Social Groups
in the Transmission of Occupational Values

In order to draw some more specific conclusions from our data, we shall outline the characteristic differences which our analysis revealed in the influences exerted by social groups on the transmission of occupational values. These differences lie in the influence exerted on the child's evaluation of various criteria for choosing a career. Graduating students are a particular sample of Estonian youth, a sample in which none of the extreme manifestations of our second set of occupational values (those dealing with external rewards for one's work), especially not the value of material remuneration, are represented. The influence of social origins on this value was less conspicuous in our data because of the exclusion of youth who had most strongly assimilated this criterion for choosing an occupation. Our respondents did not include any boys or girls who did not value the importance of self-expression in their work, since such children had dropped out of school. Thus, children with values that were less conducive to the acquisition of education were not represented for the most part. This fact, of course, tended to reduce the empirically evident differences in the extent to which social origins influenced the students' assimilation of values. Nevertheless, some differences are evident in the influence of social origins. Here we present some of the most significant of these differences.

For the purposes of our study the collective farm peasantry formed a single class which we did not attempt to subdivide into smaller social groups. Their children gave higher ratings than other students to the value of a person's usefulness to the national economy as a criterion for choosing an occupation. The mothers of this group were more effective in transmitting this value than were the fathers. The children of collective farmers showed greater individual variation in their assimilation of the value of external rewards for one's occupational activity than they did with respect to the first set of values. Material remuneration was less effectively transmitted to these children than to the children of all other social groups (except for scientists). Here, the mother placed less emphasis on transmitting this value. This situation is perfectly natural when one considers the relatively high standard of living of collective farmers.

Recognition from one's immediate environment was less important to children of collective farmers in their choice of occupation. This may be due to the fact that group consciousness in the countryside lacks any sort of scale ranking the prestige of various occupations, since almost everyone belongs to the same social environment and an individual is judged not as a representative of some profession but as an individual. At first glance it seems surprising to note the relatively high rating that children of collective farmers give to the possibility of exercising leadership over other people in their occupations. We believe that this characteristic of such children may be explained by the fact that authoritarian attitudes have been preserved to a greater degree in the countryside than in the city. Hence there is a greater respect for power as such. On the other hand, the rural setting also allows for the direct manifestation of the usefulness of this work (the concrete results of leadership are tangible).

Workers in small enterprises are quite unique in their transmission of values to their children. With respect to the value
of creativity, their influence is contradictory: fathers transmit
this value very effectively (56.4% of their children rate this
value "very important"), and it is often the overriding criterion
in their children's choice of an occupation (20.0% of the children
from this social group felt this to be true). On the other hand,
mothers — female workers in small enterprises — transmit
this value considerably less effectively (40.2% of their children
rate it as "very important," the lowest percentage of children
in any maternally-defined social group). This value functioned
less often as the dominant criterion among the children of workers in small enterprises than among other children (13.3% of
the children from this social group). Their children gave lower
ratings to the use of one's personal abilities than did other students. At the same time, however, these children did feel that
usefulness to the national economy was a basis for selecting an
occupation. In their evaluation of the importance of rewards
for one's occupational activity, the children of this group were
distinctive in two respects: they rated material remuneration
higher than any other group of workers and employees, and they
were most uneasy about their future (they were the only group
in which there was a predominance of students who rated a secure and stable future as "very important"). Their attitudes
may be due to the degree of security of their parents and the
material remuneration that their parents receive for their
work. However, they might also reflect certain petty bourgeois
attitudes held by this particular group.

Workers in large-scale industry were least effective of all
in transmitting creativity to their children as an occupational
value. Compared with other groups of workers, they placed
less emphasis on transmitting usefulness to the national economy as one of the bases for choosing an occupation.

Their children were more concerned about their futures than
other students, and this criterion entered into their choice of
an occupation. The children of workers in large-scale industry
gave very negative ratings to leadership over other people and

attainment of prominent status as occupational values (their ratings of "prominent position" were second lowest, after those of
medical workers' children; and with respect to "leadership over
other people," their ratings were the most negative given by all
the children of workers, office employees, and peasants).

Trade workers were distinguished from other workers by the
unique way in which they influenced their children's assimilation of occupational values. The most important guideline in
their children's choice of occupation was self-fulfillment (this
was the dominant value for 39.3% of the children in this group,
paternally defined, and for 43.6%, maternally defined). Their
children also gave considerably higher ratings to the use of
their personal abilities in their work; the father's influence was
especially strong in transmitting this value (22.6% of the students)*. They also gave the second highest ratings to one's
usefulness to the national economy as a basis for selecting an
occupation. Mothers were instrumental in the greater assimilation of this value.

Mothers were more effective than fathers in transmitting
values involving rewards for one's occupational activity. The
greatest discrepancy occurs in the transmission of the value
of recognition by one's immediate environment. Of all workers' children, the children of trade workers were least concerned about their future and their attitudes toward a career
were least affected by the evaluations of other people.

Office employees constitute a transitional group between the
workers and the intelligentsia. The members of this group are
not particularly distinctive in their influence on their children,
showing results very close to the mean rating for all the groups.
The differences between paternal and maternal influence are
also minimal. This suggests that the isolation of office employees as a separate group may be spurious.

With respect to their influence on their children's assimilation of creativity as a value, the technical intelligentsia more
closely resemble workers in large-scale industry than the other

---

*Here Titma presumably refers to the proportion for whom
this value was the dominant one in occupational choice.

groups of intelligentsia. The children of this group give lower ratings to the value of self-expression in one's occupation than all other children of the intelligentsia, and only 2.6% of the students from this group (paternally defined) felt that a person's usefulness to the national economy should be the main criterion in his choice of an occupation.

Students whose parents are members of the technical intelligentsia clearly place more emphasis than other children on external rewards for one's occupational activity. The value of material remuneration is most effectively transmitted to them, and students from this group rate it most highly. They constitute the group that is most interested in securing a stable future through its choice of career, and they are quite concerned about how their friends and acquaintances will judge the occupation they choose. To a greater extent than other students, they try to select an occupation that will permit them to attain a prominent position in society. On the whole, this group effectively transmits the values of external rewards. Children from this group have about the same ideas regarding the value of self-expression as the children of workers and office employees.

As we have noted earlier, medical personnel are a heterogeneous social group (though this is less true of the fathers). That is why we have made a more detailed analysis of the men in this group. Their children gave higher ratings than any others to the value of being able to use personal abilities in one's future occupation (87.5% rated this criterion as "very important"). On the other hand, they were more negative than others in their desire to be useful to the national economy. Students from this social group held material remuneration in high regard, and they were more concerned about their future than any other students from the intelligentsia (they stood second in this regard among all the groups of students). The opinion of their friends and acquaintances was of only minor importance in their choice of a career. Their attitude toward using their occupation to gain social prominence was distinctly negative (65% felt it to be "unimportant," and not a single student considered it "very important"). They also gave highly negative ratings to the value of exercising leadership over other people.

These attitudes are certainly to be expected, since neither of
these values is operative in the professional activity of the
physician.

The intelligentsia in the humanities was the largest group
(of intelligentsia) included in our study. Consequently, the
curve representing their influence on the transmission of
values may be considered representative.   Children from
this group of intelligentsia rated creativity higher than any other
students in the study: 28% of them (in both the maternally-
defined and paternally-defined groups) considered this to be the
most important of the values listed (only 14.8% of all the students felt the same way). The mothers of this group were less
effective than any other parents (except for fathers who were
medical personnel) in instilling in their children the value of
"usefulness to the national economy" as an occupational value.
Only 1% of their children considered this the most important
criterion (as opposed to 9.3% for the students as a whole). In
other words, children of the non-technical intelligentsia are
least inclined to assimilate this value.

But these children place great emphasis on material remuneration for one's work. Similarly, they are considerably more
concerned than the average student about how their future occupation will be regarded by other people close to them. The
father is considerably more effective in transmitting this value
than the mother. Social opinion (attainment of prominent status)
is also more important for them than for the other students
(except for children of the technical intelligentsia).

There are some very distinct differences in paternal and
maternal influence among the intelligentsia in the humanities.
This is the case particularly in the transmission of the values
relating to rewards for one's work ("leadership over other people," "the opinion of friends and acquaintances," and "security
of a stable future").

Personnel in leadership positions in soviets, trade unions,
and other organs have more thoroughly instilled in their children the value of "usefulness to the national economy" as a criterion in choosing an occupation than have other groups of intelligentsia. One should also note the low ratings given by their

children to material remuneration and security of a stable future. There are considerable differences between maternal and paternal influence, but this group is too small to warrant any precise conclusions. The data for this group seem to follow what is a general pattern for the entire intelligentsia, namely, that the mother is less effective in transmitting the value of rewards for one's occupational activity.

Scientists constituted a rather distinct social group in our study. As might be expected, they quite effectively transmitted the significance of individual self-expression to their children (68% of the children in this group, paternally defined, and 78.6%, maternally defined, rated creativity as "very important"; the corresponding figures for self-fulfillment were 78.8% and 92.8%; the percentages for the use of one's personal abilities were 80.6% and 92.3%). Of the students whose fathers belonged to this group, 33.3% felt that use of one's personal abilities was the most important criterion to be considered in selecting an occupation. Not a single one of these students ranked usefulness to the national economy as the main factor to consider, and this criterion was in general rated extremely low in this group.

Rewards for one's occupational activity were not as important in the eyes of scientists' children as they were for other students. The sole value in this group that had been assimilated by the children as a criterion for occupational selection was recognition by people in one's immediate social environment (rated "very important" by 58.7% of this group, paternally defined, and 61.5%, maternally defined; the corresponding percentages for those rating the value as "unimportant" were 9.8% and 0%). And it is not surprising to note that they rated material remuneration and security for the future quite low. Their ratings of the value of exercising leadership over other people were sharply negative.

Although the values relating to individual self-expression are quite effectively disseminated by other social institutions, social origins undoubtedly influence the students' assimilation of these values. This influence is even more substantial with respect to other occupational values, and it is essential for a sociological analysis of the reproduction of social structure that society be broken down into smaller groups. Of the groups we have distinguished for the present study, the following stand out clearly in their influence on children: the technical and non-technical intelligentsia, scientists, Party workers, trade workers, and workers in small enterprises. The other groups are too large and must be further subdivided, since it is apparent from our study that they do not reflect the actual social composition of our society. Medical personnel, for instance, might be further broken down into special groups depending on their educational level.

It seems evident that the intelligentsia exercise a significantly greater influence on the transmission of occupational values to their children. This influence is of an individual nature, and it is particularly conspicuous with respect to the second set of values, an area where official social policy conducted through formal channels is negatively oriented or is absent altogether. Moreover, the children of the intelligentsia are less susceptible to the influence of formal channels (schools, mass media, etc.). While the differences between classes are negligible, those between individual social groups are quite substantial — something that is also reflected in the heterogeneity of the social composition of families. Further study is called for to map out the unique features of the various groups in the population.

Notes

1) For the techniques and methods used in our empirical investigation, see M. Kh. Titma, "Techniques for Conducting an Empirical Sociological Study of the Problem of Occupational Selection," in Sbornik nauchnykh trudov Estonskoi sel'skokhoziaistvennoi akademii, Trudy po filosofii, 2, (54), Tartu, 1967.

2) See the analysis of this environment in V. I. Selivanov, "Primary Rural Collectives and Their Influence in Shaping the Personality," in Sotsiologiia v SSSR, Vol. 1, Moscow, 1965, pp. 458-470. [A substantial portion of Sotsiologiia v SSSR has been translated in the journal Soviet Sociology.]

3) G. V. Osipov, "Technological Progress and Change in the Occupational Structure of the Working Class," in Sotsiologiia v SSSR, Vol. 2, Moscow, 1965, pp. 10-27; F. G. Krotov, L. V. Fokin, and O. I. Shkaratan, Rabochii klass — vedushchaia sila stroitel'stva kommunizma, Moscow, 1965; Shkaratan, "The Social Structure of the Working Class," Voprosy filosofii, 1967, No. 1, pp. 28-39; M. T. Iovchuk, "The Social Significance of the Rise in the Cultural and Technological Level of the Workers," in Sotsiologiia v SSSR, Vol. 2, pp. 28-56; L. N. Kogan, "The Problem of Eliminating Occupational Limitations on the Worker," ibid., pp. 57-75; R. A. Kleshcheva, "Changes in the Occupational Attitudes of Soviet Workers," Voprosy filosofii, 1964, No. 7; Rabochii klass i tekhnicheskii progress, Moscow, 1965; Pod'em kul'turno-tekhnicheskogo urovnia sovetskogo rabochego klassa, Moscow, 1961.

4) See C. Wright Mills, White Collar, New York, 1951.

5) See M. N. Rutkevich, "Changes in the Social Structure of Soviet Society and the Intelligentsia," in Sotsiologiia v SSSR, Vol. 2, pp. 393-415; V. S. Semenov, "The Changes Undergone by the Intelligentsia and Office Employees in the Full-Scale Development of Communism," ibid., pp. 416-432; M. N. Rutkevich, "The Concept of the Intelligentsia as a Social Stratum in Socialist Society," Voprosy filosofii, 1966, No. 4, pp. 20-29; M. N. Rutkevich, "Social Sources of Recruitment of the Soviet Intelligentsia," Voprosy filosofii, 1967, No. 5, pp. 15-23; M. N. Rutkevich, "The Obliteration of Class Differences and the Place of the Intelligentsia in the Social Structure of Soviet Society," Filosofskie nauki, 1963, No. 5.

6) For more detail on these values, see M. Kh. Titma, "Values Influencing Occupational Choice," Voprosy filosofii, 1969, No. 9, pp. 52-61.

7) By using graphs rather than tables to present our data, we can more clearly show the influence exercised by social groups on the transmission of values to the rising generation in society.

Two of the groups of mothers included in the graphs (those who were scientists and those who served in leadership positions) were very small — only 14 members each; hence these groups can be considered representative only in certain cases. The following categories were set up for the parents' occupations:

0 — parental occupation not stated;

1 — agricultural personnel;

2 — workers in enterprises with up to 50 workers;

3 — workers in trade and public catering;

4 — workers in enterprises with more than 50 workers;

5 — technical intelligentsia (engineers);

6 — office employees in enterprises and institutions;

7 — medical personnel;

8 — intelligentsia in the humanities (teachers, journalists, etc.);

9 — leaders in trade unions, soviets, and other organizations;

10 — scientific workers;

11 — occupations not in above categories.

8) In analyzing our data, we must keep in mind that the graduating students in secondary schools constitute a sample of all the children from any given social group. A considerable proportion of young people do not go to secondary school.

9) This is the state of affairs at present, though by no means in all branches of industry. Our conclusion does characterize these occupations as a whole. See Chelovek i ego rabota, Moscow, 1967, pp. 202-234, 288-306 [published in English by International Arts and Sciences Press, 1970].

10) From here on we shall not go into such detail; we shall merely refer to the appropriate graph or table.

III.   SOCIAL MOBILITY IN THE USSR

12 Principles of the Marxist Approach to Social Structure and Social Mobility

M. N. RUTKEVICH AND F. R. FILIPPOV

There is no doubt that only Marxist dialectics and the materialist conception of history can provide a genuinely scientific basis for understanding the social structure of any society and all the processes of its change, including social mobility* (as noted above, we are using the concept of social structure in its narrow sense, as social-class structure). On these questions materialist dialectics and the Marxist theory of classes stand in opposition to structuralism as a trend in current bourgeois philosophical thought, and to the theory of social stratification in sociology referred to above. The essential differences between Marxism and these conceptions can be formulated as follows.

First, Marxist sociology, in full conformity with dialectics, requires that we examine any society not abstractly, unhistorically,

From M. N. Rutkevich and F. R. Filippov, Sotsial'nye peremeshcheniia, "Mysl'" Publishing House, Moscow, 1970, pp. 33-47.

*Rutkevich and Filippov use the term sotsial'nye peremeshcheniia ("social shifts from position to position") to refer to cases in which the unit of mobility is individuals, and they argue that the term "social mobility" should be restricted to cases in which the unit of mobility is the whole society. Since the former type of mobility is conventionally referred to as "social mobility" in Western and much of Soviet sociological literature, we have translated sotsial'nye peremeshcheniia as "social mobility" in order to avoid unnecessary confusion.

but as a historically evolved, qualitatively definite type of society. Lenin emphasized that "social organisms are just as profoundly different from one another as animal organisms are from plants." (1) This does not mean, of course, that there are no general laws of history. Marxist dialectics proceeds from the unity of the general and the particular. Just as biology reveals certain general laws of life, sociology must discover general laws of social development operating at all stages of historical progress among all the people of the earth. But the social structure of every social order is distinct from the preceding and following ones, and thus its specific features must be revealed. Therefore, the attempts of the adherents of "social stratification" to divide every society into the same layers ("strata") independently of the prevailing socio-economic order cannot be regarded as scientific. With respect to the modern epoch this means that the social-class structures of capitalist and socialist societies are fundamentally different, and thus all arguments concerning their "increasing similarity," "convergence," and the like, must be rejected. The processes of social mobility under capitalism and socialism must be examined with due regard for the fundamental differences in the social structure of the two social systems, one of which embodies the past while the other embodies the future of mankind.

Second, in analyzing social structure, scientific sociology bases itself on the materialist conception of social life. Lenin wrote that a basic idea of Marx and Engels "was that social relations are divided into material and ideological relations. The latter represent only a superstructure relative to the former, which are formed apart from the will and consciousness of human beings...." (2) Therefore, in studying the division of society into social groups, the foundation of this division must be sought in differences in their economic position. The Marxist theory of classes is based on the materialist conception of the development of society as an objective or, in Marx's expression, natural-historical process.

In contrast to this, the prevailing notion in current bourgeois sociology is that the position of individuals is determined by a "status hierarchy," and that this depends on the "scale of values"

in the given society. (3) Viewing these "values," particularly
prestige, as criteria of "social status," bourgeois sociologists
derive the social division of society from manifestations of
consciousness, public opinion, etc.

Along with the concept of status there is introduced the concept of social roles, which are varied and in their totality determine the position of the individual in society. The "social
role" of the individual is essentially his function in society,
and in this respect, therefore, the argument contains an element of truth. But, in the first place, bourgeois sociologists
treat "social role" subjectively, divorcing it from objective social position and the functions associated with it, and second,
in studying the multiplicity of "roles," the principal role (function) is either not distinguished at all or is distinguished arbi-
trarily. This reflects the eclecticism and subjectivism of "role
theory." In reality, among the variety of functions (roles) there
exists a basic one, determined by the objective position of the
individual (and the groups of which he is a member) in the system of economic relations. Marxist sociology views the social
structure, first and foremost, as a structure of objective economic relations in society. The main differences in position in
the system of economic relations are essentially differences
between social classes, and class composition and class relations determine the principal features of the social structure
of society, and thus the functions of groups and the individuals
in them, as well as the totality of "roles" belonging to them.

Third, in elucidating the social structure, Marxism and
bourgeois sociology also have a different approach to economic
characteristics. This is particularly important to consider,
since along with such features of social division as prestige,
power, and education, the works of bourgeois sociologists and
economists assign a role to such objective economic features
as income level and occupation. The eclecticism inherent in
bourgeois sociology is manifest in the fact that all these features (and frequently many others — for example, religion,
ethnic background, etc.) are examined in "parallel," without
elucidating their internal connection. If the interconnection between any two factors is examined, for example, income and

education, it is done in purely empirical terms.

However, despite methodological defects, the analyses by bourgeois researchers of the distribution of the employed population according to income levels, or of the relationship between parents' occupations and the educational level of children, etc., have some cognitive value and, with the appropriate critical approach, can be utilized by Marxists.

Only the Marxist theory of classes can provide a genuine foundation for empirical investigation of social structure and social mobility. The economic features pointed to by adherents of "social stratification," such as income level and type of employment (occupation), must be placed within the framework of the system of social production. Thus, when heads of families with annual incomes of $5,000 to $10,000 in the USA are combined within a single "stratum," the source of income remains concealed. However, this amount of annual income can be received either in the form of wages by hired workers or as the income of a small merchant or farmer. Similarly, when American statistics (and the sociologists and economists who use them) include all individuals employed in mental work in the category of "white-collar workers," the difference between the low-level employees of firms and their managers is obliterated. It is enough to glance at any statistical handbook published in the USA to become convinced that it includes "managers" and "proprietors" among "white-collar workers," along with "sales workers." (4)

As an example we may cite the book by G. Kolko, Wealth and Power in America. Promising the reader to reveal "the outlines of the actual American class structure that emerge from the inequalities of income, wealth, and economic power," Kolko states that in characterizing "class" one must also consider cultural, racial, and other factors. In many studies, he asserts, the latter "overshadow" the economic basis of class, which is usually ignored. This is "a distortion I shall endeavor to correct," he writes. (5) But when Kolko moves on to concrete analysis of the "economic features" of what he calls a "class," he concentrates his attention chiefly on the amount of income, not on its source and the form in which it is received. The income intervals presented are so wide that the same "class" includes both the employer and the skilled worker hired by this employer. In depicting the economic basis of "class," everything is thrown in: possession of a Cadillac, an account at a restaurant, membership dues in a club, etc. Despite the superficially scientific nature of his terminology and his attention to economics, Kolko's "classes" are essentially the familiar "strata." At the same time, his book contains considerable material that can be used to illustrate genuine class inequality in contemporary American society.

Therefore, the use of objective economic characteristics as criteria of social divisions is, in itself, not sufficient. When Marxist sociology elucidates social structure, it proceeds from the proposition that material production is the essence of economic activity, and that the objective differences between groups of people in the system of production relations are embodied in the existence of classes.

As we know, the fullest definition of classes, and the one generally accepted in current Marxist literature, was formulated by Lenin in 1919. "Classes are large groups of people which differ from each other by the place they occupy in a historically determined system of social production, by their relation (in most cases fixed and formulated in law) to the means of production, by their role in the social organization of labor, and, consequently, by the dimensions and method of acquiring the share of social wealth of which they dispose. Classes are groups of people, one of which can appropriate the labor of another owing to the different places they occupy in a definite system of social economy." (6)

The first part of this statement gives a brief definition of classes, pointing to the fact that each socio-economic order has its own specific social-class structure, and that the division into classes is determined by the position of classes in this structure. The definition is then made more precise by pointing to three inseparably linked characteristics of class differences, corresponding to three basic elements in production relations: relation to means of production, role in the social organization of labor, position in the system of distribution of material goods.

(We shall return to these characteristics as they apply to a socialist society.) Finally, the concluding part of the definition sums up: the fact that classes occupy different places in the system of social production makes it possible to appropriate the labor of others.

The Specific Character of Social
Mobility Under Socialism

The Leninist definition of classes applies to all socio-economic formations and their stages to the extent that they are characterized by a division into classes. It provides a key to understanding not only the division into classes but also the social structure as a whole, which includes not only classes but also nonclass social groups and the strata included in these classes and groups, insofar as they are social in nature and differ from one another by their relation to the means of production, their place in the social division of labor, and their position in the sphere of distribution. The general definition of classes also applies to a socialist society to the extent that it remains a class society, although one without exploitation and class antagonisms.

What are the common features and specific character of social mobility in a socialist society as compared to a capitalist society? The common features are conditioned by the fact that capitalism and socialism coexist in our epoch and are at approximately the same level of development of productive forces, and thus cannot help but have common features. However, despite the approximately equal level of development of their productive forces, these two social formations are fundamentally different as regards the nature of their economic and, therefore, all other social relations. From this there also follow fundamental differences in the nature and results of the process of social mobility.

Social mobility under capitalism is also distinctive as compared to precapitalist class societies, with their system of "noneconomic compulsion" (Marx), their divisions into castes and estates. Social mobility under capitalism is not restrained by such clearly expressed political and legal barriers; it depends mainly on property barriers. The classics of Marxism-Leninism noted this repeatedly. Lenin wrote: "The essence of class society (and, consequently, of class education) consists in full juridical equality, full equality of rights for all citizens, full equality of rights and access to education for the propertied.... In contrast to estates, classes always leave perfectly free the transfer of particular individuals from one class to another." (7) This freedom is formal, not real.

In a socialist society, as a result of fundamental changes in the social-class structure, most of the real barriers to social mobility disappear, the character and social consequences of mobility change qualitatively, and, finally, the nature of the stimuli which impel people to change their social position also changes. For the first time in history this mobility becomes one of the forms of the gradual elimination of social differences.

But certain common features, conditioned by the level of material production, create a number of similar tendencies in social mobility under socialism and capitalism. This applies to urbanization processes and the associated migration of the rural population, the increase in the number and proportion of individuals engaged in mental work and skilled workers in the employed population, and so on. Demographic processes also exercise a similar influence on social mobility: the decline in birth rates associated with the growth of the urban population and the employment of women in production; the increase in the average length of life and the change in the rate of "rotation" associated with this, i.e., the renewal of employed personnel in different fields of activity. Social mobility of youth under both capitalism and socialism is affected by the inevitable lengthening of the training period for work associated with scientific-technical progress. The theories of "convergence of capitalism and socialism," of a "common industrial society," and the like, which are widely accepted in bourgeois sociology, speculate precisely on these common features, studiously avoiding and ignoring the fundamental differences between capitalism and socialism, including differences in the processes of social mobility.

The boundaries of similarity between phenomena must always be clearly defined, and the essential nature of differences within these boundaries must be distinguished. There are a number of problems of this kind which are part of our theme and which require a particularly careful and specific approach. We refer, above all, to the question of the applicability to a developed socialist society, where the class hierarchy has been eliminated, of the concept of vertical mobility, i.e., social movement along vertical lines.

In our view, it is appropriate to speak of vertical gradations in the social structure of a socialist society to the extent that inequality in the degree of complexity of labor continues to prevail. This inequality is expressed in the fact that more complex labor requires higher levels of qualification and education of the individual, and is therefore more highly remunerated by society in accordance with the principles of socialism. Hence, advancement of a worker to more complex labor as a result of an increase in his educational level, higher skills, the accumulation of experience, etc., can be regarded as "vertical" mobility, i.e., as social advancement. It is in this sense that we sometimes speak of a personal "career."

Such mobility occurs primarily from one social stratum to another within a given class, for example, when an unskilled worker becomes a skilled worker, when a technician becomes an engineer, and so on. However, insofar as the labor of specialists as a whole is more skilled, and is generally remunerated at somewhat higher levels in all branches, advancement to this stratum can be regarded in a certain sense as upward vertical mobility. That is how the matter is regarded by public opinion. And that is how public opinion regards advancement to the executive staff of an enterprise or institution, which requires not only the retention of existing qualifications but also additional knowledge and effort. When an employed person advances (fully or partially) to the performance of organizational functions, his labor becomes more complex as a rule.

But this kind of mobility in our society is of a qualitatively different nature than the transformation of a small proprietor into a large one, or entry into the privileged classes and strata,

under capitalism. The attempts of some reactionary bourgeois
sociologists to "prove" the existence of a social hierarchy in
the USSR in the old sense of the word, their arguments concerning a "Soviet elite," etc., have nothing in common with Soviet
reality. Such fabrications are slanderous in nature and are
widely used by imperialist propaganda in the ideological struggle against socialist countries.

As an example, one can present some of the arguments of
S. Lipset. He states that the "phenomenon" of collective mobility has "not been studied at all by social scientists," and that
rapid changes in the position of skilled workers, for example,
may be connected with "rapid industrialization" in the so-called
developing countries (regardless of their social structure). "It
is possible that this is occurring in the Soviet Union, in other
communist countries, and in various developing countries in
other parts of the world. Social revolution, by downgrading certain classes, may improve the position of certain others and
may expand the opportunities open to them. Some communist
countries are deliberately moving to give workers and peasants,
as well as their children, greater opportunities for education
and for achieving improved positions." (8) Having thus paid his
respects to objectivity, Lipset then argues that in the Soviet
Union the opportunities for obtaining an education and the
chances of occupying "high positions" will steadily decline for
children of "simple origins" compared to those for the "elite."

It obviously never occurs to a bourgeois sociologist that the
"elite," "simple origins," and similar concepts, which are extensively used in reference to an exploitative social order, are
completely inapplicable to a socialist society.

These arguments of Lipset contain another thesis that is
readily utilized at the present time not only by bourgeois propagandists of anticommunism, but is also widely applied by
right and "left" revisionists in their anti-Soviet propaganda.
We refer to the thesis that "initially," immediately after the
revolution, large-scale social mobility occurred in Soviet society, but that "subsequently" social stability began to prevail
and that our socialist society increasingly came to "resemble"
a capitalist one, and that this similarity will increase with the

passage of time.

Contemporary socialist society differs markedly from what it was during the period of the struggle for the building of socialism, and qualitatively new features have also appeared in the processes of social mobility. But one can counterpose these two stages in the development of Soviet society against each other only by completely ignoring actual facts.

Another slanderous approach is the attempt of some anti-communists to "demonstrate" that the existence of classes under socialism allegedly "contradicts" Marxism-Leninism. Thus, with feigned amazement, L. Labedz "finds" social-class differences and social mobility in Soviet society: "Doctrinal principles," he announces, "do not correspond to the current social situation," since Marx and Engels presumably did "not foresee" that the problem of social mobility would exist in a socialist ("classless") society. (9) Labedz makes believe that he does not know that Marx, Engels and Lenin regarded a socialist society as only the first phase of a communist social order, and that in this phase certain kinds of inequality are inevitably retained. One of these is the existence of social-class differences, with which social mobility is associated under socialism. The existence of such mobility in Soviet society not only does not contradict the theory of scientific communism but, on the contrary, confirms the well-known Marxist proposition concerning the gradual character of the transition from the first phase of communist society to the second.

The absence of a class hierarchy in Soviet society has led some sociologists in the USSR and in other socialist countries to take the position that social mobility under such conditions has been completely supplanted by occupational mobility. We cannot agree unreservedly, for example, with the following treatment of horizontal and vertical mobility: "By horizontal mobility we mean the progress of a worker within his specialty, and by vertical mobility — the mastery of other specialties and occupations, the transition from manual labor to mental labor, from executor-type labor to creative labor." (10) Social mobility may not be connected with either "the progress of a worker within his specialty" or with "the mastery of other specialties and occupations." Thus, the movement of a machine-operator from a state farm to a collective farm and back again is necessarily associated with a change in social position (class position, in this case), but it is not at all connected with a change in occupation. On the other hand, a change in occupation or an increase in skills does not always involve a change in social position. There is no doubt that occupational mobility is comparatively easier to observe and measure, but beyond this we must be able to see the more profound and complex processes of social mobility, although they are sometimes more difficult to distinguish.

In measuring social mobility we can calculate the "inflow" into, and the "outflow" from, a particular social stratum. These measurements are quite feasible and can rely on mathematical methods, with which we can derive indices of the mobility of individuals comprising a given social stratum and discover the objective tendencies of this process.

In investigating and measuring social mobility in Soviet society, the differences between the processes of intergenerational mobility (here the investigation may embrace two and even more generations) and intragenerational mobility are clearly evident. In the case of the former, study of those changes which have occurred in the social position of children (and grandchildren) compared to the social position of their parents (and grandparents) not only permits us to observe social changes in society as a whole, but also to follow the reflection of these changes in the fate of each succeeding generation. In the latter case, the investigators obtain a picture of changes in the fates of individuals within the span of a single generation, or more precisely, during its period of work activity.

The study of intergenerational mobility presents greater difficulties than that of intragenerational mobility. The problem here is not only that it is more difficult to obtain data on preceding generations. There is the important methodological difficulty of determining the social origin of individuals in each succeeding generation. The greater the extent to which class and other social barriers have disappeared and been destroyed in the process of building the socialist society, the more frequently we find socially heterogeneous marriages. Therefore, determination of the social origins of children born of such marriages can only be conditional in nature (for example, according to the social position of the father), or of a dual character (with the social position of both parents being considered).

These are some of the methodological questions associated with social mobility under socialism. We have not undertaken a full survey of these questions, especially since many of them require clarification on the basis of empirical material, which is presented below in Chapters 3 to 6.*

Notes

1) V. I. Lenin, Poln. sobr. soch., Vol. 1, p. 167.

2) Ibid., p. 149.

3) A. Inkeles, What Is Sociology?, Englewood Cliffs, N. J., Prentice-Hall, 1966, p. 86.

4) Statistical Abstract of the United States, Washington, 1968, p. 225.

5) G. Kolko, Wealth and Power in America, New York, 1966, p. 6.

6) Lenin, op. cit., Vol. 39, p. 115.

7) Ibid., Vol. 2, pp. 476-477.

8) S. M. Lipset, "Problèmes posés par les recherches comparatives sur la mobilité et la développement," Revue internationale des science sociales. Les données dans la recherche comparative, UNESCO, 1964, Vol. XVI, No. 1, p. 41 [retranslated from the Russian — Eds.].

9) L. Labedz, "Structure de l'intelligentsia soviétique," La Revue Socialiste, 1962, No. 152, pp. 367, 381.

10) Rabochii klass i tekhnicheskii progress, Moscow, 1965, p. 289.

---

*Most of Chapter 4 is translated next.

13 Social Sources of Recruitment of the Intelligentsia

M. N. RUTKEVICH AND F. R. FILIPPOV

The general nature of the process of social mobility into the specialists' category, as one of the principal flows of movement from manual to mental labor, was presented above. Here we shall examine this process in greater detail, focusing on analysis of the social sources of recruitment of the intelligentsia.

Under present conditions (in contrast to the 1920s and 1930s) specialists are recruited mainly from among individuals completing secondary specialized schools and higher educational institutions either as full-time or part-time students. Advancement into this group without the corresponding education continues primarily in agriculture. In other branches the positions of technician-organizers, primary school teachers, as well as teachers of certain subjects in the 5th to 8th grades are sometimes filled by individuals without the corresponding specialized education, but they always have a 9th-10th grade general education and this makes it easier for them to acquire the necessary specialized knowledge and receive their diplomas after a certain period of time.

Thus, the principal feature of the recruitment of the intelligentsia under present conditions is that the great majority pass through the system of higher and secondary specialized educational institutions. This provides important advantages for

From M. N. Rutkevich and F. R. Filippov, Sotsial'nye peremeshcheniia, "Mysl'" Publishing House, Moscow, 1970, pp. 125-159.

sociological analysis insofar as indices of education (which, in themselves, do not signify a transfer into another social stratum!) can be used to appraise the extent of changes in the nature of labor and social mobility. In addition, students of technicums and higher schools are surveyed "automatically," so to speak, when they provide personal data at the time of their admission, although not in as great detail as is required for sociological analysis. Finally, they also represent a highly appropriate subject for supplementary investigation.

A second feature is connected with the first. A system of socially controlled competitive selections [konkursy] associated with transfers from one social group or stratum to another is characteristic of "vertical" mobility in a socialist society. True, this system by no means encompasses all transfers into and within the intelligentsia. Competitive selection in admissions to higher educational institutions and technicums is the principal link of the system. This procedure does not prevail at all times and all places: admission to many higher schools and technicums (particularly in correspondence and evening divisions) frequently does not require competitive examinations (a grade of "three" on examinations may be enough). The competitive selection system does operate with respect to faculties of higher schools, personnel of scientific institutions, and institutions of the arts. But under conditions of rapid development of science, the fact is that the competitive selection system in higher educational institutions and scientific research institutes, its operation in recruiting the scientific intelligentsia, does not always work well at the present time. However, what is important is that it exists and that in the future it will apparently play an increasing role as a special kind of screening "sieve."

The social composition of full-time students at higher schools is extremely important in understanding the process of recruitment of the intelligentsia, for it is precisely higher education which opens up the greatest prospects for further social advancement, including advancement to leading posts.

Social Composition of the Student Body

In prerevolutionary Russia the composition of the student body clearly illustrated the common situation of bourgeois countries, in which higher education was not so much an "elevator" for rising from lower to higher strata as a well-guarded barrier to the "social ascent" of youth from the working classes. In the 1914/1915 academic year the social composition of students in the principal technical higher schools of Russia was as follows: children of nobles and officials — 24.5%; children of "honored citizens" and merchants — 14%; children of clergy — 28%; children of petty bourgeois families — 31.6%; children of peasants (primarily kulaks) — 22%; children of other social strata — 3.6%. (1)

After the October Revolution the Soviet government took a number of measures designed to prepare worker and peasant youth for admission to higher educational institutions (including the creation of the workers' faculties [rabfak]), and these measures led to rapid changes in the social composition of the student body. The same purpose was served by rules governing admission to higher schools that granted preferential treatment to workers, working peasants, and their children. The liquidation of exploiting classes and the triumph of socialism in the USSR made it possible to remove restrictions on admission to higher schools for reasons of social origins and social position.

The equality of applicants, regardless of their social origins or social position, is the basic principle of recruitment to the Soviet higher school. But in order to ensure a better quality of enrollment, in certain periods and for various types of training there have been (and still are) certain privileges for various categories of secondary school graduates. Thus, in enrolling students for evening and correspondence divisions, preferential treatment is given to individuals who have work experience in the chosen or closely related specialty and are entering higher schools to raise their qualifications. In accepting people for full-time study after the war, preferential treatment was given to demobilized veterans, and for a number of years after the

educational reform of 1958, preferential treatment was given
to individuals who had two or more years of work experience.
These privileges have now been largely eliminated.

The entire Soviet student body (aside from individual cases,
such as children of priests, etc.) consists of working people and
their children. But the social composition of students still differs significantly from the structure of the population, and
therefore in the recruitment of the intelligentsia through this
channel the role of different social groups does not correspond
to the proportion of these groups in the population. Our calculations (2) yield the following approximate figures for the social composition of the country's employed population and its
change in recent years:

Table 1

Social Composition of USSR Population Employed
in Social Production, Average Annual Figures
(in %)

Social groups	1960	1966
Workers	51.9	56.4
Employees (nonspecialists)	12.5	12.6
Specialists (with diplomas)	10.0	12.6
Collective farmers	25.6	18.3
Total	100	100

As we noted earlier, the social structure of the population of
the Urals differs somewhat from that of the country as a whole:
63% of the employed population of the Sverdlovsk Region are
workers and 35% are employees and specialists, while only 2%
are collective farm peasants. (3) Naturally, the social composition of the student body in Sverdlovsk higher schools, taken in
dynamic terms, should be compared with that of the population
of Sverdlovsk Region and of adjoining regions of the Urals,
which gravitates to Sverdlovsk as a large center of higher educational institutions — third in size in terms of number of

students in the RSFSR (after Moscow and Leningrad).

General tendencies of change in the social structure of Soviet society — a rise in the percentage of workers and particularly of specialists in the country's population and a decline in the proportion of collective farm peasantry — are reflected in changes in the social composition of the student body.

The second major objective factor affecting the process under investigation here is the extremely rapid rise in the cultural and technical level of workers, collective farmers, and employees. In 1939, 15.9 million persons had a higher or secondary education (complete or incomplete), while in 1959 the figure was 58.7 million, and at the beginning of 1967 it was 84.5 million, or 80.5% of the entire working population of the country. (4)

The rise in the educational level of broad masses of working people has its greatest impact on youth. The achievement of eight-year education and the transition to universal secondary education means that the level of preparation of boys and girls from different social groups is rapidly becoming similar and there is a steady process of equalization in actual opportunities for passing the competitive examinations and enrolling in higher schools and technicums.

Both of these factors are objective and long-run in nature, but another factor is superimposed on them — changes in the rules governing admission to higher schools. This is a subjective factor in the sense that society consciously utilizes it as a means of regulating the social composition of student youth.

Changes in the social composition of the student body appear in official statistical data, which combine workers and their children, collective farmers and their children, and employees and their children. The category of children of workers, employees, and collective farmers includes only those who were students immediately prior to their admission to higher schools and did not have their "own" social position. Table 2 presents data for all higher educational institutions in the city and region of Sverdlovsk. Included in the region are the Nizhnii Tagil Pedagogical Institute and a number of branches and educational-consultation centers of Moscow and Sverdlovsk higher schools. (5)

Table 2

Social Composition of Full-Time Students at
Higher Educational Institutions of Sverdlovsk Region
(in %)

Social categories	1961	1962	1963	1964	1965	1966	1967	1968	1969
Workers or workers' children	50.0	52.0	52.5	53.0	50.0	48.6	45.3	44.6	45.3
Peasants or peasants' children	5.3	5.3	6.6	6.6	5.1	5.3	5.0	4.9	4.0
Employees or employees' children	44.7	42.7	40.9	40.4	44.9	46.1	49.7	50.5	50.7
Total	100	100	100	100	100	100	100	100	100

The figures in Table 2 do not permit us to distinguish with sufficient precision between the social position and the social origins of students; nor do they distinguish between employees and specialists, i.e., the intelligentsia proper. Finally, they aggregate students in all courses, and thus annual changes are "slurred over" since 25-50% of the student body is replaced each year.

More detailed data, which distinguish between social position and social origins and which apply to first-year students, are presented below for six Sverdlovsk higher educational institutions for a more extended period (see Table 3). (6)

What conclusions follow from the material presented in Tables 2 and 3?

If we ignore annual fluctuations, the first thing we observe is tendencies that correspond to changes in the structure of society as a whole. In the first half of the 1950s, children of workers constituted 25% to 30% of those admitted as daytime students, while in the first half of the 1960s they already represented 45% to 50%. During the same period there was some reduction in the proportion of children from peasant families, which corresponded to the decline in the proportion of collective farmers in the country's population, particularly in the Central Urals.

However, we cannot help but observe, first, that the proportion of children from employees' and specialists' families among students remains higher than their proportion in the population as a whole. Approximate calculations for recent years show that, if we take the average relative number of students from workers' families as 1 per 1,000 workers, the corresponding figures for personnel in mental labor would be 2.5 to 3. In other words, the "frequency" of admission to higher schools in the Urals among employees' families (in the broad sense) is currently 2.5 to 3 times greater than among workers' families. Insofar as collective farmers are concerned, the proportion of collective farm youth in higher educational institutions is higher than the proportion of collective farmers in the region's population, but the inflow of collective farm youth to Sverdlovsk higher schools from neighboring regions makes a

Table 3

Social Composition of First-Year Students in Daytime Divisions
in Six Sverdlovsk Higher Educational Institutions (in %)

Years	Social position				Social origins		
	workers	employees	collective farmers	students	workers	employees	peasants
1950	6.4	13.1	0.5	80.0	30.5	58.4	11.1
1953	6.3	7.5	0.4	85.8	25.5	59.0	15.5
1955	5.2	3.3	0.2	91.3	29.5	63.5	7.0
1956	10.4	10.1	0.5	79.0	30.4	62.7	6.9
1957	24.0	20.6	0.9	54.5	33.1	58.5	8.4
1958	34.0	33.9	2.1	30.3	36.8	50.6	12.6
1959	41.0	22.5	2.1	34.4	34.7	56.4	8.9
1960	40.3	31.3	5.4	23.0	44.0	48.3	7.7
1961	50.7	30.4	2.1	16.8	48.5	42.5	9.0
1962	48.0	32.6	0.3	19.1	44.8	46.8	8.4
1963	40.0	40.6	0.5	18.9	47.7	44.2	8.1
1964	41.4	28.1	0.3	30.2	50.0	43.3	6.7
1965	20.6	18.1	0.8	60.5	38.6	54.9	6.5
1966	10.1	7.9	0.2	81.8	38.5	55.6	5.9
1967	21.5	12.6	0.4	65.5	46.3	50.6	3.1
1968	19.4	13.5	0.2	66.9	41.7	55.0	3.3
1969	24.0	12.1	0.6	63.3*	47.3	50.2	2.5

*We have changed here what appeared to be an obvious misprint in the original.

more precise comparison extremely difficult.

Second, the new admissions rules introduced in accordance with the 1958 Law on the School produced certain changes of a temporary nature which were superimposed on the general picture. The greatest impact on the social position of those admitted to higher educational institutions stemmed from a decline in the percentage of those admitted directly after graduation from 91.3% of the total in 1955 to 16.8% in 1961. In 1961 more than one-half of all those accepted had the right to enter "worker" on their questionnaires. However, it is clear that many secondary-school graduates went into factories for a couple of years only to obtain credit for "work experience." Two years of work (usually as an apprentice or auxiliary and unskilled worker, conscious of the "temporary" character of his status) does not mean that the young person has become an organic part of the working class. Thus, the jump in the number of workers among applicants for higher schools during the early 1960s should be interpreted with some qualifications.

By 1966, in connection with subsequent changes in admissions rules, we returned essentially to the situation prevailing prior to the 1958 reform: more than 80% of those admitted were students currently graduating from secondary school. Individuals with workers' status constituted 41.1% in 1964; 20% in 1965; only 10% in 1966; 21.5% in 1967; 19.4% in 1968; and in 1969 the figure was the same as in 1957 — 24%.

However, this kind of temporary "peak" does not appear to the same degree when the social composition of students is viewed in terms of social origins. Workers' children averaged 40% of those admitted to six Sverdlovsk higher educational institutions during 1965-1969, which is significantly higher than the figures for the mid-1950s. This reflects the operation of the long-run objective factors discussed above.

The "peak" — connected as it was with the attempt of some young people to obtain credit for work service — appears even less sharp when examined in relation to the overall social composition of the student body. In this context the workers' category (workers and their children), which rose at one point to slightly above 50% because of "work service people" ["stazhniki"],

Table 4

Admissions to First-Year Daytime Divisions of Sverdlovsk Higher Educational Institutions, 1968

Higher educational institutions	Total	Social origin (in %)			Social position (in %)				Where from (in %)	
		workers	employees	collective farmers	workers	collective farmers	employees	students	Sverdlovsk	rural locality
Pedagogical Institute	783	41.8	56.2	2.0	13.8	0.3	25.0	60.9	30.3	18.5
Institute of National Economy	525	49.5	47.3	3.2	19.5	0.4	21.5	58.6	40.0	15.4
University	600	43.7	52.5	3.8	12.0	–	13.8	74.2	37.5	10.8
Juridical Institute	500	43.0	44.2	12.8	33.7	–	42.1	24.2	18.4	16.8
Agricultural Institute	325	43.1	22.5	34.4	10.0	16.0	9.0	65.0	3.1	65.4
Medical Institute	500	26.8	72.0	1.2	12.6	–	11.6	75.8	–	32.0
Railroad Institute	575	58.7	39.2	2.1	23.5	0.9	11.2	64.4	21.8	–
Lumber Technical Institute	900	49.8	47.0	3.2	25.7	0.1	13.4	60.8	15.6	22.2
Polytechnical Institute	2,250	34.1	64.4	1.5	14.4	0.4	10.0	75.2	39.5	8.3
Mining Institute	850	62.6	37.0	0.4	26.6	0.2	6.6	66.6	28.1	–
Total	7,808	43.5	52.1	4.4	18.8	0.9	14.9	65.4	29.6	17.8

i.e., essentially nonworkers, then declined negligibly to 44-45% during the past two years.

Analysis of 1968 admissions to ten Sverdlovsk higher schools permits us to trace the connection between social composition of students and specific institutions (see Table 4). (7)

For the ten higher schools in the city as a whole, individuals with work experience constituted 34.6% of those admitted (37% in 1967). Differences among higher schools in this respect are not very great (excluding the Juridical Institute, which has special admissions procedures). Individuals with work experience were least important in admissions to the Medical Institute (24.2%)*, and most important in admissions to the Institute of National Economy (41.1%).

The situation is different with respect to the social origins of new students. Although workers' children account for one-half or more of admissions to some technical higher schools (at the Mining Institute their share is 62.6%), their share at the Medical Institute is only 26.8%, a situation that cannot be accepted as normal. The situation is unsatisfactory with respect to admissions of collective farm youth to all higher schools except the Agricultural Institute (where more than one-third of the students come from collective farm families and 16.8% are collective farmers in terms of current social position) and the Juridical Institute (where about 13% come from collective farm families). Even among future lumber industry engineers and teachers the proportion of children from peasant families does not exceed 2-3%. But the countryside today includes more than just collective farmers. If we take another indicator, "residents of rural localities," almost 20% of the students admitted have come from the countryside, a figure which corresponds to the share of villagers in the region's population.

The statistics of the admissions committees do not distinguish the intelligentsia from the general mass of "employees" in the broad sense, i.e., individuals engaged in mental labor, employed at state institutions and enterprises. However, for purposes of investigating the role of "self-reproduction" in the

---

*We have corrected an obvious misprint in the original, which reads 14.2%. The correct figure can be calculated from Table 4.

recruitment of the intelligentsia, it is extremely important to
focus precisely on this social category in order to determine
the extent to which young people who grow up in specialists'
families are represented in the student body, i.e., the highly
qualified specialists of the future.

With this end in view, the entering class at Urals University
in 1966 was studied in greater detail by the Sociological Laboratory of the University. It is noteworthy that while children
from workers' families constituted 28.4% of total admissions
to the University in 1966, their proportion in the journalism
department was 52%. The percentage of the University entering
class coming from collective farm peasant families was insignificant (0.7%), and in many departments there simply were
none. It is also noteworthy that the employees (nonspecialists)
category provides the University with a share of entering students (up to 40%) that is out of proportion to its share in the
population as a whole, and in some departments this category
accounts for up to 50% of those admitted. Children from intelligentsia families constituted about 25% of the entering class, but
in the science departments the figures rose to 35-43% (see Table 5).
In these fields the role of the family in preparing youngsters
for the competitive examinations is particularly evident.

In the 1966 investigation, specialists were not subdivided into
the two basic categories of this stratum depending upon level of education (secondary specialized and higher). In 1968, when investigating the social composition of applicants at several departments
of the University and at other higher educational institutions in the
city, this factor was taken into account so as to determine more precisely the extent of "self-reproduction" among different strata of
the intelligentsia. Table 6 shows the percentage of applicants whose
parents had a secondary specialized or higher education.

Thus, while in the most difficult department of the University
(mechanics and mathematics), requiring the highest level of preparation, about 25% of the applicants "rely" on the higher education of
their parents, at the Agricultural Institute only 1 out of 16 do so.

The proportions were different among those actually admitted,
with the share of children from intelligentsia families rising
somewhat. But this increase was not as substantial as in the

Table 5

Social Composition of Students Admitted to Daytime Studies
at Urals State University, 1968 (in %)

Departments	Social origin					Social position				Work experience			
	workers	peasants	employees (nonspecialists)	intelligentsia (specialists)	others (a)	workers	peasants	employees (b)	students	none	less than 2 years	2-4 years	more than 4 years
Physics	27.2	1.6	32.0	35.2	4.0	5.6	0.8	4.0	89.6	89.6*	7.2	—	3.2
Mathematics and mechanics	29.0	—	30.0	35.0	6.0	1.0	—	4.0	95.0	95.0*	5.0	—	—
Chemistry	21.6	—	28.4	43.4	6.6	6.6	—	10.0	83.4	83.4*	6.6	10.0	—
Biology	30.0	—	44.0	26.0	—	10.0	—	10.0	80.0	80.0	6.0	10.0	4.0
Economics	29.0	—	49.0	18.0	4.0	10.0	—	11.0	79.0	79.0	13.0	5.0	3.0
Philosophy	22.6	2.6	40.0	29.4	5.4	13.3	—	9.4	77.3	77.3	4.0	9.3	9.4
Philology	35.0	1.2	50.0	11.3	2.5	6.2	—	7.5	86.3	86.3	8.7	3.7	1.3
History	30.0	—	40.0	22.0	8.0	4.0	—	16.0	80.0	80.0	14.0	4.0	2.0
Journalism	52.0	—	28.0	10.0	10.0	28.0	—	52.0	20.0	20.0	22.0	20.0	38.0

(a) This category includes pensioners' children (where the previous social position is unknown), youngsters raised in children's homes, and those who did not answer the questionnaire precisely.

(b) This category combines employees and specialists since very few worked as specialists prior to admission to the University.

*We have changed here what appeared to be obvious misprints in the original.

Table 6

Educational Level of Applicants' Parents, 1968

Institute and department	Number of applicants questioned	Applicants with family head having secondary specialized education		Applicants with family head having higher education	
		no. of applicants	% of applicants	no. of applicants	% of applicants
Agricultural Institute (10% sample)	185	21	11.4	11	6.0
University: mathematics and mechanics department (50% sample)	202	40	19.8	48	23.8
Urals Polytechnical Institute: physics and chemical technology departments (50% sample)	600	134	22.4	98	16.3
Medical Institute (10% sample)	289	50	17.3	36	12.5

case of Rostov State University, where the percentage of specialists' children among first-year students in 1966 was almost
double their proportion among applicants. (8) This problem
requires further investigation. But it is perfectly clear that
we must differentiate employees (in questionnaires) into nar-
rower and more precise social categories in sociological
analysis.

Thus, on the basis of the objective tendencies noted above,
we can observe that the social composition of students and the
social structure of society are becoming increasingly similar.
However, the composition of full-time students at higher educational institutions (in contrast with technicums) still differs very
significantly from the social composition of the country's population, and especially from the population of the area from
which our higher schools recruit their students.

What are the reasons for this? The most important is that
the full legal equality of all citizens and social groups under
socialism does not yet signify their complete actual equality.
Objective factors do operate in the direction of greater conformity between the composition of the student body and the
changing structure of our society. But conscious direction of
these important social processes must play an important role.
As V. N. Stoletov correctly pointed out, the higher school must
make certain that "the social composition of the student body
reflects the specific social features of the USSR population, for
this is the basic foundation of the genuine democracy of Soviet
higher education." (9)

It is quite obvious that, given equal abilities of youngsters,
those families in which the parents have higher educational
attainments provide greater opportunities for preparing young
people for the competitive examinations. This emerged in the
mid-1950s in a number of higher schools (particularly in regional capitals) in the form of an uncontrolled increase in the
proportion of children of intelligentsia families among the student body.

The school reform of 1958 was designed (among other things)
to correct this situation. The enrollment procedure for daytime
divisions of higher educational institutions was changed so that

two years of work experience was enough to open the doors of any department, even if the applicant's performance in the entrance examinations was only moderately satisfactory. But several years of experience demonstrated that this procedure was not justified, primarily because it led to poorer preparation of students. This meant an increased drop-out rate from higher schools, a deterioration in the relationship between admissions and graduations, and an irrational use of public resources. The result was a sharpening of a contradiction which is inherent in the selection system for higher schools and is one of the manifestations of a most important contradiction inherent in socialism — that between the full legal equality of citizens and their incomplete actual equality.

The essence of this contradiction consists in the following. Socialist society is interested in selecting those individuals who will yield maximum benefits in the future as skilled specialists. Competitive examinations for higher educational institutions, generally speaking, enable us to choose those who are best prepared to master a given specialty. But it is well known that the degree of preparation of an applicant depends not only on his natural abilities, but also on the material and cultural level of the family in which he was raised, on the quality of teaching in the secondary school that he attended, and on many other factors that promote the early development of abilities and the acquisition of greater knowledge by the time of the examinations. Other things being equal, therefore, greater opportunities for admission to higher schools are available to children from more well-to-do families, especially from families in which the parents' educational level is higher, from larger cities, where the qualifications of schoolteachers are typically higher, and so on.

Given the number of applicants, which is now several times greater than the number of vacancies in first-year courses at higher schools, society is interested in selecting those who in a few years are capable of becoming the best specialists, both in terms of general and specialized knowledge as well as in the ability to lead people in a politically mature way, and also those who are prepared to work permanently in the countryside and sparsely settled areas. But of all of these factors, the greatest weight is given to the level of knowledge, although other factors may play a role in admissions to certain higher educational institutions (for example, pedagogical and agricultural institutes, where preference is given to rural youth, and art schools, where not only knowledge but particular talents are considered). In ignoring the conditions under which applicants are trained, and in making judgments based only on the applicants' knowledge, admissions committees in effect sanction inequality of opportunity.

Competition for admission to higher schools undoubtedly involves a contradiction: competition among the participants. It is on these grounds that it is sometimes argued that the very principle of competitive selection contradicts the socialist principle of mutual assistance. Indeed, during the competitive examination period the studying on the part of the entering students is highly individual in nature, although this by no means excludes mutual assistance among the applicants in preparing for examinations and after passing the examinations. In reality the competitive selection procedure involves a competition that is profoundly socialist in nature, for our society is vitally interested in choosing, for future specialists' positions, those who are best prepared. In capitalist countries, competition for admission to higher educational institutions does not exist in our sense of the word. Everything depends on the ability to pay for one's studies and to bear the necessary costs for the whole period of education. Competition in knowledge and abilities is replaced by the "competition" of the purse. But competitive selection in our higher schools is, of course, a special form of socialist competition, and the usual, "standard" approach to it is inappropriate. It is a competition not in the course of performing work set by society as, for example, competition between factory brigades, but competition for the right to perform a certain type of work. Problems involving the relationship between competition and mutual assistance are, of course, solved differently than in the case of competition between brigades.

The contradiction examined here is by no means something

"external" to socialism, but expresses the dialectics of development of socialist social relations.

Does all this mean that socialist society must simply record
passively the resulting contradiction and do nothing to resolve
it? Of course not. However, it is all the more important to reject the arguments of some foreign sociologists to the effect
that any attempts to ease the path to a higher education for
workers and their children must be rejected on the grounds
that this would be "antidemocratic." Slanderously labeling as
"conservatives" those Communists who are struggling to expand the admission of working class youth to higher educational
institutions, these sociologists regard the increased influx of
workers to higher schools as "a violation of the social independence of students."

As an example we may cite the arguments of L. Makhachek
(of Czechoslovakia), presented in a report to the symposium in
Nitra in 1967. This report argued, in part, that students in contemporary society represent "a new force capable of participating in the criticism of society or in revolutionary acts directed not only at reforming the schools but society as a whole."
"The revolutionary student movement," Makhachek asserts,
"does not recognize any boundaries separating social orders.
Prague, Warsaw, Belgrade...these are not the only and apparently...not the last cities of socialist countries to have seen
open conflict between students and the government." Thus, in
Makhachek's opinion, students represent some kind of ahistor-
ical force. A familiar theme! H. Marcuse and other "renova-
tors of Marxism" have long argued that the working class has
abandoned its revolutionary role to "youth." Makhachek states
further: "Conservative groups most often...use the slogan
'send more workers' children to higher educational institutions.'" But in his opinion this "violates democratic conditions
for all strata and groups." Thus the praise of "democracy" is
transformed essentially into an antidemocratic and anti-working-
class policy with respect to higher education. And the thesis
that workers' children "are not interested in higher education"
is just as false. A survey conducted in Poland showed that, out
of 76,000 graduates of secondary schools wanting to enter

higher schools, 46,000, or more than 60%, were from worker
and peasant backgrounds. (10)

Socialist society is not only interested in ensuring the influx
of the most able young people into higher educational institutions, but also in making certain that the talents and abilities
of all young citizens are rapidly and fully revealed. Achievement of full, genuine equality in this sphere urgently requires
equalization of the material and cultural conditions of families,
decisive and effective assistance to rural schools, further development of out-of-school children's institutions, and well-
prepared work in the vocational guidance of youth. The creation
of boarding schools for gifted youth from remote localities can
also play an important role. These policies can provide the preconditions for ensuring that the fate of young people will be decided in full accord with their actual abilities, and that the frus-
tration of career plans associated with failure in entrance examinations will be as painless as possible.

To resolve these problems, to accelerate the scientific, technical, and cultural progress of the country, to ensure full and
genuine equality in this sphere (as in others), we must utilize
the incentives inherent in socialism that arise from the partial
inequality of citizens, so that the young people admitted today
to higher schools will become the best specialists in a few years.

It is frequently proposed that we solve the problem of equalizing actual opportunities for admission to higher educational
institutions by introducing admissions rules which would give
priority to particular categories of youth depending on their social characteristics. It seems to us that adoption of such policies in general form (special cases will be discussed below) is
unacceptable, since it would contradict the principle of equality
of citizens under Soviet law. But this is not all that is involved.
Enrollment in higher schools is a matter of great public importance. Both the number of specialists graduating five years
from now (a smaller drop-out rate!) and — what is particularly
important — their quality depend directly on the composition of
today's first-year students. The rates of scientific-technical
progress and the development of culture and public health are
determined by the quality of specialists. That is why the

accelerated progress of socialist society urgently requires the
admission of youth to higher educational institutions in accordance with the main criterion — the ability to master a future
specialty. As yet there is no other method of determining these
abilities than competitive entrance examinations, with decisive
importance attached to the major subjects. Proposals to re-
place examinations or interviews by "certificate competition"
["konkursom attestatov"] cannot withstand criticism, since the
requirements of our secondary schools and technicums are still
highly unequal. That explains why a large number of medal
winners receive unsatisfactory grades on competitive examinations.

However, in recent years admissions rules do give certain
advantages to some categories of young people in enrollment
for daytime studies, and as a whole these are justified. We refer, first of all, to the preferential admission of rural youth
(assuming, of course, satisfactory grades on examinations) to
training in a number of specialties requiring work in the
countryside upon graduation from a higher school. What counts,
of course, is not only the quality of the specialist's knowledge,
but also his readiness to work where his knowledge is especially
needed by society. As a rule, young specialists from urban
areas do not adjust well to the countryside. The result is that
rural schools, hospitals, clubs, and some collective and state
farms experience a shortage of skilled cadres and suffer from
their frequent turnover. This factor has a significant effect on
the speed with which we can overcome social differences between the city and countryside. For example, without raising
the level of rural schools to that of urban schools we cannot attain genuine equality of opportunity in admissions to higher educational institutions for succeeding generations of rural youth,
and in order to raise this level we must now have a larger number of rural youth in pedagogical institutes, despite the inadequate training they receive in secondary schools. This "vicious
circle" can be broken only by taking special measures. That is
why preferential treatment for rural youth in access to specialties in teaching, agriculture, agricultural economics, biology,
medicine, library work, and a number of other specialties is a

fully justified temporary measure.

The second major step involves special assistance in preparing for higher schools those young people who are raised in less favorable cultural circumstances. Such measures, aimed at the fuller and more rapid discovery and development of youngsters' abilities, are extremely important, particularly at factories and in the countryside. They should help to reduce the advantages possessed by youngsters in large cities compared to children of the same age in the countryside and in workers' settlements, and the advantages of children from intelligentsia families compared to those from workers' and collective farmers' families. The problem of the specific measures that should be taken is the subject of lively discussion in the press, particularly in Pravda. Most participants lean in the direction of finding means of raising the actual level of knowledge of applicants from among working class youth and residents of villages. (11)

The most radical measure, which will have considerable social consequences, is the creation, in accordance with a decree of the CPSU Central Committee, of preparatory divisions at higher educational institutions for working youth, persons demobilized from the Soviet armed forces, and residents of villages, beginning in the 1969/1970 academic year. All of this — the provision of full-time instruction at the preparatory divisions during the school year by the academic staff of these institutions and their best teachers, the provision of state stipends, living quarters, etc., to the students — has the objective of eliminating the actual gap in knowledge between children from various social groups that shows up so sharply in the higher school entrance examinations. The preparatory divisions, of course, should not be regarded as simply a repetition of the workers' faculties of the 1920s. The general circumstances and needs are different now, and in many ways the process of instruction at the preparatory divisions is organized differently than it was in the workers' faculties. But in terms of their social role, the preparatory divisions have a great deal in common with the workers' faculties, which earned such well-deserved and enduring fame.

The solution of this problem has its peculiar features in other socialist countries. In those countries in which socialist social relations are still in the process of formation, where remnants of propertied classes still exist, regulation of the social composition of higher educational institutions encompasses organizational-political measures. Insofar as assistance to those entering higher schools is concerned, it is based, as a rule, on a class approach. Thus, in Poland, where remnants of a kulak class remain, assistance to rural youth desiring to enter higher schools is granted in accordance with the social origins and social position of the rural applicants. In admissions to higher educational institutions, peasant youth (whose families have an annual income of not more than 67,000 zlotys) and children of working-class families receive additional points which give them preferential opportunities to enroll, and 10% of vacancies are guaranteed to working-class and peasant youth. As a result of the measures taken, the number of students from workers' and peasants' families in Poland has increased by 15% during the last two years (1968-1969). (12)

In recent years a great deal has been done in our country to help applicants to prepare for entrance examinations to higher educational institutions. Considerable positive experience has been accumulated in the higher schools of Cheliabinsk and Magnitogorsk.

The Sverdlovsk higher schools have also gained a certain amount of experience that has yielded favorable results. Thus, the proportion of rural youth admitted to the Sverdlovsk Pedagogical Institute has been a steady 20% or more in recent years, which is extremely important for assuring a stable number of teachers in the countryside in the future. Technical higher schools are also adopting special measures to assist working youth. Part-time courses are being organized at large enterprises to prepare people for higher schools. This helps to raise the level of knowledge among production workers and makes it possible for them to receive higher point scores in the competitive examinations. In the 1967/1968 academic year the Urals Polytechnical Institute organized a broad network of courses which were attended by almost 6,000 persons, 63.5% of whom were working-class youth. Such courses were in operation at a number of large enterprises in Sverdlovsk, Nizhnii Tagil, Neviansk, Baranch, at the Beloiarsk Atomic Electric Station, etc. A considerable number of the newly admitted students at the Urals Polytechnical Institute in 1968 had completed these courses. In the 1968/1969 academic year a workers' faculty was organized at the Institute, and in the 1969/1970 academic year preparatory departments were organized in Sverdlovsk and Nizhnii Tagil.

Third, we attach special importance to recent changes in the system of vocational-technical education that trains cadres of skilled workers for industry and construction, and machine-operators for agriculture. Some of the vocational-technical schools, drawing their students from the eight-year schools, are currently being shifted to a new curriculum which simultaneously provides the students with a workers' specialty and a complete secondary education. The working youth trained at these schools will have a higher level of general education, and this will provide additional opportunities for tens of thousands of young workers to take the competitive examinations for admission to higher educational institutions with greater confidence. In the spring of 1969 there were already 156 of these schools. In the Sverdlovsk Region the reorganization has been carried out in three such schools with an enrollment of more than 600 persons who are being trained as steel workers in Nizhnii Tagil, Serov, and Pervouralsk. The decree of the CPSU Central Committee and the Council of Ministers adopted in the spring of 1969, "On Measures to Further Improve the Training of Skilled Workers at Educational Institutions in the System of Vocational-Technical Education," provides for the gradual transformation of a considerable number of these schools into three- to four-year institutions simultaneously providing a skill and a certificate of complete secondary education. In 1969 these institutions were expected to enroll 50,000 persons (3% of the total enrollment of 1.7 million), and by 1975 the figure is scheduled to rise to 300,000, which will represent more than 16% of the total enrollment of 1.9 million persons. (13) Sooner or later, apparently, we will have to consider removing the requirement that

working youth who complete these schools must work for three
years at assigned enterprises in those cases where the individual has successfully passed the entrance examinations for admission to a higher educational institution.

Some assistance and preferential treatment in admissions,
following examinations, is necessary for some categories of
youth even when their point scores are the same as those of
other applicants. In our view such preferential treatment may
be justified for applicants who are being sent by enterprises —
assuming they have been carefully selected — and for rural
youth entering a number of specific specialties, as we noted
earlier. But those advantages in admission to higher schools
that prevailed earlier for young people who had acquired two
years of work experience are not justified, and it is hardly appropriate to retain them. As we know, remnants of these privileges continued during 1967-1969 in the sense that vacancies
were distributed between the two categories of entering students
in proportion to the number of applications submitted by the two
categories, and the passing grades on examinations required
for admission were not the same for these groups. Whatever
advantages may be acquired in mastering special knowledge
through work experience in the particular specialty should necessarily be revealed in the entrance examinations in the major
disciplines, and only in this way should they "accrue" in favor
of the individual with work experience.

Fourth and last, the problem of improving the quality of students admitted, including their quality in the sense of social
composition, depends on the functioning of secondary schools.
It is not only a matter of the quality of knowledge, but also of
the prompt development of abilities in particular directions, of
the occupational and social orientations of secondary-school
graduates. A considerable number of applicants still make the
decision to enter a higher school, and select the institution and
the department, on the basis of random circumstances, without
a firm conviction that their future specialty is really "in their
hearts."

It is our view that we must introduce specialization [profili-
rovannoe obuchenie] in the secondary schools on a wider scale

if we are to do a better job of discovering and developing the abilities of young people. Such specialization would enable young people to make a more conscious choice of their major fields, and higher educational institutions to recruit a higher quality of students. On the other hand, it would help in discovering the abilities of the older schoolchildren and thereby would hasten the process of "equalization" of opportunities for admission to higher education among youngsters growing up under differing material and cultural circumstances. This kind of specialization, of course, cannot be implemented everywhere. But it is definitely possible in the large cities. Higher education personnel have long been propagandizing for specialized training in the secondary schools, but thus far substantial experience has been acquired only in physics and mathematics schools, and in classes and schools where various subjects are taught in a foreign language. The introduction of elective courses in the schools for the purpose of more intensive study of particular disciplines is a step in this direction. As for specialized schools, there are not many of them thus far. According to data of the RSFSR Ministry of Education, there were 222 such schools in the 1967/1968 academic year, of which 110 specialized in mathematics, 51 in physics and radioelectronics, 48 in chemistry and chemical technology, 2 in biology and agro-biology, and 11 in the humanities. In the 1968/1969 academic year there were 258 specialized schools, and in addition there were 266 schools in which various subjects were taught in a foreign language in the senior classes. An increase in the number of such schools will undoubtedly have an impact on the quality of students admitted to higher educational institutions.

But the issue is not only one of specialized training. The patronage of higher educational institutions over secondary schools, the participation of teaching personnel from the higher schools in various kinds of olympiads, as well as in the schools for young mathematicians, economists, biologists, etc., organized at higher educational institutions, and a multitude of other kinds of work with youngsters can play an important role in the early identification of different abilities among the whole mass of schoolchildren, and thereby in orienting the most capable secondary-school graduates toward particular departments and specialties.

Our purpose here has not been to list all of the possible measures that could help to hasten closer conformity between the social composition of students and the changing social structure of the socialist society. In this situation the dialectics of interaction between subjective and objective factors under socialism assumes the following form: The more precisely we understand the objective regularities of changes in the social composition of student youth, and the more use that is made of the results of sociological studies by leading agencies at the center and in the localities, and also by the higher educational institutions themselves, the more effective will be the management of the process of recruitment to higher education.

The Social Composition of Evening-Division and Correspondence Students

The preparation of specialists is also conducted through part-time studies at evening and correspondence-type higher schools. These forms of training have played a considerable role in the creation of the Soviet intelligentsia. In the 1940/1941 academic year, 31.2% of the total number of students were attending evening divisions and taking correspondence courses, while in 1968/1969 the figure was 54.5%. (14) However, because of the longer period of training and the higher drop-out rate, the share of evening and correspondence education in the graduation of specialists is not that large. In 1960, 33.5% of the diplomas awarded by higher educational institutions were received by full-time students, while in 1967 and 1968 the figures were 48% and 48.6% respectively. (15) Recent years have been characterized by an increasing role for daytime instruction in higher schools.

It is our view that daytime instruction should be the principal form of training for specialists. The role of correspondence and evening instruction will evidently decline gradually as the "praktiki" stratum [individuals performing specialists' jobs without the corresponding education] is "washed away."

Table 7

Social Composition of Evening-Division Students
at Higher Educational Institutions,
Sverdlovsk Region (in %)

Social composition	Years				
	1959	1962	1965	1968	1969
Workers or workers' children	54.3	55.0	51.5	51.8	58.8
Peasants or peasants' children	0.4	0.8	1.3	0.5	0.9
Employees or employees' children	44.4	44.2	47.2	47.7	40.3
Others	0.9	—	—	—	—
Total	100	100	100	100	100

Nonetheless, even in the future the socialist society will undoubtedly take advantage of the great social effect yielded by
training specialists from among individuals directly employed
in production who wish to advance to more complex kinds of
work.

Evening-division and correspondence students are workers,
employees, and collective farmers who are raising their general educational level and skills in their own specialties or are
changing their specialties in the process. The social composition of the evening-division students at Sverdlovsk higher educational institutions is revealed by the above data (see Table 7).

It is apparent from Table 7 that the composition of evening-
division students reflects more closely the relative proportion
of workers and employees in the region's population than is the
case with daytime students. There is a clear predominance of
workers in evening education. Nonetheless, even here the proportion of employees is somewhat higher than their share of the
total population, since many specialties in mental labor are

Table 8

Social Composition of Evening-Division Students
at Higher Educational Institutions
of Sverdlovsk, 1968 (in %)

Higher educational institutions	Categories of students		
	Workers or workers' children	Peasants or peasants' children	Employees or employees' children
Polytechnical Institute	63.0	0.3	36.7
Mining Institute	74.0	—	26.0
University	36.6	4.4	59.0
Railroad Institute	53.0	—	47.0
Juridical Institute	32.5	—	67.5
Conservatory	21.6	1.1	77.3

more likely to require a higher education and an increase in skills than is true of workers' occupations. For workers, study at an evening higher school is frequently connected not only with a rise in skills but also with a change in specialty. The relatively small proportion of peasants among evening-division students is explained by the fact that this form of education is designed for urban residents, for individuals who are able to attend classes four times a week. A more concrete analysis requires that we examine the composition of this category of students at individual institutions (see Table 8).

Thus, depending upon the area of specialization of the institution, evening-division students are either predominantly workers (at the technical institutes) or employees (at institutions specializing in the humanities and at the University).

The territorial boundaries of higher schools permit a considerable extension of correspondence education, which is reflected in the social composition of its students. In comparison with evening-division students, there is a larger percentage of peasants in correspondence education, although it has declined

Table 9

Social Composition of Correspondence-Division Students
at Higher Educational Institutions of Sverdlovsk Region
(in %)

Social composition	Years				
	1959	1961	1964	1966	1969
Workers or workers' children	29.5	43.7	39.1	34.3	38.9
Peasants or peasants' children	25.3	8.6	7.5	4.9	0.6
Employees or employees' children	44.9	47.7	53.4	60.8	60.5
Others	0.3	—	—	—	—
Total	100	100	100	100	100

in recent years (see Table 9).

The sharp decline in the proportion of peasants' children between 1959 and 1961 is explained by changes in the social composition of the region's population connected with the transformation of a considerable number of collective farms into state
farms. The somewhat higher proportion of employees, compared to the situation in evening education, is associated with
the greater relative share of humanities specialties (teachers,
economists, etc.) in correspondence education.

Again, to be more concrete, let us examine the data on the
social composition of correspondence students in those institutions for which we presented data on evening-division students
(see Table 10).

Since these figures are generally based not on social origins
but on the social position of correspondence students, there is
no doubt that a considerable number are children of peasants.
But those who are taking correspondence courses are primarily
workers and employees (teachers, lawyers, economists, etc.)

Table 10

Social Composition of Correspondence-Division Students
at Higher Educational Institutions
of Sverdlovsk, 1966 (in %)

Higher educational institutions	Categories of students		
	Workers or workers' children	Peasants or peasants' children	Employees or employees' children
Polytechnical Institute	42.2	—	54.8
Mining Institute	58.4	0.4	41.2
University	34.8	10.2	55.0
Railroad Institute	38.3	—	61.7
Juridical Institute	17.2	0.3	82.5
Conservatory	35.9	—	64.1

whose social origins (i.e., the social position of their parents)
are not considered in compiling the statistical data. In the technical institutions, as in the evening divisions, workers predominate, while in the humanities it is employees and middle-level
specialists.

Students at Secondary Specialized
Educational Institutions

We observe a highly characteristic phenomenon in comparing
the social composition of students at higher educational institutions with those at secondary specialized schools. In the 1968/
1969 academic year, the social composition of students at secondary specialized schools of Sverdlovsk Region was as follows:
workers' children — 70.5%, collective farmers' children —
3.1%, nonspecialist-employees' children — 13.9%, specialists'
children — 6.3% (the remaining 6.2% fell into the category of
"others" — young people raised in children's homes, children

Table 11

Social Composition of Students at Secondary Specialized Schools of
Sverdlovsk Region, 1967/1968 Academic Year (in %)

Secondary specialized schools, by branches	Social origins					Social position			Place of origin	
	workers	collective farmers	employees (nonspecialists)	specialists	others	workers	collective farmers	employees and specialists	urban	rural
Industry	68.3	3.6	13.9	6.8	7.4	95.8	2.8	1.4	90.0	10.0
Construction	65.4	3.9	15.0	7.1	8.6	87.5	—	12.5	90.7	9.3
Transport and communications	76.9	2.1	11.7	0.8	8.5	84.6	7.7	7.7	94.5	5.5
Economics	88.4	1.4	5.3	1.4	3.5	90.5	—	9.5	83.4	16.6
Public health	67.5	3.9	18.4	7.3	2.9	91.8	—	8.2	88.6	11.4
Education	76.7	2.8	12.4	4.6	3.5	70.6	—	29.4	89.7	10.3
Art	25.5	1.1	32.6	36.3	4.5	25.0	—	75.0	100.0	—
Total	70.5	3.1	13.9	6.3	6.2	91.5	1.3	7.2	91.0	9.0

of pensioners whose previous social position could not be determined, etc.). These figures approximate the social composition of the region's population.

Table 11 gives a more detailed picture of the social composition of students at secondary specialized schools. The table
presents data concerning the students' social origins, as well
as their social position prior to their enrollment. (16)

It is apparent from Table 11 that most students of secondary
specialized schools are urban youngsters. The proportion of
workers' children at these institutions (except for art schools)
is much higher than at higher schools, primarily because the
time required to acquire a specialty through secondary specialized
education is much shorter than through higher education. Completion of an 8-year and a secondary specialized school requires about 12 years in all, while 15 years or more are required to complete secondary school and a higher educational
institution. Workers and their children are much more likely
to choose the shorter path to the acquisition of a specialty and
a skill, while children of persons in mental work, particularly
specialists' children, show greater preference for higher education. This by no means signifies that children of persons in
mental work do not join the ranks of workers and peasants, but
here we are not examining this aspect of social mobility.

In the near future, secondary specialized education must develop considerably more rapidly than higher education. At the
present time, the number of specialists with higher education
is 40% of the total, while those with secondary specialized education constitute 60%. This relationship remained essentially
stable during the 1960s. But for every employed engineer there
should be several technicians, and for every doctor in a hospi-
tal there should be several nurses, etc. This situation has been
noted frequently in the press. Appropriate measures have now
been taken, and already in 1969 the number of graduates from
secondary specialized schools (more than one million) was almost double the number from higher educational institutions
(565,000). (17) The growing national economic significance of secondary specialized education means that its role as a "channel" of
recruitment of the intelligentsia will become increasingly important.

Notes

1) See Ts. E. Chutkerashvili, Razvitie vysshego obrazovaniia v SSSR, Moscow, 1961, p. 8.

2) See M. N. Rutkevich, "Quantitative Changes in Social
Structure During the 1960s," Sotsial'nye razlichiia i ikh
preodolenie.

3) Data from the Sverdlovsk Region Statistical Administration.

4) Calculated from the statistical handbook Narodnoe
khoziaistvo SSSR v 1968 godu, pp. 34, 423, 548.

5) Data from the Sverdlovsk Region Statistical Administration.

6) This table encompasses the following higher educational
institutions: Urals Polytechnical Institute, Urals State University, Sverdlovsk Mining Institute, Urals Lumber Technical Institute, Sverdlovsk Medical Institute, and Sverdlovsk Juridical
Institute (data provided by L. I. Sennikov).

7) Data from the Sociological Laboratory of Urals University.

8) See B. Rubin and Iu. Kolesnikov, Student glazami sotsiologa, Rostov, 1968, p. 70. This question has been discussed
more fully in M. N. Rutkevich's article "Competitive Selection,"
Izvestia, December 9, 1967. It is clear that V. Mishin is wrong
in reproaching us for wanting to simply "abstain from the direct
regulation of the social composition of the student body" (see
V. Mishin, Obshchestvennyi progress, Gorkii, 1970, pp. 245-
248).

9) V. N. Stoletov, "Student and Society," Komsomol'skaia
pravda, May 11, 1968.

10) See Kh. Iablon'skii, "A Ticket to Students' Status,"
Komsomol'skaia pravda, December 21, 1969.

11) See V. Eliutin, "The Competitive Examination, the Student, and Occupations," Pravda, July 19, 1969.

12) Iablon'skii, op. cit.

13) See "Both a Skill and a Graduation Certificate," Pravda,
May 7, 1969.

14) See Narodnoe khoziaistvo SSSR v 1968 godu, p. 679.

15) Ibid., p. 688.

16) Data provided by V. I. Lipatnikova.

17) See "Communication of the Central Statistical Administration of the USSR. The Results of the Fulfillment of the State
Plan for the Development of the National Economy of the USSR
in 1969," Pravda, January 25, 1970.

14 The Social Conditioning of Occupational Choice

L. F. LISS

The choice of an occupation requiring a corresponding level of education is a complex and protracted social process which can be divided into the following main stages:

The preliminary stage involves the formation of occupational plans. This is the period in which occupational interests and inclinations arise and develop, and having become consolidated in the course of their development, are transformed into a definite occupational focus which forms the area of occupational preference. This is the foundation on which the choice of a future occupation is made. It is during this stage that an orientation toward a definite activity and the mode of life associated with it is developed. When it is a matter of selecting the first occupation, this stage corresponds, as a rule, to the training period in general-education schools.

The stage of adopting and implementing the decision is characterized by the fact that the individual, having made a choice, then attempts to implement it by gaining admission to an appropriate educational institution. During this stage an important role is played by the individual's perception of his interests, inclinations, and actual abilities, as well as by his conceptions about the occupational spectrum and the demands which the chosen occupation makes on those engaged in it and the chosen educational institution makes on its students. Not only does the

From Tartuskii Gosudarstvennyi Universitet, Materialy konferentsii "Kommunisticheskoe vospitanie studenchestva," Tartu, 1971, pp. 137-150.

individual choose an occupation at this stage, but the occupation selects the individual (the selection system in admissions to specialized educational institutions).

The stage of occupational training consolidates the previously apparent occupational interests and inclinations on the basis of a fuller conception of the content of the chosen specialty acquired in the process of training. Occupational knowledge, skills, habits, and value orientations are developed during this period. The process of selection continues simultaneously — those who change their occupational interests leave the educational institution, as do those who show an inability to study there.

In the formation of an occupational direction, the general social conditions of the socialist society create a common foundation in the form of the corresponding value orientations. As numerous studies have shown (1), the orientations which are most characteristic of Soviet youth are associated with essential matters — the content of the future occupation and the individual's relation to society, his yearning to be useful to society. Among university applicants this is a yearning to understand and discover the new: a yearning for labor that is creative and useful to society, and that is connected with an interest in the chosen sphere of knowledge, and that is based on the conception of the scholar as a creator, a discoverer, whose activity is among the most useful for society. The predominance of these values reflects the shared world outlook of Soviet youth, its high moral aspirations, and that romantic elevation which is characteristic of young people.

It is against this background, and under the influence of both common and specific social circumstances (which still differ substantially under socialism), that the area of occupational preference is developed and becomes the basis on which the concrete choice is made. Given the variety of channels through which the individual is connected with society (school, out-of-school institutions, the system of mass communications) and its strata and groups (through family, friends, neighbors, etc.), the specific character of the individual (socially determined on the basis of native characteristics) predetermines the variety

of types of behavior even within similar social circumstances
of individual development. Among university applicants, formation of the area of occupational preference and the concrete
choice are influenced by such factors as the study of particular
subjects at school; the reading of books, journals, and newspapers; various personal contacts (with friends, teachers, specialists); activities in specialized classes and schools, in various clubs; participation in olympiads, etc.

Study of the composition of applicants' families and of their
places of settlement shows the connection between social origins and the formation of occupational orientations. Although
individuals from the most varied strata and groups of our society aspire to gain admission to the University,* the applicants' parents are mostly employed in primarily mental work (2)
(64-66% of the men and 63-66% of the women) and are characterized by a high educational level (65-67% of the men and 58-
60% of the women have a higher, secondary-specialized, or
secondary-general education). The most sizable groups among
the men are engineering-technical personnel, executives of enterprises or their structural subdivisions, personnel in the sciences and in education, as well as industrial workers. Among
women the major groups are personnel in the sciences and education, engineering-technical personnel, medical personnel,
and planning and accounting workers.

Although the occupations and educational levels of the parents
are closely connected, a clearer picture of the character of the
families and their connections with different social strata is
obtained by considering family structure with regard to both
parents (see Table 1).

Families which include specialists with higher or secondary
specialized education predominate (60-66%). In a third of the
families the parents are employed in primarily manual labor.
Families from different places of settlement have different
characteristics with respect to occupation and, especially, education. Thus, while higher education predominates among

---

*The data and general discussion are based on Liss's studies
of applicants and students at Novosibirsk State University.

Table 1

Family Structure of Applicants to Novosibirsk State University, 1970, by Education of Parents (in % of total)

		Education of mothers						Single fathers	Total, fathers
		H	SS	SG	IS	P	Total		
Education of fathers	H	18.3	7.3	2.2	1.7	0.5	30.0	0.3	30.3
	SS	3.6	9.1	2.5	5.4	1.0	21.6	0.1	21.7
	SG	0.4	1.0	1.5	2.0	0.6	5.5	0.2	5.7
	IS	1.0	3.5	1.1	8.0	3.6	17.2	0.2	17.4
	P	0.3	1.0	0.7	2.8	6.3	11.1	0.5	11.6
Total		23.6	21.9	8.0	19.9	12.0	85.4	1.3	86.7
Single mothers		3.2	3.8	0.8	3.2	2.3	13.3		
Total, mothers		26.8	25.7	8.8	23.1	14.3	98.7		

Note: Education groups are: H — higher education; SS — secondary specialized; SG — secondary general; IS — incomplete secondary; P — primary or less.

applicants' families from large cities in which both parents are employed in mental work requiring either a higher or secondary specialized education, secondary education is predominant among analogous rural families. We should note an essential stability in the distribution of different types of families over the last five years (both with respect to occupation and education), which means a stability in the orientation toward a university education for youth among the various social strata which they represent.

The distinctive nature of University applicants' families, as an index of the influence of a social stratum on the formation of occupational orientations, is clearly revealed when we compare these families with the social structure of society (according to data from the All-Union Population Census of 1959 for the RSFSR). (3)

We take the age group closest to the age of the bulk of applicants' parents, and also the families of secondary school graduates (using 1966 data from V. N. Shubkin's study of the Novosibirsk Region). The general results reveal considerably more individuals employed in skilled mental work among families of secondary school graduates compared to the employed population as a whole, and the same is true of University applicants' families compared to the families of secondary school graduates. (4) Moreover, the relative shares of different groups of occupations among applicants' parents vary unevenly compared to the employed population as a whole. The proportion of agricultural workers is particularly low compared to other groups of workers, while the proportion of personnel in science and education and engineering-technical personnel is high compared to other groups employed in primarily mental work. The same tendency is revealed in the dynamics of educational levels. While among urban males from the corresponding groups of the whole population, 6.3% have a higher education and 11.5% have a secondary specialized education, among parents of secondary school graduates the figures are 20.0% and 12.0% respectively, and among applicants' parents they are 39.9% and 23.0%. The comparable figures for urban females are, for higher education, 6.4%, 13.4%, and 26.9%, and for secondary education — 12.8%,

9.0%, and 23.0%.

University applicants come from different regions of the country, but the bulk are from Siberia and the Far East. Large cities (with a population of 100,000 or more) are the most typical places of settlement, accounting for 56-60% of the applicants, while villages account for 15-18% (these types of settlements comprise 34% and 39%, respectively, of the population of the RSFSR, and 33% and 37%, respectively, of the population of Siberia and the Far East). (5)

Given the differences in the composition of applicants' families from areas of different degrees of urbanization, it must be recognized that the formation of occupational objectives by young people is connected with both the character of the family and the area of residence. Both of these factors are, so to speak, superimposed on each other, and ultimately determine the specific features of behavior.

Although the applicants for the various specialties have much in common as regards their social origins, which affects their integrating attraction to the scientific sphere, certain specialties are chosen by applicants who have distinctive features with respect to both the composition of their families and the extent to which they come from different types of settlements. All of the data show that the orientation of different strata to the education of their children, as well as the occupational focus of youth from different social strata, vary depending on the sphere and character of labor, the level of education, and the nature of the place of settlement which is specific to the given social stratum.

This tendency may be observed in the evaluation of the attractiveness of occupations by graduates of secondary schools from different social strata (6), in their career plans, in the differing composition of applicants to the individual higher educational institutions, and indirectly — in the differing social composition of students at individual higher schools and technicums. (7) Thus, studies conducted in the Novosibirsk Region show that at technicums, during the last five years, workers and their children comprised 62-65% of the students, and employees and their children — 22-24%. At higher schools the corresponding figures

were 40-42% and 49-52%. Moreover, the social composition of
the students at specific higher educational institutions and technicums varies depending on the kind of specialized training offered. During this period, for example, workers and their children comprised 19-28% of the students at the University, 28-
40% at the Medical Institute, 37-47% at the Electrical Engineering Institute, and 55-63% at the Institute for Railroad Engineers.

Thus, the specific nature of applicants' social origins observed in our study of University applicants reflects objectively
existing tendencies in society for the formation of young people's occupational goals to be connected with the character of
the social stratum from which they derive. This connection is
revealed both at the level of general plans (to continue one's
education) and particular ones (the choice of a specific occupational direction). It must be emphasized that there is no social
exclusiveness in the formation of occupational inclinations of
youth under socialism, that the occupational goals of youth from
the different strata are varied. But the very fact of belonging
to a certain social stratum, the greater familiarity with the kind
of employment typical for its members, and the greater opportunity for assimilating its mode of behavior, create the conditions
for developing the kind of occupational orientation which is more
typical for this stratum. To the extent that the impact of the social stratum is exercised against the background of many other
influences operating through the schools, the mass communication media, and various personal contacts, it manifests itself
as a tendency toward a high degree of preference for a definite
group of occupations.

Both the sex and age of the individual have a certain impact
on the choice of occupation. Data covering the last nine years
show that physics is most popular among male applicants —
40-53% seek admission to physics departments, followed by 13-
21% who apply for mathematics and 10-14% who aspire to applied mathematics. Chemistry, geology, and history each account for 5-8%, economic cybernetics for 4-6%, biology for 3-
5%, and linguistics for 0.3-0.7%. Girls are distributed more
evenly among the various specialties: 15-20% seek admission
to chemistry departments, while the figures for mathematics,

biology, economic cybernetics, and history are 11-16% in each
case; 7-11% apply for physics; applied mathematics and linguistics each account for 7-9%; and geology attracts 3-4%. The
consequence is a clear division of all University specialties
into "primarily male" — physics, geology, applied mathematics,
and mathematics (with the shares of male applicants accounting
for 86-90%, 67-72%, 67-69% and 57-64% respectively) — and
"primarily female" — chemistry, history, economic cybernetics,
biology, linguistics (with the shares of female applicants accounting for 71-76% in 1962-1965 and 59-62% in 1967-1970,*
62-66%, 71-75%, 66-74%, and 89-94% respectively).

The relationship between the applicants' sex and the preference for particular specialties may also be observed among applicants at more homogeneous technical higher educational institutions. (8) Analysis of applicants' questionnaires shows that
the selective attitudes of boys and girls toward different kinds
of activities emerge at an early school age, and continue during
the period of intensive formation of interests and inclinations.
All this testifies to the existence in society of certain stereotypes of occupational preference according to sex, which is confirmed by differences in the ratings of occupations by secondary
school graduates and teachers, and by the actual feminization
of a number of occupations in whole branches of the economy.
Under current conditions these stereotypes are not always connected with the essence of the occupation itself, and apparently
they have deep historical-psychological causes which call for
special study. At the same time, the attitudes of boys and girls
toward individual specialties are not completely static, and are
subject to change as a result of purposeful activity. But stereo-
typed preferences are so deep that the process of change is
proceeding slowly and, apparently, has a definite limit.

A study of the age composition of applicants shows that in recent years they have become younger (this has also been noted

---

*These figures, for 1962-1965 and 1967-1970, presumably
apply to chemistry. The ones which follow presumably apply
to history, economic cybernetics, biology, and linguistics, in
that order, and are for the whole period 1962-1970.

in other studies). (9) Most are 17-18 years old and have completed secondary school in the year of enrollment or in the preceding year. Although this is the general tendency, there are
some differences in age composition among individual specialties. One consequence of the "youthful" composition of the applicants is that their life experience is limited (to schooling in
most cases), and the same is also true with respect to the channels through which they are connected with society. This also
applies to those who have worked after completing secondary
school, 75% of whom worked for no more than a year. Although
this year, spent in new surroundings, has not passed without
leaving any mark at all, we can hardly say that there has been
any important change in the applicants' social status compared
with that of their families, or that they have assimilated new
value orientations and norms of behavior. Therefore, in appraising the social composition of applicants and students at
higher schools, it is not enough to study only their own social
position just prior to admission, without considering the social
position of their families.

Thus, the formation of occupational orientations is determined through different channels of influence which are connected with both general and specific social circumstances.
Within this framework the individual himself is an active par-
ticipant in the ongoing process. As analysis of questionnaires,
school references and other materials shows, he strives to express the interests which have emerged in the form of some
kind of activity — a search for and reading of literature, club
activities, participation in olympiads, conversations with specialists, heightened attention to the particular subjects in
school, etc. Perception of his own abilities in performing these
activities also has an impact on the consolidation of his occupational orientation. An indicator of abilities is success in those
kinds of activities, accessible to young people, which are connected in some way with the chosen occupation. The role of external factors in this situation consists in providing greater or
lesser opportunities for involvement in these activities.

Analysis shows that in selecting a specific higher educational
institution and a specialty within it, the applicants consider,

directly or indirectly, many factors: the geographic location
and character of the institution; the peculiarities of its operation; whether it includes specialties which interest them, or related specialties; the economy's need for specialists in those
areas (which is reflected in the institution's admissions plans);
the intensity of competition and associated factors; and the difficulty of admission associated with the institutions's examination requirements.

When we consider differences in the occupational aspirations
of boys and girls, differences in the social composition of applicants for the individual specialties, and so on, we can conclude
that the attractiveness of a specialty is determined both by societal needs for the corresponding specialists, as well as by the
nature and intensity of the interest in it on the part of boys and
girls, and of youth from different social strata. The role of interest is particularly evident in heightened striving for certain
specialties despite the unfavorable situation created by the high
degree of competition for them. Thus, the prestige of occupations is formed on the basis of societal needs as these are re-
fracted through societal, group, and individual interests. The
resulting contradiction between societal and individual interests
is resolved by means of competitive selection of the most deserving, prepared, and capable individuals who have passed their
entrance examinations. This kind of selection process, although
it basically satisfies the needs of society (which is interested in
the most qualified performance of every occupational activity)
and the interests of particular individuals (who are interested
in the realization of their creative potentials in the kind of activity for which they are most suited), nonetheless contains certain contradictions. The social character of the contradictions
arising in the process of competitive selection requires special
study. Here we shall examine some of those connected with the
influence of the personal qualities and social characteristics of
applicants on the results of University entrance examinations.
Performance on entrance examinations is an indicator of the
possibility of attaining one's occupational choice at the stage of
admission to a higher school.

In the case of difficult entrance examinations whose emphasis is predominantly on subjects in the physics-mathematics cycle, boys do significantly better than girls (this divergence already begins with the mathematics results). The influence of the degree of interest and purposefulness may be observed in the fact that among physics applicants whose secondary school references directly or indirectly noted an interest in subjects in the physics-mathematics cycle, one out of every two passed the examinations, while among the others it was only one out of every six. Moreover, the closer the content of the examination subjects to the specific features of a specialty, the less the impact of different social factors. The influence of levels of ability is shown indirectly in the fact that among a homogeneous group of youth from large Siberian cities, the examination results in mathematics were distributed in accordance with their secondary school performance in this subject.

Examination results are also connected with the social position of applicants' parents. Among those who come from families in which both parents are employed in highly skilled mental work, 59% passed the examinations, while 55% did so where the parents are in less skilled mental work, and 39% where the parents are in primarily manual labor. The examination results are most clearly differentiated with respect to the educational level of the family (see Table 2).

A more detailed analysis shows that the greater or lesser role of the family is also connected with the degree of urbanization of the place of residence (which affects the character of the family and the school), the sex of the applicant, and the nature of the specialty. The more the applicant is oriented to a specialty and the closer the connection between the examination and the specialty, the less the influence of the family on examination results, and vice versa. The role of the family's educational level is not only explained by the fact that it determines how favorable or unfavorable the circumstances and atmosphere will be to development, and the intensity of the orientation to inherit this educational level, but also by the fact that this characteristic synthesizes in itself the influence of a number of others: the parents' employment status, the family's place of residence, etc. It is as though the family's education contains

Table 2

Results of Entrance Examinations,
Novosibirsk State University, 1967, 1968, 1970,
Depending on Educational Level of Applicants' Parents,
Where Both Parents Have Same Educational Level
(% Passing Examinations)

	Education of parents				
Year	higher	secondary specialized	secondary general	incomplete secondary	primary or less
1967	57	41	37	28	23
1968	66	54	43	48	38
1970	71	50	42	36	33

within itself the essence of the specific social circumstances
of the individual's development, and this strengthens its differentiating function.

Although in statistical terms the applicants' examination results are distributed in accordance with their secondary school
performance, the differences in the quality of schools is reflected in the fact that even among applicants who received the
highest ratings in their graduation certificates we find the whole
gamut of examination grades (including unsatisfactory grades).
The best results were obtained by those who had been in specialized classes and schools (specializing in mathematics or
physics-mathematics). The greater the demands made on entering students, the closer the connection between the place of
residence and examination results. Applicants from large cities show better results than those from rural areas (54% and
46%, respectively, of these groups passed the examinations).*

---

*It is not clear whether the figures refer to the relative
shares of these two groups in the total number who passed the
examinations, or the proportion of individuals in each group
who passed the examinations. The latter seems more likely.

All this material shows the dependence of University entrance examination results on both the applicants' personal characteristics and individual orientations and the specific social circumstances of their development.

The degree of success in studies at higher schools is also connected with both the students' personal qualities and their social origins. Study of data for the University that cover a number of years shows the dual nature of this connection: on the one hand, the connection is with the earlier conditions of development of the student, and on the other — with the results of the University entrance examinations. Thus, while 1/3 of the workers' children who were admitted during 1966-1968 dropped out, and 1/4 of employees' children did so (the chief reason for dropping out was manifest or latent failure in studies), among those who received the highest grades on entrance examinations only 1/5 dropped out, and among those who received lower grades, 2/5 dropped out. This testifies to the fact that the social circumstances of the individual's earlier development leave their mark on his success at the higher school to the degree that they are reflected in the extent of his preparation for higher education.

Thus, the social conditioning of occupational choice may be observed at all the main stages of this process. While at the stage of formation of occupational orientations it is primarily connected with the existence of certain models of behavior among the different social strata and groups, at the stage of implementation of occupational choice and during the period of occupational training the primary factors are the differences in the cultural levels of these groups and in the quality of the educational system and the character of different places of settlement, all of which, in combination, create more or less favorable external conditions for the development of young people.

Notes

1) Our material was obtained in studying applicants and students at Novosibirsk State University.

2) Our classification of employments is based on that used in the All-Union Population Census of 1959.

3) Itogi Vsesoiuznoi perepisi naseleniia 1959 g. RSFSR, Moscow, 1963.

4) L. F. Liss, "On the Stability of the Characteristics and Specific Features of the Social Origins of University Applicants," Sotsial'noe prognozirovanie v oblasti obrazovaniia, Novosibirsk, 1969.

5) Narodnoe khoziaistvo RSFSR v 1967. Statisticheskii ezhegodnik, Moscow, 1967.

6) See V. V. Vodzinskaia, "Orientations Toward Occupations," Molodezh' i trud, Moscow, 1970; Kolichestvennye metody v sotsiologicheskikh issledovaniiakh, Novosibirsk, 1964.

7) See V. V. Vodzinskaia, "On the Problem of the Social Conditioning of Occupational Choice," Chelovek i obshchestvo, II, Leningrad, 1967; O. I. Zotova, A. G. Ashkinazi, and Iu. P. Kovalenko, O nekotorykh sotsiologicheskikh aspektakh vybora professii vypusknikami srednykh shkol, Moscow, 1970; M. N. Rutkevich and F. R. Filippov, Sotsial'nye peremeshcheniia, Moscow, 1970; Effektivnost' podgotovki spetsialistov, Kaunas, 1969.

8) L. T. Pesochina, "Some Generalized Characteristics of a Higher Educational Institution and Its Structural Subdivisions," Materialy seminara po programmirovannomu obycheniiu i nauchnoi organizatsii uchebnogo protsessa, No. 4, Novosibirsk, 1968.

9) See B. Rubin and Iu. Kolesnikov, Student glazami sotsiologa, Rostov State University Publishing House, 1968; M. N. Rutkevich and L. I. Sennikova, "On the Social Composition of the Student Body in the USSR and Its Changing Tendencies," Sotsial'nye razlichiia i ikh preodolenie, Sverdlovsk, 1969.

15 Social Ties and Social Mobility

O. I. SHKARATAN

The material we have collected on social ties embodied in friendship patterns and in family and marriage relations permits us to study more concretely the degree of "openness" of social groups, i.e., the intensity of intergroup contacts.

Let us begin with the friendship patterns of the respondents.* The instructions made it clear that we were interested in individuals who were not members of the respondents' families. As far as we know, this question has not been posed in current or past sociological studies. The absence of comparable material requires that our findings be checked in other surveys. It should

From O. I. Shkaratan, Problemy sotsial'noi struktury rabochego klassa, "Mysl'" Publishing House, Moscow, 1970, pp. 426-455. Notes numbered 1-9 below correspond to footnotes numbered 116-124 in Chapter 3 of Shkaratan's book. Tables numbered 1-7 below correspond to Tables 59-65 in Shkaratan's book.

*This selection covers the same categories of employed personnel and the same areas as those covered in the selection on pp. 63-105. Shkaratan's data are based on empirical investigations conducted among employed personnel of (1) seven machine-building enterprises in Leningrad in 1965-1966, (2) the firm Krasnaia zaria, with plants in Leningrad, Pskov, Porkhov, and Nevel, in 1967, and (3) a variety of economic enterprises in three cities of the Tatar Republic — Kazan, Almetevsk, and Menzelinsk — in 1967-1968. For details on sample size and characteristics of the cities see pp. 63-64 above.

Table 1

Social Contacts Depending on Membership in Socio-Occupational Group,
Leningrad Machine-Building Personnel, 1965 (in %)

Groups of respondents	Closest friend (friends)							
	worker	technician, others with secondary specialized education	engineer, others with higher education	other categories of employees	collective farmer	student	housewife	total
Unskilled personnel in manual labor	77.6	9.2	5.0	2.5	1.6	4.1	—	100
Personnel in nonmanual labor of medium skills	46.5	17.6	13.2	11.8	0.4	7.4	3.1	100
Personnel in skilled, primarily manual labor, employed on machines and mechanisms	68.8	12.5	6.7	4.3	1.2	4.7	1.8	100
Personnel in skilled, primarily manual, hand labor	60.3	13.3	11.0	4.3	1.4	7.0	2.7	100
Highly skilled personnel combining manual and mental work	60.9	18.9	14.4	2.9	—	2.9	—	100
Personnel in skilled mental work	20.2	27.3	32.5	7.9	1.2	7.2	3.7	100
Personnel in highly skilled scientific and technical work	9.1	21.5	50.3	6.7	—	8.6	3.8	100
Organizers of production collectives (from foremen to enterprise executives)	21.2	23.3	41.7	5.4	1.2	5.4	1.8	100
Total	51.9	15.9	16.4	6.0	1.1	6.0	2.7	100

be clear that there could be two or three answers to this question and that the total number of answers exceeds the number of respondents. (1)

It is evident from Tables 1 and 2 that varied social ties are exhibited by all the socio-occupational groups, that there is an absence of "exclusiveness," of caste-like elements, of avoidance of contacts with individuals in the extreme socio-occupational groups. Although their friends are chiefly other workers, unskilled workers employed in manual labor have extensive contacts with individuals employed in positions requiring secondary specialized or higher education. On the other hand, personnel in highly skilled mental work have a certain proportion of their friends among workers. It is characteristic that among executives of production collectives, whose social ties are more varied by virtue of their work activity, the proportion of friendships with workers exceeds 21% in Leningrad and 10% in Pskov. The executives of our labor collectives are recruited from individuals who are in active contact with representatives of all social groups, and consequently they do not themselves form a caste-like, exclusive group, but rather one which is open and actively absorbing information from different strata of the population. Personnel in nonmanual labor of medium skills and skilled workers have the most widely dispersed social ties.

We obtained the same findings in Kazan, where the classification of both the respondents and their friends was close to the one utilized in Leningrad and Pskov. The fact that the association between socio-occupational status of respondents and social position of their friends is not very "strong" is apparent from the Chuprov coefficients, which in this case were: $T = 0.140$ in Kazan, $T = 0.126$ in Almetevsk, and $T = 0.101$ in Menzelinsk.

The data for Kazan confirmed that two groups of working people — skilled workers and executive personnel in various branches of the economy — had the widest range of ties. Moreover, the most open category of workers consisted of those who were employed in highly complex labor which combined manual and mental functions in the work process. Only 14.3% of this group's friendships were with urban workers. A considerable

Table 2

Social Contacts Depending on Membership in Socio-Occupational Group,
Automatic Telephone Station Factory, Pskov, 1967 (in %)

Groups of respondents	Occupational status of friends (in %)								Number of respondents
	collective farmers	workers in agriculture	unskilled workers in city or workers' settlement	skilled workers in city or workers' settlement	employees without specialized education	personnel with secondary specialized education	personnel with higher specialized education	others	
Unskilled personnel in manual labor	–	–	47.0	15.6	18.7	–	–	18.7	32
Personnel in nonmanual labor	–	1.4	22.6	25.3	16.9	19.7	9.9	4.2	71
Personnel in skilled hand labor	–	0.7	6.1	67.1	3.0	10.7	4.5	7.9	265
Personnel in skilled manual labor, employed on machines and mechanisms	0.9	0.9	6.9	74.0	5.2	7.8	1.7	2.6	146
Personnel in skilled mental work and scientific and technical work	–	–	–	20.8	22.2	22.2	32.0	2.8	72
Executives of labor collectives	–	–	–	10.0	5.0	30.0	50.0	5.0	20

proportion of its friends came from the countryside (7.6% were agricultural workers and 5% were collective farmers). A high proportion of friendships were with individuals having a specialized secondary or higher education (42.9% of friendships were accounted for by these groups). This is the most open of the groups employed in executor-type labor.

It must be assumed that these results of our observations are not accidental. Labor that combines mental and manual functions is the most promising type of work; it is the work of the future. This group, which is the most advanced socially, is characterized by broad contacts with all groups, including those far removed from its direct occupational and socio-occupational surroundings.

The second group — executives — whose formation reflects the results of Party and state policy in the selection of executive personnel, is also characterized by social ties that are adequate for the nature of our social structure (21.5% of the friends of this group are workers and collective farmers, 17.5% are employees without specialized education, etc.).

Let us now examine family and marriage relations.

The investigation of Leningrad machine-building personnel provided data on the association between an individual's membership in a particular socio-occupational group and his social-class origins (the social position of his parents). Table 3 shows that the offspring of different classes and social strata may be found in all the groups. At the same time, it is characteristic that among all personnel in skilled, primarily manual labor, among those employed on jobs which combine mental and manual labor, and among personnel in nonmanual labor of medium skills, we find that a particularly large proportion — significantly more than one-half — are the children of workers. On the other hand, among personnel employed in scientific and technical work, children from employees' families predominate, while workers' children account for 31.9% of this group and collective farmers' children account for 3.5%, i.e., less than in any of the other categories of personnel employed in industrial production. This latter indicator testifies to the fact that there is still an inadequate flow of individuals of rural

Table 3

Influence of Social Position of Parents on Socio-Occupational Status
of Employed Personnel in Leningrad Machine-Building, 1965

Groups of employed personnel	Social position of father (in %)				Number of respondents
	worker	collective farmer, individual farmer	employee	other	
Unskilled personnel in manual labor	43.9	37.5	8.4	10.2	107
Personnel in low-skilled labor of mixed type (storeroom personnel)	47.9	37.9	11.6	2.6	269
Personnel in skilled, primarily manual labor, employed on machines and mechanisms	55.6	24.7	15.4	4.3	693
Personnel in skilled, primarily manual, hand labor	58.6	17.9	19.0	4.5	829
Personnel in nonmanual labor of medium skills	57.9	14.2	20.6	7.3	316
Highly skilled personnel combining mental and manual work	53.5	22.4	15.5	8.6	58
Personnel in skilled mental work	46.6	10.6	33.9	8.9	245
Personnel in highly skilled scientific and technical work	31.9	3.5	54.0	10.6	113
Executives of production collectives, including lower group (from foremen to enterprise executives)	42.8	20.5	31.5	5.2	248
Total	52.9	20.8	20.8	5.5	2,878

origin into the ranks of the scientific and technical intelligentsia.

These conclusions were verified in the more thorough investigation conducted in the Krasnaia zaria combine in 1967. Here
it turned out that the family background of unskilled workers
was as follows: collective farmers' children — 36.4%; agricultural workers' children — 15.2%; urban unskilled workers' children — 16.7%; urban skilled workers' children — 21.2%; and
children of nonmanual, including skilled mental, workers —
only 10.5%.

The situation was markedly different among workers in
skilled, primarily manual, hand labor. Children of different social categories of the country's population were widely represented in this socio-occupational group: children of collective
farmers constituted 18.7%; children of agricultural workers —
2.2%; of unskilled urban workers — 17.2%; of skilled urban
workers — 34.9%; of employees without specialized education
— 13.8%; of personnel with specialized secondary education —
3.4%; and of personnel with higher education — 4.9% (about 5%
were children of "others," i.e., those with a social status other
than the ones we have considered).

Let us now turn to scientific and technical personnel (designers, scientific workers). In this group there are considerably
fewer collective farmers' children — 3.9%, no children at all
of agricultural workers, a relatively small proportion of unskilled urban workers' children — 7.8%, a substantial proportion of children from families of skilled urban workers — 17.9%,
of employees without specialized training — 25.1%, of personnel
with secondary specialized education — 16.4%, and of personnel
with higher education — 20.3%. The children of "others" comprise 8.6%.

The findings for the Krasnaia zaria firm deserve particular
attention because the grouping of parents is based on a more
detailed classification of social groups in our society. These
findings also confirm the observations summarized above for
the survey of Leningrad machine-building personnel.

And the findings obtained in the survey of urban residents of
the Tatar Republic are not significantly different. As Table 4
shows, all social strata of our population are broadly represented

here in all the socio-occupational groups. Only two special features should be noted. First, most groups in Kazan have a larger proportion of individuals from rural backgrounds than is the case in Leningrad.

Second, in many groups the children of all categories of employees constitute a smaller proportion than they do in Leningrad, with their share of the total constituting 12% compared to 19% in Leningrad. However, the data on children from employees' families are not fully comparable since the investigation in Kazan covered all branches of the economy while in Leningrad it covered only machine-building, and naturally there is a greater inflow of the more socially advanced groups into machine-building. Therefore, we can only repeat that in the second half of the 1960s all the socio-occupational groups were recruited from the same social sources, although a certain inequality in socio-occupational status still remained because of the different conditions in which children were reared. This is particularly evident in the groups of highly skilled personnel employed in scientific and technical work and in the so-called "creative occupations." In Kazan, for example, the proportions of these groups drawn from children of collective farm families were 8.2% and 4.6% respectively, and the proportions coming from unskilled workers' families were 7.2% and 9.3%, while the proportions drawn from families of highly skilled personnel in mental work reached 27.0% and 25.6%. (2)

The material available from the investigation of Leningrad machine-building personnel included information on the current social position of the individual, on the jobs held by his adult children and, finally, on the social-class status of his parents. Thus, it was possible to trace the fates of families of working people over a span of three generations. Naturally, the group of employed personnel with grown children was a relatively small one, and thus it is difficult to accept the data for this group as representative. Nonetheless, the available information is highly interesting from the standpoint of identification of trends. The group of individuals who had grown children currently employed and whose fathers were workers comprised 252 persons. Thirty-seven percent of this group's children

Table 4

Distribution of Employed Personnel Depending on Social Position of Family Head of Respondent, Kazan, 1967

Groups of respondents	Social position of family head of respondent* at the start of the latter's work activity (in %)								Number of respondents
	collective farmers or individual peasants	agricultural workers	unskilled manual workers	personnel in skilled, primarily manual labor	employees not requiring specialized secondary education	employees requiring specialized education	employees requiring higher education	those who did not answer	
Unskilled personnel in manual labor and low-skilled personnel in non-manual labor without specialized training	41.7	7.4	16.7	18.6	2.6	4.4	0.8	7.8	562
Personnel in skilled, primarily manual labor, employed on machines and mechanisms	25.9	8.4	23.5	22.7	5.2	5.3	1.9	7.1	1,045
Personnel in skilled, primarily manual, hand labor	33.2	6.1	18.0	22.6	5.6	4.9	2.2	7.4	1,049
Personnel in skilled nonmanual labor without specialized education	24.3	4.4	18.4	26.9	7.9	9.2	2.0	6.9	452
Highly skilled personnel combining mental and manual functions	13.3	16.7	13.3	20.1	3.3	10.0	10.0	13.3	30
Personnel in skilled mental work	10.4	2.3	15.4	12.3	14.9	21.5	16.8	6.4	656
Personnel in highly skilled scientific and technical work	8.2	1.2	7.2	17.6	14.1	18.8	27.0	5.9	85
Highly skilled personnel in the so-called "creative occupations"	4.6	2.3	9.3	9.3	20.9	23.4	25.6	4.6	43
Executives of labor collectives and state organizations	27.9	1.1	9.7	23.7	12.9	10.7	8.6	5.4	93

*Shkaratan's "respondent" covers all those who were questioned, including those who did not answer.

(93 persons), i.e., the grandchildren of workers, became workers themselves. But not all of their fathers (the intermediate
generation) were workers: in 27 cases (out of 93) they were engineers, technicians, and employees. Thus we do not find a con-
tinuous series in the succession of occupations. This is understandable, since a high level of social mobility, the rapid intermingling of social strata, and the absence of caste-like elements
are distinctive features of our society's social structure. Among
the grandchildren of workers, in addition to the 93 persons who
also became workers in primarily manual labor, there were 56
technicians, 30 engineers, and 45 who were students at higher
educational institutions or technicums.

The fate of collective farmers' grandchildren is an interesting one. The proportion who have become workers in primarily
manual labor (34.1%) is about the same as in the case of workers' grandchildren. Moreover, the fathers of this group (the
intermediate generation, i.e., those who were surveyed) were
workers themselves in 49 cases out of 56, while in 4 cases they
were engineers and technicians, and in 3 cases they were employees. Thus, in contrast to the intermediate generation of
workers' children, the intermediate generation of peasants'
children is more homogeneous in its social composition. In
other words, the representatives of the generation which begins
work in the city for the first time remain workers as a rule,
but their offspring follow the same path in life as do the children of hereditary workers. We traced the genealogy of a total
of 164 grandchildren of collective farmers and individual peasants, and of these, 56 became workers, 41 became technicians
and entered other fields requiring a secondary specialized education, 13 became engineers, doctors, etc., 14 became employees without specialized education, and 26 were pursuing
their studies at higher schools or technicums. All this testifies
once again to the high social mobility of the population.

Let us now examine in greater detail what happens to grown
children depending on the jobs and differing socio-occupational
status of the surveyed parents. We should note, first of all, that
in the present generation we do not find a social rigidity of employments. Among workers' children, 34.9% became workers

themselves, 7.9% became employees without specialized education, while the remainder were either pursuing their studies or
had already received a secondary specialized or higher education. Among executives of enterprises, heads of shops, and other
executive personnel, 8.4% of the children had become workers,
11.6% had become employees without specialized education, and
the remainder had either received a secondary specialized or
higher education or were continuing their studies. We see that
there was not a single category of employed personnel in industry that was not represented, through its grown children, in the
different social groups. There is clearly no evidence of caste-
like elements or of rigidity of groups. It is true, however, that
a certain amount of continuity may still be observed in the employments of groups in intellectual or primarily manual work.

The same conclusion follows from Table 5, which groups the
respondents according to the nature of their labor. It is noteworthy that even in the group of highly skilled workers combining mental and manual labor, in which the material possibilities
and conditions of life provided by the families create all the necessary prerequisites for the children to enter preferred occupations and to acquire the corresponding social status (although
the small number of individuals in the sample limits the significance of our conclusions), 40% of the grown children have taken
the same path as their parents and have also become workers.
At the same time, even among personnel in highly skilled mental work, a considerable proportion (26.3%) of the grown children have chosen workers' occupations. It should be noted once
again that such a high level of social mobility is evidence of the
deep-rooted nature of socialist democracy.

This is also suggested by our findings on the association between educational level and the social origins of the respondents' children. In the latter group the proportion having an education of up to 7 grades is greatest among the children of peasants (31.1%), followed by the children of workers (16.9%) and
the children of employees (7.6%). The proportion of individuals
with an education of 8 to 11 grades is highest among the children of workers (64.9%), followed by the children of peasants
(53.2%) and the children of employees (52.6%). The proportion

Table 5

Employment Status of Grown Children Depending on Socio-Occupational Status of Parents, Leningrad Machine-Building (in %)

Groups of respondents	Employment status of grown children (in %)						
	workers	personnel with secondary specialized education	personnel with higher education	employees	students	housewives	total
Unskilled personnel in manual labor	37.3	20.9	11.6	13.9	16.3	—	100
Personnel in nonmanual labor of medium skills	37.6	22.8	11.3	7.9	15.9	4.5	100
Personnel in skilled, primarily manual labor, employed on machines and mechanisms	43.2	21.6	7.5	7.5	16.5	3.7	100
Personnel in skilled, primarily manual, hand labor	34.4	23.4	14.3	7.5	17.7	2.7	100
Highly skilled personnel combining manual and mental work	40.2	19.9	—	—	34.9	5.0	100
Personnel in skilled mental work	28.6	27.0	17.5	4.7	14.3	7.9	100
Personnel in highly skilled scientific and technical work	26.3	10.6	26.3	5.3	31.5	—	100
Organizers of production collectives (from foremen to enterprise executives)	13.0	39.4	19.7	6.5	15.9	5.5	100
Total	32.9	24.8	13.2	8.1	16.6	4.4	100

of specialists with higher or secondary education is highest among the children of employees (39.5%), followed by the children of workers (17.7%) and the children of collective farmers (15.3%).

Other data indicate that with the passage of time the role of social-class differences in determining the amount of education received is declining. For example, 15% of the grown children of employed personnel with a 5th-6th grade education are students, while among employed personnel with a 7th-9th grade education and among specialists with a secondary or higher education, 13% of the grown children are students.

The information on the social composition of students who are combining work and study is of particular interest. Of this group, 47% are workers' children, 25% come from a collective farm background, and 23% are employees' children.

Among workers' children, a total of 24% are continuing their studies, while among collective farmers' children the figure is 23%, and among employees' children — 31%. But the differences between the social-class groups are greater when we consider the proportions of children from each of the groups who are combining work and higher education or postgraduate study. Among workers' children the proportion of such individuals is 5.5%, among collective farmers' children — 6.9%, and among employees' children — 10.1%.

The first stages in the working careers of youth are significantly affected by social origin and the cultural and educational level of the family. But in the subsequent advancement of youth the role of these factors is substantially reduced by the social institutions of the socialist society operating through the system of correspondence and evening education. The performance of the individual in production and his social and political activity assume increasing importance.

In this connection, V. N. Shubkin's findings in his study of the realization of the career plans of youth completing secondary school in the Novosibirsk region in 1963 are significant. It was determined that a certain association exists between the realization of the career plans of secondary school graduates and the social position of their parents. Most young people aspire

to the creative occupations. However, the social status of parents exercises a definite influence even in the development of
orientations toward the choice of an occupation.

Thus, the children of collective farmers and agricultural
workers do not expect to begin their working careers in mental work, but in contrast to the position of their parents, they
see their advancement through transfer to employment in the
city, in industry. Among urban children, the career plans of
those who come from families employed in primarily manual
labor differ relatively little from the plans of those whose families are employed in mental work.

It is true, of course, that the conditions of life in intelligentsia families provide their youth with greater opportunities for
achieving their career plans. Nonetheless, a considerable proportion of workers' children achieved theirs as well. Collective
farmers' children were less successful in solving their problems. (3) It should also be noted that some of the children from
the lower-paid and less cultured groups of the population drop
out of school in the senior grades.

The authors of a Moscow study present the following data for
the first half of the 1960s: in the 10th-11th grades of secondary
school, 42.8% of the pupils are children whose fathers have
highly skilled jobs, while in trade schools and factory schools
this group of children constitutes 4% of the student body; in 4th
grade classes the proportion of children having both a father
and mother accounts for 81.4% of the pupils, while in vocational-
technical schools such children comprise 57.6% of the pupils.
The writers' justifiable conclusion is: "As we move from class
to class, a considerable number of children whose parents are
employed in unskilled and average-paid work drop out, and the
percentage of children whose parents are employed in highly
skilled work increases sharply." (4)

Similar findings were obtained by I. M. Musatov in Novosibirsk. He showed that pupils from the socially less advanced
groups drop out because of poor performance. This circumstance, of course, is not biologically predetermined; it is socially conditioned by the level of cultural development in the
pupils' environment. According to the results of Musatov's

sample study of the performance of schoolchildren in the Novosibirsk secondary schools in the 1963/1964 academic year, an average of 8% of all pupils did unsatisfactory work, but among the children of unskilled workers this proportion was 15.6%, and among skilled workers' children it was only 7.8%; among the children of low-skilled employees it rose to 8.8%, while among the children of highly skilled personnel it fell to 3.2%. Although only 16% of all pupils were the children of unskilled workers, this category accounted for 40% of all retarded children and 34% of those who had to repeat a grade. (5)

According to the findings of the State Committee of the Council of Ministers on Vocational-Technical Education, children from low-income groups of the population, because of all the factors indicated here, frequently do not complete a full secondary education but enroll in vocational-technical schools after the 8th grade. Thus, 30.9% of the pupils in the schools studied (who accounted for 65.5% of all students in this system) did not have one or both of their parents. Of those who did have both parents, 56% came from families with an income per family member of up to 20 rubles per month, 22.3% — with an income of 21-30 rubles per month, and only 4.3% — with an income of more than 50 rubles per month. (6)

Hence the fundamental importance of the decree of the CPSU Central Committee and the USSR Council of Ministers providing for the gradual transformation of schools of the vocational-technical type into special kinds of educational complexes which will provide three to four years of instruction and in which youngsters who have no parents or who come from low-income families will be able to obtain a complete secondary education and thereby will have a real possibility of choosing a life path corresponding to their abilities and inclinations.

We may also add that, according to the findings of the already cited investigation of students graduating from Leningrad secondary schools in the 1963-1967 period (with E. K. Vasil'eva and G. G. Zaitsev heading the project, and the author of this book acting as consultant), the proportion of those who could not pursue a higher education because of financial difficulties fell from 21.4% in 1963 to 7.3% in 1967, relative to the number of employed secondary school graduates.

Thus, by the end of the 1960s our socialist system had, in effect, eliminated in the great majority of cases the influence of economic circumstances on the achievement of the career plans of children from different social groups. However, the influence of inequality in social and cultural background still remains. Thus, the same investigation of graduates of Leningrad secondary schools shows that 52% of those entering higher schools were youngsters whose parents had a higher education (this comprised 80% of all such youngsters), and 31% came from families in which the parents had a secondary specialized education.

Is the influence of family status on the future social position of the individual just as strong as it is on the start of his independent working life? The investigation conducted in the Tatar Republic permits us to verify to some extent the hypothesis of the equalizing effect of social institutions on the individual's subsequent work career. Our findings show that in Kazan the association between social origins and education at the start of an individual's work career can be expressed as $T = 0.198$, while the association between social origins and education at the time of the survey was $T = 0.203$*. In the language of statistics this appears as follows. Of the Kazan residents who had a higher education, 7.8% were the children of collective farmers, while only 2.9% of those who began their work careers with a higher education were the children of collective farmers. Of all residents with a higher education, 10.3% were the children of workers in unskilled manual labor, but the latter category constituted only 7.4% of those who began their work careers after completing a higher education. The gap for children of skilled urban workers is less — 11.4% and 10.3% respectively. But the relationship is reversed among children from families employed in positions requiring a higher education. Such children comprised 25.6% of all personnel with a higher education, and 32.5% of those who began their work careers after receiving such an education.

Similar findings, testifying to the declining influence of social origins on the social status of the individual in the course

---

*In the light of the material that follows, the values for T given here by Shkaratan appear to be reversed.

of his work career, were obtained for Almetevsk and Menzelinsk.

Let us now examine the influence of social origins on work performance and social and political activity.

According to data obtained in the study of Leningrad machine-building personnel, the average skill grades of workers were as follows: 3.75 for children of workers in manual labor, 3.67 for children of collective farmers, and 4.55 for employees' children.* These differences are closely related to differences in the average length of vocational training, which was 12 months in the first case, 9 months in the second, and 20 months in the third.

The value orientations of hereditary workers are of special interest to enterprises. Among children of workers in manual labor, the majority (56%) were satisfied with their specialties. Among employees' children, partial satisfaction was typical ("In general I like the work").

No clear association between work performance and social origins can be observed among workers in today's Soviet industry. Thus, among Leningrad machine-building personnel, 36.8% of workers' children overfulfilled their shift assignments, while 39.4% of collective farmers' children did so. On the other hand, there were hardly any hereditary workers who failed to fulfill their shift assignments (only 0.8% of the total), while 4.2% of those of rural origin failed to do so. The reason for this does not lie in differing attitudes toward work (such differences do not exist) but in the special circumstances of being raised in the countryside. Most of those who do not fulfill their shift assignments are rather young children of peasants who have not yet become accustomed to the city or to the enterprise. The slight superiority of children of rural origin with respect to the overfulfillment of output norms is associated with the longer work experience of this group, and also with the fact that the children of workers in manual labor are actively moving into the ranks of the technical intelligentsia, a process which embraces the most energetic and professionally capable portion of hereditary workers. This also explains the difference in the

---

*Like a number of other Soviet wage scales, that for machine-building workers normally has six skill grades.

extent of participation in rationalization activity (8.2% among workers' children compared to 10.5% among collective farmers' children). There are also certain differences in pay: the average wages of collective farmers' children are 5% higher than those of workers' children. But at the present time it is the length of employment that exercises a considerable influence on many aspects of the work performance of individuals, and this is about three years longer among collective farmers' children than among hereditary workers, which is also the approximate gap in age of these groups. This is fully understandable. Until the mid-1950s the countryside served as the principal source of workers' cadres. Only in recent years has the role of the working class in replenishing itself increased sharply, with the result that the proportion of individuals of peasant origin in the current generation of Leningrad machine-building workers has fallen to 12.3%.

Differences in length of employment, and consequently in social and political experience, also explain differences in indicators of Party membership. Among machine-building personnel who are hereditary workers, 15.2% are Communists, while among collective farmers' children in machine-building the figure is 26.8%. The proportions of Komsomol members are 19.5% and 10.4% respectively. Participation in community life (the holding of elective posts, community assignments) closely follows the same lines: the proportion of hereditary workers who have community assignments is 56.9%, while among collective farmers' children it is 61.5%.

All this makes it clear that social ties in the form of parents-to-children (i.e., social origins) do not have a significant impact on the intensity of manifestation of basic class characteristics. However, in some aspects of daily life and culture these ties (more accurately, the differences between city and countryside that still remain) do show themselves. For example, hereditary workers have more books in their personal libraries (an average of 74 compared to 60 for those of peasant origin), and they read more books per month. Those who have arrived from the countryside are more strongly attracted to television (they regularly view all programs), while the proportion of

Table 6

Employment Status of Wives (Husbands) Depending on Socio-Occupational Status of Respondents, Leningrad Machine-Building, 1965

Groups of respondents	Employment status of wives (husbands) (in %)						
	workers	personnel with secondary specialized education	personnel with higher education	employees	students	housewives	total
Unskilled personnel in manual labor	66.4	8.1	5.3	5.3	–	14.9	100
Personnel in nonmanual labor of medium skills	65.2	13.7	6.6	7.0	3.1	4.4	100
Personnel in skilled, primarily manual labor, employed on machines and mechanisms	61.5	15.3	5.4	13.0	1.0	3.8	100
Personnel in skilled, primarily manual, hand labor	52.9	17.3	6.3	16.1	1.7	5.7	100
Highly skilled personnel combining manual and mental work	47.9	14.8	6.2	24.9	–	6.2	100
Personnel in skilled mental work	27.9	22.1	31.5	10.7	2.9	4.9	100
Personnel in highly skilled scientific and technical work	10.5	23.2	53.8	6.3	3.1	3.1	100
Organizers of production collectives (from foremen to enterprise executives)	25.7	17.4	27.9	17.8	1.7	9.5	100
Total	51.2	16.3	12.6	12.7	1.7	5.5	100

workers' children who attend theaters and concerts is higher. These circumstances primarily reflect not differences in material well-being (income per capita and housing space are about the same for both groups) but differences in social traditions and general cultural levels.

Let us now examine the extent of social ties between different groups of employed personnel in industry, and whether there are purely workers' families, for example, or whether families of mixed social composition are now typical. We have already ascertained how complex are the genealogies, how interwoven are the social employments among three generations. Tables 6 and 7 are of interest in this respect. They present data which portray the association between the socio-occupational status of respondents and the employment status of their wives (husbands).

It is clear from Tables 6 and 7 that family and marriage ties are formed in such a way that they embrace the whole society and are not locked within given social groups. However, we cannot help but note that within the extreme groups (workers in unskilled manual labor, on the one hand, and personnel employed in highly skilled mental work, on the other) there is a high degree of homogeneity of marriage ties. The greatest heterogeneity of family and marriage ties prevails among skilled workers, particularly among highly skilled personnel combining manual and mental functions (adjusters, repair-mechanics). Less than one-half of the married couples in this group (47.9%) are of the purely workers' type, while the remainder are of mixed social composition. Marriage ties are also highly dispersed among personnel in skilled mental work requiring primarily a specialized secondary education. In Leningrad the marriage ties of this category are almost equally distributed among three groups: in 27.9% of the cases the spouse is a worker, in 22.1% of the cases — an individual with secondary specialized education, and in 31.5% of the cases — an individual with higher education. A similar situation may be observed at the Pskov automatic telephone station plant, where personnel in skilled mental work are married to workers in 23.8% of the cases and to employees without specialized education in 19% of

Table 7

Employment Status of Wives (Husbands) Depending on Socio-Occupational Status of Respondents, Automatic Telephone Station Plant, Pskov, 1967

Groups of respondents	Employment status of wives (husbands) (in %)								Number of respondents
	collective farmers	workers in agriculture	unskilled workers in city or workers' settlement	skilled workers in city or workers' settlement	employees without specialized education	personnel with secondary specialized education	personnel with higher specialized education	others	
Unskilled personnel in manual labor	—	—	23.0	26.8	38.6	7.7	3.9	—	26
Personnel in nonmanual labor	—	—	13.2	51.0	5.6	22.7	7.5	—	53
Personnel in skilled, primarily manual, hand labor	—	—	10.2	45.7	9.8	21.6	8.5	4.2	166
Personnel in skilled manual labor, employed on machines and mechanisms	1.2	1.2	13.4	61.0	8.6	14.6	—	—	82
Personnel in skilled mental work, and scientific and technical work	2.4	—	—	23.8	19.0	28.6	23.8	2.4	42
Executives of labor collectives	—	—	—	27.3	9.1	27.3	36.3	—	11

the cases. It is important to note that the dispersion of family and marriage ties, viewed in a social framework, promotes social progress.

Among Leningrad machine-building personnel whose wives (husbands) were workers, 10.9% were continuing their education, with 2.1% attending higher educational institutions, while among those whose spouses were technicians the corresponding figures were 39% and 10.5%. Among those whose wives (husbands) were students, 59.8% were continuing their education, with 17.6% attending higher educational institutions. However paradoxical it may seem, when the spouse was a housewife the husband was less likely to be continuing his education (the corresponding figures were 24% and 5%). Similar results were obtained for the reading of books, theater attendance, and other aspects of the cultural development of employed personnel. Naturally, the data apply to identical (comparable) age groups. Thus, it appears that being married to a housewife does not create better conditions for continuing one's education and for the social advancement of the husband. On the contrary, other things being equal — including age categories — our findings show that the more active participation of the wife in the life of society promotes the social growth of the husband.

In order to obtain a more precise picture of social ties, in the investigation conducted in the Tatar Republic we attempted to examine the integrated socio-occupational status of members of the families of respondents (excluding the latter). The results were highly interesting. The degree of correlation between the socio-occupational status of respondents and that of the members of their families was higher than it was between the socio-occupational status of respondents and that of their friends. This was to be expected of course, although, as we noted earlier, families of mixed social composition predominate in our society. The Chuprov coefficients expressing the relationship between the socio-occupational status of the respondents and that of the members of their families were as follows: $T = 0.172$ in Kazan, $T = 0.150$ in Almetevsk, $T = 0.171$ in Menzelinsk.

In considerable measure the material presented above has

already revealed the nature of social mobility in contemporary Soviet society.

Analysis of the dynamics of the social position of families from generation to generation is especially important in examining social mobility.

The family chart included in the questionnaire used in the investigation conducted in the Tatar Republic contained information on all members of the family who were employed or on pension at the time of the study. The families were divided into ten groups:

1) families in which there was a rise in social level without a transition of members of the family to groups employed in positions and jobs requiring a higher education;

2) families in which the rise in socio-occupational status from generation to generation was associated with the transition of some members of the family to jobs requiring higher education;

3) families in which the younger and older generations retained approximately the same socio-occupational status, but within a range of jobs requiring no more than a secondary specialized education;

4) families in which there was no rise in social status between the older and younger generations, but in which both generations included individuals employed in jobs requiring higher education;

5) families in which there was a fall in status, a shift of the younger generation to a lower socio-occupational status, with both generations remaining within a range of jobs not requiring more than a secondary education;

6) families in which there were individuals in the older generation who had jobs requiring a higher education while there were no such individuals in the younger generation;

7-10) families in which the representatives of three generations were employed. The number of such families, of course, was relatively small, and thus our data are not representative in a statistical sense. However, they may be used to characterize certain processes. The seventh group included families in which the younger generation experienced more progressive changes than the middle generation but remained in jobs not requiring a higher education. The eighth group consisted of families in which the younger generation underwent more progressive changes than the middle generation and also included individuals employed in jobs requiring a higher education. The ninth group comprised families in which the changes in the younger generation were less progressive than in the middle generation, but the social status of the younger generation remained higher than that of the older generation, with higher education characterizing both the middle and younger generations. The tenth group comprised families in which the changes in the younger generation were less progressive than in the middle generation, with the changes in all cases remaining within the types of jobs requiring no more than a secondary education. In each case the social status of the family was determined by considering the position of the respondent. (7)

Let us now turn to some quantitative indices. Given the statistics available, we must confine ourselves to the data for Kazan.

The first group included 36.2% of the families investigated, while the second included 14.5%. This means that more than one-half of the families (50.7%) were characterized by a high level of social mobility.

A considerable percentage of the families remained at a stable social level. This applies to families of the third (27.6%) and fourth (2.9%) groups.

It is characteristic that families which experienced a decline in family social status represented an immeasurably smaller proportion — 17.1%. The fifth group included 10.5% of the families, and the sixth — 6.6%. But in families of the sixth group, where members of the younger generation had a secondary education, there were still prospects of social advancement. Therefore, it would be rash to accept the figure of 6.6% as representing the proportion of families with declining social status.

Families of the seventh to tenth groups constituted an insignificant proportion of the total, only 1.8%. Hence we need not consider them.

Thus, we do not have the kind of distribution, let us say, in which 50% of the families raised their social status and 50% experienced a decline. What we have is a situation in which there have been fundamental changes in social structure accompanied by intensive growth in the proportion of upwardly mobile families and an active process of increasing social homogeneity in society.

It is obvious from the material presented here that an extremely important feature of the social structure of socialist society is the absence of stable, self-reproducing, exclusive, "closed" social strata.

The same findings can also be used to characterize the social sources of recruitment of the working class. They show that all socio-occupational groups of personnel in industry are formed today from representatives of different social strata, and that these groups are increasingly similar with respect to sources of recruitment. This conclusion is confirmed by an analysis of data on the social-class origins of different age groups of employed personnel in Leningrad machine-building.

For the older age groups the initial structure of recruitment was different, naturally, than the one recorded in our investigation. Apparently it included more individuals of working class background, who subsequently shifted into the ranks of the intelligentsia, regular armed forces personnel, etc. However, there is no need to introduce such strong qualifications as were necessary in interpreting the data of the census of workers and employees conducted by the All-Union Central Council of Trade Unions in 1929. The data obtained at that time really could not be used, without risking serious mistakes, to analyze the sources of recruitment of the working class during the Imperialist and Civil Wars, since the qualitative migration processes which occurred in the 1920s completely changed the structure of the older age groups of the working class in comparison with the initial structure. There are no grounds for assuming that such great distortions were also introduced during the Great Patriotic War and the subsequent period of peaceful socialist construction, since, as analysis of the material presented above shows, social mobility both within the working class and beyond it embraces descendants from all social strata more or less evenly.

For purposes of analysis we took three age groups of Leningrad machine-building personnel: 20-24 years, 30-34 years, and
50-54 years. The youngest age groups are not included because
they are not firmly attached to their jobs. As for the 55 and
over age group, its representation in our sample is too small.
The data for the three basic age groups permit us to analyze
the structure of recruitment of the working class at the end of
the 1920s and the early 1930s, at the end of the 1940s, and during the current period.

Among the older generation of the working class, 58% were
of worker origin, 27.7% were children of collective farmers,
10.9% were employees' children, and 3.4% were in the "others"
category. Among the postwar generation of the working class,
49.5% were children of workers, 19.8% were children of collective farmers, 24.1% were employees' children, and 6.6% were
children of "others." In the current generation of workers,
55.3% are of worker origin, 12.3% are children of collective
farmers, 25.9% are employees' children, and 6.5% are children
of "others."

Despite possible inaccuracies in these figures associated with
the social migration of the past, they suggest conclusions which
coincide with the observations of journalists and the testimony
of managerial personnel and Party workers: the proportion of
collective farmers' children is declining sharply (it is less than
50% of the level prevailing at the end of the 1920s and early
1930s); the proportion of employees' children is rising markedly; and the proportion of workers' children — following a natural decline in the postwar years — is rising somewhat.

In 1965 the Central Committee of the Komsomol conducted a
sociological study of the factors determining the degree of satisfaction of youth in automobile and tractor plants with their
jobs and their advancement in production (see Chapter 1).* It
turned out that among the workers of these plants, which are
very typical of contemporary Soviet industry as regards sources
of recruitment of the work force, 49.6% were the children of urban workers, 9.8% were the children of agricultural workers,

_____

*This section was not included in the present volume.

15.5% were the children of collective farmers, 21.1% were employees' children, and 4% were the children of "others." However, the figures differ markedly among cities. In Kutaisi and Minsk the cadres are drawn largely from the countryside, while in Lvov and Kharkov, on the other hand, some 75% of the recruits are the children of urban residents.

In a book issued in 1959, the economist M. Ia. Sonin noted that the ranks of manual workers were being replenished both by the children of workers as well as by the children of collective farmers and the intelligentsia. These were also the sources of recruitment of the intelligentsia. The collective farm peasantry is being reproduced primarily from its own ranks, although to a certain extent it is being replenished by working-class and intelligentsia children. Thus, a distinguishing feature of the reproduction of classes in our socialist society is the systematically increasing similarity of the sources of their reproduction. In this connection, the classification of sources according to indicators of social class is inadequate and should be supplemented by several other indicators. Sonin proposes that in regulating the sources of recruitment, primary consideration should be given to two features: (a) the division of the population into urban and rural, in connection with significant differences in their conditions of life; (b) sex and age, as well as the degree of preparation for social labor. (8) In our view these correct conclusions will continue to be significant in the near future.

It is difficult to agree with N. A. Aitov's statement that "at the present time the peasantry is the main source of recruitment of the working class in our country." (9) Aitov cites the following data in this connection: 48% of the workers in Kazan enterprises in 1963 were the children of collective farmers (or peasants); at some Lithuanian enterprises (note the "at some"), 53-56.7% of the workers were the children of peasants (data from Razvitie rabochego klassa v natsional'nykh respublikakh SSSR, Moscow, 1962, pp. 111-112); in 1960, 37% of the workers participating in communist labor at nine enterprises in Moscow were the children of peasants (from Voprosy organizatsii i metodiki konkretno-sotsiologicheskikh issledovanii, Moscow, 1963, p. 124).

Aitov has not considered two circumstances: (1) his examples rely chiefly on areas of high inflow of labor from the country-side; (2) the figures apply to all age groups, while the study of sources of recruitment requires the adjustment of the data on social origins according to the period in which the individual began work in industry. Finally, the figures themselves not only fail to corroborate but seem to conflict with Aitov's conclusion. Aside from the data for Lithuania, they refer to predominantly nonrural sources of recruitment of the working class.

For the contemporary theory and practice of the management of social processes, it is not enough to rely exclusively on social-class categories in analyzing sources of recruitment of the working class. Nor can we confine ourselves to studying these sources only with respect to the working class taken as a whole. By relying on the kind of differentiation of the working class presented in the preceding section of this chapter,* we could then analyze the sources of its recruitment from the stand-point of the socio-occupational status of the heads of families of individuals belonging to different socio-occupational groups. Thus, the analysis should be based on a combination of data relating to the class status, socio-occupational status, and area of origin (village versus city, with subdivisions according to type of city) of recruits to the working class.

Unfortunately, basic data of this type are not at our disposal. All of the findings presented above on the socio-occupational status of the respondents and their grown children help us to understand, in some measure, the main tendency in the development of sources of recruitment of different social groups of the working class, a tendency which reveals a process of steady intermingling of these sources.

*   *   *

On the basis of all the material presented in this chapter, the process of formation of the principal social, intraclass groups

_____
*Shkaratan is referring here to the material on pp. 63-105 of this volume.

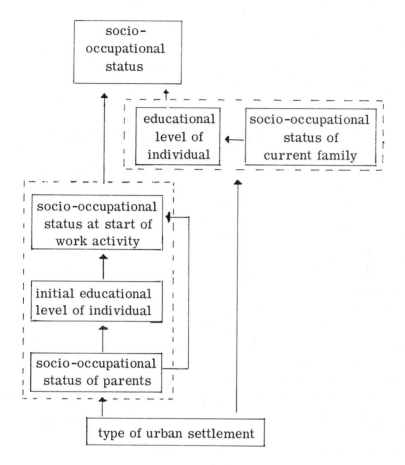

may be presented in the form of the above scheme.

The interaction of the individual elements in this scheme has been the subject of our study. As the scheme shows, the socio-occupational groupings are determined by the initial condition of social relations in society, as these are expressed in indicators of the social status of families in which the rearing of new recruits to the social groups proceeds. The educational level of the individual at the start of his work activity is to a large degree predetermined by the family, and this has a significant impact on the distribution of new members of the work force among the socio-occupational groups. The investigation showed that education acquired in the process of work activity, and the

adjusted [usrednennyi] social status of the new family formed
by the individual, have a relatively independent impact on the
ultimate socio-occupational status of this individual.

Moreover, there is a rather clear-cut connection between
types of urban settlements and the characteristics of socio-
occupational groups. It seems clear in general that, as we move
from a larger to a smaller city, the demands made on the socio-
occupational and social-cultural potential of an individual of
given socio-occupational status decline. We may also observe
a declining level of social expectations and more modest claims
on the part of the population with respect to social advancement.
This is explained to a large extent by the fact that a small city
expels its surplus, socially active population, while a large city,
with a stabilized and relatively conservative system of social
groups, retains and redistributes the socially mobile part of
city-dwellers within its own limits.

We can recognize that large cities represent a type of intensive, organic urbanization of society, and therefore should be
evaluated as a kind of standard, a model of the near future of
society. Other types of urban settlements represent less developed types of aggregates of social relations. It is no accident that our scheme includes the type of urban settlement, influencing as it does both the initial as well as the subsequent
stages of an individual's social career. The socio-occupational
structure itself is set by the type of urban settlement, and this
structure — as we have seen — differs markedly among cities
primarily in the proportions of socio-occupational groups, and
therefore in the scale and rates of social mobility.

Notes

1) It should be noted that, naturally, we could not distribute
the friends of the respondents according to the same gradations
as were applied to the respondents. Individuals frequently did
not have sufficiently precise information on the socio-occupational
status of their friends. That is why the friends of the respondents in the 1967 studies were classified into the following categories: collective farmers, agricultural workers, unskilled

urban workers, skilled urban workers, employees without specialized education, technicians and others with specialized secondary education, engineers and others with higher education,
students, housewives, and others. In Kazan, as well as in other
cities, hardly anyone (from 1% to 2%, depending on the group)
was included in the "others" category, i.e., those who were not
covered by the selected gradations. We may assume that our
classification was satisfactory for the purposes for which it
was used in the survey. [Shkaratan may be referring here only
to cities in the Tatar Republic. Table 2 shows that in Pskov
more than 18% of unskilled workers' friends were in the "others" category.]

2) We omit the data for Almetevsk and Menzelinsk, which do
not contribute anything fundamentally new to the investigation
of this problem.

3) See V. N. Shubkin, "The Choice of Occupation Under Conditions of Communist Construction (Results of an Empirical
Sociological Investigation of Occupational Inclinations of Schoolchildren)," Voprosy filosofii, 1964, No. 8, pp. 18, 24, 27; "Youth
Enters Life," Voprosy filosofii, 1965, No. 5, p. 65.

4) Rabochii klass i tekhnicheskii progress, Moscow, 1965,
p. 258.

5) See I. M. Musatov, Sotsial'nye problemy trudovykh
resursov v SSSR (Opyt konkretnogo ekonomiko-sotsiologiche-
skogo issledovaniia), Moscow, 1967, p. 47.

6) From data obtained in the All-Union Scientific Research
Institute of Vocational-Technical Education by the author's
diploma candidate, L. A. Kesti.

7) The method of classification was worked out by E. K.
Vasil'eva. It seems to us that the principles on which it is
based can be useful in further studies which rely on more extensive statistical data.

8) See M. Ia. Sonin, Vosproizvodstvo rabochei sily v SSSR
i balans truda, Moscow, 1959, p. 59.

9) Voprosy filosofii, 1965, No. 3, pp. 7-8.

16 Social Mobility in the Countryside

IU. V. ARUTIUNIAN

A need for change is the preliminary and internal condition for mobility, while the actual movement is its external mani- festation and implementation. Thus, we now shift our attention from the analysis of social needs to their realization by means of social mobility. Radical changes in the social structure of the population and the rapid increase in its professionalization are naturally accompanied by the intensive and large-scale so- cial movement of both groups and individuals from one social stratum to another, from the collective farm-cooperative sec- tor to the state sector, and so on. Social mobility is a matter of fundamental significance. People change not only their jobs and occupations, but their very mode of life, and this is some- times accompanied by the restructuring of the whole social- psychological cast of the individual.

The processes of social mobility have their own peculiarities under rural conditions. They are simultaneously simpler and more complex than in urban areas. They are simpler to the ex- tent that the socio-occupational structure of the countryside is not as multilayered as in the city. There are no social groups such as the creative, scientific-technical, and higher adminis- trative intelligentsia. But at the same time the countryside has

---

Our title. From Iu. V. Arutiunian, Sotsial'naia struktura sel'skogo naseleniia SSSR, "Mysl'" Publishing House, Moscow, 1971, pp. 304-333. Tables 1-14 below correspond to Tables 94- 107 in the Arutiunian book. This is Chapter 8 of Arutiunian's volume and is entitled "The Realization of Social Mobility."

its own peculiarities connected with the existence of an additional social feature. That is, here we find a boundary between
two forms of property, and classes associated with these forms
of property. Here the collective farm peasantry interacts directly with the rural working class and intelligentsia.

Despite the existence of complex differentiation, the countryside is characterized by a large-scale shifting of population that
promotes processes of integration. Mobility within the village
proceeds unimpeded both between sectors and between social
strata of the population.

Most important, the division between social spheres of employment of labor — between the collective farm-cooperative
and state sectors — is becoming less and less clear-cut. The
erasure of boundaries between these sectors is conditioned both
by the organic inclusion of the collective farm-cooperative sector in the uniform system of national economy and by the steadily increasing similarity of the social, economic, and production
foundations of collective farms and state enterprises. We have
already mentioned the mass transfers — so familiar in the modern history of the Soviet countryside — from one sector to another, transfers of machine operators from machine tractor
stations to collective farms in 1958-1959, of collective farmers
to state farms in connection with the transformation of collective farms into state farms, and organized recruitment of individuals from collective farms for industry and construction
projects. Such transfers in themselves suggest the provisional
nature of interclass differences and the ease with which movements can occur between sectors.

The main direction of horizontal mobility (mobility not directly connected with a change in socio-occupational status) is
from collective farms to the state sector — to state farms, industrial enterprises, and institutions. The collective farms appear most frequently as the system of diffusion, and the state
sector as the system of absorption. Movements in the opposite
direction are considerably less frequent. Population transfers
to cities are a particular form of social mobility, where social
mobility is combined with territorial mobility, or migration.

The peasantry is the principal social reservoir from which

Table 1

Role of the Peasantry in the Formation of Social Groups in the Collective
Farm-Cooperative and State Sectors of the Countryside
(individuals of peasant origin in % of total number in group)

Socio-occupational groups	Kalinin Region			Krasnodar Territory			Tatar ASSR		
	collective farms	state sector		collective farms	state sector		collective farms	state sector	
		state farms	other enterprises		state farms	other enterprises		state farms	other enterprises
Higher-level managerial personnel and specialists (A$_1$)	50	47.1	71.4	55.1	44.0	n.a.*	91	57	67
Middle-level managerial personnel and specialists (A$_2$)	60	63.6	55.7	88.0	52.0	52.6	83	50	n.a.*
Employees (B)	90.8	47.1	60.1	83.8	63.7	62.8	91	53	61
Machine operators (C)	88.6	54.9	57.9	80.0	58.3	53.1	96	58	77
Skilled workers and collective farmers (D$_1$)	85.5	79.3	79.8	87.4	60.2	77.8	97	83	69
Common laborers (D$_2$)	89.5	86.1	63.8	88.8	69.0	53.7	94	82	79
Total	87	78	63	87	63	64	95	77	n.a.*

* — not available.

the rural working class and intelligentsia, including all their
component socio-occupational groups, are formed (see Table 1).

The role of the peasantry as a social source varies depending
on the type of enterprise. While almost all collective farmers
are hereditary peasants (85-90%), the latter group accounts for
a smaller proportion (65-75%) of personnel in state farms and,
particularly, nonagricultural enterprises. Although we may observe certain differences between the social origins of rural
workers and collective farmers, they are not of great importance since in all cases these groups are the offspring of essentially similar classes. In the villages of Krasnodar Territory
and the Tatar ASSR only 10-12% of the employed population are
children of private peasants, while about 90% are children of
working people in the public sectors — the state and collective
farm-cooperative sectors. In the Kalinin Region, where the
population is older, children of private peasants still comprise
only about 20% of the employed population. Moreover, the proportion of children of private peasants does not differ much as
between collective farms and state enterprises (see Table 2).

Essentially, the present generation of rural working people
has not seen, and does not know, forms of conducting economic
activity other than the currently existing public forms. This
feature of the social biography of rural residents is important
for understanding the social-political situation in today's Soviet
village.

The role of the peasantry as a social source of recruitment
is not the same among the different socio-occupational groups.
The peasantry is somewhat more important among groups employed in manual labor, and less important among those in mental labor, especially skilled mental labor (see Table 1). Differences in modes of recruitment of the various socio-occupational
groups from the peasantry are even more clear-cut.

Former peasants now employed in manual labor at enterprises of the state sector began work, as a rule, at collective
farms, and only later shifted to the state sector. But for those
who are now employed in mental labor, especially of the skilled
kind, a state enterprise was generally their first place of employment. (1) This difference is of great importance. It reflects

Table 2

Class Origins of Collective Farmers, Workers,
and Employees in the Countryside
(in %)

Parents	Employed population	Krasnodar Territory			Kalinin Region		
		collective farmers	workers and employees		collective farmers	workers and employees	
			state farms	other enterprises		state farms	other enterprises
Workers and employees in state sector		13	37	36	13	22	37
Collective farmers		77	53	60	56	58	51
Private peasants, others		10	10	4	31	20	12

the specific character and noncorrespondence of the social and production roles of the collective farm as a source of labor resources.

The structure of production in collective farms is not so developed that they can supply a sufficient amount of skilled labor, particularly mental labor, to the state sector. Therefore, those who shift from collective farms are chiefly individuals employed in manual labor, above all, low-skilled labor. The large-scale recruitment of these individuals by state farms was connected, in particular, with the transformation of some collective farms into state farms in the late 1950s and early 1960s. They are not simply collective farmers' children, but "the children of collective farms," production workers whose potential is determined by the production training they obtained in the economic unit.

In contrast to the traditional cadres of collective farms, we find children of collective farmers who are employed in "job positions" requiring certain skills and who are the bearers of the social (as distinct from the production) "current" of the collective farm order. They are school graduates whose potential is not determined by production experience but depends on school and family training, on the immediate environment in which they are reared, on the social opportunities for growth, and these have been equalized relative to other social groups in the countryside. Children from a collective farm background have the same opportunities as all rural residents to realize their potential and to occupy leading positions in all social groups of the state sector in the countryside.

The social opportunities for collective farmers, relative to those for other village strata, have been equalized to the extent that they not only can move easily into the state sector in the countryside, but they also are in an equal position with individuals reared in the state sector of the village insofar as migrating to the city and thus acquiring urban occupations are concerned. It is true that in moving to the city, collective farmers' children continue their studies somewhat less frequently than the children of rural workers and employees (Table 3). But this difference is explained only by the somewhat more backward occupational structure of collective farmers, among whom there are fewer families with skilled individuals. It is no accident that the advantages of the offspring of families employed in the rural state sector disappear when we examine collective farmers and rural workers in similar socio-occupational groups. As a whole, the offspring of identical socio-occupational groups in different sectors of the countryside continue their studies to the same extent. The equality of mobility opportunities for those employed in the collective farm-cooperative and state sectors is particularly apparent from the data revealing the final results of mobility — the proportion of individuals employed in skilled mental labor. In this respect individuals reared in the collective farm-cooperative sector are not in the least bit disadvantaged compared to those reared in the rural state sector. However, in both sectors, and to an equal degree, significant differences exist in mobility opportunities depending on the skills of the parents.

Table 3

Children of Rural Residents in the City
(in % of total number of "emigrants" from the indicated socio-occupational group)

Socio-occupational groups of parents	Krasnodar Territory				Kalinin Region				Tatar ASSR			
	% continuing their studies upon arrival in city		% of rural "emigrants" employed in skilled mental work in city (a)		% continuing their studies upon arrival in city		% of rural "emigrants" employed in skilled mental work in city (a)		% continuing their studies upon arrival in city		% of rural "emigrants" employed in skilled mental work in city (a)	
	total	of these, children of collective farmers	total	of these, children of collective farmers	total	of these, children of collective farmers	total	of these, children of collective farmers	total	of these, children of collective farmers	total	of these, children of collective farmers
Higher-level managerial personnel and specialists (A_1)	75	100	53	100	60.0	100	71.4	100	73		58	n.a
Middle-level managerial personnel and specialists (A_2)	58	45.2	50	100	59.5	58.5	40.7	24.8	76	75	38	34
Employees (B)	59	63.7	46	80.4	50.2	62.4	50.0	50	77	62	35	28
Machine operators (C)	53	46.5	52	74	51.2	67.0	16.7	0	61	76	24	25
Skilled workers and collective farmers (D_1)	46	47.0	22	20.2	44.4	41.7	29.2	41.9	57	50	19	24
Common laborers, others (D_{2-3})	32	27.7	26	34.1	34.4	27.9	21.1	24.5	45	36	13	17
Total	41	35	29	39	39	33	24	29	54	40	24	23

(a) Higher-level and middle-level managerial personnel and specialists.

Among the rural population, the rate of social advancement is affected not by class position but by socio-occupational status.

Thus, the collective farm as a social institution does not impede or restrict the opportunities for social advancement of collective farmers compared to other groups of the rural population. This situation also has its ethnic aspect. Since we know that in the national republics the collective farms contain chiefly non-Russian population, equalization of opportunities for the collective farm-cooperative and state sectors in the countryside promotes the equalization of mobility chances (social advancement) for the indigenous nationalities and Russian population in the countryside.

Large-scale mobility proceeds (see Chart I) not only between sectors (1), i.e., not only along horizontal lines, but also between social strata, intraclass groups (2), i.e., along vertical lines. Socio-occupational advancement is also frequently associated with changes in the sphere of employment, movement to another region, i.e., it proceeds as a combination of both vertical and horizontal mobility (3). This kind of mobility, of course, frequently has the most far-reaching consequences for the mobile population, particularly when it involves long distances.

Chart I

Direction of Social Mobility of the
Collective Farm Population

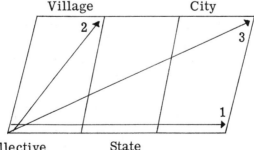

Village   City

Collective
farm cooperative   State
sector   sector

Mobility:
1. horizontal   2. vertical   3. combined

The collective farm-cooperative sector, whose social structure is simpler than that of the state sector (for example, many public and state institutions are absent in the former), provides fewer opportunities for advancement in social status within the sector itself. That is why cases of combined mobility are most frequent: movement from the collective farm-cooperative sector to the state sector and, simultaneously, an advancement in socio-occupational position (see Table 4).

Collective farmers continue their socio-occupational advancement more actively outside the collective farm-cooperative sector. As the data in Table 4 show, that part of the population which was not mobile in socio-occupational terms was most likely to remain permanently in the collective farms. As for the mobile part of the population, some 50% shifted to the state sector in the course of their work activity. More precisely, they moved on to employment in mental work in various rural institutions.

The intensity of vertical mobility, or to be more accurate, the consequences of vertical mobility, are demonstrated by the highly varied social origins of the socio-occupational groups in the village (see Table 5).

As Table 5 shows, only a few rural residents with skills are "repeating" the status of their parents. This is understandable. Many currently existing types of occupations were unknown to the previous generation in the countryside. The socio-occupational structure of the contemporary village has been largely created anew. Only among common laborers is a high degree of self-reproduction typical. All other social groups of the population are recruited primarily from "alien" groups. "Hereditary" occupations are rare. The major characteristic and result of this process is the predominance in all groups of the descendants of individuals in primarily unskilled and low-skilled manual labor. Today's rural intelligentsia is the flesh and blood of the people, drawn from the very depths of the people, and organically connected with them through its whole past.

Intensive vertical mobility is equally characteristic of the different ethnic groups of the rural population whom we investigated. More than one-quarter of the Tatars (26%) and Russians

Table 4

Distribution of the Population by Sectors and Forms of Production
in the Process of Work Activity

(in % of number in each mobile and stable group) (a)

Forms of production	Krasnodar Territory				Kalinin Region				Tatar ASSR			
	occupationally mobile DC-BA N = 212		occupationally stable DC-DC N = 973		occupationally mobile DC-BA N = 186		occupationally stable DC-DC N = 816		occupationally mobile DC-BA N = 230		occupationally stable DC-DC N = 1,419	
	at start of work career	at time of survey	at start of work career	at time of survey	at start of work career	at time of survey	at start of work career	at time of survey	at start of work career	at time of survey	at start of work career	at time of survey
Collective farms	54.8	40.6	62.5	42.0	45.4	20.3	57.4	37.0	62	33	77	63
State farms	13.4	26.4	15.9	51.0	2.5	26.6	3.4	40.2	10	12	10	21
Enterprises, construction projects	20.4	12.7	13.2	3.4	29.3	20.5	13.1	14.6	20	6	7	7
Service sphere	2.3	4.1	1.0	1.3	4.3	11.4	5.9	4.5	3	9	1	3
Institutions	2.1	14.7	0.3	1.0	5.5	20.1	0.5	2.8	3	38	1	4

(a) Mobile refers to individuals shifting from groups in manual labor (D, C) to groups in mental labor (B, A); stable refers to those remaining in manual labor.

Table 5

Composition of Socio-Occupational Groups by Social Origins (Father's Employment)
(in % of each group of respondents)

Socio-occupational status of parents	Kalinin Region				Krasnodar Territory				Tatar ASSR			
Socio-occupational status of respondents	intelligentsia	employees	machine operators	common labor-ers and others	intelligentsia	employees	machine operators	common labor-ers and others	intelligentsia	machine operators	employees	common labor-ers and others
Higher-level managerial personnel*	25	4	11	50	15	5	5	75	27	13	—	60
Middle-level managerial personnel*	25	2	2	69	21	6	13	60	21	10	5	64
Higher-level specialists*	30	9	17	46	27	14	8	51	21	18	5	56
Middle-level specialists*	28	9	9	60	14	6	12	68	23	7	6	64
Employees	20	7	7	66	19	12	10	60	12	10	9	69
Machine operators and others in industrial labor	14	8	9	70	8	7	19	66	8	5	10	77
Skilled workers in nonindustrial labor	4	6	4	86	15	4	12	69	3	3	7	87
Low-skilled workers in manual labor	6	3	3	88	9	5	13	73	2	5	6	87
Common laborers	5	4	2	89	7	4	7	82	4	4	2	91

*In Kalinin Region the totals presented by Arutiunian for these groups diverge from 100% by more than can be accounted for by rounding.

Table 6

Increase in Socio-Occupational Status of Tatars
and Russians in Comparison with Parents
(number of times greater) (a)

Socio-occupational groups	Tatars	Russians
Higher-level managerial personnel and specialists	2.01	1.85
Middle-level managerial personnel and specialists	1.42	1.40
Employees	1.36	1.25
Machine operators	1.34	1.19
Common laborers and others employed in primarily un-skilled, manual labor	1.13	1.05
Total	1.16	1.12

(a) Socio-occupational status is measured by taking account of three indices: earnings, education, and influence in the producing enterprise. Data pertaining to these factors are the basis for assigning each status position a certain rank. An approximate step corresponds to the interval between middle-level and higher-level specialists. For greater detail see the Appendix [not included in the present volume]. An increase in status among individuals in primarily unskilled labor occurred as a result of certain changes in skills within this group.

(31%) had higher social status than their parents. However, if we consider not only the overall frequency of mobility but the distance moved, the Tatars have an advantage. Given the less advanced initial positions of the Tatars, they have traveled a longer distance in their social growth. The comparative rates of social advancement of Tatars and Russians in the village may be seen in Table 6.

The fact that Tatars are improving their status more rapidly than Russians in all cases is also confirmed by data on intra-generational mobility (changes in social status in the process of work activity, i.e., between the start and completion of a work career). In this connection, not only the rates but also the scale of mobility are greater among Tatars.

This situation may also be characteristic, to one degree or another, of other national minorities among the rural population. Since they frequently started from a worse position than the Russians, they naturally had to travel a relatively longer distance in the course of their work careers. The great majority of individuals in every ethnic and socio-occupational group occupy better social positions than their parents. Moreover, they achieve a higher status in the course of their own work activity, and this obviously promotes the social optimism of these most influential social groups of the population, who determine the situation in the village (see Table 7).

Chart II brings together indices of intergenerational and intra-generational mobility. It shows us what proportion of individuals in the various occupational groups were already ahead of their parents at the start of their work careers, and to what degree their final advantage was due not to their initial positions but to advancement in the course of their work activity. The one group that was most frequently ahead of its parents even at the start of its members' work careers was that of higher- and middle-level specialists. This is understandable. Prolonged studies lead directly to intelligentsia-type occupations. Jobs as agronomists, livestock specialists, and engineers are frequently the first ones appearing on an individual's service record. This stems from the special manner in which socio-occupational groups of specialists are recruited. Only a certain proportion (approximately 1/3 to 1/2, judging by our figures) move into this category in the course of their own work activity. In this respect specialists are sharply distinguished from managerial personnel who, like members of other socio-occupational groups, move into their positions step by step during their work careers rather than as a result of completing studies at an educational institution. About 80-90% of higher-level managerial personnel and 96%

Table 7

Proportion of Individuals in Various Socio-Occupational Groups
Attaining Higher Status than Their Parents
(in % of each socio-occupational group)

Socio-occupational groups	Krasnodar Territory			Kalinin Region			Tatar ASSR		
	total	at start of work career	in course of work career	total	at start of work career	in course of work career	total	at start of work career	in course of work career
Managerial personnel									
higher-level	95	13	82	91	5	86	87	7	80
middle-level	79	0	79	86	0	86	79	0	79
Specialists									
higher-level	90	34	56	84	23	61	89*	53	27
middle-level	86	30	56	72	26	46	77	36	41
Employees (a)	60	46	14	74	25	49	77	20	57
Machine operators (a)	67*	17	40	69	21	48	75	22	53

(a) The status of employees and machine operators is treated as being the same.

*There is a misprint in these series of figures. The components do not add up to the total.

Chart II

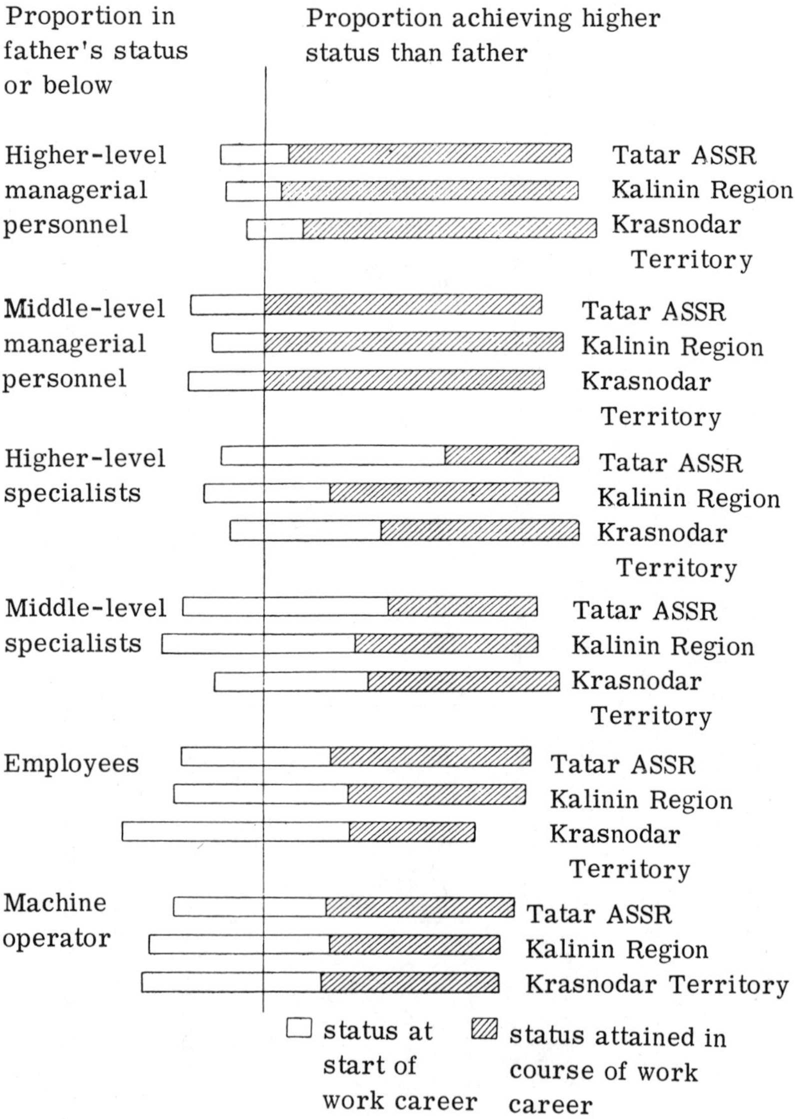

Proportion in
father's status
or below

Proportion achieving higher
status than father

Higher-level
managerial
personnel

Tatar ASSR
Kalinin Region
Krasnodar
Territory

Middle-level
managerial
personnel

Tatar ASSR
Kalinin Region
Krasnodar
Territory

Higher-level
specialists

Tatar ASSR
Kalinin Region
Krasnodar
Territory

Middle-level
specialists

Tatar ASSR
Kalinin Region
Krasnodar
Territory

Employees

Tatar ASSR
Kalinin Region
Krasnodar
Territory

Machine
operator

Tatar ASSR
Kalinin Region
Krasnodar Territory

☐ status at
start of
work career

▨ status attained in
course of work
career

of middle-level managerial personnel in the countryside began
their work careers in other socio-occupational groups, predominantly in those of lower status. (2)

The social position of managerial personnel, as well as of
middle-level specialists, employees, and machine operators, is
not primarily the result of specialized training but of work experience, and quite possibly this leaves its imprint on the psychological characteristics of these groups.

The emergence of new strata of skilled personnel from a rural population which had previously been occupationally and cul-
turally quite homogeneous is evidence of the socio-occupational
differentiation of this population. Thus, the dialectics of development toward a homogeneous society is a complex process.
The village is moving toward unification via differentiation. This
is a progressive process, for it signifies the material and cultural advancement of newly emerging groups of the rural population, and thus the gradual approximation of the latter to the
urban population.

Intraclass, as well as interclass, differentiation is not absolute in nature. New strata which emerge from the people do not
lose their ties to the people. The large number of socially mixed
families, for example, is evidence of social unification (see
Table 8).

Above all, the figures in Table 8 reveal the socially mixed
nature of the rural intelligentsia, in one-half of whose families
either the husband or wife is employed in manual labor. In the
intelligentsia category, relatively homogeneous families are
found only among higher-level specialists. These families are
often formed outside the village, in urban circumstances. One
can understand that individuals in manual labor are less likely
to marry outside their group. They marry members of the intelligentsia infrequently, if only because the number of the latter in the countryside (and thus the possibility of marrying them)
is limited.

Not only the boundary lines between socio-occupational groups,
but also those between workers and collective farmers associated with different forms of property, frequently disappear
within the family unit. Moreover, the higher the socio-occupational

Table 8

Proportion of Wives (Husbands) Employed
in Manual Labor
(in % of total number of families, by
socio-occupational groups)

Socio-occupational groups	Krasnodar Territory	Kalinin Region	Tatar ASSR
Higher-level managerial personnel	48.4	25.0	46
Middle-level managerial personnel	49.9	50.9	65
Higher-level specialists	34.5	34.3	27
Middle-level specialists	61.7	58.3	51
Employees	60.1	60.5	54
Machine operators	79.8	60.0	85
Skilled and low-skilled workers and collective farmers	83.8	86.4	91
Common laborers	83.4	87.4	96

status of a group, the more frequent are socially mixed marriages. In families of the collective farm intelligentsia (according to data for the Tatar ASSR), almost 1/2 of the spouses are
employed at enterprises and — even more frequently — state
institutions, while in families of machine operators the figure
is 1/4, and in families of common laborers — 1/7. These ratios
correspond to the dialectics of the general trend of social development. With each step up the occupational ladder, the existence
of common occupational traits among identical groups of both
the collective farm-cooperative and state sectors is increasingly apparent. These traits are associated with similar levels
of general and specialized training and education, similar levels
of material compensation, and so on. Thus class differences,
which are eroded as individuals advance occupationally from

group to group, become less and less clear-cut. And this factor, in particular, is also reflected in the social composition of collective farm families.

The ramified social ties which promote close contacts and intermingling among the population are naturally supplemented by, and interwoven with, ties between ethnic groups. The facts show that the increasingly sharp national self-consciousness of the intelligentsia, and of other social groups as well, does not impose barriers which separate national groups from each other and does not lead to their isolation. The current mode of life requires contacts and interaction, and independently of the wills of people, this objectively promotes the multiplication of ties between ethnic groups, including family ties. Working in the same enterprises and economic units, associating with each other in regional and urban centers, Tatars and Russians form friendships and increasingly enter into mixed marriages. Naturally, the number of such marriages is greater in multinational villages (with Tatar and Russian populations) than in those containing a single national group. Of the surveyed residents in multinational villages, 10% had entered into mixed marriages, and more than 25% responded that they had relatives who were married to an individual of a different nationality. In Tatar villages there were practically no nationally-mixed families.

Ties with other ethnic (as well as social) groups are particularly noticeable among occupationally advanced groups, especially those who have frequent contact with other nationalities. While less than 1% of Tatar common laborers had entered into mixed marriages with Russians, among the intelligentsia the figure was 4-5%. The situation was approximately the same among Russians. Similarly, about 1/3 of the Tatar intelligentsia and the same proportion of Russian intelligentsia answered that they had relatives who were married to individuals of a different nationality, while among common laborers the corresponding proportion was no more than 1/6.

Ties between ethnic groups are greatly facilitated by the creation of a common international cultural foundation which promotes mutual understanding between people and draws them closer together. It is no accident, for example, that almost 20%

of Tatars who are fluent in Russian are married to Russians, while among those who are not, the figure is no more than 1%.

The operation of processes of integration and high rates of mobility of ethnic and social groups are evidence of the rapid and intensive social development of society. For a considerable proportion of the rural population the improvement in conditions of life is experienced not only as an objective fact but also as a subjective phenomenon. This ensures the viability and healthy functioning of the social organism.

The available data, however, do not permit us to conclude that opportunities for social mobility have been fully equalized among the different socio-occupational groups. We have already seen (Table 5) that the largest proportion of individuals — 50% at the very least — in all social groups, including the intelligentsia, come from families of common laborers. But this does not mean, for example, that common laborers have the same oppor-tunities as others to attain membership in all social groups of the rural population. Inasmuch as common laborers comprise a majority (and the intelligentsia — a minority) of the population in the countryside, even a small proportion of the children of common laborers may be sufficiently numerous to constitute a significant fraction of the intelligentsia. Therefore, to obtain a more precise picture of the relationship between the occupations and educational levels of parents and their children, we must recalculate the data in Table 5. First of all, let us determine whether a relationship exists between the education of parents and that of their children (see Table 9).

As the reader can see, the relationship is quite significant. The proportion of children obtaining a higher education is 3.4% for those whose parents are illiterate, 8-9% for those whose parents have up to six years of schooling, 10% for those whose parents have seven to ten years of schooling, 44% for those whose parents have a specialized secondary education, and 64% for those whose parents have a higher education.

Under the conditions of socialism, where skill — as appraised by the state — rather than property is the most important factor in the social position of the individual, education operates as the decisive condition for social advancement. According to specially

Table 9

Relationship Between Educational Level of Parents and Children,
Data for Tatar ASSR (in %)

Education of father	Number of respondents	Education of respondents, in %*							
		illiterate, barely literate	less than 4 grades	4-6 grades	7-9 grades	10 grades	secondary specialized education	higher education
Illiterate	1,029	18.3	18.5	21.1	27.3	5.0	4.0	3.4
Less than 4 grades	358	2.4	13.3	18.7	31.8	14.1	9.5	9.0
4-6 grades	253	2.8	7.9	17.4	39.5	14.6	9.9	8.3
7-9 grades	62	3.2	4.8	6.4	38.7	21.0	9.7	9.7
10 grades	40	2.5	—	2.5	22.5	27.5	30.0	10.0
Secondary specialized education	16	—	—	—	6.3	12.5	37.5	43.7
Higher education	22	4.5	—	9.0	—	18.2	4.5	63.8

*The sums of the percentage figures in the first five rows differ from 100% by more than can normally be accounted for by rounding.

calculated coefficients of determination, the educational level of parents predetermines the educational level of children to the extent of 50%.*

We would naturally expect a similarly close relationship to prevail between the socio-occupational status of parents and children. The data presented below (see Table 10) do, in fact, confirm such a relationship.

As Table 10 shows, only 8% of the children whose fathers were common laborers became members of the intelligentsia, while about 50% of those whose fathers were higher-level specialists did so. The remaining population groups — with some degree of variation — are distributed between these two extreme "parental poles." The coefficient of determination between the social status of parents and that of children (with respect to the initial place of work and type of job) is 53.5%, i.e., in more than 50% of the cases the social position of the children at the start of their work careers was determined by the status of their parents. It is interesting to observe that the mother has a greater influence on both the educational level and socio-occupational status of the child than the father. An increase in the mother's education by 1.0 units (from the 1st grade to the 4th, from the 5th grade to the 8th, etc.) is associated with an increase in the child's education by 0.58 units, and a rise of 1.0 units in the mother's socio-occupational status is associated with a 0.69 unit increase in the child's status (with respect to the initial place of work); the corresponding figures for the father's influence are 0.47 and 0.42.**

Although rural residents frequently shift from one social group to another during their work careers, the positions attained in one's youth exercise an influence on one's ultimate status. The coefficient of determination between the "final" socio-occupational status of village residents and that of their

_____

*The calculations underlying this conclusion are found in the Appendix to the Arutiunian book, which has not been included in this volume.

**Arutiunian notes here that the details underlying these calculations appear in the Appendix to his work.

Table 10

Relationship Between Socio-Occupational Status of Parents
and Children, Data for Tatar ASSR
(in % of number of children in each socio-occupational group)

Socio-occupational status of father	Number of children	Socio-occupational status of children at start of work career, in %								
		1	2	3	4	5	6	7	8	9
Higher-level managerial personnel (1)	23	–	4.4	4.4	17.4	4.3	8.7	–	8.7	52.1
Middle-level managerial personnel (2)	48	2.1	4.3	10.6	10.6	14.9	14.9	8.5	–	34.1
Higher-level specialists (3)	35	–	3.0	36.5	12.1	6.0	9.1	3.0	3.0	27.3
Middle-level specialists (4)	31	–	–	25.0	17.8	7.2	7.2	7.2	–	35.6
Employees (5)	96	–	–	16.6	7.8	18.9	7.8	4.5	6.7	37.7
Machine operators and others in industrial labor (6)	76	–	–	8.2	5.5	13.7	24.6	9.6	6.9	31.5
Skilled personnel in nonindustrial labor (7)	112	–	–	5.9	4.9	8.8	10.8	11.8	7.8	50.0
Low-skilled personnel (8)	86	1.2	–	7.2	8.3	11.9	5.9	–	17.8	47.7
Common laborers (9)	1,044	0.1	0.9	4.3	3.0	3.3	6.0	2.6	5.7	74.1

Chart III

Intergenerational Mobility*

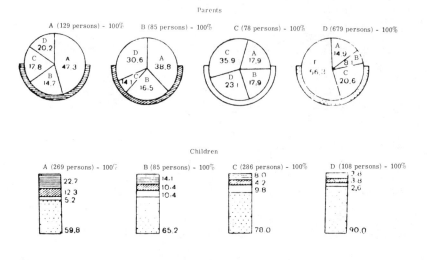

*The social groups that Arutiunian designated by A, B, C, D are
shown in Tables 1 and 3.

parents is rather high (0.5).

Chart III reveals the direction and results of social mobility
of the rural population of the Tatar ASSR.

It is apparent from this chart that although low-skilled socio-
occupational groups "send" a rather modest proportion of their
offspring into skilled occupational groups, these offspring account for a significant proportion of the more skilled groups.
Thus, the group engaged in predominantly unskilled labor (D —
parents) "sent" only 14.9% of its children into the intelligentsia,
but these children accounted for 59.8% of the relatively small
category of rural intelligentsia (A — children).

How do we explain the influence of the socio-occupational status of parents on the fates of children? It is obvious that this is a matter of the unequal and dissimilar economic and cultural circumstances in the immediate environment surrounding the child.

In most cases the intelligentsia is concentrated in relatively large population centers which provide favorable opportunities for the development of individuals' capacities and potentials. The children of the more well-to-do and more educated parents begin to work later than others. Almost 75% of the children whose parents were employed in unskilled labor began to work before the age of 16, both because of material considerations as well as because of underestimation of education as a social value. The point at which children embark on their own working lives varies rather systematically with the educational level and — to a certain extent — the socio-occupational status of their parents (see Table 11).

Among those employed in unskilled manual labor, the bulk (from 2/3 to 3/4) began to work before the age of 16, while among specialists — particularly higher-level specialists — there were relatively few who did so, no more than 17%. As for managerial personnel, in this respect they differ from the intelligentsia and are closer to the great mass of working people. Personifying the leading role of the working class, their biographies, so to speak, reveal a close link with the fate of the broad masses of people.

Personnel in specialized mental work begin their work careers at a later age, and thus settle down into married life at a later age. In the Tatar ASSR, 22% of the immobile population group were married before the age of 20, while the figure for the mobile group was 14%. The corresponding proportions in Krasnodar Territory were 21% and 12%, and in the Kalinin Region — 21% and 9%.

Starting a family, particularly the appearance of children, frequently operates to obstruct the socio-occupational advancement of women, and this is reflected in the overall indicators of mobility. Of particular importance in stimulating mobility are the immediate surroundings, above all the cultural atmosphere and

Table 11

Proportion of Rural Residents Who Began
to Work Before the Age of 16
(in % of each socio-occupational group)

Socio-occupational groups	Krasnodar Territory	Kalinin Region	Tatar ASSR
Common laborers	66	83	79
Low-skilled workers in manual labor	66	76	78
Skilled workers in non-industrial activity	54	62	72
Machine operators and others in industrial labor	56	52	66
Employees	36	37	44
Middle-level specialists	28	16	16
Higher-level specialists	17	11	11
Middle-level managerial personnel	51	46	55
Higher-level managerial personnel	29	41	40

general climate in the family, especially the extent to which the family knows and uses Russian. More than 60% of the individuals in the mobile population group of the Tatar ASSR are fluent in Russian or in both the Russian and Tatar languages, while in the immobile group the corresponding figure is about one-half as great — 34%.

It is important, from a practical standpoint, to determine at what stage in the socio-occupational advancement of an individual the favorable impact of the advantages available to the highly-skilled groups makes its appearance. Or, to put it differently, what is the barrier, the obstacle, to the socio-occupational advancement of the low-skilled groups of the rural population?

In order to clarify this problem we analyzed the social

background of pupils in the secondary schools of one of the surveyed districts of the Tatar ASSR.

It appears that the proportion of children in all grades of the
incomplete and complete secondary school whose parents are
employed in unskilled labor remains unchanged and corresponds
to the share of this group of working people in the district's
population (see Table 12). District organizations now keep records of each child of school age, and nonattendance at school is
regarded as an extraordinary event — the district department
of public education is held responsible for each child not attending school. There are even special reporting procedures in effect to determine the number of children not attending school in
the district. According to these records only 38 of 2,103 children (7 to 15 years of age) were not attending school in the
Almetevsk District.

Secondary education is now available to rural residents in
practically the same degree as it is to urban residents. This is
evident from data in statistical reports (see Table 13).

After finishing the incomplete secondary and secondary school,
approximately the same proportion of students in cities and villages continue their studies in the system of general and secondary specialized education. Moreover, there are no differences
between the graduates of Tatar rural schools and Russian
schools in this regard. Judging by the data for the Almetevsk
District (Table 12), the proportion of Tatar pupils at all levels
of the secondary school corresponds to their share of the population. A very slight decline in their relative share may be observed only in the Russian and mixed schools (32% of the pupils
in the 5th-6th grades were Tatars, and 24.8% in the 9th-10th
grades were Tatars), which is apparently connected with difficulties in mastering the Russian language. After completing
secondary school, 20.7% of the graduates in Tatar districts enter higher educational institutions and technicums, compared to
19.4% of graduates in predominantly Russian districts. A distinct difference may be observed only in the distribution of those
secondary school graduates in Tatar and Russian districts who
begin to work after completing school. We find a more clear-cut
agrarian orientation among Tatars. In the Tatar districts, 19%

Table 12

Social and National Composition of Pupils in Secondary Schools
of Almetevsk District, 1967–1968 (a)

Grades	Russian and mixed schools			Tatar schools			All schools		
	number of pupils	children of unskilled workers and collective farmers (in %)	Tatar children (in %)	number of pupils	children of unskilled workers and collective farmers (in %)	Tatar children (in %)	number of pupils	children of unskilled workers and collective farmers (in %)	Tatar children (in %)
5–6	1,742	50.2	32.5	1,174	65.2	100	2,916	56.3	59.7
7–8	1,579	46.2	31.5	962	66.7	99.7	2,541	54.2	57.3
9–10	1,705	53.9	24.8	894	60.5	99.9	2,599	56.2	50.6
Total	5,026	50.3	29.5	3,030	64.3	99.9	8,056	55.6	51.0

(a) Data were collected for each school by using a standardized form. The data were gathered with the assistance of the Department of Public Education of the Almetevsk District Executive Committee.

Table 13

Distribution of Graduates of Rural and Urban Schools
of the Tatar ASSR, 1967-1968, in % (a)

Activities of graduates	Rural schools			Urban schools			Total for republic		
	all grad-uates	8th grade grad-uates	10th grade grad-uates	all grad-uates	8th grade grad-uates	10th grade grad-uates	all grad-uates	8th grade grad-uates	10th grade grad-uates
Continued their studies	71	83	37	71	89	39	71	86	39
At higher educational institutions	3	–	10	8	–	23	5	–	17
Began to work	27	16	60	26	9*	55	27	13	57
In industry	6	2	16	18	7	39	12	4	28
In agriculture	17	12	31	2	4	4	10	7	17

(a) The data were brought together by districts. In addition to the division into rural and urban localities, the data were grouped separately for Tatar and Russian districts, as well as for districts adjoining Kazan and suburban districts as a whole (including districts adjoining Kazan).

*This figure is probably a misprint. It is less than the sum of those who began to work in industry and agriculture.

of the graduates begin to work in agriculture, whereas 11% of those in Russian districts do so.

Both the Tatar and Russian rural populations undergo substantial "losses" in the transition to higher education. Only about 10% of the graduates of rural secondary schools go on to higher educational institutions, compared to some 20% of the graduates of urban schools. Thus, while collective farmers are represented in secondary schools approximately in proportion to their share of the population (about 30%), within the city limits their opportunities for receiving a higher education (as well as the opportunities of the rest of the rural population) are diminished. (3) True, this does not apply to an agricultural education, for collective farmers predominate in this system of higher education. Thus, the proportions of collective farmers at all higher schools and technicums in 1967-1968 were 17.9% and 23.8% respectively, while at agricultural higher schools and technicums they were 72.8% and 63%.

The enrollment of collective farmers and their children at the University and at technical higher educational institutions is particularly small. They constitute 11% of the students at Kazan University, 7% at the Aviation Institute, and 17% at all higher schools of the Tatar ASSR. This situation is also typical of other higher educational institutions. Among Moscow higher schools it is only at the Agricultural Academy that the proportion of collective farmers (and their children) approximates their share in the population (26% in 1964), while at all other institutions it is considerably lower (6% at Moscow State University, 3% at the Moscow Higher Technical School, 4% at the Lenin Pedagogical Institute).

These figures testify to the relatively low quality of training received by pupils in rural secondary schools in comparison with that of urban schools. The actual level of secondary education in the countryside does not correspond to the formal requirements (as specified in official documents), although the gap between formal requirements and actual education, between rural and urban education, is narrowing significantly as time passes. (4)

The preparatory departments of higher schools, which have

Table 14

Proportions of Russians and Tatars at Different
Stages of Education, Tatar ASSR
(in %)

Stage of education	Tatars	Russians
Graduate study	27	56
Specialists with higher education	35	55
Higher educational institutions	37	56
Agricultural institutions	76	24
Secondary specialized schools	38	54
Agricultural schools	63	27
Rural secondary schools	60	40
Population of republic	60	40

recently been established by decision of the Party and government for working youth, demobilized soldiers and rural residents, are expected to have a considerable impact on equalizing
opportunities for rural youth to gain admission to higher educational institutions.

The factors that we have been considering here affect the formation of a national intelligentsia in a number of the country's
regions. Those national groups which reside primarily in rural
localities naturally have less opportunities for social advancement than the more urbanized national groups. It is no accident,
for example, that the relative share of primarily "urban" national groups in the student body is disproportionately high (Russians, Armenians, Estonians, Latvians), while the share of most
predominantly rural national groups (Kirgiz, Moldavians, Tad-
zhiks, etc.) is disproportionately low. (5) Moreover, the more
advanced the level of professional training, the more apparent are
the differences associated with the extent of urbanization of national groups (see Table 14).

The dominant element in the problem of mobility of nationality
groups clearly shows through in Table 14. Its solution is connected

Chart IV

Probability of Employment in
Mental Labor for Different
Social Groups of the Rural
Population of the Tatar ASSR*

Opportunities

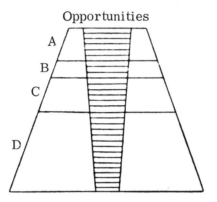

* The social groups designated by Arutiunian as A, B, C, and
D are shown in Tables 1 and 3.

with the overall development of the countryside to the level attained by the city. This is precisely the means by which the
equalization of socio-occupational opportunities for different
nationalities must proceed, and is actually proceeding.

Inasmuch as the formation of the rural intelligentsia proceeds
through the system of "urban" higher education, it is understandable that those employed in rural unskilled labor lose out to individuals in skilled labor — above all to individuals in mental
labor — precisely at the urban "zigzag" of their careers. The
relatively small number of rural intelligentsia have comparatively great opportunities for social advancement. The pyramid
of social structure and the pyramid of opportunities are, so to
speak, inversely related to each other (see Chart IV above,

based on the data in Table 10).

It is precisely in the city that the decisive influence of family background is manifested. The greater opportunities for social advancement open to children whose parents are employed in relatively skilled labor stem from their greater utilization of the possibilities for mobility afforded by the city.

What are the prospects for social mobility in the future? In essence, two contrasting trends are possible. Abstractly speaking, we can conceive of the possibility that mobility opportunities for low-skilled population groups will diminish as a result of the growth in numbers of the intelligentsia who, having additional opportunities for advancement, will increasingly satisfy the demand for skilled labor. Such a conclusion is incorrect, however, inasmuch as the tendency for the intelligentsia to reproduce itself is more than offset by other processes. The main trend in social mobility is determined by the general extension of education and the steadily increasing similarity between the intelligentsia, on the one hand, and the working class and peasantry, on the other. The new five-year plan should be a significant stage in this process. The plan provides for a decline in the use of manual, heavy, and unskilled labor in all branches of the economy, as well as for completing the transition to universal secondary education. As the materials presented above have shown, we have already reached the point where children of low-skilled parents do not drop out of the incomplete secondary school, and their drop-out rate is very low at the complete secondary school. Some differences in the educational opportunities of different socio-occupational groups are found only at the secondary specialized and higher levels of education. The diffusion of universal secondary education will alter the situation fundamentally. In order to see this, let us turn again to the regression coefficients. Not only do they reveal the influence of parents' education and social status on children's opportunities, but also the declining impact of this influence,* i.e., among more skilled and educated families, status differences have a

---

*Arutiunian refers here to the Appendix to his volume, which we have not reproduced.

steadily weaker influence on the statuses of children.

In other words, differences in opportunities for children of common laborers and employees — groups which are one status rank apart — are considerably greater than those for children of middle-level and higher-level specialists, who are also separated by one status rank.* This is extremely important inasmuch as we are moving in the general direction of equalizing educational levels of the population, of reducing and then eliminating the least skilled types of labor. Thus we can expect that the boundaries of the pyramids of opportunity for different social groups will become increasingly similar, not primarily because of special measures which facilitate the access of low-skilled strata to specialized and higher education, but chiefly because of the narrowing of the very foundations of the social pyramid, i.e., changes in the social structure of society. Inevitable and increasingly strong integrating tendencies constitute the basis upon which processes of social and national integration and unification will develop.

Notes

1) In the Tatar Republic, for example, only about 20% of the higher-level managerial personnel and specialists employed in the state sector (who are of peasant origin) began their work careers at collective farms, while almost all (more than 80%) of the low-skilled and unskilled workers first worked at collective farms.

2) According to data for the Tatar ASSR, only 12.5% of higher-level managerial personnel and 7.4% of middle-level managerial personnel began their work careers in positions of equivalent status, i.e., as specialists.

3) See also D. L. Konstantinovskii and V. N. Shubkin, "Personal Plans and Their Realization," Voprosy filosofii, 1970, No. 7.

4) The lagging quality of education in rural schools is mainly

---

*See the note to Table 6 for Arutiunian's method of assigning a rank to occupational positions.

accounted for by the comparatively poor quality of teachers. In 1967, for example, about 50% of the teachers in the 5th-11th grades of rural schools in the Almetevsk District had a higher education, while in urban schools the figure was 86%. Some years earlier the gap between rural and urban teachers' training was considerably greater.

5) The proportion of Russians in the country's population in 1959 was 56%, while the proportion of Russians among students was 61%. For Armenians the corresponding figures were 1.4% and 1.66%, while for Moldavians, on the other hand, they were 1.1% and 0.5%, and so on.

Commentary: Social Stratification Research and Soviet Scholarship

S. M. LIPSET

The revival of Soviet sociology in the post-Stalin era is indicative of the changes in that society made possible by de-Stalinization. In a real sense, academic sociology is not possible in a totalitarian society since the need to shed light on the distribution of privileges is inherent in the very nature of the discipline. Regimes such as the Nazi, the Stalinist, or seemingly the Maoist, which cannot tolerate the slightest opposition to the party line, also cannot permit sociologists to find out who does what, and particularly who does what to whom. Since there always must be a gap between social reality and the ideological self-justification of social systems, the sheer opportunity to analyze "reality" quantitatively must always supply ammunition to the critics of the system, to those who are motivated to point up the existence of such a gap.

In the United States and other Western countries, sociology has been a "critical discipline." Here, its practitioners have documented almost ad nauseum the extent to which American reality and the American creed of an egalitarian society are at odds. Sociologists have emphasized the failings of the school system in reducing the differences in ability and motivation among children from families of varying income and cultural levels. They have shown the limits of the efforts to curtail wealth or income differentials through progressive tax policy. They have documented the punitive consequences of low status on personality and health. With few exceptions, such writings have been cast in the context of criticism of the society and various of its institutions for repressing opportunity and inhibiting

355

equality. American and other Western sociologists as a group
have been more supportive of "liberal" or "left" egalitarian
politics than those in any other field in academe. (1)

Although only slightly more than a decade old in its revived
empirical form, Soviet sociology bears clear resemblance to
the field in other countries both in its value orientations and in
findings, particularly in the field of social stratification. (2)
Thus, as a perusal of the selections in this book makes evident,
almost all Soviet, like American, students of stratification discuss their findings in the context of a positive concern for a
more egalitarian society. Accepting the communist goal of
equality, they document the existence of considerable inequality
within their country in terms of power, income, status and opportunity, variations which are associated in the research literature with family socio-economic background, sex, community of origin (metropolitan to rural), and less frequently with
national or ethnic background.

The Soviet sociologists differ, publicly at least, from their
American and other Western counterparts in assuming that
their society and governmental regime are in a transitional
stage which will lead increasingly and inevitably to the achiev-
able goal of real equality, i.e., communism, a system without
differentiated strata or variations in reward. Unlike most Western students of stratification, they do not link the existence of
inequality in their country to the desire of the privileged to
maintain their superior position for themselves and their kin.
Their data are rarely presented in the context of an explicit
critique of some major aspect of the society. And although
quantitative comparisons with the results of comparable research in non-Soviet society are rarely made, there are frequent comments in Soviet academic journals that the research
findings demonstrate that the Soviet Union is more egalitarian,
offers more opportunity, than the United States or the West, or
that the situation is steadily improving, i.e., becoming more
egalitarian. "Unpleasant facts," for example, the lesser economic or educational achievements of some ethnic groups, are
explained away in non-invidious terms, e.g., as a consequence
of disproportionate rural background.

Much Soviet sociological literature is written in the context
of refuting contentions made by Western writers about Soviet
society. Yet the answers to the Western statements are so weak
or so clearly counter to the findings which the authors themselves, or other Soviet scholars, have published as to make one
wonder what message they are trying to communicate. In a selection included as Chapter 5 in this volume, Iu. E. Volkov refers
to bourgeois ideologists who "circulate fabrications" concerning "a 'new ruling class,' a new 'elite,' etc." in the Soviet Union,
which depict them as that stratum "engaged in performing management functions in administrative-political, economic and
other organs." In answering this contention, Volkov acknowl-
edges that the functions of management appear to be the same
under capitalism and socialism, but insists that the essence is
different because the only masters "are the working masses."
He argues that management under socialism "cannot be the expression of the self-seeking interests of a minority.... It can
only be a more or less exact expression of the will and interests of the whole society." And he contends, in a statement
which certainly is at odds with almost all the empirical work of
Soviet sociology, that "aside from working people there is no
one else in a socialist society."

There are limited references to variations in power linked to
occupation. Soviet sociology as yet has not been able to face up
to the problem of power, although it was once openly discussed
in the one classic communist work which sought to confront the
work of "bourgeois" sociology, Historical Materialism: A System of Sociology by Nikolai Bukharin. This book, first published
in the Soviet Union in 1921, was a required Party text during
Lenin's lifetime. In it, Bukharin dealt with the arguments of
Robert Michels who, in a section "in his very interesting book"
Political Parties, so described and quoted by Bukharin, con-
tended that socialism "assigns at least as much power to the administrators as would possession of their own private property."
Hence for Michels, socialism "seems to be nothing more than
a substitution of one group of leaders for another," the masses
cannot govern.

Bukharin recognized that Michels' argument could not be

easily dismissed. In answering him, he acknowledged that it was not certain who would turn out to be right, Michels or the Marxists. He insisted, however, that Michels was wrong because he made certain assumptions about the working class's inability to govern which are in error.

> [W]hat constitutes an eternal category in Michels' presentation, namely the "incompetence of the masses," will disappear, for this incompetence is by no means a necessary attribute of every system; it likewise is a product of the economic and technical conditions, expressing themselves in the general cultural being and in the educational conditions. We may state that in the society of the future there will be a colossal overproduction of organizers, which will nullify the stability of the ruling groups.
>
> But the question of the transition period from capitalism to socialism, i.e., the period of the proletarian dictatorship, is far more difficult.... There will inevitably result a tendency to "degeneration," i.e., the excretion of a leading stratum in the form of a class-germ. This tendency will be retarded by two opposing tendencies; first, by the growth of the productive forces; second, by the abolition of the educational monopoly. The increasing reproduction of technologists and of organizers in general, out of the working class itself, will undermine this possible new class alignment. The outcome of the struggle will depend on which tendencies turn out to be stronger. (3)

Presumably the abundant empirical Soviet sociological studies could shed light on Bukharin's judgments, but his book and particularly his thesis, once Party doctrine, that "the ruling groups," the "class-germ" would be prevented from dominating by the "over-production" of working-class activists who would "undermine this possible new class alignment," are ignored even in post-Stalinist Russia. Yet some of the descriptive analyses of contemporary Soviet sociology may relate. For example, O. I. Shkaratan's report, presented here, on the results of studies of the working class, notes that "although the members of society are equal co-owners of socialist property, they do not participate equally in the organization and improvement of production, they contribute unequally to the development of the economy and culture, and they are unequal in the degree to which they are the subjects of social activity."

Social Mobility and Education

Some Soviet sociologists both denounce and at the same time implicitly acknowledge the possible validity of analyses of limitations on upward mobility into the elite. Two scholars, M. N. Rutkevich and F. R. Filippov, take me to task for anticipating a decline in such opportunities as the society stabilizes following the end of the rapid growth demanded by early industrialization and the needs of post-Revolutionary and postwar eras. (4) But though they denounce this analysis as being "readily utilized at the present time not only by bourgeois propagandists of anti-communism, but...[as] also widely applied by right and 'left' revisionists in their anti-Soviet propaganda," they go on in another section of their book, also reprinted here, to present data completely in line with my discussion. Since the numbers seeking entrance to institutions of higher education are increasing much more rapidly than places, they conclude: "Competitive selection in admissions to higher educational institutions...in the future...will apparently play an increasing role as a kind of screening 'sieve.' "

The growth of the competitive pressures can be seen in the admission statistics reported for the 1972/73 academic year. Only 22 percent of secondary school graduates could enter daytime higher education. This may be contrasted to 25 percent in 1960, 50 percent in 1950, and 80 percent in 1940. (5) The large majority of secondary school graduates take the examinations to continue their education. Consequently, as the ratio of failures to successful candidates increases steadily, the chances of those from less privileged backgrounds inevitably decrease. (6)

Rutkevich and Filippov reiterate the results of the many Soviet studies which document a considerable correlation between family socio-economic background and school achievement on every level. And they emphasize the extent to which such stratification biases, in the context of greater competition for university place, results in a steady increase in the proportion of students from intelligentsia backgrounds, while that from working-class and peasant origins declines:

> Given the number of applicants, which is now several times greater than the number of vacancies in first-year courses at higher schools, society is interested in selecting those who in a few years are capable of becoming the best specialists.... It is quite obvious that, given equal abilities of youngsters, those families in which the parents have higher educational attainments provide greater opportunities for preparing young people for the competitive examinations.... In ignoring the conditions under which applicants are trained, and in making judgments based only on the applicants' knowledge, admissions committees in effect sanction inequality of opportunity.*

But though analyzing the discriminatory processes, Rutkevich and Filippov (as well as other Soviet sociologists who have written on the subject) reject, as an egalitarian or "socialist" solution, giving "priority to particular categories of [deprived] youth depending on their social characteristics...[as] unacceptable, since it would contradict the principle of equality of citizens under Soviet law." And they argue further that, since social progress depends on putting the most capable and best qualified in leading positions ("specialists"), "the accelerated progress of socialist society urgently requires the admission of youth to higher educational institutions in accordance with the main criterion — the ability to master a future specialty." (7)

These comments, of course, have a familiar ring in Western and American ears since they have been debated here in the context of "open enrollment," or special preference "quotas," for admission to higher education for those from deprived ethnic, racial, or class backgrounds. A large segment of higher education in the United States and other countries has adopted policies designed to make it easier for underprivileged and less trained youth to attend college. Though the issues and the relevant research are highly comparable, it is noteworthy that Rutkevich

---

*All quotations which are not footnoted are from selections in this book.

and Filippov reject any possible comparison, stating flatly:

> In capitalist countries, competition for admission to
> higher educational institutions does not exist in our sense
> of the word. Everything depends on the ability to pay for
> one's studies.... Competition in knowledge and abilities
> is replaced by the "competition" of the purse.

Still, there can be little doubt that Soviet sociologists are
sensitive about the implications of these trends. Thus, L. I.
Sennikova, who also pointed up the "decline in the proportion of
workers and peasants (in terms of social composition) among
the students," sought to answer the criticism that this change
violates socialist values. She wrote that this drop "does not by
any means signify that Soviet higher schools have lost in the
slightest degree their distinguishing feature — their genuinely
public character. Employees and the intelligentsia are also
part of the people, the working people." (8)

The bias in favor of academic achievers, heavily of privileged
origins, goes beyond admission to higher education. In the fall
of 1972, the regulations for granting and paying stipends to students were changed to increase the emphasis on "achievement"
and downgrade financial need. "The amount of the stipend is increased by 25% for students who have received excellent grades
and distinguished themselves in public, scientific or technical
work." (9) In awarding stipends to students with grades of "satisfactory," an "educational institution's stipend committee may
in individual cases consider the students' financial situation." (10)

The commitment of the Soviet leadership to "elitism," an emphasis on supporting the education of the best, rather than
"egalitarianism," a concern for upgrading the bottom in higher
education, is also exhibited in their position with respect to the
"teaching" versus "research" debate. In the United States, the
more left-inclined populist educators and activist student radicals, and increasingly most American state officials, have con-
tended that higher education should be primarily concerned with
teaching, with helping students, particularly those from underprivileged backgrounds, to cope with their situation. A focus on
research is seen as antithetical to such objectives, and as a
form of self-serving "careerism" on the part of the leading
scholars who insist on good research facilities and a light

teaching load. The Soviets, however, have come down hard on the research side of the debate and give the same arguments presented by Western scholars. I. Obraztsov, the Minister of Higher and Specialized Secondary Education for the RSFSR, argued in these terms in December 1972:

> Sometimes one encounters a tendency to denigrate the role of scientific research in the higher schools vis-à-vis the study process. However, it is known that the best Soviet and foreign scientific schools that train highly qualified cadres were created on the basis of major research laboratories, that the "pure" academic process [teaching] in the higher schools makes it possible to train only standardized personnel, that the denigration of the role of research work in the higher schools leads inevitably to the lowering of the teachers' qualifications and that research work protects the study process from scholasticism and stagnation. (11)

It is significant to note that the Chinese Communists became quite sensitive to the stratification biases inherent in a competitive examination system for determining entry to higher education and consequent elite positions during the 1960s and actually eliminated examinations during the Cultural Revolution. Chinese writers noted the existence of "extreme inequality" between the children of the rich and poor in the Soviet educational system. (12) Yet with the end of the Cultural Revolution, as China seeks to create a stable developing society again, its leaders appear to be reverting to policies comparable to those of the Soviets. Examinations, denounced as capitalist devices, were restored in 1972. Teachers had complained that their classes were "slowed to the pace of the poorest students," that automatic promotions led to incompetents being certified as qualified. At the university level there is a "swing away from the worker-peasant-soldier applicant toward the academically better prepared, but ideologically less well qualified graduates of the city middle school." (13)

Occupational Prestige and Attitudes to Work

One of the ideological whipping boys of Soviet sociology is any form of convergence theory, hypotheses which assert that societies at comparable levels of technology, whether socialist or not, will develop similar significant behavior patterns. Hence, although it is clear that many Soviet sociologists are intimately acquainted with the writings of Western sociologists and that they frequently make use of their ideas in analyzing Soviet society, they cannot acknowledge this. L. F. Liss, for example, presents a Soviet version of the functionalist theory of stratification which has been attacked by Western radicals as an ideological rationalization for inequality. (14) Liss states that the "prestige of occupations is formed on the basis of societal needs." This means that many will compete for entrance to higher education and consequent chance for high-status occupations, although relatively few will succeed. "The resulting contradiction between societal and individual interests is resolved by means of competitive selection of the most deserving, prepared, and capable individuals who have passed their entrance examinations."

Considerable Soviet writing and sociological research, such as that by Vodzinskaia in this volume, document the low esteem evidenced by many Soviet youth for farm or manual work. Upon leaving secondary school many will refuse to take any job while they seek to maneuver themselves into some higher education institution.

Various articles published in the second half of 1972 that report on research on the prestige of occupations conducted among secondary-school youth in different parts of the country note the serious problem for the economy created by the fact that the majority want to go on to higher education to secure a prestigeful upper-level position. Thus Iu. P. Averichev reports: "Many former tenth-graders [graduates] go into production work under pressure and consider such work to be temporary. A total of 80% of the young people who come to the borough employment commissions in Krasnodar have failed higher-school entrance exams. The working conditions do not interest them.

What they care most about is the opportunity to prepare for the next competitive examinations...." (15) The Kiev Young Communist League asked 5,000 schoolchildren what they wanted to be, and an article summarizing the results points up the problem that the predominant reluctance to consider manual jobs poses:

> Let us transport ourselves magically to a desert island where each of the pupils has become what he wanted to be. We find many designers, but only seven construction workers and one work superintendent. Every tenth person is a doctor, but there are only five nurses. Manufacturing is hopelessly bad, with only 80 factory workers. There are nearly 300 teachers and state security officials. There are hundreds of journalists and writers, but no printers to publish their work. We find one restaurant director, 23 cooks and no waiter — but with only seven livestock specialists, one tractor driver and one fisherman it is hard to feed all the scientists, actors and coaches at work on the island. (16)

Following the publication of a survey of the occupational preferences of a sample of Russian youth, the manager of an industrial plant wrote to the press asking "where am I to find my turners and milling machine operators," occupations which placed 75th and 76th out of 80 occupations in one community. Two articles in Pravda by Georgi Kulagin, the manager of a Leningrad factory, complain that the emphasis on classes for "gifted children" and the rewards for higher education serve to denigrate manual occupations. As he notes:

> Families and children fight for admittance to such courses, because otherwise they would feel "inferior." Naturally not all are of a high enough standard, and many who could be excellent workers become very bad technicians and functionaries, thus providing a loss to society twice over. "Enough of the classes for the elite," appeals Kulagin. "The school must ensure a more realistic preparation for a working life. And we must remember that we need engineers, but we need workers too." (17)

Concerns of this type have been repeatedly voiced by Soviet scholars and policymakers since research on these topics revived.

V. Kantorovich noted with dismay that the distaste exhibited by Russian youth for farm and manual work "is not as exceptional as it might seem."

Sociologists have noted a highly critical attitude toward physical labor, bordering on squeamishness, exists among some upper-grade secondary school students in Leningrad. It was this, actually, that the Resolution of the Central Committee of the Party on the School Reform (1958) dealt with: "Some of those who graduate from school regard it as demeaning for them to engage in physical labor."

...[I]n our country (and this is by no means limited to the ranks of the salaried professionals) people are prepared to condemn a juvenile — and, even more, the parents of one — who will work for pay.... Abroad, children from diverse strata of society (except the elite, of course) regularly earn money by working as baggage-handlers, salesmen, dish-washers, maintenance workers, and so forth. Should one be surprised that having been trained from childhood only for mental work, for study, the Leningrad secondary students...had decided that they were born only for the professions and not for any other kind of work? When life compels them to "become a worker," this is taken as demeaning and even as a catastrophe.

...It is dinned into the ears of the young person that he has free access to all occupations which enjoy standing in his eyes, and that he can advance to the highest status in our society.... In effect, this aphorism strips all but the thoroughly intellectual occupations of all attractiveness, and thus misleads young people by picturing as excessively easy the difficult choice of a "place in life." (18)

Although the main concern about work values reiterated both in sociological and Party writings deals with the lack of respect for manual labor, some Soviet leaders, sounding like American conservatives, have even begun to complain about the decline of any interest in work among the more privileged youth. The First Secretary of the Lithuanian Communist Party Central Committee, in a speech in June 1972, explained such behavior as a result of affluence among the Soviet elite.

It is no secret that, with the higher material standard of living, many families seek to protect their children from any kind of work. Then we are surprised when families of good and industrious people rear softies, people with no sense of responsibility. It is gratifying that today children do not have to undergo the poverty and misfortune that many people of our generation experienced. But it is bad that the content of their lives becomes idleness and the search for casual adventures and friends.

...it is necessary to take a more decisive stand against the frame of mind in which young people demand only rights and privileges of various kinds for themselves but have no sense of duty and refuse to give anything to society....
The cultivation in young people of a sense of order and self-discipline should not end with the "hair" problem. It is good that many bitter words were spoken at this congress about long-haired sloppy individuals who no longer look like human beings.... (19)

Kantorovich's suggestion that the Soviet ideological emphasis on equality of opportunity has the effect of demeaning occupations which require less training is comparable to the analyses of the dysfunctional consequences for American society of the stress that "all should strive for the same lofty goals since these are open to all." (20) This comparison may not be as foreign to East European scholars as one might think. Poland's most influential sociologist, the late Stanislaw Ossowski, pointed out that the "American conception [of stratification] combining classlessness with the maintenance of great differences in national income, which is contained in a certain version of the American Creed, is by no means alien to the Soviet Union and the People's Democracies in relation to their own societies."

The Socialist principle "to each according to his merits" is in harmony with the tenets of the American Creed, which holds that each man is master of his fate, and that a man's status is fixed by an order of merit. The Socialist principle allows of the conclusion that there are unlimited opportunities for social advancement and social demotion; this is similar to the American concept of "vertical social mobility." The arguments directed against uravnilovka [equalization or leveling of wages] coincide with the arguments put forward on the other side of the Atlantic by those who justify the necessity for economic inequalities in a democratic society. "The maximization of effort in an achievement-oriented society calls for considerable inequality" — wrote [the American sociologist, J. J.] Spenger in 1953. This sentence could equally well have been uttered by a statesman in the Soviet Union or the Peoples' Democracies. (21)

In specifying the consequences of the emphasis on opportunity for all, Robert Merton has suggested that failure to achieve success is felt more severely in a "classless" society than in cultures which place more overt emphasis on hereditary social position, or in which the ideology dominant in the less affluent strata explains their position as a consequence of structural discrimination. This leads him to assume that in societies stressing equality, "the greatest pressures toward deviation are exerted upon the lower strata.... Several [American] researchers have shown that specialized areas of vice and crime constitute a 'normal' response to a situation where the cultural emphasis upon pecuniary success has been absorbed, but where there is little access to conventional and legitimate means for becoming successful. The occupational opportunities of people in these areas are largely confined to manual labor and the lesser white-collar jobs. Given the American stigmatization of manual labor which has been found to hold rather uniformly in all social classes, and the absence of realistic opportunities for advancement beyond this level, the result is a marked tendency toward deviant behavior.

"...It is the combination of the cultural emphasis [on opportunity] and the [limitations in] the social structure which produces intense pressure for deviation.... Despite our persisting open-class-ideology, advance toward the success goal is relatively rare and notably difficult for those armed with little formal education and few economic resources." And in a note, Merton goes on to emphasize that "numerous [American] studies have found that the educational pyramid operates to keep a

large proportion of unquestionably able but economically disadvantaged youth from obtaining higher formal education." (22)

Soviet social scientists have not argued (publicly at least)
that similar processes produce criminal or other forms of de-
viance in their society. Their empirical findings, however, are
congruent with Merton's analysis. Thus, Kantorovich points out
"that sociologists take a skeptical attitude [of the image] that it
is...the professional-and-intellectual (higher earning) section
of young people who take that path of crime. It turns out that
the percentage of young criminals is high in another environment — that of those who have dropped out of school, those in
what is called inadequate families, and then [among] those whose
parents have little education and low levels of skill and, moreover, suffer from alcoholism." (23)

Soviet sociology, of course, cannot accept an interpretation
which emphasizes similar components and behavioral consequences of the ideologies of Americanism and communism. And
in a selection published here, O. I. Shkaratan comes up with an
ingenious alternative explanation which is both compatible with
the Marxist emphasis on varying property-relations defining
class differences, and also places Soviet society in a favorable
light. He suggests that "the significance of differences between
workers in mental and manual labor" actually increases in socialist society as compared to others because "they move to the
foreground by comparison with the more rapidly disappearing
interclass differences." He goes on to describe how under socialism one finds salient division "between executive-type and
executor-type labor and, in the case of the latter, between mental and primarily manual labor and between skilled and unskilled
labor." Under socialism the "significance of differences associated with one's role in the social organization of labor is
heightened," particularly among the higher occupations which
tend to get quite differentiated in status, skill, and reward. And
Shkaratan suggests, not unlike some leading American sociological methodologists, that the way to find the best set of categories for analyzing differentiation is "by determining the range
of fluctuations of the principal socio-economic characteristics
of groups with respect to mobility, income, wages, cultural

level, family ties, etc., since the most adequate classification is the one that yields the lowest coefficient of variation." Such an analysis is important, for the actual "social position of a category of individuals is not fully determined by the position of each category in the formal structure of the enterprise: it is also defined by indices of the individual's position in the community, the social status of those associated with them, including, above all, members of their families, etc." Shades of Lloyd Warner.

The similarities which may be drawn between communist countries and Western societies are not, of course, limited to the consequences of values on behavior. Purely structural factors, such as those stemming from differences in the character and rewards attached to varying occupations, also affect the potential for mobility. The various Soviet surveys of job satisfaction and occupational prestige indicate a hierarchical rank order linked to a subjective sense of the possibilities for creative and interesting (non-routine) work, and the objective factor of income. (24) As in Western countries, the results of Soviet research dealing with workers' conceptions indicate that "Men in occupations calling for higher skills wanted their work to be interesting. Those in lower-skill jobs tended to put much more stress on pay." The American Sovietologist, George Fischer, notes that these findings bear out the contention of Alex Inkeles "that in all modern societies a relation seems to exist between the nature of an occupation and what part of it led to the most satisfaction." (25)

Communist ideology and many Soviet writers suggest that their system is eliminating such differences by various measures designed to combine manual and mental work. Again, more empirically minded analysts have challenged these optimistic beliefs.

> Nonetheless, the replacement of physical by mental work is not going at nearly the headlong pace that one might like and that literary men sometimes picture.... Unfortunately, this is the same old substitution of the wish, or of the desirable, for the reality. It is a fact that trends in the opposite direction are under way at the same time. For example,

today we find, in machine-building enterprises, very many fewer of the all-round machinists or mechanics, the real creators of metal products, than we used to. More and more frequently one sees in their stead operators of semiautomatic machinery who perform just a few operations, repeated over and over all day long. The introduction of conveyors, with the extreme division of labor characteristic of them, continues....

It follows that neither the sociologist nor the writer dealing with a theme based on the working class...[can] ignore all the actually existing groups of which the working class consists — including, particularly, the large category engaged in physical labor, which is especially monotonous particularly in jobs at machine tools. It is these types of work that are most oppressive for young people, particularly those who have a secondary education. Here lies the root of one of the factors making for labor turnover — even for population migration. (26)

Soviet scholars continue to contradict those in their country who suggest that economic growth and mechanization provide the solution to the high level of job dissatisfaction reported in many studies among unskilled workers. V. Churbanov reports, as of June 1972, that "50% of our industrial workers perform unmechanical labor at present, and the proportion has declined only two or three percent during each of the last two five-year plans. In fact, in absolute terms the number of such workers is increasing.... [O]ne worker in three in our country works on an assembly line. Indeed, most of the laborers whose work is to be mechanized by 1975 (50% of all manual laborers) will then be performing even more limited tasks with even less intellectual content."

Churbanov goes on to suggest that the problem of job dissatisfaction in the Soviet Union will worsen because educational attainment is increasing much more rapidly than is the growth in the proportion of more interesting non-routine jobs. As he puts it, the problem "would in fact be better formulated as 'educated youth and uninteresting work,'" a phenomenon not unknown in the United States.

The higher a young person's educational level, the greater his need for interesting work. Yet most industrial work presently requires no more than a sixth to eighth grade education, and the scientific and technical revolution is not expected to keep pace with the spread of education in the next few years. The transition to universal secondary education, otherwise so desirable, will only exacerbate this problem. (27)

Finally, it should be emphasized that in both communist and non-communist industrial societies, the sources of unrest among those employed in jobs which require low levels of skill cannot be limited to dissatisfaction with low status, or with monotonous work. Real poverty exists, a fact abundantly documented by Western social scientists and increasingly also by Soviet ones in recent years. The latter reports are still little known in the West.

Official public admission of poverty in the Soviet Union came in the mid-sixties.... The euphemistic term, maloobespechennost, or "underprovision," now came into use....

Soviet researchers put a figure on this poverty line in terms of rubles ... [needed for] a "normative minimal budget for a Soviet urban family"... at 51.4 rubles ... a month per head.

[T]here are some recently published results of family budget surveys. One, covering some 10,000 workers of all kinds in Leningrad between 1962 and 1963, showed that over 40 percent of their families had not reached a per capita income of 51 rubles per month.... Perhaps the most intriguing distribution, however, was published by a Soviet economist called S. P. Figurov in 1962. Though his cate-- gories were vague, his figures seemed to suggest that among workers and white collar families in the Soviet Union as a whole just over 30 percent were, by Soviet standards, poor.

Second, there are some data on the distribution of wages.... A handbook of Soviet labour statistics, published in 1967, showed that over 20 percent of the people employed in the highly-paid building industry, and 60 percent of those in the low-paid building industries, were probably earning less than was needed to ensure the minimum per capita coverage. (28)

A recent comprehensive work on Soviet stratification by the British Sovietologist, Mervyn Matthews, seeks to explain the great class gap in ways which would obviously not be acceptable within the Soviet Union. He suggests that the upper classes in Soviet education "were for many decades 'elitist' in character, and in some ways more comparable to private rather than state schools in the west." Hence, those who came through the Soviet schools would much more strenuously object to taking a non-elite position. And as a student of Soviet living standards, he suggests as a second factor the possibility "that the distinctions in living standards between the upper and lower layers of Soviet society are more keenly felt than material differences in richer societies. The Soviet working class has to suffer many more immediate shortages than its counterparts in more fortunate lands, and the desire of individuals to rise above them may be correspondingly greater." (29)

Family Factors

Thus far, Soviet sociologists have avoided comparative studies of stratification and social mobility, although it would be rather easy for them to replicate the many surveys conducted in the United States and other Western countries, much as has been done by sociologists in Poland, Hungary, and Yugoslavia. (30) The Soviet mobility surveys are limited to special noncomparable samples of employees in given plants, industries, special districts, and various categories of students. While, as noted earlier, all these studies presented in this volume and elsewhere point to strong relationships between parental social origin and status of their offspring, they also indicate that a considerable minority have shifted position, up or down the socio-economic hierarchy. These results are invariably presented as demonstrating the absence of "caste-like" tendencies in Soviet society, unlike the situation in the Western capitalist countries where

mobility is allegedly declining. In spite of their stress on increased equality of opportunity, however, Soviet sociologists do
not avoid pointing to the continuity of privileged status within
the higher levels of society. Thus, L. I. Sennikova found — in
line with the results presented in this volume — that the more
prestigious the school (university as compared to technical institute) the higher the background of those enrolled. She com-
mented on her findings: "This is a completely understandable
phenomenon. Such higher educational institutions as the Medical Institute and the University are attended by larger numbers
of children of doctors, teachers, and the like, for among the intelligentsia these occupations are often 'hereditary.'" (31) Another Soviet sociologist, V. N. Shubkin, also suggested that such
patterns of intergenerational occupational continuity in high-
level positions are to be expected since "the greater the scope
for creative work provided in any occupation, the greater the
continuity between the occupations of the parents and the children. . . . This close correlation of the occupations of fathers
and children is based on community of creative demands and interests. It has nothing in common with the social predestination
in the type of society in which private property and inequality
prevail." (32)

While the intergenerational continuity of elite status in the
Soviet Union may have "nothing in common" with the similar
phenomena in the West, it would seem that what these Russian
scholars are saying is that it is perfectly understandable that
those reared in a privileged ("interesting," "creative") environment will be highly motivated to continue living at that level.
And abundant reports in Soviet publications indicate that affluent
Soviet parents can do much to assure that their offspring also
do well. (33)

Shubkin, who has been much involved in mobility research,
has not attempted to quantify the "close correlation," but a more
recent study published in this volume by Arutiunian includes
such an estimate. He reports a "coefficient of determination"
for the relationships between parents' educational and occupational level and that of their children of 50 percent or more, the
equivalent of a correlation coefficient of over 0.7. While it is

impossible to make any exact comparison with American re-
search, given the variation in classifications employed, few
American studies have ever reported a relationship as high as
Arutiunian's.

These findings clearly may be explained in traditional economic terms. Yet increasingly both Western and Soviet sociologists look for the determining factors in cultural values associated with varying socio-economic positions, rather than for
the direct effect of economic advantage or disadvantage. Thus,
in his study here, Shkaratan contends that by the end of the
1960s, the "socialist system had, in effect, eliminated in the
great majority of cases the influence of economic circumstances
on the achievement of the career plans of children from different social groups. However, the influence of inequality in social
and cultural background still remains." Various sociologists in
Eastern Europe, like their Western counterparts, stress the
causal role of class-linked culture as transmitted in the family,
which affects propensity to take advantage of educational opportunity even when economic barriers do not appear to exist. Thus
Soviet sociologist V. V. Ksenofontova, in interpreting varying
job goals, states: "The differences in career plans of workers'
and specialists' [children] are not caused primarily by material
circumstances.... A much greater role in this matter is played
by family traditions, particularly by the family's cultural level
and general living conditions." (34) A group of Novosibirsk
scholars who have devoted much energy to analyzing the determinants of occupational choice and of social mobility are as
pessimistic as their American counterparts about efforts to affect the correlations with family-related factors by manipulating
the school curriculum. (35)

Sex Differences

American sociologists and others will find additional familiar
ground in the material in this volume dealing with sex differences or, conversely, male chauvinism (a term never used) in
the Soviet Union. Once again, the facts which contradict the ideological self-image are presented in the context of pointing up

how much improvement has been made. Still, Gordon and Klopov report women workers have "half the free time" of men because they do much more of the housework. They "have fewer possibilities for raising their qualifications, for mastering the more complicated and responsible types of jobs. It is characteristic that the average wages of women are lower than those of men." Arutiunian found that in contrast to men, "women have a more enduring orientation toward the family than toward work." Two different studies, those by Vodzinskaia and Liss, report surveys indicating "the existence... of certain stereotypes of occupational preference according to sex." Fields requiring mathematics are predominantly chosen by male students, while in a subject like languages, 90 percent are female. Not surprisingly, therefore, Liss notes "the actual feminization of a number of occupations in whole branches of the economy."

Although Soviet women attend higher schools in about the same proportion as they are in the population, the statistical data indicate their participation relative to men is declining in the more advanced and prestigious scientific and professional fields, e.g., research. And British Sovietologist G. R. Barker stresses that some Soviet sociologists justify these trends by suggesting that "women represent bad investments if the main social goal is the maximization of productivity." (36)

Other statistical data assembled by Soviet sociologists point up both the extensive participation of women — they are over half the wage and salary earners — and the extent to which they remain underprivileged politically as well as economically. Thus, they form but a fifth of Party members, five percent of those holding ministerial posts in all republics, four percent of the members of the Party Central Committee, one percent of the Council of Ministers of the USSR, and "zero percent at the summit, in the Politburo." (37) Within given occupational categories which are heavily female, such as education or health, it seems clear that women are much more likely to be found in the lower echelons than men. Thus women constitute about four-fifths of all schoolteachers, but less than 30 percent of all school principals. (38) As of 1970, 39 percent of all scientific workers, including academics, were women. Within the category,

however, they formed 50 percent of the assistants, 26 percent
of the research associates, 21 percent of the professors, and
but 10 percent in the most prestigious sector, the members of
the Academy. (39) A detailed study of rural structures in Belo-
russia reports that women are considerably underrepresented
"among administrators of various enterprises and organizations." The author, Z. I. Monich, says "this is a clear under-
valuation of a woman's capabilities, since when candidates are
put forward, preference in the absolute majority of cases is
given to men. At the same time, women themselves often refuse leadership posts because of the double burden placed on
them by housework and family." (40) Within industry a similar
pattern is reported. As of 1963, women constituted 38 percent
of all engineers, 16 percent of chief engineers, 12 percent of
factory managers and their assistants, and 6 percent of directors of industry. (41)

It is not easy to obtain a clear picture of sex stratification in
the Soviet economy since the classifications used by occupational statisticians sometimes blur significant differences.
Titma points up this problem in his chapter here in discussing
his effort to relate varying occupational orientations of youth to
the occupations of their mothers and fathers. He found confus-
ing results for medical personnel, a category which ranges
from physicians to attendants. Almost all men in the category
are physicians, while it is a very heterogeneous classification
for women, many of whom are paraprofessional physicians or
nurses.

In seeking to account for such differences, Soviet sociologists
point to many continuing variations in the family roles of men
and women which serve to handicap the latter. Thus, it is clear
that although relatively few Soviet women do not work outside
the home, they continue to bear most of the burden of maintaining the household, cooking, shopping, and taking care of the children. Over half the men do little or nothing in the house. Conversely, women prepare most meals, they give 73 percent of the
parental help in their children's schoolwork, are involved in
75 percent of the visits to their children's schools, and supply
over four-fifths of the general assistance to small children. (42)

The situation of working Soviet women is more difficult than that of their sisters in the West because of the lesser availability of consumer services, such as supermarkets, and goods. Among working-class families, 15 percent have a washing machine, 17 percent a refrigerator, and 20 percent a vacuum cleaner. Commercial services are relatively rare. Thus for 244 million people there are only 33,500 shoe-repairers, 3,600 laundries, and 1,100 dry cleaners. It has been estimated that auxiliary services only cover 5 percent of the work of women. Restaurants are relatively scarce compared to Western nations. In 1962 only 4 percent of all meals were taken outside the home. (43) According to a recent study, "in 1970 only 50 percent of all urban children were attending preschool facilities, while the figure for rural children was a low 30 percent." (44)

On the subjective side, Soviet opinion surveys still produce large minorities willing to endorse "chauvinist" attitudes which run counter to official ideology. Thus in one rural district near Moscow, Arutiunian found that 30 percent of those queried in a sample survey thought it better for the wife to devote herself exclusively to the home and the children. Even more surprising, 25 percent of the intelligentsia agreed that it "was proper for a husband to punish his wife." (45)

In evaluating reports such as these, it is important to remember that as with the studies of occupationally related stratification, American research points up the comparable pattern of privilege and inequality associated with sex roles. Thus the Columbia sociologist Harriet Zuckerman has noted that women "comprise something like 6 percent of the PhDs" in the scientific fields in the United States, but that only 8 out of the 866 members of the highly honorific National Academy of Sciences were women in 1971. In Britain, women make up about 3 percent of the members of the Royal Society. (46) Similarly, medicine, which is increasingly becoming a feminine profession in the Soviet Union, even though men still predominate at the upper levels, is overwhelmingly reserved for males in the United States. Clearly, Americans can have no reason to point to the existence of sex-linked inequalities (or any others) as evidence of the moral superiority of their own society.

Ethnicity

The one major aspect of stratification found in the Western
literature which is almost missing from this book is race or
ethnicity. (47) Anti-Semitism and the special role of the Jews
in certain occupations are certainly not treatable as a scholarly
topic in the Soviet Union. Neither is a subject which has been
studied in Yugoslavia, the relation of differences in value systems among different ethnic groups to economic behavior. (48)
The problem posed for the Soviet Union by disparate national
values and rates of development has been pointed up by journalists. Thus, a New York Times dispatch from Baku, the capital
of the Azerbaijan Soviet Socialist Republic, discusses the way
in which the "Azerbaijani style of life, reflecting centuries of
Moslem influences, refuses to conform to the communist model":

> No less a figure than Geldar A. Aliyev, the Communist
> party chief, has been complaining about nepotism, forced
> child marriages, corruption on a grand scale, the urge for
> private ownership and the penchant for private trading —
> "plundering of socialist property for mercenary reasons,"
> he called it — and the practice of bribing examiners at uni-
> versities for entrance or graduation. . . .
>
> The clannishness of the Azerbaijanis, their skill at ar-
> ranging deals under the table and their general undisciplined
> ways have long been a problem for Communist leaders —
> apparently at a greater scale than in many other regions.
> Some local Communists blame centuries of Moslem domi-
> nation over this southern territory. . . .
>
> "Islam is more aggressive and more reactionary than
> other religions," asserted Gasham Asianov, editor of the
> Communist youth paper Yunost. . . . "This religion teaches
> people to think about themselves and their families. . . . We
> lived about 1,300 years by this religion, by this ideology,"
> he explained. "We have lived under Soviet power only 50
> years. During 50 years it is very difficult to change human
> nature." (49)

Similar criticisms have been voiced about the values and behavior of the Georgians. They, too, seemingly "are clearly

determined to preserve as much of their own way of doing things as possible — which includes a notorious addiction to private enterprise of all kinds." (50)

Discussion at a Plenary Session of the Georgian Party Central Committee called attention to many other ills within that Republic, including considerable evidence of corruption and "a tolerant attitude toward vestiges of the past, toward remnants of private-ownership psychology, personal enrichment, and money-grubbing." Although clearly not a specific Georgian trait, the Minister of Local Industry complained of "more and more cases of the selection, placement and evaluation of cadres not according to ability and on-the-job qualities but according to who was acceptable to whom. The Party principle of cadres selection was often replaced by the family principle, and selection was determined by kinship and acquaintance...." (51)

The Secretary of the Tadzhik Party Central Committee noted recently that in "our work of internationalist upbringing we are paying special attention to eradicating the opposites of communist morals and ethics and remnants of the past in people's consciousness and daily life. Such manifestations are on the decrease. But they do exist, and their chief danger lies in the fact that they are sometimes passed off as national traits and national traditions." He noted, however, that "again and again, hackneyed fabrications to the effect that in the Soviet Union, including Tadzhikistan, national traditions are supposedly being stifled, national art eliminated, etc., etc., are brought forward." The Tadzhik Party Central Committee, reacting to such problems, has "pointed out the need to wage an uncompromising struggle against bourgeois ideology and any manifestations of national narrowness and parochialism." (52)

Complaints concerning an influx of Russians who succeed in securing a disproportionate share of economic, housing, and educational advantages in minority republics are common. A group of 17 Latvian Party members published an appeal to Western Communist Parties in 1971 to intervene on behalf of minority peoples. The document complained about the increased presence of Russians in leading positions, and the importation of specialists and other highly skilled personnel from outside.

All of this made for forced assimilation. (53)

One selection in this volume, by Arutiunian, discusses some aspects of this problem in reporting on mobility and stratification in the Tatar Autonomous Soviet Socialist Republic. The Tatars, a predominantly rural people, though including a large upwardly mobile segment, are much less likely to go on to higher education than Russians living in the area. Though Tatars constitute 60 percent of the population, they form only 37 percent of those who attend higher educational institutions and 27 percent of those in graduate work. In the Almetevsk District, the percent of students who were Tatars in 1967-1968 was 59.7 percent in grades 5-6, but only 50.6 in grades 9-10. Arutiunian, who presents these data while repeatedly stressing the improvement in the achievements of the Tatars, furnishes a "materialistic" explanation for such ethnic differences:

> Those national groups which reside primarily in rural localities naturally have less opportunities for social advancement than the more urbanized national groups. It is no accident, for example, that the relative share of primarily "urban" national groups in the student body is disproportionately high (Russians, Armenians, Estonians, Latvians), while the share of most predominantly rural national groups (Kirgiz, Moldavians, Tadziks, etc.) is disproportionately low. Moreover, the more advanced the level of professional training, the more apparent are the differences associated with the extent of urbanization of national groups.

This interpretation makes sense and undoubtedly explains a large part of the ethnic variations. (54) Yet a look at Table 12 in Arutiunian's study clearly suggests that the children of Russian unskilled workers and collective farmers do much better in school than Tatar offspring. Seemingly there are differences in the situation of Russians and Tatars living in the Tatar Republic beyond these subsumed under the heading of rural-urban variations that affect their achievement potential. Arutiunian indicates some of the underlying processes at work in his comment that "of particular importance in stimulating mobility are the immediate surroundings, above all the cultural atmosphere

and general climate in the family, especially the extent to which
the family knows and uses Russian. More than 60% of the individuals in the mobile population group of the Tatar ASSR are
fluent in Russian or in both the Russian and Tatar languages,
while in the immobile group the corresponding figure is about
one-half as great — 34%." In other words, assimilation to the
dominant minority's culture facilitates upward mobility in the
USSR much as it does elsewhere.

Scholarship and Social Criticism

Yet, after pointing to the repeated patterns of convergence (if
that word may be allowed) in findings and interpretation between
Soviet and Western sociologists dealing with stratification, it
must be reported that in one important respect the Soviet scholars seemingly differ: they are much less likely to supply members of the political opposition than their American counterparts. As noted earlier, American survey data indicate that sociologists have been more disposed to be involved in varying
kinds of radical and anti-war protest than those in other fields;
they are more prone to favor left or radical views than their
academic colleagues. In the Soviet Union, however, where natural scientists have constituted the core group of protestors in
the 1960s, sociologists have simply not been visible among the
various dissident groups and publications. (55) The MIT Sovietologist Zev Katz notes that "in contrast to the situation in the
literary field, not a single piece of sociological writing sup-
pressed in the U.S.S.R. has been published abroad; there is not a
single Soviet sociologist who is an expatriate in the West; nor
do the signatures of Soviet sociologists usually appear on protest documents." (56)
These differences in political behavior of American and Soviet sociologists clearly do not reflect the fact that the latter
have been less unable or unwilling to study and publish unpalat-
able facts exposing the "contradictions" of their society. But
the Soviet scholars operate in a country in which the governing
regime takes adherence to its ideology seriously, demanding
that the social sciences support the dominant dogma. In effect,

social science, and sociology in particular, are allowed freedom
to do research on the condition that none of their findings appear
to challenge communist ideology. In a speech delivered in December 1971 to the heads of social science departments at
higher educational institutions, M. A. Suslov, the Secretary of
the Central Committee of the CPSU, told them explicitly that
"the most important conditions for the fruitful development and
effective utilization of the social sciences in communist construction are the allegiance of these sciences to Marxist-
Leninist methodology...," that they must help intensify "the
Marxist-Leninist tempering of all Soviet students." (57)

Some indication of the pressures under which Soviet sociologists live may be found in a detailed report of a five-day-long
meeting "of the departments of philosophy of the Academy of
Social Sciences and the Higher Party School of the Central Committee of the CPSU" held from November 20 to 25, 1969 to discuss the first effort to present a textbook in the field, Iu. A.
Levada's Lectures on Sociology (1967). Twenty major scholars
spoke, each one attacking the errors of the work, basically for
not emphasizing the "contradiction between capitalist-oriented
and Marxist sociology." One speaker sensed "in the Lectures
a certain influence of Talcott Parsons and other bourgeois sociologists." The last critic to speak condemned the book because it dealt with "a sociology above classes" and attempted
to find links between Marxism and Western sociology. Sociology
cannot be "neutral with respect to the class struggle, the struggle of ideologies." (58)

More recently, in August 1972, a Pravda editorial discussed
"significant shortcomings" in the work of social science institutes. It noted "serious mistakes and confusion in the interpretations of certain fundamental theoretical propositions. It is
necessary to adhere without deviation to the principle of the
Marxist-Leninist Party line...in analyzing the social processes
of our times." (59)

Natural scientists in the Soviet Union may be much more
critical and active politically because, not being as overtly politically relevant in their actual work, they are less hampered
than the social sciences by political controls. Social scientists,

particularly sociologists, as Katz observes, are under much
greater pressure to present their criticisms, their exposés, in
the context of reinforcing Marxism-Leninism and to recommend
changes as a means of helping the system evolve "in the direction of the humanist ideals of Marxism and the Bolshevik Revolution.... Indeed, such an attitude may be an indispensable pre-
condition for a major contribution by sociology to a positive
transformation of Soviet society." (60) Yet, given the increasing
recognition of the importance of sociology, the Party leaders
"— and indeed, the sociologists themselves — find themselves
in a painful dilemma. For if sociology is to be a truly effective
instrument for improving the Soviet system, it must be somewhat independent and critical, to point out where the failings of
the system lie.... The Party is as yet reluctant to do this, and
it therefore continues to try to keep sociology within safe
bounds." (61) The sociologists, perhaps because they publish
so much which is genuinely critical, may feel it necessary to
voice a much greater formal ideological loyalty than do those
in other fields, whose work, as such, does not touch the Party
line.

Yet it should be noted in conclusion that such overt "conform-
ist" behavior does not completely protect the Soviet sociologists.
Another account of their situation notes that the discipline still
faces considerable opposition from within the Party leadership
and remains "in constant turmoil." Alexei M. Rumiantsev, the
first director of the Institute of Concrete Social Research, established to coordinate work in the field, was recently removed
"in a shuffle apparently intended to make the sociologists more
responsive to Party officials in the Central Committee. This
was followed by a purge at the Institute by a special Central
Committee commission which reviewed the professional qualifications of all the sociologists...." (62)

Writing in Kommunist in July 1972, V. Iagodin, the Secretary
of the Moscow Party Committee, attacked the "Institute of Concrete Social Research, the U.S.S.R. Academy of Sciences' Institute of World History, and certain other scientific institutions...
[for] doing a poor job in mobilizing scholars to produce fundamental works in the social sciences, raising the scientific and

ideological-theoretical level of research, intensifying the struggle for the purity of Marxist-Leninist theory, and strengthening
effective ties between theory and the practical tasks of communist construction. Individual scholars, including Communists,
are not displaying the requisite Party spirit or the necessary
class and concrete-historical approach in posing and resolving
scientific problems, are failing to take account of the full complexity of the ideological struggle in today's conditions, and are
not engaging in active, aggressive criticism of bourgeois and
revisionist concepts. Certain research projects are being done
on a low scientific, ideological and theoretical level, and contain
serious methodological and political mistakes in their treatment
of fundamental problems of Marxist-Leninist theory and the
practice of communist construction." (63) An East European sociologist, well acquainted with the situation in the Soviet Union,
interprets these events as reflecting the fact that the young Soviet sociologists "began serious work in the 1960s, forgetting
that the taboos of Marxism-Leninism would make it impossible
to conduct unfettered empirical research." (64)

It is interesting to note that a solution to the problems of increasing research effectiveness and ideological purity at scientific institutes both in the natural and social sciences, fostered
by the Party, is to stimulate "the further development of socialist competition at research institutes." Among other things this
means "a system that makes researchers' earnings directly dependent on the results of their work.... The basic indices for
determining the amount of incremental pay a researcher is to
receive are as follows: qualitative level and significance of the
work performed; observance of plan deadlines; and results of
the utilization of research findings in applied science and in
practice." (65)

Finally, I would like to note again that the patterns of inequality in the Soviet Union documented in this volume can easily be
paralleled with reports from American and other Western sociological works. Although many of my comments have been implicitly comparative, I have avoided explicit comparisons for
the most part, assuming that the readership of this book will
largely be drawn from the ranks of Western sociologists who

are intimately acquainted with the evidence demonstrating the patterns of steep inequality in non-communist countries. Those readers who are not familiar with that literature should turn to it before drawing any conclusions about the degree of inequality in different social systems. Clearly, no citizen of the United States, Western Europe, or the communist world who believes in equality can find reason for smugness about the situation in his own part of the world. Structural factors favoring the enlargement of privilege and inheritance of social position characterize all existing social systems. If any conclusion can be drawn from the evidence concerning the recurrence of stratified differentiation following on deliberate efforts to sharply reduce it, it is that the struggle to limit inequality requires a constant conscious effort to restrain elites from exploiting the masses. And insofar as sociology points up the nature of inequality, particularly in systems such as the American and the Soviet, which proclaim the objective of a "classless" society, it furthers efforts to approach that goal. (66)

These are some of the issues raised by reading the materials covered in this important collection of writings by Soviet sociologists. The selections attest to how much our colleagues have accomplished in little more than a decade of work. We can look forward eagerly to their research in the next few decades. Hopefully, now that some of the bitterness occasioned by cold and hot wars between East and West has declined, it may be possible to undertake systematic comparative investigations, to compare sources and patterns of mobility, family behavior, educational achievement, and many other topics. The editors and publisher of this excellent book are to be congratulated for this contribution to international knowledge. Its existence should push forward teaching and research in comparative sociology among English-language scholars.

Notes

1) S. M. Lipset and E. C. Ladd, Jr., "The Politics of American Sociologists," American Journal of Sociology, 78 (1972), pp. 67-104.

386   Commentary / S. M. Lipset

2) I have previously compared Soviet research in stratification with Western work in S. M. Lipset, "Social Mobility and Equal Opportunity," The Public Interest, No. 29 (Fall 1972), pp. 90-108; and Lipset, "La mobilité sociale et les objectifs socialistes," Sociologie et sociétés, 4 (November 1972), pp. 193-224. For other reports dealing with stratification and social mobility in the USSR and other communist countries, see Zev Katz, Hereditary Elements in Education and Social Structure in the U.S.S.R. (Glasgow: Institute of Soviet and East European Studies, University of Glasgow, 1969); David Lane, The End of Inequality? Stratification Under State Socialism (Baltimore: Penguin Books, 1971); Frank Parkin, Class Inequality and Political Order: Social Stratification in Capitalist and Communist Societies (New York: Praeger, 1971); Zev Katz, Patterns of Social Mobility in the U.S.S.R. (Cambridge: Center for International Studies, MIT, 1972); and Mervyn Matthews, Class and Society in Soviet Russia (New York: Walker and Co., 1972).

3) Nikolai Bukharin, Historical Materialism: A System of Sociology (New York: International Publishers, 1925), pp. 309-311 (emphases in original).

4) A similar analysis has been presented by a Hungarian scholar. See R. Adorka, "Social Mobility and Economic Development," Acta Oeconomica, 7, No. 1 (1971), pp. 40-41.

5) See P. Oldak and V. Gruber, "The Higher School: Wide-Open Doors and Crowded Steps," Literaturnaia gazeta, No. 42, October 18, 1972, p. 10, as abstracted in The Current Digest of the Soviet Press, 25 (February 7, 1973), pp. 15-16.

6) See V. N. Shubkin, "Youth Starts Out in Life," Soviet Sociology, 4 (Winter 1965-1966), p. 11, and S. S. Voronitsyn, "Class Distinction in Soviet Higher Education," Bulletin of the Munich Institute for the Study of the U.S.S.R., 17 (November 1970), pp. 39-40.

7) For comparable arguments by other Soviet scholars against giving special admission preference to those from underprivileged social backgrounds, see Shubkin, op. cit., p. 11, and V. Kantorovich, "Sociology and Literature," Soviet Sociology, 7 (Summer 1968), p. 35.

8) L. I. Sennikova, "Higher Education as a Factor in Social

Mobility," in M. N. Rutkevich, ed., The Career Plans of Youth (White Plains, N.Y.: International Arts and Sciences Press, 1969), p. 14. This translation of a Russian volume contains 16 articles, most of which present statistical data from different parts of the country which document the sharp correlation between socio-economic background and educational achievements. Similar trends have occurred in Yugoslavia, as Tito himself recently noted in an interview: "There are fewer and fewer worker- and peasant-youths at the universities, because there is a fairly large number of those who are well off and who can afford to study." Tito, however, views these developments in negative terms. They distress him deeply. See: Interview with President Tito, "We Must Have a Vanguard and United Party," Vjesnik, October 8, 1972, translated in Socialist Thought and Practice, No. 49 (August-December 1972), pp. 21, 11, 13.

9) E. Rozanova, "The Student Stipend," Izvestia, September 30, 1972, as abstracted in The Current Digest of the Soviet Press, 24 (October 25, 1972), p. 31.

10) Izvestia Legal Service, "Stipends for Technicum Students," Izvestia, January 31, 1973, as abstracted in The Current Digest of the Soviet Press, 25 (February 28, 1973), p. 43.

11) I. Obraztsov, "For Science and Production," Izvestia, December 14, 1972, p. 5, as abstracted in The Current Digest of the Soviet Press, 24 (January 10, 1973), p. 9.

12) See Donald J. Munro, "Egalitarian Ideal and Educational Fact in Communist China," in John M. H. Lindbeck, ed., China: Management of a Revolutionary Society (Seattle: University of Washington Press, 1971), pp. 256-301.

13) John Burns, "China Restoring Exams in Her Schools," New York Times, September 25, 1972, p. 3.

14) For an effort to indicate the variations and similarities in various sociological theories of stratification, especially the Marxist, Weberian and functionalist, see S. M. Lipset, "Issues in Social Class Analysis," in Lipset, Revolution and Counter-revolution (Garden City: Doubleday-Anchor, 1970), pp. 157-202.

15) Iu. P. Averichev, "Guiding Pupils into Trades," Sovet-skaia pedagogika, 1972, No. 7, pp. 12-19, as abstracted in The Current Digest of the Soviet Press, 25 (February 7, 1973), p. 14.

16) Val. Rushkis, "And Here We Are on the Island," Komso-molskaia pravda, September 21, 1972, p. 4, as abstracted in The Current Digest of the Soviet Press, 25 (February 7, 1973), pp. 14, 27.

17) "Young Soviet Citizens No Longer Wish to Be Workers," (a summary of an article by the Moscow correspondent of the Corriere della Sera (Milan), Giuseppe Josca, in SIPE (International Student Press Service, Rome), 3 (October/November, 1971), pp. 12-14.

18) Kantorovich, op. cit., pp. 32-33.

19) A. Snieckus, "The Soviet Woman Is an Active Creator and Educator," as abstracted in The Current Digest of the Soviet Press, 24 (July 26, 1972), p. 6.

20) Robert K. Merton, Social Theory and Social Structure (New York: The Free Press, 1968), p. 193. See Merton's discussion on pp. 185-248.

21) Stanislaw Ossowski, Class Structure in the Social Consciousness (New York: The Free Press, 1963), pp. 110, 114.

22) Merton, op. cit., pp. 198-199 (emphases in the original).

23) Kantorovich, op. cit., p. 32.

24) See V. N. Shubkin, "Social Mobility and Choice of Occupation," in G. V. Osipov, ed., Industry and Labour in the USSR (London: Tavistock, 1966), pp. 90-93; A. G. Zdravomyslov and V. A. Iadov, "Effect of Vocational Distinctions on the Attitude to Work," in ibid., pp. 99-129 (see p. 114 for data on the interrelationship of creativity and pay in determining satisfaction).

25) George Fischer, "Current Soviet Work in Sociology: A Note in the Sociology of Knowledge," The American Sociologist, 1 (May 1966), pp. 127-132. A detailed translated report of Soviet research in this field is A. G. Zdravomyslov, V. P. Rozhin, and V. A. Iadov, Man and His Work (White Plains, N.Y.: International Arts and Sciences Press, 1970). See pp. 159-160 for the findings cited by Fischer.

26) Kantorovich, op. cit., p. 29.

27) V. Churbanov, "The Young Worker and Uninteresting Labor," Molodoi Kommunist, 1972, No. 6, pp. 64-71, as abstracted in The Current Digest of the Soviet Press, 25 (February 7, 1973), pp. 13-14.

28) Mervyn Matthews, "Poverty in Russia," New Society, 19 (January 27, 1972), pp. 174-175. A more extensive analysis by Matthews may be found in his book Class and Society in Soviet Russia, op. cit., esp. pp. 81-90, and passim.

29) Ibid., pp. 314-315.

30) For a discussion of some of these comparative analyses, see Lipset, "Social Mobility...," op. cit., pp. 98-100; Philips Cutright, "Occupational Inheritance: A Cross-National Analysis," American Journal of Sociology, 73 (1968), pp. 400-416; Lipset, "La mobilité sociale...," pp. 195-199.

31) Sennikova, op. cit., p. 148.

32) Shubkin, "Social Mobility and the Choice of Occupation," op. cit., pp. 92-93.

33) Lipset, "Social Mobility...," op. cit., pp. 102-103; Lipset, "La mobilité sociale...," pp. 203-213.

34) V. V. Ksenofontova, "Career Plans of 8th and 9th Grade Students and Their Realization," in Rutkevich, ed., op. cit., p. 49.

35) V. N. Shubkin, V. I. Artemov, N. P. Moskalenko, N. V. Buzukova, and V. A. Kalmyk, "Quantitative Methods in Sociological Studies of Problems of Job Placement and Choice of Occupations [Part 1]," Soviet Sociology, 7 (Fall 1968), p. 24.

36) G. R. Barker, "La femme en Union Soviétique," Sociologie et sociétés, 4 (November 1972), pp. 180-181. This article is an exceptionally good detailed account of the Soviet sociological literature dealing with the situation of women.

37) Ibid., p. 185.

38) See "Women in the USSR: Statistical Data," Soviet Sociology, 11 (Summer 1972), pp. 57-86, esp. pp. 63, 69-75.

39) Barker, op. cit., p. 175.

40) Z. I. Monich, Intelligentsiia v strukture sel'skogo naseleniia (iz materialakh BSSR), Minsk, "Nauka i tekhnika" Publishing House, 1971, as abstracted in ABSEES Soviet and East European Abstracts, series 2 (April 1972), pp. 77-78.

41) Barker, op. cit., p. 175.

42) Ibid., p. 176; see also Matthews, op. cit., pp. 102-105.

43) Barker, op. cit., pp. 177-178.

44) Bernice Madison, "Social Services for Families and

Children in the Soviet Union," Slavic Review, 31 (December 1972), p. 831.

45) Barker, op. cit., pp. 184-185.

46) These data are drawn from an important, as yet unpublished, paper by Harriet Zuckerman, "Women and Blacks in American Science: The Principle of the Double Penalty" (Lecture at the California Institute of Technology, 1971).

47) There is a considerable literature by Soviet sociologists dealing with ethnic differences, attitudes and patterns of behavior. For examples of these, see articles in Stephen P. Dunn, ed., Sociology in the USSR (White Plains, N.Y.: International Arts and Sciences Press, 1969), esp. pp. 42-106, 145-197, and passim, and "Ethnosociology and Ethnic Relations," a special issue of Soviet Sociology, 11 (Winter-Spring 1972-73), pp. 211-422. Many other issues of Soviet Sociology contain relevant articles.

48) See Gary K. Bertsch, Nation Building in Yugoslavia (Beverly Hills: Sage Publications, 1971). For an article from Yugoslavia on the subject, see V. St. Erlich, "Value Orientation and Culture Contact: The Yugoslav Example," International Journal of Sociology, 1 (Spring 1971), pp. 4-26.

49) Hedrick Smith, "Islamic Past of Azerbaijan Republic Frustrates Moscow's Marxist Plans," New York Times, December 13, 1971, p. 25.

50) "Dissidents Among the National Minorities in the USSR," Radio Liberty Research Bulletin, 16 (August 30, 1972), CRD 224/72, pp. 4-5.

51) Report of Plenary Session of the Georgian Communist Party Central Committee, "On the Tasks of the Republic's Party Organization in Improving the Work of Industry and on Measures for Ensuring the Production Growth Rates Envisaged by the Five-Year Plan," Zaria Vostoka, November 4, 1972, pp. 1-4, as abstracted in The Current Digest of the Soviet Press, 24 (December 20, 1972), pp. 7-11.

52) D. Rasulov, "Under the Leninist Banner of Internationalism," Pravda, September 23, 1972, pp. 2-3, as abstracted in The Current Digest of the Soviet Press, 24 (October 18, 1972), p. 28.

53) "Dissidents Among the National Minorities...," op. cit.

54) Sharp differences in proportions receiving higher education from "the more advanced" and the "most backward republics" are presented in Raymond Poignant, Education and Development in Western Europe, the United States and the U.S.S.R. (New York: Teachers College Press, 1969), p. 202.

55) S. M. Lipset and Richard B. Dobson, "The Intellectual as Critic and Rebel: With Special Reference to the United States and the Soviet Union," Daedalus, 101 (Summer 1972), pp. 148-163, 166-168.

56) Zev Katz, "Sociology in the Soviet Union," Problems of Communism, 20 (May-June 1971), p. 28.

57) From "The Social Sciences Are a Combat Weapon of the Party," Pravda, December 22, 1971, p. 2, as abstracted in The Current Digest of the Soviet Press, 23 (January 18, 1972), p. 10.

58) V. E. Kozlovskii and Iu. A. Sychev, "Discussion of Iu. A. Levada's Course of Lectures on Sociology," Soviet Sociology, 9 (Winter 1970-71), pp. 475-494.

59) Editorial — "Current Tasks in the Social Sciences," as abstracted in The Current Digest of the Soviet Press, 24 (September 13, 1972), p. 24.

60) Katz, op. cit., p. 28.

61) Ibid., pp. 38-40.

62) Robert G. Kaiser and Dan Morgan, "East Europe Turning to Sociologists for Some Answers," The Washington Post, December 23, 1972, p. A14.

63) V. Iagodin, "Party Life in Scientific Collectives," Kommunist, July 1972, pp. 51-64, as abstracted in The Current Digest of the Soviet Press, 24 (November 8, 1972), pp. 10-11.

64) Kaiser and Morgan, op. cit.

65) Iagodin, op. cit., p. 10.

66) I have elaborated on some of my ideas on the subject of inequality in "Ideology and Mythology: Reply to Coleman Romalis (and Other Critics)," Sociological Inquiry, 42, No. 3-4 (1972), pp. 233-265. Much of the discussion here about Soviet stratification and sociology has been treated in further detail in Lipset and Richard B. Dobson, "Social Stratification and the Role of Sociology in the Soviet Union," Survey, 19 (Summer 1973).

Selected Bibliography

SOVIET MATERIALS

Aganbegian, A. G., Osipov, G. V., and Shubkin, V. N., eds. Kolichestvennye metody v sotsiologii. Moscow: "Nauka" Publishing House, 1966 [selections translated in Soviet Sociology, Vol. VII, Nos. 1 and 2].

Aitov, N. A. "Social Aspects of Receiving an Education in the USSR." In Akademiia nauk SSSR, Sotsial'nye issledovaniia, vypusk 2, pp. 187-196. Moscow: "Nauka" Publishing House, 1968.

_____. "Some Features of Changes in the Class Structure of the USSR." Voprosy filosofii, 1965, No. 3, pp. 3-9.

Akademiia nauk Belorusskoi SSR. Struktura sovetskoi intelligentsii. Minsk: "Nauka i tekhnika" Publishing House, 1970.

Akademiia nauk SSSR, Sibirskoe otdelenie, Institut istorii, filologii i filosofii. Sotsial'naia struktura naseleniia Sibiri. Novosibirsk: "Nauka" Publishing House, Siberian Division, 1970.

Ambrosov, A. A. Ot klassovoi differentsiatsii k sotsial'noi odnorodnosti obshchestva. Moscow: "Mysl'" Publishing House, 1972.

Arutiunian, Iu. V. Opyt sotsiologicheskogo izucheniia sela. Moscow: Moscow University Publishing House, 1968 [selections translated in Soviet Sociology, Vol. X, Nos. 1, 2, 3, and 4].

_____. "Social Aspects of the Cultural Growth of the Rural Population." Voprosy filosofii, 1968, No. 9, pp. 119-131.

_____. "The Social Structure of the Rural Population." Voprosy filosofii, 1966, No. 5, pp. 51-61.

_____. Sotsial'naia struktura sel'skogo naseleniia SSSR.
    Moscow: "Mysl'" Publishing House, 1971.
Belykh, A. K. Upravlenie i samoupravlenie. Leningrad: "Nauka"
    Publishing House, 1972.
Bliakhman, L. S., Sochilin, B. G., and Shkaratan, O. I. Podbor i
    rasstanovka kadrov na predpriiatii. Moscow: "Ekonomika"
    Publishing House, 1968.
El'meev, V. Ia., Polozov, V. R., and Riashchenko, B. R. Kom-
    munizm i preodolenie razdeleniia mezhdu umstvennym i
    fizicheskim trudom. Leningrad: Leningrad University Pub-
    lishing House, 1965.
Glezerman, G. E. "From Class Differentiation to Social Homo-
    geneity." Voprosy filosofii, 1963, No. 2, pp. 39-49.
_____. "Social Structure of Socialist Society." Kommu-
    nist, 1968, No. 13, pp. 28-39.
Gordon, L. A. and Klopov, E. V. "The Social Development of
    the Working Class of the USSR." Voprosy filosofii, 1972,
    No. 2, pp. 3-18.
Grushin, B. Svobodnoe vremia. Moscow: "Mysl'" Publishing
    House, 1967.
Iovchuk, M. T. and Kogan, L. N. Dukhovnyi mir sovetskogo
    rabochego. Moscow: "Mysl'" Publishing House, 1972.
Kochetov, G. M. "Occupational Inclinations and Job Placement
    of Secondary-School Graduates." Shkola i proizvodstvo,
    1968, No. 7, pp. 23-25.
Kolbanovskii, V. N. Kollektiv kolkhoznikov: sotsial'no-
    psikhologicheskoe issledovanie. Moscow: "Mysl'" Publish-
    ing House, 1970.
Kolesnikov, Iu. V. "On the Social Functions of the Leader of a
    Socialist Production Collective." In Nauchnoe upravlenie
    obshchestvom, vypusk 6, edited by V. G. Afanas'ev, pp. 85-
    130. Moscow: "Mysl'" Publishing House, 1972.
Konstantinov, F. V., ed. Stroitel'stvo kommunizma i razvitie
    obshchestvennykh otnoshenii. Moscow: "Nauka" Publishing
    House, 1966.
Konstantinovskii, D. L. and Shubkin, V. N. "Personal Plans
    and Their Realization." Voprosy filosofii, 1970, No. 7,
    pp. 32-42.

Kravchenko, I. I. and Faddeev, E. T. "On the Social Structure of Soviet Society." Voprosy filosofii, 1966, No. 5, pp. 143-154.

Kravchenko, I. I. and Trubitsin, O. N. "Problems of Changes in the Social Structure of Soviet Society." Voprosy filosofii, 1972, No. 6, pp. 137-147.

Krivushin, L. T. "On the Structure and Concept of Political Power." In Chelovek i obshchestvo, vypusk V, edited by B. G. Anan'ev and D. A. Kerimov, pp. 3-14. Leningrad: Leningrad University Press, 1969.

Kugel', S. A. "Changes in the Social Structure of Soviet Society Under the Impact of the Scientific and Technical Revolution." Voprosy filosofii, 1969, No. 3, pp. 13-22.

_____. Novoe v izuchenii sotsial'noi struktury obshchestva. Leningrad: 1968.

_____. Zakonomernosti izmeneniia sotsial'noi struktury pri perekhode k kommunizmu. Moscow: Ekonomizdat, 1963.

Kugel', S. A. and Nikandrov, O. M. Molodye inzhenery. Moscow: "Mysl'" Publishing House, 1971 [selections translated in Soviet Education, Vol. XIV, No. 8-9].

Kugel', S. A. and Shkaratan, O. I. "Some Methodological Problems in the Study of the Social Structure of Society." Nauchnye doklady vysshei shkoly, filosofskie nauki, 1965, No. 1, pp. 55-64.

Kurylev, A. K. Kommunizm i ravenstvo. Moscow: Political Literature Publishing House, 1971.

Lebin, B. D. and Perfil'ev, M. N. Kadry apparata upravleniia v SSSR. Leningrad: "Nauka" Publishing House, 1970.

Ministerstvo vysshego i srednego spetsial'nogo obrazovaniia Litovskoi SSR, Kaunasskii politekhnicheskii institut, Motivatsiia zhiznedeiatel'nosti studenta. Kaunas: 1971.

Ministerstvo vysshego i srednego spetsial'nogo obrazovaniia RSFSR, Gor'kovskii gosudarstvennyi universitet im. N. I. Lobachevskogo. Sotsiologiia i vysshaia shkola. Gorky: 1970.

Monich, Z. I. Intelligentsiia v strukture sel'skogo naseleniia. Minsk: "Nauka i tekhnika" Publishing House, 1971.

Mutagirov, D. Z. "Methodological Problems in the Study of the Social Structure of the Working Class." In Chelovek i obshchestvo, vypusk V, edited by B. G. Anan'ev and D. A. Kerimov, pp. 25-36. Leningrad: Leningrad University Publishing House, 1969.

Novosibirskii gosudarstvennyi universitet. Kolichestvennye metody v sotsiologicheskikh issledovaniiakh. Novosibirsk: 1964.

Osipov, Gennadii V., ed. Industry and Labour in the USSR. London: Tavistock, 1966.

_____. Town, Country, and People. London: Tavistock, 1968.

Osipov, G. V. et al., eds. Rabochii klass i tekhnicheskii progress. Moscow: "Nauka" Publishing House, 1965.

Osipov, G. V. and Shchepanskii, Ia., eds. Sotsial'nye problemy truda i proizvodstva. Moscow: "Mysl'" Publishing House, 1969.

Podmarkov, V. G. "Man in the World of Occupations." Voprosy filosofii, 1972, No. 8, pp. 53-62.

Rubin, B. and Kolesnikov, Iu. Student glazami sotsiologa. Rostov: Rostov University Publishing House, 1968.

Rutkevich, M. N. "Education in the USSR as a Factor in Social Mobility." In Sotsiologiia i ideologiia, edited by L. A. Volovik, pp. 91-100. Moscow: "Nauka" Publishing House, 1969.

_____. "Problems of Change in the Social Structure of Soviet Society." Nauchnye doklady vysshei shkoly, filosofskie nauki, 1968, No. 3, pp. 44-52.

_____, ed. Izmenenie sotsial'noi struktury sotsialisticheskogo obshchestva. Sverdlovsk: 1965.

_____. "On the Concept of the Intelligentsia as a Social Stratum in Socialist Society." Nauchnye doklady vysshei shkoly, filosofskie nauki, 1966, No. 4, pp. 20-28.

_____. "Processes of Social Movement from Position to Position and the Concept of 'Social Mobility.'" Nauchnye doklady vysshei shkoly, filosofskie nauki, 1970, No. 5, pp. 14-21.

_____, ed. Protsessy izmeneniia sotsial'noi struktury v

sovetskom obshchestve. Sverdlovsk: 1967.
_____. "Social Sources of Replenishing the Soviet Intelligentsia." Voprosy filosofii, 1967, No. 6, pp. 15-23.
_____, ed. Sotsial'nye razlichiia i ikh preodolenie. Sverdlovsk: 1969.
_____, ed. Zhiznennye plany molodezhi. Sverdlovsk: 1966.
Ryvkina, R. V., ed. Sotsiologicheskie issledovaniia, voprosy metodologii i metodiki. Novosibirsk: 1966.
Semenov, V. S. "The Erasure of Social-Class Differences and the Transition to a Classless Society." Voprosy filosofii, 1965, No. 9, pp. 141-151.
_____. Sfera obsluzhivaniia i ee rabotniki. Moscow: "Izdatel'stvo politicheskoi literatury" Publishing House, 1966.
_____. "The Social Structure of Soviet Society." Kommunist, 1965, No. 11, pp. 39-48.
Shkaratan, O. I. "The Ethno-Social Structure of the Urban Population of the Tatar ASSR." Sovetskaia etnografiia, 1970, No. 3, pp. 3-16.
_____. "Problems of Social Structure of the Soviet City." Nauchnye doklady vysshei shkoly, filosofskie nauki, 1970, No. 5, pp. 22-31.
_____. Problemy sotsial'noi struktury rabochego klassa SSSR. Moscow: "Mysl'" Publishing House, 1970.
_____. "The Social Structure of the Soviet Working Class." Voprosy filosofii, 1967, No. 1, pp. 28-39.
_____. "The Working Class of the Socialist Society in the Epoch of the Scientific and Technical Revolution." Voprosy filosofii, 1968, No. 11, pp. 14-25.
Shubkin, V. N. "Occupations: Problems of Choice." Nauka i zhizn', 1971, No. 5, pp. 68-73.
_____. "Reflections on Occupational Pyramids." Literaturnaia gazeta, December 9, 1970.
_____. "Some Problems of Adaptation of Youth to Labor." In Akademiia nauk SSSR, Sotsial'nye issledovaniia, pp. 118-139. Moscow: "Nauka" Publishing House, 1965.
_____. "Some Social and Economic Problems of Youth." In Nekotorye problemy politicheskoi ekonomii, edited by

V. E. Shliapentokh, pp. 265-280. Novosibirsk: 1965.

_____. Sotsiologicheskie opyty. Moscow: "Mysl'" Publishing House, 1970.

_____. "Youth Starts Out in Life." Voprosy filosofii, 1965, No. 5, pp. 57-70 [translated in Soviet Sociology, Vol. IV, No. 3].

Sotsiologiia v. SSSR. 2 vols. Moscow: "Mysl'" Publishing House, 1965 [selections translated in Soviet Sociology, Vol. VI, No. 1-2].

Stepanian, Ts. A. and Semenov, V. S., eds. Klassy, sotsial'nye sloi i gruppy v SSSR. Moscow: "Nauka" Publishing House, 1968.

_____, eds. Problemy izmeneniia sotsial'noi struktury sovetskogo obshchestva. Moscow: "Nauka" Publishing House, 1968.

Taganov, I. N. and Shkaratan, O. I. "Investigation of Social Structures by the Method of Entropy Analysis." Voprosy filosofii, 1969, No. 5, pp. 74-82.

Tartuskii gosudarstvennyi universitet. Materialy konferentsii 'Kommunisticheskoe vospitanie studenchestva." Part I. Tartu: 1971.

Titma, M. Kh. "Factors Determining Occupational Choice." In Molodezh' i trud, edited by V. A. Iadov, pp. 65-79. Moscow: "Molodaia gvardia" Publishing House, 1970.

_____. "The Role of Social Origins in the Formation of Values of Occupations." In Uchenye zapiski Tartuskogo gosudarstvennogo universiteta, No. 273. Trudy po filosofii. Tartu: 1970.

_____. "Values Affecting Occupational Choice." Voprosy filosofii, 1969, No. 4, pp. 52-61.

Trufanov, I. P. "Time Budgets as an Instrument for Investigating Daily Life of Working People." In Akademiia nauk SSSR, Sotsial'nye issledovaniia, vypusk 6, pp. 128-149. Moscow: "Nauka" Publishing House, 1970.

Vittenberg, E. Ia. "Problems of Social Mobility in the USSR in Recent Bourgeois Historiography." Istoriia SSSR, 1971, No. 5, pp. 174-194.

Vodzinskaia, V. V. "On the Problem of the Social Conditioning

of Occupational Choice." In Chelovek i obshchestvo, vypusk
II, edited by B. G. Anan'ev, V. Ia. El'meev, and D. A. Kerimov, pp. 74-91. Leningrad: Leningrad University Publishing House, 1967.

_____. "Orientations Toward Occupations." In Molodezh'
i trud, edited by V. A. Iadov, pp. 79-101. Moscow:
"Molodaia gvardia" Publishing House, 1970.

_____. "The Sociological Aspect of the Problem of Occu-
pational Choice." In Chelovek i obshchestva, vypusk VI,
edited by B. G. Anan'ev and D. A. Kerimov, pp. 43-54.
Leningrad: Leningrad University Publishing House, 1969.

Volkov, Iu. E. "The Organization of Management of Society and
the Character of Social Relations." Voprosy filosofii, 1965,
No. 8, pp. 13-24.

Zhuravleva, G. A. and Sikevich, Z. V. "The Social Conditioning
of the Preparation of Applicants for Higher Educational Institutions." In Chelovek i obshchestva, vypusk VI, edited
by B. G. Anan'ev and D. A. Kerimov, pp. 55-65. Leningrad:
Leningrad University Press, 1969.

NON-SOVIET MATERIALS

Bialer, Seweryn. "Soviet Political Elite: Concept, Sample, Case
Study." Columbia University: Ph.D. Dissertation, 1966.

Bottomore, T. B. Classes in Modern Society. London: George
Allen & Unwin, Ltd., 1965.

_____. Elites and Society. London: C. A. Watts, 1964.

Broderson, Arvid. The Soviet Worker: Labor and Government
in Soviet Society. New York: Random House, 1966.

Cliff, Tony. Russia: A Marxist Analysis. London: Socialist
Review Publishers, 1964.

Conquest, Robert, ed. Industrial Workers in the USSR. London:
Bodley Head, 1967.

Deutscher, Isaac. The Unfinished Revolution, Russia, 1917-
1967. New York: Oxford University Press, 1967.

Djilas, Milovan. The New Class. New York: Praeger, 1957.

Dunn, Stephen P. and Dunn, Ethel. The Peasants of Central

Russia. New York: Holt, Rinehart & Winston, 1967.

Feldmesser, Robert A. "Aspects of Social Mobility in the Soviet Union." Harvard University: Ph.D. Dissertation, 1955.

_____. "Social Classes and Political Structure." In
Cyril E. Black, ed. The Transformation of Russian Society,
Aspects of Social Change Since 1861. Cambridge, Mass.:
Harvard University Press, 1960, pp. 235-252.

_____. "Social Status and Access to Higher Education."
Harvard Educational Review, 27, 2, pp. 92-106.

_____. "Stratification and Communism." In Allen Kassof,
ed. Prospects for Soviet Society. New York: Praeger, 1968,
pp. 359-385.

_____. "Towards the Classless Society?" In Reinhard
Bendix and Seymour M. Lipset, eds. Class, Status and
Power, 2nd ed. New York: Free Press, 1966, pp. 527-534.

Fischer, George. The Soviet System and Modern Society.
New York: Atherton, 1968.

Goldthorpe, John H. "Social Stratification in Industrial Society."
In Bendix and Lipset, eds. Class, Status and Power, 2nd
ed., pp. 648-659.

Granick, David. The Red Executive. New York: Doubleday,
1960.

Inkeles, Alex. Social Change in Soviet Russia. Cambridge,
Mass.: Harvard University Press, 1969.

Inkeles, Alex and Bauer, Raymond. The Soviet Citizen: Daily
Life in a Totalitarian Society. Cambridge, Mass.: Harvard
University Press, 1959.

Katz, Zev. "The Soviet Sociologists' Debate on Social Structure in the USSR," "Soviet Dissenters and Social Structure
in the USSR," and "Patterns of Social Stratification in the
USSR." Papers nos. 1, 2, and 3 of Project on Sociology of
Soviet Audiences, Center for International Studies, Mass-
achusetts Institute of Technology, Cambridge, Mass.,
1971-72.

Kiss, Gabor. Marxismus als Soziologie. Reinbek bei Hamburg:
Rowohlt, 1971.

Lane, David. The End of Inequality? Stratification under State
Socialism. Baltimore, Md.: Penguin Books, 1971.

Lipset, Seymour M. "Social Mobility and Equal Opportunity."
    The Public Interest, 29(Fall 1972), pp. 90-108.
_____ . "La mobilité sociale et les objectifs socialistes."
    Sociologie et sociétés, 4 (November 1972), pp. 193-224.
Markiewicz-Lagneau, Janina. Éducation, égalité, et socialisme.
    Paris: Éditions Anthropos, 1969.
Matthews, Mervyn. Class and Society in Soviet Russia. New
    York: Walker Publishing Co., 1972.
Meissner, Boris, ed. Social Change in the Soviet Union. Notre
    Dame, Ind.: Notre Dame Press, 1972.
Osborn, Robert J. Soviet Social Policies: Welfare, Equality,
    and Community. Homewood, Ill.: The Dorsey Press, 1970.
Ossowski, Stanislaw. Class Structure in the Social Conscious-
    ness. New York: Free Press, 1963.
Parkin, Frank. Class Inequality and Political Order: Social
    Stratification in Capitalist and Communist Societies. New
    York: Praeger, 1971.
Vucinich, Alexander. "Peasants as a Social Class." In James
    R. Millar, ed. The Soviet Rural Community. Urbana, Ill.:
    University of Illinois Press, 1971, pp. 307-324.
Wiles, P. J. D. and Markowski, Stefan. "Income Distribution
    under Communism and Capitalism. Some Facts about
    Poland, the UK, the USA, and the USSR." Soviet Studies,
    22, 3, pp. 344-369 (Part 1); 22, 4, pp. 487-511 (Part 2).
Yanowitch, Murray. "The Soviet Income Revolution." Slavic
    Review, 22, 4, pp. 683-697.
Yanowitch, Murray and Dodge, Norton. "Social Class and Ed-
    ucation: Soviet Findings and Reactions." Comparative Ed-
    ucation Review, October 1968, pp. 248-267.
_____ . "The Social Evaluation of Occupations in the So-
    viet Union." Slavic Review, 28, 4, pp. 619-642.

Partial List of Contributors

IU. V. ARUTIUNIAN is a Doctor of Historical Sciences. He holds the rank of Professor and is a Section Head, Institute of Ethnography, USSR Academy of Sciences, Moscow.

F. R. FILIPPOV is a Candidate of Philosophical Sciences. He is a Docent at Urals State University, Sverdlovsk.

L. A. GORDON is a Candidate of Historical Sciences. He is a Senior Research Associate at the Institute of the World Labor Movement, USSR Academy of Sciences, Moscow.

E. V. KLOPOV is a Candidate of Historical Sciences. He is a Senior Research Associate at the Institute of the World Labor Movement, USSR Academy of Sciences, Moscow.

IU. A. LEVADA is a Doctor of Philosophical Sciences. He is a Senior Research Associate at the Central Mathematical Economics Institute, USSR Academy of Sciences, Moscow.

M. N. RUTKEVICH is a Corresponding Member of the USSR Academy of Sciences. He is Director of the Institute of Sociological Research, USSR Academy of Sciences, Moscow.

O. I. SHKARATAN is a Doctor of Historical Sciences. He is a Section Head, Institute of Sociological Research, USSR Academy of Sciences, Leningrad.

M. KH. TITMA is a Candidate of Philosophical Sciences. He is a Docent at Tartu State University, Estonian SSR.

V. V. VODZINSKAIA is a Candidate of Philosophical Sciences. She is a Senior Research Associate at the Institute of Sociological Research, USSR Academy of Sciences, Leningrad.

IU. E. VOLKOV is a Doctor of Philosophical Sciences. He is a Section Head, Institute of Marxism-Leninism, CPSU Central Committee, Moscow.